INDIGENOUS AND DECOLONIZING STUDIES IN EDUCATION

Indigenous and decolonizing perspectives on education have long persisted alongside colonial models of education, yet too often have been subsumed within the fields of multiculturalism, critical race theory, and progressive education. Timely and compelling, *Indigenous and Decolonizing Studies in Education* features research, theory, and dynamic foundational readings for educators and educational researchers who are looking for possibilities beyond the limits of liberal democratic schooling. Featuring original chapters by authors at the forefront of theorizing, practice, research, and activism, this volume helps define and imagine the exciting interstices between Indigenous and decolonizing studies and education. Each chapter forwards Indigenous principles—such as Land as literacy and water is life—that are grounded in place-specific efforts of creating Indigenous universities and schools, community organizing and social movements, trans and Two Spirit practices, refusals of state policies, and land-based and water-based pedagogies.

Linda Tuhiwai Smith is a Professor of Māori and Indigenous Studies at the University of Waikato in New Zealand.

Eve Tuck is Associate Professor of Critical Race and Indigenous Studies, Ontario Institute for Studies in Education, and Canada Research Chair of Indigenous Methodologies with Youth and Communities, University of Toronto.

K. Wayne Yang is the Director of Undergraduate Studies in the Ethnic Studies Department at the University of California, San Diego.

Indigenous and Decolonizing Studies in Education

Series Editors: Eve Tuck and K. Wayne Yang

Indigenous and Decolonizing Studies in Education

Mapping the Long View

Edited by Linda Tuhiwai Smith, Eve Tuck, and K. Wayne Yang

INDIGENOUS AND DECOLONIZING STUDIES IN EDUCATION

Mapping the Long View

Edited by Linda Tuhiwai Smith
Eve Tuck
K. Wayne Yang

Routledge
Taylor & Francis Group

NEW YORK AND LONDON

First published 2019
by Routledge
711 Third Avenue, New York, NY 10017

and by Routledge
2 Park Square, Milton Park, Abingdon, Oxon, OX14 4RN

Routledge is an imprint of the Taylor & Francis Group, an informa business

Library of Congress Cataloging-in-Publication Data
A catalog record for this book has been requested

ISBN: 978-1-138-58585-0 (hbk)
ISBN: 978-1-138-58586-7 (pbk)
ISBN: 978-0-429-50501-0 (ebk)

Typeset in Bembo
by Apex CoVantage, LLC

CONTENTS

ARTIST STATEMENT ON THE COVER ARTWORK

Lisa Boivin (Deninu Kue First Nation)

This painting came to me while I was completing course requirements for graduate school. I study rehabilitation science which is the branch of medicine concerning rehabilitation and disability. I chose this academic discipline because I have always questioned the limits of the medical model; a measure of wellness based on the presence or absence of disease. My father, a Dene man, navigated the world with a mobility impairment but I never considered him unwell or disabled. It was only when he was diagnosed with the medical model that he was disabled. Furthermore, his rehabilitation did not take place in a clinic, rather he stepped on a dog sled and all was well.

I entered the Rehabilitation Science Institute at University of Toronto Faculty of Medicine with lofty ideas of challenging notions of disability based on the medical model. Eventually, the content I was studying restricted my intellectual mobility. The simplest of required tasks were impossible. I no longer had the language for conversations with my peers, seminars, and papers. I shut down, literally immobilized by colonial methods of study and research in rehabilitation science.

One afternoon, I started to think about how I would tell my supervisor that I was withdrawing from graduate school. As I was tearfully looking out of my window, Hawk appeared and circled in my line of sight. He was very generous with his time, staying with me long enough to remind me of my teachings. Hawk Medicine appears when we need to take a wider view. He sees everything. Just like Hawk we must circle above to take a wider view to make sense of what is around us. From this view, we recognize the gifts we have already received and we can open ourselves up to new gifts that we will be given.

In this painting each flower represents a gift of knowledge that I have received. I identify these knowledges as medicine teachings passed on to us by the ancestors. In this instance the ancestor was my father, who died earlier that year. When

I was telling the story of Hawk to a community member she said, "That was your father checking up on you." At that moment, I could hear what my father would say to me when I cried. "My, girl you are forgetting who you are." This was his way of telling me to be stronger. He reminded me many times while he was alive that as an Indigenous person I am supported by thousands of years of Indigenous knowledge.

Hawk Medicine is reminding me that I need to interact with Indigenous knowledge systems to endure my graduate research journey. Situating myself in the colonial process of writing a thesis has been painful. The academy is not built for Indigenous people. Accordingly, it does not support me or provide me with suitable research methods to translate Dene arts-based knowledge. And so, I continue to take a wider view. I recognize the gifts I have received and keep myself open for the gifts that are coming.

SERIES EDITORS' INTRODUCTION

Eve Tuck (Unangax̂) and K. Wayne Yang

Indigenous and decolonizing perspectives on education have long persisted alongside colonial models of education, yet too often have been subsumed under broader domains of multiculturalism, critical race theory, and progressive education. In addition to many other unique attributes, Indigenous and decolonizing studies engage incommensurabilities fashioned by (settler) colonialism and our relations within and outside it. By attending to Indigenous worldviews and decolonizing theory as distinct philosophical traditions, this provocative series hones the conversation between social justice education and Indigenous and decolonizing studies. Timely and compelling, the *Indigenous and Decolonizing Studies in Education* series features research, theory, and foundational reading for educators and educational researchers who are looking for possibilities beyond the limits of liberal democratic schooling.

This series brings together the central concerns of Indigenous and decolonizing studies with the innovative contributions of social justice education. The books in this series have a commitment to social change with a specific material politics of Indigenous sovereignty, land, and relationships. Because the material politics of decolonization and Indigeneity connect and sometimes abrade with social justice educational research and practices, the books in this series will engage the political incommensurabilities that generate possibilities for education. Topics addressed by the series have drawn increased attention in recent years, and the series is poised to speak to ongoing social and educational challenges including education reform, climate change and environmental degradation, school control and decision-making, and the very purposes of schooling and education. In the sections that follow, we discuss the domains of Indigenous and decolonizing studies and social justice education in order to describe the ideas which form the foundation for the series.

Indigenous Studies and Decolonizing Studies

Writing about the founding of Native American studies in the early 1970s, Elizabeth Cook-Lynn describes the primary commitments of the field as concerned with Indigenous land, Indigenous sovereignty, and the "*endogenous* study of First Nations cultures and history" (1997, p. 11, italics original); that is, the study of Indigenous lives and issues *by* Indigenous peoples. Linda Tuhiwai Smith (2012), Shawn Wilson (2008), Margaret Kovach (2009), and Bagele Chilisa (2011) describe corresponding central commitments within Indigenous studies emerging in New Zealand, Australia, Canada, and Botswana. Contemporary works in Indigenous studies are dynamically diverse and interdisciplinary, yet the very best works attend to those first commitments: land, sovereignty, and Indigenous perspectives.

As an extension of Indigenous studies, Indigenous methodologies of inquiry seek to regenerate Indigenous ways of knowing and research, and craft educational spaces for Indigenous peoples, by Indigenous peoples (Smith, 2012). Many discussions of Indigenous methodologies highlight the role of Indigenous cosmologies, axiologies, and epistemologies in the design and implementation of research (Smith, 2012; Wilson, 2008; Kovach, 2009; Chilisa, 2011). Indigenous research methodologies emerge from Indigenous epistemologies or knowledge frameworks so they are always people- and place-specific (Smith, 2012; Tuck & McKenzie, 2015). The same Indigenous research methods may be used across many contexts but will always need to be tailored to that context to match community needs and understandings of knowledge and knowing.

Indigenous research methods are distinct from other research methods not because they are so vastly different—many Indigenous methods include interviews, focus groups, surveys, archival research, and other tried-and-true methods of social science—but because of the theories that guide them. One of the distinguishing features of Indigenous research methodologies is that they are built upon the concept of relational validity or "relational accountability" (Wilson, 2008, p. 77). In other words, what is most "important and meaningful is fulfilling a role and obligations in the research relationship—that is, being accountable to your relations" (Wilson, 2008, p. 77). Creating and maintaining respectful and mutually beneficial relationships between researchers and Indigenous communities (even when the researcher comes from the community) is of utmost importance, in part because Indigenous peoples have sometimes been mistreated and misled by academic researchers, both in the distant and recent past (Smith, 2012; Wilson, 2008; Tuck & Guishard, 2013). Theories accountable to these relations between land, sovereignty, belongingness, time and space, reality, and futurity shape Indigenous research methods (i.e., Goeman, 2013; Byrd, 2011; Salmón, 2012).

Decolonization studies are informed by Indigenous theory, history, epistemology, and futurity. Decolonization studies emphasize the ways that colonization and decolonization are time-specific and land-specific (Fanon, 1963; Tuck & Yang,

2012). Theories of colonialism have largely focused on what is sometimes called exogenous domination (Veracini, 2011), exploitation colonialism, or external colonialism—three names for the same form. In this form of colonization, small numbers of colonizers go to a "new" place and dominate a local labor force in order to send resources back to the metropole; for example, the spice trade that impelled the colonization of India by several different European empires. Exploitation colonialism, its nature, consequences, endgame, and post-possibilities have been the focus of (what would become) the field of postcolonial studies for the past 50 years. Though settler colonialism has been resisted and systematically critiqued by Indigenous philosophers since its outset, it has only been in the last two decades that *settler* colonialism has been more comprehensively theorized in academe, mostly via the emergence of the field of settler colonial studies. Settler colonialism is a form of colonization in which outsiders come to land inhabited by Indigenous peoples and claim it as their own new home (Tuck, McKenzie, & McCoy, 2014; see also Hinkinson, 2012).

In settler colonial contexts like the US, Australia, Canada, and New Zealand, theories of decolonization bring together critiques of settler colonialism, borders, and conceptualizations of antiblackness. That is, settler colonialism in the US, for example, is the context for the destruction of Indigenous peoples to acquire land, and the enslavement of people from the continent of Africa as units of capital for trade, labor, and disposal (Smallwood, 2007). Thus, decolonization from settler colonialism in the US will require a repatriation of Indigenous land and abolition of slavery in all its forms (Tuck & Yang, 2012). Since the technologies of slavery and land appropriation are reapplied in novel ways to new lands and bodies, understandings of empire (Byrd, 2011), borders (Calderon, 2014), queerness (Morgenson, 2010), disability (Erevelles, 2011), labor, and antiblackness (King, 2014) elucidate the features of settler colonialism.

Theorizations of Blackness and interrogations of antiblackness consider the ways that societal structures in the West require the invention of race, the specificity of Blackness as criminal, landless, and forgone. Such analyses seek to understand how antiblackness determines relationships to the state, land, geography, and other peoples (in the tradition of Wilderson, 2010; Spillers, 2003; McKittrick, 2006). Theories and conceptualizations of blackness that engage the possibilities in Blackness for agency, futurity, fugitivity (Harney & Moten, 2013; Moten, 2013), monstrosity (Kaplan, 2007), and relationships to Indigeneity (King, 2013; Tuck, Guess, & Sultan, 2014) are particularly relevant to theorizing decolonization within settler colonial contexts.

Decolonizing studies at the border attend to how coloniality shapes and severs human and non-human relationships across land, nation-state, waters, and time (Calderon, 2014). These efforts learn from analyses at the intersection of Chican@ studies and Indigenous studies, Pacific Islander studies and Indigenous studies, Black studies and Indigenous studies, diasporic studies and Indigenous studies, and critical Muslim/Arab studies and Indigenous studies.

Decolonizing studies, when most centered in Indigenous philosophy, push back against assumptions about the linearity of history and the future, against teleological narratives of human development, and argue for renderings of time and place that exceed coloniality and conquest.

Social Justice Education

Whereas Indigenous and decolonizing approaches are attentive to relational validity as described previously, social justice education is concerned with catalytic validity (Lather, 1991; see also Fine, 2008). That is, what is valid in research is that which resonates with people's lives and informs their power to make change. Social justice education in this respect has a general commitment to social change, even though that change is not necessarily decolonizing. Nonetheless, the drive to create theory and research that matters to people's lives is relevant to decolonizing and Indigenous studies. The contributions of social justice in education have broad implications for pedagogy, curriculum, schooling, educational policy, and social movements.

Critical pedagogy is one site of radical critique of education, rooted in sometimes Marxist (McLaren, 2003), sometimes postmodern (Giroux, 1991) desires for social transformation. Current scholarship on critical pedagogy interrogates pedagogy not simply as effective classroom practice, but as a source of praxis that has a present purpose and future purpose toward change (Picower, 2012; Au, 2012; Duncan-Andrade & Morrell, 2008). Postcritical pedagogy (Lather, 1995) is concerned with challenging and deconstructing the patriarchal tendencies of critical pedagogy, especially tendencies that install barriers for everyday people to speak for themselves (p. 180).

Overlapping with critical pedagogy is curriculum studies (Malewski, 2010), which arose from examinations of how schooling as well as other state institutions inculcate people for their place within capitalism. On the surface, curricular content is taught in schools, but the deeper lesson entails a "hidden curriculum" (Apple, 2004) that normalizes class, gender, sexuality, citizenship, and race. Thus, curriculum studies is fundamentally concerned with articulating how the disciplinary procedures in schooling connect to unequal relations of power in society. Critical race scholars in education have taken the class-centric, poststructuralist analyses of curriculum studies and fractured them through the fundamental difference that difference makes at the intersections of race, gender, and sexuality. These analyses of race (gender, sexuality) might be seen by some as a development in or reconceptualization of curriculum studies (Jupp, 2013). However, Rubén Gaztambide-Fernández (2006) forwards the idea of "browning" of curriculum studies as a refusal of the linear narrative of curriculum studies as "originating" from white fathers of critical theory, then progressing toward a multicultural inclusion of non-whiteness into the curriculum studies. Browning is a kind of stain that resurfaces, that calls to attention the continuing reassertions of white supremacy and colonialism not only in curriculum, but in curriculum studies and thus the theorizations of how power operates and how change occurs. Browning gestures toward the possibilities for Indigenous and decolonizing studies to refuse settler colonial replacement (Tuck & Gaztambide-Fernández, 2013; see also Calderon, 2014); that is, the re-assimilation and re-incorporation of Indigenous theory under a patrilineal critical theory.

Beyond pedagogy and curriculum, educational research also seeks to understand the role of institutions, especially schools, to compel or constrain social change. Social change is most conventionally conceived of in educational research as, "How can we make schools (and society) less unjust?" Or, "How can we improve schooling outcomes?" These approaches to change might be best described as "harm reduction" (Jacobs, 2009) and expansion of "public good." Harm reduction models seek to alleviate the consequences of white supremacy and colonialism—by treating their symptoms as historical inequities to be mitigated. Expansion treats the idealized white, middle-class, unrestrained citizen-consumer as a uninterrogated standard for the empowered social actor, and thus the social, cultural, and economic benefits of whiteness as public goods to be gradually expanded to non-white peoples. Such approaches to change are often framed by the premise of "gaps" in achievement and wealth to be narrowed. Scholarship on social transformation, by contrast, challenge these paradigms of reducing harm and expanding good, by insisting that the distribution of harm and good reflects a fundamental social structure of which schools are a part—and it is that structure that must be transformed. By refusing notions of gaps in achievement and opportunity (Ladson-Billings, 2006), such scholarship works to uncover debts: the actively accumulating cost of colonialism that accrues to racially othered bodies in order to produce (settler) white wealth and privilege.

A lens of social transformation critically examines the relationship between change and institutions, but does not necessarily assume institutions of schooling to be vehicles of social change in and of themselves (Anyon, 2014; Noguera, 2003). Anyon (2014) examines the "radical possibilities" of connecting social movements to school transformation. Her concern is how to organize meaningful relationships between educational practitioners, learners, and community members in effecting social change. Similarly, Noguera (2003) is interested in how to "break the cycle of poverty"—a cycle that is raced and classed—and he looks at schooling as one of multiple institutions that must be transformed to do so.

As such, educational research unravels the tangles of complicity, contradictory relationships with the institution, and contradictory relationships with the state (Dimitriadis, 2003; Camangian, 2013; Patel, 2013a). This dis/entanglement attempts to render an understanding of agency within and despite structures (Willis, 1990), for researchers and the researched communities both. Thus, critical educational research intervenes in poststructural analyses that reify the disciplinary power of institutions and the sheerness of hegemony. Such scholarship is animated by agency, by contradictory desires for access to (Patel, 2013a) and for escape from (Fine, 1991; Tuck, 2012) states and institutions.

Indigenous and Decolonizing Studies in Education

Now that we have identified the most salient features of Indigenous and decolonizing studies and social justice education, we turn to their intersections and implications. This discussion is intentionally brief because this is the terrain of the proposed series—we have chosen three exemplars to demonstrate what becomes possible in bringing Indigenous and decolonizing studies into conversation with social justice education and educational research.

Red Pedagogy

Sandy Grande (2004), drawing upon McLaren (2003), describes the importance of a revolutionary critical pedagogy for Indigenous education. In particular, Grande highlights how critical pedagogy is a *collective process* that utilizes a Freirian dialogical learning approach that is *critical* of the underlying structures of oppression, *systematic* in its inquiry into the theory and practice, *participatory* in involving communities members and organizations in change making, and *creative* in employing popular texts and people's cultural productions to re-read society (Grande, 2004, p. 25). Grande writes, "Such principles are clearly relevant to [Indigenous communities] and their need for pedagogies of disruption, intervention, affirmative action, hope, and possibility" (p. 26). Grande observes that non-Indigenous revolutionary pedagogies fail to consider a fundamental difference between revolutionary democracies and Indigenous sovereignty (see also Brayboy, 2005). This difference is made evident in critical pedagogy's frequent promotion of practices that foster an empowered critical citizenry for greater participation and integration in the nation-state (Morrell, 2008; Dewey, 1997), in contrast to Indigenous approaches that seek self-determination from a colonizing state (Smith, 2012; Grande, 2004; Brayboy, 2005; Abdi, 2011; Coulthard, 2014). Grande describes a "red pedagogy" as one that attends to decolonization in its material politics in order to recognize and nurture Indigenous practices of present and future change.

Decolonial Participatory Action Research

Consistent with concepts of sovereignty and decolonization is education research that centers the expertise of youth and communities about the neighborhoods and institutions they inhabit, as well as the saliency of that expertise in making policy and social change (Cammarota & Fine, 2008). Participatory Action Research (PAR) describes one set of methodological approaches that attempts to accomplish this ground- and grassroots-knowledge production. That people come to know things through their lived lives and that knowledge matters is often attributed only to PAR. Yet educational researchers develop this kind of positionality in terms of their participation and in terms of the theory of knowledge through a range of methodological approaches, such as critical ethnography, public science, collaborative interviews, participatory performance, and community mapping, to name a few (Guishard & Tuck, 2014). These different methodologies deconstruct the power of research and researcher to construct knowledge that is valid for empowered communities. Decolonizing participatory research approaches make explicit how knowledge is territorialized (Simpson, 2007); namely, the university is settler colonial in its acquisitions of "data" on Indigenous and non-white communities (Tuck & Yang, 2014), in its framing of these communities as pathologically Other (Patel, 2013b), and in its theorizing of how change ought to happen to these communities (Tuck & Yang, 2014). Thus the acquisitive ethics of research, the archives of data, and the theorizations are part of an academic knowledge territory. Decolonizing participatory methods draw limits to this territory by refusing to hand over anything and everything to the academic enterprise, by drawing attention to power's code of ethics (Tuck & Guishard, 2013), by re-presenting the taken-as-natural knowledge territories of Indigenous thought-worlds (Smith, 2012), and by "theorizing back" at power about its abuses in the guise of change (Smith, 2012; Guishard & Tuck, 2014).

Culturally Responsive and Sustaining Education for Indigenous Students

Although culturally responsive education has been a concern for Indigenous education since the emergence of colonial boarding schools (Brayboy, 2005; Brayboy & Castagno, 2009; Lomawaima & McCarty, 2006), and for Black education (Walker, 1996), Chican@/Latin@education (Solorzano & Yosso, 2000), and "urban" education as a general marker for minoritized communities of color (Delpit, 1995; Ladson-Billings, 1995), the impact of Indigenous epistemologies that engage the metaphysical, the communal, the intergenerational, and the past, present, and future possible has been profound in recent scholarship (Villegas, Neugebauer, & Venegas, 2008). Django Paris (2012) proposes a need for a "change in stance, terminology and practice" beyond what is commonly called culturally responsive pedagogy to "culturally sustaining practice" (p. 93). Such a stance focuses not so much on the translation of schooling into culturally responsive materials for the purposes of achievement, but positions education as the vehicle for sustaining cultural knowledges that have otherwise been targeted for extinction. In this way, Paris's work draws from Indigenous philosophies of education.

Research methods, particularly those driven by an ethics of community participatory design, have developed greatly through different Indigenous understandings of reciprocity and intergenerational relationships. For example, inspired by the Mother Earth Walks that began in 2003, community members and Indigenous academic researchers who were members of the Chicago intertribal American

Indian community created an intergenerational community research project that would bring together more than 100 Indigenous community members to design and implement innovative science learning environments for Indigenous youth and community in Chicago (Bang, Marin, Faber, & Suzukovich, 2013).

The Timing for This Work Is Now

In the past 20 years, around the globe, Indigenous and decolonizing studies have grown dramatically. Doctoral and master's programs in Native American, American Indian, Maori, Aboriginal, Native Hawaiian, and Alaska Native Studies have been established in the US, Canada, Australia, and New Zealand. In the past few years, several relevant journals have been founded, including *Decolonization: Indigeneity, Education, and Society* (Open access, 2012), *Settler Colonial Studies* (Open access now subscription, 2011), *Critical Ethnic Studies* (subscription, 2013–2014), and *Native American and Indigenous Studies* (subscription, 2013). The Native American and Indigenous Studies Association (NAISA) was founded in 2007.

Some of the most exciting work in Indigenous/decolonizing studies is being done by scholars from education, and many of the most germane and provocative ideas in education are being produced by Indigenous and decolonial scholars. Though Native American studies and Indigenous studies have traditionally been engaged by disciplines such as history, anthropology, art history, humanities, and archeology, NAISA's annual meeting now regularly features the contributions of scholars in education. Likewise, major education associations including the American Educational Research Association (AERA), the American Educational Studies Association (AESA), and their international counterparts have highlighted the work of scholars in Indigenous education in major plenary sessions, journal special issues, and working groups. Every other year since 1987, the World Indigenous Peoples Conference on Education (WIPC:E) meets, bringing several thousand academic and non-academic educators, researchers, teacher educators, and community members to discuss issues of Indigeneity and education. Further, memberships of the Indigenous Peoples of the Americas Special Interest Group and the Indigenous Peoples of the Pacific Special Interest Group in AERA have grown exponentially in the past decade.

In part, the increased attention to Indigenous and decolonizing issues in education can be attributed to the reach of several high-impact books, including Linda Tuhiwai Smith's, 1999 *Decolonizing Methodologies* (Zed Books) and Sandy Grande's, 2004 *Red Pedagogy* (Rowman & Littlefield). Both books now have second editions that expound upon earlier ideas in light of the growth of the field. But the increased attention can also be attributed to the ways the field uniquely responds to educational concerns related to culturally responsive education, diversity and multicultural/multilingual education, environmental education and climate change, school dropout, and teacher education. People are paying attention to what Indigenous and decolonizing studies in education have to say.

We invite you to keep reading other books in this series and to consider this series as a potential home for your work in Indigenous and decolonizing studies in education.

Series Editors
Eve Tuck and K. Wayne Yang

References

Abdi, A. A. (2011). *Decolonizing philosophies of education*. Rotterdam, The Netherlands: Sense Publishers.

Anyon, J. (2014). *Radical possibilities: Public policy, urban education, and a new social movement*. New York, NY: Routledge.

Apple, M. W. (2004). *Ideology and curriculum*. New York, NY: Routledge Falmer.

Au, W. (2012). *Critical curriculum studies: Education, consciousness, and the politics of knowing*. New York, NY: Routledge.

Bang, M., Marin, A., Faber, L., & Suzukovich, E. S. I. I. I. (2013). Repatriating indigenous technologies in an urban Indian community. *Urban Education, 48*(5), 705–733.

Brayboy, B. M. J. (2005). Toward a tribal critical race theory in education. *The Urban Review, 37*(5), 425–446.

Brayboy, B. M. J., & Castagno, A. E. (2009). Self-determination through self-education: Culturally responsive schooling for indigenous students in the USA. *Teaching Education, 20*(1), 31–53.

Byrd, J. A. (2011). *The transit of empire: Indigenous critiques of colonialism*. Minneapolis, MN: University of Minnesota Press.

Calderon, D. (2014). Speaking back to manifest destinies: A land education-based approach to critical curriculum inquiry. *Environmental Education Research, 20*(1), 1–13.

Camangian, P. R. (2013). Seeing through lies: Teaching ideological literacy as a corrective lens. *Equity & Excellence in Education, 46*(1), 119–134.

Cammarota, J., & Fine, M. (Eds.). (2008). *Revolutionizing education: Youth participatory action research in motion*. New York, NY: Routledge.

Chilisa, B. (2011). *Indigenous research methodologies*. London, UK: Sage Publications, Inc.

Cook-Lynn, E. (1997). Who stole native American studies? *Wicazo Sa Review, 12*(1), 9–28.

Coulthard, G. (2014). From wards of state to subjects of recognition? Marx, Indigenous peoples, and the politics of dispossession in Denendah. In A. Simpson & A. Smith (Eds.), *Theorizing native studies* (pp. 56–98). Durham, NC: Duke University Press.

Delpit, L. D. (1995). *Other people's children: Cultural conflict in the classroom*. New York, NY: New Press.

Dewey, J. (1997). *Democracy and education: An introduction to the philosophy of education*. New York, NY: Free Press.

Dimitriadis, G. (2003). *Friendship, cliques, and gangs: Young black men coming of age in urban America*. New York, NY: Teachers College Press.

Duncan-Andrade, J. M. R., & Morrell, E. (2008). *The art of critical pedagogy: Possibilities for moving from theory to practice in urban schools*. New York, NY: Peter Lang.

Erevelles, N. (2011). *Disability and difference in global contexts: Enabling a transformative body politic*. Basingstoke, UK: Palgrave Macmillan.

Fanon, F. (1963). *The wretched of the earth*. New York, NY: Grove Press.

Fine, M. (1991). *Framing dropouts: Notes on the politics of an urban high school*. New York, NY: SUNY Press.

Fine, M. (2008). An epilogue, of sorts. In J. Cammarota & M. Fine (Eds.), *Revolutionizing education: Youth participatory action research in motion* (pp. 213–234). New York, NY: Routledge.

Gaztambide-Fernández, R. A. (2006). Regarding race: The necessary browning of our curriculum and pedagogy public project. *Journal of Curriculum and Pedagogy, 3*(1), 60–65.

Giroux, H. A. (1991). *Postmodernism, feminism, and cultural politics: Redrawing educational boundaries.* Albany, NY: State University of New York Press.

Goeman, M. (2013). *Mark my words: Native women mapping our nations.* Minneapolis, MN: University of Minnesota Press.

Grande, S. (2004). *Red pedagogy: Native American social and political thought.* Boulder, CO: Rowman & Littlefield.

Guishard, M., & Tuck, E. (2014). Youth resistance research methods and ethical challenges. In E. Tuck & K. W. Yang (Eds.), *Youth resistance research and theories of change* (pp. 181–194). New York, NY: Routledge.

Harney, S., & Moten, F. (2013). *The undercommons: Fugitive planning & black study.* Wivenhoe, UK: Minor Compositions.

Hinkson, J. (2012). Why settler colonialism? *Arena Journal, 37/38*(1), 1–39.

Jacobs, A. (2009). *Undoing the harm of white supremacy.* (Unpublished master's thesis). The Gallatin School, New York University.

Jupp, J. (2013). Undoing double binds in curriculum: On cosmopolitan sensibilities in US curriculum studies. *Journal of the American Association for the Advancement of Curriculum Studies, 9.* Retrieved from www.uwstout.edu/soe/jaaacs/upload/v9_Jupp.pdf

Kaplan, S. C. (2007). Love and violence/maternity and death: Black feminism and the politics of reading (un)representability. *Black Women, Gender & Families, 1*(1), 94–124.

King, T. J. (2013). *In the clearing: Black female bodies, space and settler colonial landscapes.* (Doctoral dissertation). Retrieved from DRUM. (1903/14525).

King, T. L. (2014, June 10). Labor's Aphasia: Toward Antiblackness as constitutive to settler colonialism. *Decolonization: Indigeneity, Education and Society.* Retrieved from http://decolonization.wordpress.com/2014/06/10/labors-aphasia-toward-antiblackness-as-constitutive-to-settler-colonialism/

Kovach, M. E. (2009). *Indigenous methodologies: Characteristics, conversations, and contexts.* Toronto, ON: University of Toronto Press.

Ladson-Billings, G. (1995). Toward a theory of culturally relevant pedagogy. *American Educational Research Journal, 32*(3), 465–491.

Ladson-Billings, G. (2006). From the achievement gap to the education debt: Understanding achievement in US schools. *Educational Researcher, 35*(7), 3–12.

Lather, P. (1991). *Getting smart: Feminist research and pedagogy with/in the postmodern.* New York, NY: Routledge.

Lather, P. (1995). Post-critical pedagogies: A feminist reading. In P. McLaren (Ed.), *Postmodernism, postcolonialism and pedagogy* (pp. 167–186). Sommerville, Albert Park, Australia: James Nichols Publishers.

Lomawaima, K. T., & McCarty, T. L. (2006). *"To remain an Indian": Lessons in democracy from a century of native American education* (pp. 2–3). New York, NY: Teachers College Press.

Malewski, E. (2010). *Curriculum studies handbook—the next moment.* New York, NY: Routledge.

McKittrick, K. (2006). *Demonic grounds: Black women and the cartographies of struggle.* Minneapolis, MN: University of Minnesota Press.

McLaren, P. (2003). *Life in schools: An introduction to critical pedagogy in the foundations of education.* Boston, MA: Allyn and Bacon.

Morgensen, S. (2010). Settler homonationalism: Theorizing settler colonialism within queer modernities. *Glq: A Journal of Lesbian and Gay Studies, 16*, 105–131.

Morrell, E. (2008). *Critical literacy and urban youth: Pedagogies of access, dissent, and liberation.* New York, NY: Routledge.

Moten, F. (2013). Blackness and nothingness (mysticism in the flesh). *South Atlantic Quarterly, 112*(4), 737–780.

Noguera, P. (2003). *City schools and the American dream: Reclaiming the promise of public education* (Vol. 17). New York, NY: Teachers College Press.

Paris, D. (2012). Culturally sustaining pedagogy: A needed change in stance, terminology, and practice. *Educational Researcher, 41*(3), 93–97.

Patel, L. (2013a). *Youth held at the border: Immigration, education and the politics of inclusion.* New York, NY: Teachers College Press.

Patel, L. (2013b). What does the acquittal of Zimmerman have to do with educational research?" *Decolonizing Educational Research.* Retrieved from http://decolonizing. wordpress.com/2013/07/15/what-does-the-acquittal-of-zimmerman-have-to-do-with-educational-research/.

Picower, B. (2012). *Practice what you teach: Social justice education in the classroom and the streets.* New York, NY: Routledge.

Salmón, E. (2012). *Eating the landscape: American Indian stories of food, identity, and resilience.* Tucson, AZ: University of Arizona Press.

Simpson, A. (2007). On ethnographic refusal: Indigeneity, 'voice' and colonial citizenship. *Junctures, 9*, 67–80.

Smallwood, S. E. (2007). *Saltwater slavery: A middle passage from Africa to American diaspora.* Cambridge, MA: Harvard University Press.

Smith, L. T. (1999/2012). *Decolonizing methodologies: Research and indigenous peoples.* London, UK: Zed Books.

Solorzano, D., & Yosso, T. (2000). Toward a critical race theory of Chicana and Chicano education. *Charting New Terrains of Chicana (o)/Latina (o) Education*, 35–65.

Spillers, H. (2003). *Black and white in color: Essays on American literature and culture.* Chicago, IL: University of Chicago Press.

Tuck, E. (2012). *Urban youth and school pushout: Gateways, get-aways, and the GED.* New York, NY: Routledge.

Tuck, E., & Gaztambide-Fernández, R. (2013). Curriculum, replacement, and settler futurity. *Journal of Curriculum Theorizing, 29*(1), 72–89.

Tuck, E., Guess, A., & Sultan, H. (2014, June 26). Not nowhere: Collaborating on selfsame land. *Decolonization.* Retrieved from http://decolonization.wordpress.com/2014/06/26/not-nowhere-collaborating-on-selfsame-land/

Tuck, E., & Guishard, M. (2013). Uncollapsing ethics: Racialized sciencism, settler coloniality, and an ethical framework of decolonial participatory action research. In T. M. Kress, C. S. Malott, & B. J. Portfilio (Eds.), *Challenging status quo retrenchment: New directions in critical qualitative research* (pp. 3–27). Charlotte, NC: Information Age Publishing.

Tuck, E., & McKenzie, M. (2015). *Place in research: Theory, methodology, and methods.* New York, NY: Routledge.

Tuck, E., McKenzie, M., & McCoy, K. (2014). Land education: Indigenous, post-colonial, and decolonizing perspectives on place and environmental education research. *Environmental Education Research, 20*(1), 1–23.

Tuck, E., & Yang, K. W. (2012). Decolonization is not a metaphor. *Decolonization: Indigeneity, Education and Society, 1*(1), 1–40.

Tuck, E., & Yang, K. W. (Eds.). (2014). *Youth resistance research and theories of change*. New York, NY: Routledge.

Veracini, L. (2011). Introducing settler colonial studies. *Settler Colonial Studies, 1*, 1–12. Retrieved from http://ojs.lib.swin.edu.au/index.php/settlercolonialstudies/article/view/239

Villegas, M., Neugebauer, S. R., & Venegas, K. R. (2008). *Indigenous knowledge and education: Sites of struggle, strength, and survivance*. Cambridge, MA: Harvard Education Press.

Walker, V. S. (1996). *Their highest potential: An African American school community in the segregated South*. Chapel Hill, NC: University of North Carolina Press.

Wilderson, F. (2010). *Red, White, and Black: Cinema and the structure of US antagonisms*. Durham, NC: Duke University Press.

Willis, P. E. (1990). *Common culture: Symbolic work at play in the everyday cultures of the young*. Milton Keynes, UK: Open University Press.

Wilson, S. (2008). *Research as ceremony: Indigenous research methods*. Blackpoint, NS: Fernwood Publishing.

ACKNOWLEDGMENTS

We acknowledge that everything that we know that feels like knowing is because someone who loved us taught it to us. We acknowledge the rest of it, that which doesn't quite feel like knowing, but something more like what we have learned the hard way; we acknowledge that, too. This is a book for all of us, a dramatic yet still-true thing to say. This is the book we always wanted, the book that still escapes us, because that is what it is like to grow.

As editors of this book, this flow, we are grateful to one another, to the people in each other's lives who do so much to make the space for writing and thinking, for hurrying up around the swift bends and slowing down across the long stretches. The pacing of this book was completely, ethically, beautifully managed by Nisha Toomey, a graduate student at the Ontario Institute for Studies in Education at the University of Toronto. Her work has been vital to the coming-true of this book.

We are so thankful for our ongoing collaborations with Catherine Bernard, our brilliant editor at Routledge. Now, on the occasion of the publication of the first book in this new series on Indigenous and Decolonizing Studies in Education, Eve and Wayne remember our friend and mentor Greg Dimitriadis, who guided us in all aspects of making books and now a book series. We celebrate Greg's work and life with the launch of this series.

Dear authors in this book, and authors who will read and respond to this book, thank you for your words, and for all the presences and absences that those words convey. To one another, to you, to all our relations, we express our appreciation.

INTRODUCTION

Linda Tuhiwai Smith (Ngāti Awa, Ngāti Porou),
Eve Tuck (Unangax̂), and K. Wayne Yang

Water is life.
Land is our first teacher.

This is a book about these, perhaps the most foundational ideas in Indigenous and decolonizing studies in education. All the pages that follow come back to these ideas. But these ideas can be perceived to be more simple than they are. Their simplicity can mask the deep implications involved, their resounding consequences. For example, to say *water is life, land is our first teacher,* and to ignore Indigenous presence and relationship with those lands and waters, is to miss the point entirely. Indigenous feminist scholarship has been especially careful to remind: there is no decolonization without Indigenous presence on Indigenous land and waters (Hunt, 2013; Simpson, 2016).

Part of the planning and decision-making for this book happened along the curve of the Yanaguana, the San Antonio river. If you have ever been to San Antonio, you may be familiar with its distinctive downtown feature called the River Walk, which wends along the banks of the river at many stretches well below street level. If you have traveled this path, you have shared space with many other travelers earthly and celestial, as we were taught by Gary Pérez, an Indigenous knowledge keeper who presented Coahuiltecan teachings at the Indigenous Pre-conference of the American Educational Research Association in April 2017. The river Yanaguana has a unique horseshoe-shaped path that is mirrored in the sky by a constellation, a celestial river of the same shape, known also as the constellation Eridanus. Not only can the shape of the river be mapped as an overlay upon the shape of the stars, but according to Pérez, the two rivers, water and celestial, also meet to make a path that ancestors use to travel between worlds. The Yanaguana is a path between these worlds for ancestors traveling during profoundly symmetrical moments, such as the solstice, when the earthly and celestial rivers meet exactly on the horizon. It is also for ancestors traveling at more quotidian times, because those two rivers also touch and separate whenever they share sky, as ordinary occurrences.

If you have been near the river during Fiesta San Antonio, as we were when planning this book, then you have perhaps experienced the massive, now 10-day party that is often likened to Mardi Gras. It is historically connected to a commemoration of the battle of the Alamo, a symbol for Anglo settler revenge against the Mexican army and for the grand narrative of Texan exceptionalism. Let us remember the Alamo was the Spanish *Misión San Antonio de Valero*, a site where Native children were abducted and schooled and buried, where Anglo settlers who supported slavery and who pretended to convert to Catholicism in hopes of securing land grants tried to stage a seizure of Native land then occupied/claimed by the new nation-state of Mexico.

Fiesta is an affair of complex desires, with people of many generations taking a hard-earned stroll in a vibrant nightlife that is often missing in norteamericano society. Payday advances increase just before Fiesta, an indication that many of the people celebrating are living paycheck to paycheck. Lovely people from many communities—many of whom are no doubt Indigenous, many Mexican, many of whom are critical of the monumentalization of the Alamo—come out to celebrate Fiesta. Some, like ourselves, are visitors to the river, arriving by way of a large carbon footprint.

We start here, at the river's edge, to do more than locate our book or to put the labor that made this book in a particular place. We start here to ask: what does it mean to celebrate colonialism, as Fiesta does, when water is life—even the water in the seemingly human-made curves of the river walk? What does such a "celebration" do to the water? Yes, there are many plastic cups and flakes of confetti that remain on streets and the water walk the morning after; but what does the commemoration of colonial violence do to our relations with water? Further, what does our planning of this book along the Yanaguana do to the water?

In September 2017, at an event in Toronto called Water is Life (But Many Can't Drink It), Winona LaDuke described the deathly short-sightedness of the extractive fuel industry. In this discussion, LaDuke shared images of water crystalline structures before and after human prayer (this is also something that you can look up online, a few keywords revealing images like those LaDuke shared). The "before" images were comprised of deflated-looking mushy droplets, whereas after human prayer, droplets had been restructured with the gorgeous symmetries that we might associate with snowflakes. This is evidence that human prayer can have a healing effect with regard to the microscopic structure of water. In sharing these images, LaDuke was reminding us that humans have a relationship to water that is reciprocal, that people can heal water that heals us.

At the same event, Métis artist Erin Marie Konsmo was one of the invited respondents to LaDuke's lecture, along with Christi Belcourt and Isaac Murdoch, all members of the Onaman Collective. We were so engaged by Konsmo's remarks that we asked permission to share some of their notes here, in this introduction. We also asked them to provide the essay that would become the afterword of this volume, on accessing Indigenous land/water and bodies. In response to LaDuke's lecture, Konsmo asked,

> What might "Water is Life" mean in the context of a city like Tkaronto? How/does urban life change the way we engage and protect water, life, and each other?
>
> Sometimes it feels really hard to hear "water is life" when we're losing young people to the river in Thunder Bay almost every month. Many of our youth and women have been found beside or in water sources.
>
> We need to think about life at all times of creation. Even under dire circumstances of climate change. How can we love and build right relation with profoundly polluted water, water that we are entangled in harming through the infrastructures and systems we have to live through (sewers, garbage, industrialism)?
>
> This question brings me to thinking about disabilities, desirability and disposability.
>
> In order to love and build good relations through ongoing colonialism and environmental destruction we need to get rid of concepts of purity (which also ultimately harm our city kin). They also harm gender and sexuality-complex folks and people with disabilities. Myself included. I also hear purity concepts weaponized against people who have experienced sexual violence.
>
> Rarely do we hear people talk about environmental justice and disability. I think coming to terms with and identifying that purity is a destructive and isolating concept is important to how we treat cities and our kin who live there. Whether that's purity around the water or land or purity around cultural and ceremonial knowledge. We are in a time where we are entangled in infrastructure. We need to not force dogmatic practices of land/water on our people, because it's ultimately ableist, incorporates shame if you don't meet that standard and leaves very specific people behind.
>
> Finally, how do we think about water and gender? Often these things are segmented and isolated in building social movements, but they overflow. How can water help us approach gender differently?
>
> Water brings us together. If we could rally together for trans youth like we do for water, what would that look like? How can we make sure people are bringing Two Spirit youth with them and then making supportive ceremonial environments, not essentialist ceremonies? Almost every Two Spirit person I know faces barriers to ceremony. It is important that we start mentoring Two Spirit people to hold those ceremonies.
>
> Water is self-determining. You're not going to go to the lake in August (a hot month) and tell it to be an ice cube. If we love water in all the various forms that it takes, then we can love our family in all the complex ways that they exist. If we could model more of our relationship to the land in the

ways that we have relationships with other people, we may see the ways that
Two Spirit, Trans and gender complex people already have their existence
in our worlds.

(Konsmo, 2017)

We are grateful to Erin Marie Konsmo for allowing us to print these words from
their conversation with Winona LaDuke. Konsmo's connective threads between
murdered and missing Indigenous women, girls, and two-spirit people; the shore-
lines of polluted rivers that can become final resting places for Indigenous peoples; gender, sexuality, disability; and the harms of purity discourses do a great deal
of work to bring complexity to saying that water is life.

As we have only begun to indicate here, the abiding ideas that *water is life* and
that *Land is our first teacher* bear much complexity in their seemingly simple phrasing.
Among the Indigenous scholars who have written about the notion of Land as first
teacher across generations, Sandra Styres is one of those who have most directly taken
up these ideas in her work. Styres writes, "Land as first teacher is a contemporary
engagement with Indigenous philosophies derived from a land-centred culture and
based on *very old pedagogies*" (2011, p. 717, emphasis original). The article emphasizes
how creating pedagogy and curricula to reflect and engage the notion of Land as
first teacher can mean centering and grounding student learning "to the land that
holds their stories, (re)membered experiences, and has recorded tracks of both their
and their ancestors' journeying" (*ibid.*, p. 726). Styres locates the learning she has done
to generate this writing in work with students in Sioux Lookout, and in the teachings of Ojibwe-Anishinabe traditional teacher Eddie Benton-Benai. She engages
Benton-Benai's 1988 book, *The Mishomis Book*, to reflect on the implied responsibilities in the understandings within Land as first teacher. "What tracks are we leaving
as educators? What tracks are we teaching our students to leave?" Styres asks (*ibid,*.
p. 728). These questions are but one way to describe the generational ethic required
in forming theories and systems of education that are wholly influenced by water as
life and Land as first teacher. Styres continues to consider this ethic and many of the
themes that are important to this book in her chapter, *Literacies of Land* (Chapter 1),
which serves to open the remainder of the volume.

Prompting the Fields and Waters of Indigenous and Decolonizing Studies in Education

This the first volume of a new books series in Indigenous and decolonizing studies in education, edited by Eve Tuck and K. Wayne Yang. The creation of this book
series is, like many Indigenous efforts in education, a next step in a long history
or long path taken by so many others. The book series is one of many efforts to
widen a field that has at times been characterized as a trail of letters: Indigenous
writers and educators writing to one another, across generations and colonized
territories. Notes scribbled in margins, reaching across the page to one another,

becoming the page. Messages in bottles, gathering together in an eddy. In the next section, Eve Tuck and Linda Tuhiwai Smith have crafted brief missives, in part to one another, but mostly for you, the anticipated readers, and for the anticipated Indigenous and decolonizing authors who will create books that will also appear in this series.

Writing to One Another—Eve Tuck

One thing that I feel like I have learned from Linda Tuhiwai Smith is how to engage our writing as letters out to other Indigenous people, who are working in their own ways to decolonize their home territories and the other spaces they move within. Because we are spread across great distances, because our homelands and our worksites (if separate, like mine) are geographically dispersed and our time is taxed by university demands (the emergencies that always pop up), our writing is our way of saying, "I am still thinking of you, and the last conversation we had." Once, when I was still a graduate student, Linda and I talked about the idea that Indigenous women and non-binary people are always writing to each other in our footnotes. I have held that idea in my heart, and over time, have grown the courage to move what would have been footnotes to the body of my writing. Now, we have a whole book series on what was once only sayable in footnotes.

Several summers ago, Linda and I were on a panel speaking to graduate students and early career scholars. Their questions, I realized, were nearly identical to the questions I asked Linda when we first met nearly a decade before. How do we get the space to do the work that is meaningful here? How do we keep writing when it feels like no one gets it? Linda's answers—take the space; do the writing; we are out here reading you—continue to resonate, to reverberate across the decisions I make as a scholar. Her book *Decolonizing Methodologies*, but even more, her insistent presence in the academy and in the field, show what those answers—take the space, do the writing, we are out here reading you—mean when applied to a life's work.

So the relationships have been fruitful, the writing has been fruitful, the moving of whispers in the footnotes to discussions happening deep within the body, the lands of our work, has been exceedingly fruitful. I have a mix of fury and gratitude, always, for the opportunity to do this work.

Writing in the Field(S) of Education and Indigenous Studies Feels Different Now—Linda Tuhiwai Smith

Writing in the field(s) of education and Indigenous studies feels different now than it did when I initially published *Decolonizing Methodologies* in 1999. These days I feel that I am not alone, writing into an emptiness or vacuum to a colonial system that is intent on destroying Indigenous peoples. My early efforts seemed like a cry in the wilderness or message in a bottle or whisper in the dark, hoping to catch the attention of someone somewhere who would accept the message and respond. I knew the message was worth writing. I thought the message needed to be carried at an international level and be aligned to the work being done on the rights of Indigenous peoples and deeply connected and engaged with our communities. These fields did not exist as fields of Indigenous scholarship when I began my career or when I wrote *Decolonizing Methodologies*.

My observation of earlier Maori or Indigenous scholars was that the academy consumed them, changed them, distracted them, and isolated them from the Indigenous world and that we, as a community, could not trust all of them to work for us. My critique of colonialism was not just about looking at the colonizer but also looking at what colonial hegemony was doing within our own Indigenous minds, spirits, and behaviors. I saw the need for a decolonizing agenda that dealt with the whole of the dialectic of colonizer-colonized and recognized the role of education as a means to transform colonialism at deep levels of knowledge, pedagogy, the shaping of minds and discourses.

Now, I feel that I am writing as part of a community of Indigenous scholars who have deepened understandings of the work of decolonizing education and, importantly, created new approaches to education that theorize, revitalize, enhance, and produce Indigenous educational experiences that support Indigenous futures.

There is much that feels the same, however. There are still more scholars working with deficit approaches who are trying to either "save" us from ourselves or fix us up, sort us out, and, in some cases still, convince us that they "know best." I am reminded quite often that faculties of education are still dominated by academic staff who are ignorant and hostile to Indigenous peoples. I feel a sense of déjà vu that some of my early work still needs to be restated.

On Institutionalizing Indigenous Studies/Maori Studies—Linda Tuhiwai Smith

Institutionalization of Indigenous studies and Maori studies in Western-dominated academies is not, in itself, a thing to aspire to, but creating "safe" places is often a practical response to isolation and marginalization. Of course, decolonization teaches us that putting a group of Indigenous academics together does not naturally translate to safe, healthy, and stimulating environments. As scholars, we are not immune to, or above, the historic trauma of our peoples and we have to work purposively to create healthy decolonized academic spaces. The severing of Maori studies from anthropology and linguistics was seen as an important stance of self-determination that, in the academy, represents a major academic debate and academic "win." It only works, however, if Maori studies reimagines itself at the same time. That project has proven more challenging to achieve than what was initially imagined. In a fundamental sense, the day after the declaration of decolonization and formal transfer of power becomes the first day of work to decolonize.

I like the idea of, and have worked to create, networks and communities that cut across institutions and communities. When I was a student, an Indigenous conference was primarily a conference during which white scholars discussed their research about Indigenous people. Now, I see a growing body of Indigenous scholars in research programs, in networks and collaborations, in journals, at conferences, in symposia, and in special interest groups that have formed in recent times. I think these structures of Indigenous collegiality have proven to be very powerful in advancing our scholarship, creating the academic language we need, and mentoring our researchers. Talking with each other is a far more stimulating way to advance Indigenous intellectual work than trying to talk to each other through the mediating presence of non-indigenous scholars.

My own academic background is multidisciplinary. I majored in history and politics at the bachelor's level, did a master's degree starting in counseling and then transferring to sociology. My Ph.D. supervisors in education were a sociologist and psychologist. I do not have any particular loyalty to a single discipline. I am intrigued, as my work shows, in how academic disciplines work to discipline language and thought, as well as to institutionalize and legitimate knowledge. Understanding the nature of academic disciplines and their underlying philosophies and methods has helped me deconstruct the power of disciplines to define and represent Indigenous peoples and our ways of knowing and being, and to entrap us in their sense of reality. A decolonizing agenda has to help Indigenous peoples to create and revitalize our own frameworks, language, theories, methodologies, and practices that work for us.

For readers who wonder whether or not you should be attending more meaningfully to the work of institutionalizing Indigenous studies, you are probably used to going it alone but have established networks and good, strong collaborations that give you a place to be and a sense of a shared community. The questions become ones such as, *Where do you find your community? Who do you consider your peers? Who is the audience for our/your work? Who do we love spending time with?* I tend to see us as growing community rather than institutionalizing decolonial and Indigenous studies.

There does not need to be a rush to establish Indigenous studies in any mainstream university nor to take up Indigenous research by agencies. I think the Indigenous studies trend is a repositioning trend to strengthen kinds of teaching and research that is often fragmented and piecemeal and unsatisfying to teach. That trend is part of a process that may lead somewhere else in 20 years' time. The other trend mostly occurring in Canada and Australia is to seek ways to "Indigenize" the academy, which can often mean simply adding more Indigenous people to university settings. This aspiration is an entirely different proposition and is not about Indigenous studies per se but often about inclusion, equity, and reconciliation. Somewhat cynically, it can also be viewed as about mainstreaming, dispersing, infusing, or shoring up white privilege by keeping it firmly in positions of power. The critical questions in terms of the call to "Indigenize" are, *Who is making the call? Who is controlling the way that call is articulated? What Indigenous capacity is being developed and how is that being sustained over the long term?* Sometimes these new ideas are opportunities to advance Indigenous thought and scholarship, Indigenous engagement and participation, but sometimes they simply add more work on to the shoulders of the few Indigenous scholars and other staff available in an institution with little attention being given to growing capacity, developing careers, improving relationships, or indeed transforming institutional practices.

Locating Our Work in Education, When It Might Have Had a Home in Other Fields—Eve Tuck

Part of how I ended up locating my work in education has to do with the way that my story has unfolded—that I worked with mentors who located *their* work in education, that the community organizing that I learned from early in my career was across environmental, education, and anti-carceral system movements. I was doing participatory educational design, participatory curriculum development, and participatory action research in my role as a community educator in a community youth organization before I learned the words and terms for what I was doing later in university. This isn't to say that I am somehow advanced or unique, but that community learning spaces already do so much of what gets legitimated and valued as research in the academy. So, part of how I found myself in the field of education has to do with the types of organizing that I saw as most urgent at the time that I was entering graduate school: school policy, environmental racism, policing, and community-led social change.

I also sometimes pause to consider why I have *stayed* in the field of education, rather than move to another interdisciplinary field. This has to do with what I experience as the disciplinary advantages of working in education, rather than fields that also engage Indigenous studies, community organizing, local schooling, participatory approaches to knowledge creation, and intergenerational learning. I could have located my work in another field, and still be able to get at those same questions and practices that have mattered so much to me. So what keeps me here in education, at least for now?

First, this is a field that, when it is at its best, embraces and anticipates change. Change, the likelihood of change, the certainty of change with uncertain outcomes, are foundational to questions of education and learning. The whole field pivots on how change happens and how our efforts as humans can bring about the changes we want to see. This is at the level of the individual, at the level of communities, and at the level of societies or polities—and this is not an ordered scaling; change does not necessarily go in the order from individual to polity, or from polity individual. I like working in a field in which change is at the core of what we talk about. However, sometimes our field tries to discuss or deal with change by making things static when they definitely are not static. Education in this way, when it tries to make itself too much like other fields, makes humans and human activities into predictable boxes that can be stacked to add up to certain things/certainty. I disbelieve in those research practices and disbelieve in their centrality to our field.

I also like working in a field that is concerned with relationality. This is why teacher education, teacher research, and teaching are so integral to educational research more broadly. The relationality of teaching is so immediate, so urgent, that it doesn't allow itself to be overshadowed. It helps to remind that much of what we are looking at, what we are studying when we are doing educational research, is engaging in and simultaneously seeking to know more about relationships and relationality. So, there are questions in my work that would be addressed very differently if I were a historian or an anthropologist. One prominent example has to do with my more recent collaborations to understand more about Black peoples' and Indigenous peoples' relationships to each other within and beyond settler nation-states. To attend to those connections in a way that prioritizes history will yield different results than attending to them in ways that prioritize ongoing relationality, as my collaborators and I have been doing. Opaskwayak Cree scholar Shawn Wilson (2008) discusses the concept of *self as relationship* in Indigenous research, a concept he attributes to his father Stan Wilson (2001). Shawn Wilson writes,

> Identity for Indigenous peoples is grounded in their relationships with the land, with their ancestors who have returned to the land and with future generations who will come into being on the land. Rather than viewing ourselves as being *in* relationship with other people or things, we *are* the relationships that we hold and are part of.
>
> *(p. 80)*

The relationality that I am emphasizing as being especially possible, especially legible within the field of education (as opposed to other fields) is an indelible feature of Indigenous research and Indigenous studies. There is a productive compatibility that I have experienced in working in both these fields.

What has always kept me interested in the field of education as an Indigenous scholar is the way that international conferences on education, such as the American Educational Research Association (AERA) and the World Indigenous People's Conference on Education (WIPCE), draw a critical mass of Indigenous educational scholars from around the globe. It should be said that this is not necessarily attributable to the design of AERA, whereas WIPCE does intentionally engage Indigenous scholars by design. Nonetheless, education is a field that attracts Indigenous scholars, and not only because of exclusion from other fields. Maybe education is a field that Indigenous people have greater access to because so many of us are educators. Maybe it is because the field is so large that proportionally as an "asterisk" group (Shotton, Lowe, & Waterman, 2013)—as numbers too small to be reported—that at a large conference like AERA we are quite sizeable even if we are less than a percentage point. Yet education also attracts Indigenous scholars because of the role of compulsory schooling in colonization, the necessary future-building work that must take place to interrupt practices of assimilation/eradication in schools, and the space made by generations of Indigenous educators for us to meet and forward Indigenous futures.

Thus, Indigenous perspectives on education have never been limited to the liberal values of increasing equity and citizenship in the nation-state; in other words, have never been delimited by the field of education. Indigenous educators pragmatically enact decolonizing work while settler scholars can only imagine decolonization as philosophical and theoretical. Indigenous educators carry forward Indigenous teachings and carry forward the relations—circling back to the teaching-as-relation and self-as-relation—that is the heart of Indigenous futurity. This book series is dedicated to this work, Indigenous + decolonizing work in education, which is not a small intersection in the field of education; it is already beyond the field of education.

Bringing Your Work Home—Linda Tuhiwai Smith

Indigenous graduate students and Indigenous scholars often ask me what it can look like to bring our work home. It is a question about how you understand your work and understanding that there are multiple ways to articulate your work to multiple audiences, including home. If we problematize the national tone, then there are multiple and complex audiences at home, as well.

The trick is recognizing that bringing your work home involves a number of elements. One is to bring yourself home. It's not a "Pack up the thesis and I'm done, I'm graduated, I'm going home, wow." It doesn't happen like that, I think. As someone who has gone in pursuit of advanced education, how do you bring yourself home as an intellectual? That can be quite challenging. You can be home as a daughter, as a niece, as a branch out, as a descendant, as a member, but how do you bring yourself home as an intellectual? I wouldn't recommend you arrive home with a newly minted Ph.D. and say, "I'm here! I'm your intellectual." That probably won't go down well.

The idea of bringing your work home has the element of bringing yourself home, and then there's the element of how your work speaks. How do you want your work to speak? Who do you want your work to speak to? In some senses, advanced degrees give you a platform to speak. I think advanced degrees also give you an opportunity to expand your work further afield.

If I look at what I've tried to do over the long years of my career, probably the least effective way to bring my work or to take my work home to my different communities is to get them a research report. Boring, boring, boring to them.

I have returned home with poems and short stories. And then there is talking, conversing with people about ideas and approaches, trying to apply them to strategies that they can use at home, trying to expand the way we think about the issues at home. I recently went home and spoke to our governance entity about food and food governance. People were enthusiastic because food resonated with every single person in the room. But they were sort of baffled with the governance part until we talked about what it means to govern our food, starting from the production of food from the earth and the ocean, to what we put in our mouths. They got really excited about governance and then, organically, I talked about the background policy for the tribe and suggested some strategies that they could use to implement community-level food sovereignty.

It's so easy sometimes to be disappointed at home because things often take so long to change. You're trained in a way to see the implications of decisions. You can be at home, and you can see decisions being made, and you almost feel like you know what the consequences of decisions are, and you really, really want to feel compelled to intervene and say, "You can't do this" and "You should know this." That's a really tricky space to be in unless you've got lots of strategies for influencing change that you're not just going to learn in a Ph.D. program. You actually have to learn those strategies in the world of community activism, because they're subtle. I don't know about your communities, but my communities have long memories. They have especially long memories for when you mess up. They're forgiving if you carry on trying, but I just think that's another part of the work.

I have sort of dipped in and out of community work, but quite frankly, sometimes, being involved in projects has just made me frustrated and I want to scream. That's a flagrant indicator that maybe I shouldn't be doing that work; I should give all my information and become an adviser to someone else who is prepared to do that kind of work.

For some of us, our work is most effective at the borders of our homes, not in our homes. Our role might be to be outside speaking for our communities or speaking into those communities that are hostile to our homes or speaking to those communities that potentially could support what we do at home, but essentially, working at the borders of your homeland, you're not working within home. You have a role, and it's like a sentinel at one level, sentinel on the border, or you might be beyond the border. You might actually be somewhere else trying to do work for your home.

But I think it's just always about taking yourself home and being connected and understanding that that's a particular role. I would not say that it is an easy role. I would say that it is always a challenging role. I don't have easy solutions for how you manage that role if you come out of an Indigenous or First Nation. Even in the community—communities are complicated.

Revisiting "Insiders" and "Outsiders" in Indigenous Research—Linda Tuhiwai Smith

When I wrote *Decolonizing Methodologies* (1999), discussions of being an insider or outsider in ethnographic research were prevalent. Anthropology departments now teach people how to be a research insider, and there is an industry around making yourself inside, as though that is the solution to the kinds of tensions that are raised in considering who is inside and who is outside a community. I think really, in practice, there is no inside. Even if you are researcher in your own community, by being a researcher, you're positioned in relation to the community in a complicated way. You might know the community. You might have the language of the community. You might have relationships in the community. But the role of research always positions you in a somewhat different space with different responsibilities, including ethical responsibilities and intellectual responsibilities, let alone managing relationship responsibilities if you are a researcher.

Interestingly, some anthropology research still clings to traditional ideas of being able to immerse oneself in primitive cultures. Here in New Zealand, we still endure graduate students from European universities who come to our communities to do research without any ethical documents or pre-established relationships with a host New Zealand institution. Some arrive unannounced to a community event. They look so hopeless and pathetic that a community member feels sorry for them and takes them into their homes and feeds them. Then the community member finds out that they're there to do research and are seeking "contacts" and "networks." The act of taking them in and sharing food obligates their host to try and help them. In fact, researchers need to approach the community in more formal ways. This is kind of subterfuge of innocence where one arrives like some naïve traveler saying, "Oh, I've just been sent to do my Ph.D. Help me, help me!"

That example of the insider/outsider notion was really common when I started writing *Decolonizing Methodologies*. It shocks me that the practice still happens, that people can come literally from the other side of the world and think that they can immerse themselves in our community and think they can become like an insider. When I am teaching about insider/outsider, I make clear that it is a very kind of crude binary if you think about it. It is much more complicated in terms of what is the outside, what is the inside, and whether there are really sides anyway. More and more, we are teaching our own students about positioning and positionality, the responsibilities of yourself as a researcher, but also understanding that you can position yourself in different ways when you understand that context.

I have undertaken research with my own communities, with Indigenous communities that are not my own and with communities that transgress traditional notions of geopolitical and genealogical community such as urban youth, social service providers, women. One of the reasons I have enjoyed working with communities to which I do not belong is because I am not drawn into all the domestic dramas of my community. I just smile when they look at me and say "Oh, did you hear the latest?" I can just say, "No," and get on with our work. If I am in my own community, all that stuff is always in the room. You hear the latest gossip and little dramas. That is what comes with me working in my community. But I have also enjoyed working in other Indigenous contexts where I have been able to focus on the particular aspects of research of interest to me. I have been able to do that in a good way with that Indigenous community and develop a really good partnership in research. Increasingly, I am more concerned with the deeper issues that empirical research hints at but often fails to pick up upon, or with connecting different parts of a puzzle that cannot be answered in a single project. This may be a question about the ways in which Indigenous values inform multiple strands of work, or how Indigenous knowledge is being utilized across different domains, or ideas about resilience and resistance, well-being, and hospitality.

These days, when I am thinking about the insider/outsider, I think it is what a beginner needs to know about boundaries, borders, liminality, and intersectionality. An Indigenous researcher needs to know so much more than that. It comes back to how you position yourself, how you understand yourself, your intentions and capacity to work in a good way, your skills at negotiating complexity and your ability to work in relation with community, with land and water, with a wider sense of the world.

Losing Patience for the Task of Convincing Settlers to Pay Attention to Indigenous Ideas—Eve Tuck

Learning from Linda Tuhiwai Smith's work, much of my writing has expressed some impatience with regard to research practices *on* Indigenous peoples. I have been critical of damage-centered research (Tuck, 2009), which focuses solely on the supposed damage of Indigenous people in the supposed aftermath of colonization (supposed because settler colonialism continues to violently shape Indigenous life). I have also written with Wayne (Tuck & Yang, 2012) to critique superficial, additive employs of the term decolonization in education discourse, and have argued for using the term with specificity, not just as an emptied synonym for whatever project someone was already wanting to make happen. To say that decolonization is not a metaphor is to resist using decolonization as a trendy term, and in settler colonial contexts, to resist delinking decolonial projects from the rematriation of Indigenous land and life. In settler states that are also antiblack states founded through the violence of chattel slavery, decolonization also must involve abolition.

So, I'm somewhat used to expressing impatience in my work, but more recently, I have become frustrated by the way that Indigenous scholarship is taken up in the settler academy. For most of my career, I have advocated for the centrality of Indigenous social thought in fields of education. Most of my interventions have focused on the possibilities afforded by attending to Indigenous writings, worldviews, teachings, approaches to relationship, ethics, histories, and futurities. I have done this because I am convinced that Indigenous texts, for the most part, do the work to teach readers how these texts need to be read.

One extended analogy that I have made to describe the relationship between Indigenous social thought and Western theory is that of the New York City subway system. I was a New Yorker for much of my adult life, and I hold the NYC subway system in high regard (note I am describing the network of tracks, not necessarily the company that runs the trains!). A map of the criss-crossing routes is something to behold. Trains go all over the city, taking one below rivers, beneath stone and skyscrapers, above avenues and through the most sacred parts of the city. Subway lines route from this corner to that corner, from this neighborhood to that beach. Entryways from the street are well marked, often with a glowing green ball, or one that glows red to convey that it is closed for now. Signs from the street indicate "downtown only," or "uptown only," and where a train will go to (and not go to) is clearly marked on the platforms. For me, thinking of this underground world of connectivity and travel and hubs and pathways is a good way to think about Indigenous knowledges. Indigenous knowledges have many of these characteristics and are also usually sign-posted—*this will take you in this direction, but not in this direction. This is open for you now. This is how you get to your destination, but this is also how you get to other destinations.*

To extend this analogy, sometimes listening to a person who is trying to understand something only by engaging Western theory is like listening to a person who keeps trying to take a taxi cab in rush-hour traffic. They complain about getting stuck, the slow ride, the cost of the trip. Being an Indigenous scholar in the settler academy is like listening to someone go on and on about the dilemmas of cab rides while knowing that the subway system is just beneath the surface.

Again, I feel that I have spent much of my time in education encouraging people to take just a short journey on a subway, or at least check out a map. I feel that I have been standing at the subway entrance, calling to colleagues and students as they hop in their individual taxi cabs into gridlock traffic.

I find myself less willing to do this now. I am weary after so many conference presentations in which Indigenous scholars present work and then someone in the audience asks them a question that expects them to do more work. When I was in graduate school, I hated conference presentations because no matter how carefully I articulated my project, there was always someone in the audience who wanted me to do more labor for them; either tell them what they can do or help them see how they can save all the "Indian" children. In most cases, this question was posed even if my presentation critiqued the ways in which white settlers make their experiences the center of life and work. Now, especially when I am serving as chair or discussant on panels with new Indigenous scholars, I warn audiences away from asking self-serving questions or questions that make Indigenous scholars create honey-do lists for settlers.

There have been several "turns," including the ontological turn, the material turn, the spatial turn, each of which is actually a turn to where Indigenous people have always been (see also Tuck & McKenzie, 2015). I recently became totally exasperated when I saw a social media post by a white settler colleague asking for recommendations of "more practical" readings by Indigenous scholars, which would provide more detail about what decolonization looks like "in reality." To watch settler scholars sift through our work as they effectively ask, "Isn't there more for me to get from this?" is so insulting. It seems like the tacit (and sometimes arrogantly explicit) request for more (details, explanation, assurance) is actually a form of dismissal. It is a rejection of the opportunity to engage with Indigenous texts on their own terms. It is a deferral of responsibility through asking, "Isn't there something less theoretical? Isn't there something more theoretical? Something more practical? Something less radical? Can't you describe something that seems more likely or possible?" These insistences upon Indigenous writings contradict themselves while also putting all the onus of responsibility on Indigenous people to make the future more coherent and palatable to white settler readers. In reading Indigenous work, they ask for more work, even if they have done little to fully consider what has already been carefully and attentively offered. Often it seems that settler readers read like settlers (that is, read extractively) for particular content to be removed for future use. The reading is like panning for gold, sorting through work that may not have been intended for a particular reader, sorting it by what is useful and what is discardable. Again, something being purportedly too theoretical is often the reason that Indigenous work is discarded or disregarded, whereas that "too theoretical" idea may be entirely practical, life-sustaining, and life-promoting for an Indigenous reader.

I spent almost all my career, up until recently, believing that if white settlers would just read Indigenous authors, this would move projects of Indigenous sovereignty and land rematriation in meaningful ways. I underestimated how people would read Indigenous work extractively, for discovery. I underestimated how challenging it would be for settlers to read Indigenous work, after all these years of colonial relations.

Indigenous and decolonial theories are unfairly, inappropriately expected to answer to whiteness and to settler relationships to land in the future. At the end of *Decolonization is Not a Metaphor*, Wayne and I write about the importance of incommensurability. We write that incommensurability is an ethic that contests reconciliation—reconciliation is about rescuing settler normalcy, about ensuring a settler future. A settler future is preoccupied by questions of, *What will decolonization look like? What will happen after abolition? What will be the consequences of decolonization for the settler?*

Wayne and I close the article with the insistence that decolonization is not obliged to answer questions concerned with settler futures. "Decolonization is not accountable to settlers, or settler futurity. Decolonization is accountable to Indigenous sovereignty and futurity. The answers to those questions are not fully in view" (Tuck & Yang, 2012, p. 35). What I am coming to more fully understand is that the questions of "What will decolonization look like?," when posed by settlers, are a distraction to Indigenous theorizations of decolonization. They drain the energy and imagination of Indigenous scholarship—they pester, they think they are unique, and they are boring. I want time and space to sketch the next and the now to get there. Decolonization is not the endgame, not the final outcome of a long process, but the next now, the now that is chasing at our heels. I am lucky to come from the long view.

A Preview of the Chapters in This Book

One thing that readers will immediately notice is that the chapters and organization of this book do not readily adhere to the more typical divisions within education as a broad field. Chapters drift between things that elsewhere get called higher education, curriculum and instruction, out-of-school learning, special education, educational research. This is part of the river-like design of this book, a way of showing how interventions afforded by Indigenous and decolonizing studies in education re-order and re-imagine the divisions within education that have been naturalized. These divisions do not have to be the way that we approach our teaching and research in education. They have an impact on what gets constructed as a problem and what can be understood as a solution. They do not need to have so much influence. They can be washed away.

We have found that water—in its insistence on being what it is (as Erin Marie Konsmo points out), in its profound relationship to places, to its multiplicity of forms, in its fluidity, and its worldwide connections to all places and peoples—has become an appropriate organizing principle for this book. This introduction began with a discussion of Yanaguana river and its celestial river companion, the constellation Eridanus. To live and make research as though water is life necessarily means attending to ways that water as relation is regenerated through ceremony, through restoring and establishing good relations with water. It means turning away from water as a colonial commodification. The connection of these two distinct but related projects of Indigenous relation-making and decolonization can inform approaches to education. As such, readers will notice that chapters highlighting the centrality of water as teaching, as relation, and as place have been distributed throughout the chapters—to signal difference/diversity in Indigenous thought but to also weave a connective pathway within the chapters. Ocean, rivers, reef—waters and their interconnected lands—thread and flow throughout this book.

Our opening chapter, "Literacies of Land: Decolonizing Narratives, Storying and Literature" offers important frameworks about reading, teaching, and writing from an emplaced perspective that is based on classroom practices by Sandra Styres (Kanien'kehá:ka), residing on Six Nations of the Grand River Territory in Oniatari:io. Space is connected but different from place, different from land, and different from Land—and Styres takes us quickly and meaningfully to appreciate literacies of Land as decolonizing and Indigenous knowledge-making praxis. Choosing to capitalize "Land" is to recognize Indigenous Land as source of philosophy, of cosmology, of spirituality. Thus Styres extends and perhaps explodes the theories of critical literacy and place-based literacies. Literacies of the Land are "about reading all of the things around us that are not necessarily the written word." The Land teaches us both pathways beyond colonization and original instructions on being-in-relation, and thus teaches us what we hope the words "Indigenous and Decolonization in Education" would mean in this book series. As the opening chapter for this book, "Literacies of Land" articulates so many principles about Land as sentient, as consciousness, as teacher, as relation that are shared in the chapters in this book.

Along the spirit of water as relation, and as a relation that teaches, Naadli Todd Lee Ormiston (Northern Tutchone, Tlingit) describes "paddling as pedagogy" in his chapter, "Haa Shageinyaa: 'Point Your Canoe Downstream and Keep Your Head Up!'" Naadli shares his learnings from and meditations upon a 55-day, 850-mile journey in a canoe on the Eagle, Bell, Porcupine, and Yukon rivers. Readers might be struck by the contrast between critical Western philosophies of pedagogy as reading and writing the world—acting upon the world—and Tlingit philosophies of knowledge creation where learning and teaching are in collaboration with the world: the waters, the weather, the wildlife. Certainly, paddling and living on the water is an embodied practice of persons-in-movement, but it is also a collaborative practice where living is interdependent with one's paddling companion, the plants and animals, and the trails and traces left behind by previous travelers. Along Ormiston's journey is evidence of settler encroachment in forms of physical violations that are so clearly epistemological violations as well, yet still the river life is all around, collaborating, flowing, teaching.

Chapter 3, "Rez Ponies and Confronting Sacred Junctures in Decolonizing and Indigenous Education," is an artful engagement of colonial incommensurabilities and decolonial embodiment through the connections between horse, rider, and land. Diné author Kelsey Dayle John compels us to think about the Diné horse and riding as relation, as methodology, as knowledge transmission. "The way I was taught, Diné call this hózhǫ . . . walking in beauty." Diné receive instruction on relations with animal nations, and on navigating the borders of colonial/decolonial, through observing and participating in the embodiment acts of respect for horses amidst a landscape scarred by colonization. Weaving narratives about riding horses together with careful writings on decoloniality and Indigeneity, Kelsey Dayle John takes us on a ride that reverberates with a grounded Diné epistemology about incommensurability and decolonization without privileging these academic terms and, indeed, without using academic theory as the carrier and conduit of thinking on these matters. "Horses are a gift," in so many ways, including an active source of dynamic knowledge of ground and movement, that teaches the Diné rider decolonizing pathways.

In Chapter 4, "River as Lifeblood, River as Border: The Irreconcilable Discrepancies of Colonial Occupation from/with/on/of the Frontera," Marissa Muñoz (Xicana Tejana) speaks as a restorying and, indeed, restorative guide along the banks of the Rio Grande/Rio Bravo—the waters that have come to be the geopolitical boundary separating Laredo, Texas from Nuevo Laredo, Tamaulipas. These borderlands are Muñoz's home and her grandmother's home before her. Grounded in place-based knowledges, Muñoz meditatively addresses incommensurabilities of Mexican/Indian/American colonial relations and realities. Deliberately not heavy with borderland theory, this chapter opens possibilities for an evolving Xicanx epistemology that engages Indigenous and decolonizing pasts, presents, futures through place-based conocimiento. Marissa Muñoz navigates us through the borderlands, taking the Rio Grande rather than any border wall or political demarcation as the place of restorying, "in order to remember who we were before our river became an occupied, armed, international border."

"Indigenous Oceanic Futures: Challenging Settler Colonialisms and Militarization" offers a critical framework for addressing (de)militarization in Indigenous and decolonizing studies in education. Noelani Goodyear-Ka'ōpua (Kanaka Maoli) insightfully situates projects of decolonization in the "global" conditions of empire built upon and maintained by militarization. Goodyear-Ka'ōpua uses the fluidity of oceanic boundaries and movements to unsettle the naturalization of land-as-territory with stable landscapes readily available for cartographic borders. This chapter begins with a story of contemporary 2014 Oceanic voyaging on double-hulled sailing canoes as a practice of navigating to an Indigenous future—a voyage that necessarily connects oceanic (de)toxification, border crossings, and regeneration of Indigenous relations connected by the Pacific. In the same year, a voyage of massive firepower by the US Pacific Fleet around the "Rim of the Pacific" enacts a settler futurity—and puts into perspective the geopolitical stakes of demilitarization and Indigenous oceanic futures. By "looking at lands from vantage points on the ocean," this chapter connects thinking about futurities by Indigenous scholars across lands and oceans. Readers will appreciate the scope of ideas covered in accessible and storytelling manner, such as futurities, futurisms, resurgence. This chapter combines many of the existing tools in Indigenous and decolonizing studies for "visions for and practices of decolonial future-making."

Chapter 6, "The Ixil University and the Decolonization of Knowledge" details contemporary efforts of an autonomous university dedicated to Indigenous land, culture, and resource preservation, created and run by the Maya in the Ixil Region of the western highlands of Guatemala. Author Giovanni Batz (K'iche' Maya) shares the contexts of nation-state mining, hydroelectric dams, resource extraction, and the negative effects of nation-state educational institutions on distancing Indigenous students from their communities. These conditions of Indigenous place and communities may resonate with many readers. The Ixil University, in response to these conditions, prepares students to defend their territories, resources, cultures, and communities, and does so without seeking state recognition. Batz writes about Indigenous efforts with great care and respect—rooting his perspectives in modern Mayan epistemologies and carefully sharing only what is permissible and necessary for the reader. This chapter is an important contribution in considering Indigenous educational institution-building beyond the parameters of the nation-state.

In Chapter 7, "Decolonizing Indigenous Education in the Postwar City: Native Women's Activism from Southern California to the Motor City," Kyle T. Mays (Saginaw Chippewa) and Kevin Whalen engage history, place, and Native feminisms in the creation of Indigenous urban educational institutions. They tell the story of Judy Mays, a Saginaw Anishinaabe woman who was instrumental in the development of Detroit's Indian Educational and Cultural Center, founded in 1975, and Medicine Bear American Indian Academy, founded in 1994. They also tell of a connected but radically different context, Sherman Institute in Southern California's Inland Empire, an off-reservation boarding school originally intended to assimilate Native American youth into whitestream society. They detail the labors of Native women, with particular attention to Lorene Sisquoc (Cahuilla/Apache), to "transform Sherman Institute from a place of dispossession into a hub for intertribal cultural survival." Mays's and Whalen's writing moves across space and time, with specificity to place and history, a motion that offers broader insights into the interplay between Indigeneity, class, place, and race—particularly Blackness in the case of Detroit. And through all this, they focus on urban Indigenous feminisms in revitalizing pedagogies and institutional transformation.

Chapter 8, "Queering Indigenous Education," is a talking chapter by Alex Wilson (Neyonawak Inniniwak) in an interview with Marie Laing (Kanyen'kehá:ka). Discussing land-based education with a perspective attuned to two-spirit and Indigenous LGBTQ communities, Wilson describes the inseparability of land sovereignty and body sovereignty. This perspective rethinks pedagogical practices that may substitute Indigenous traditions for colonial traditions in education, yet nonetheless reproduce the colonial commitments to fixity and to hierarchizations embedded in Western pedagogical paradigms. This means women and two-spirit people bear the "whiplash" politics on their very bodies, in forms of violation, in the murdered and missing, in the un-understood suicide. In restoring traditional understandings of bodies to land, fluidity and tradition become complementary. Wilson offers both teachings that are translatable to other settings and roots their discussion in the specificities of the land-based education master's program at the University of Saskatchewan, LGBTQ2S activist histories, and land epistemes of Opaskwayak Cree Nation.

"What makes research ethical?" is the question that opens Madeline Whetung's (Nishnaabeg) and Sarah Wakefield's chapter, "Colonial Conventions: Institutionalized Research Relationships and Decolonizing Research Ethics." Their discussion learns from a half century of Indigenous critiques of the colonizing impact of research. This history includes institutional attempts to correct for the worst violations of research, while simultaneously reaffirming the power of university ethic boards to evaluate and approve research as ethical. Their purpose is not to just critique, but to pragmatically ask what can be done to create genuinely ethical research in relationship to people and places, as well as to foster accountability to embedded Indigenous knowledge. They account for how the academy is porous, with Indigenous presence inside and outside, even though institutional ethics codes presume Indigenous people to be non-researchers. Written in an engaging dialogic style between an Indigenous graduate student and a non-Indigenous professor who has served on university ethics boards, the chapter forwards challenges to the power of universities and ethics as "something we *do*" rather than something adjudicated.

What would it mean to move from learning about Indigenous peoples to learning from Indigenous peoples? This is the paradigm shift that Adam Gaudry (Métis) and Danielle Lorenz envision for mandatory university Indigenous Course Requirements (ICRs), in Chapter 10, "Decolonization for the Masses? Grappling with Indigenous Content Requirements in the Changing Canadian Post-Secondary Environment." The advent of ICRs in the Canadian context ought to be critiqued as another attempt by the settler state to sidestep the transformative project of decolonization with a liberal project of curricular inclusion of Indigenous content. The authors reject the notion that simply providing more information about Indigenous peoples and cultures will remedy colonial relations. However, they suggest that ICRs can be a decolonizing program if education on treaty relations and practical experience become a primary concern of ICR policies. The authors synthesize the debates over these mandatory course requirements—which were exciting developments from the reconciliation movement—attending closely to the pedagogical, ideological, and practical questions that arise for university faculty, students, and administrators.

"E Kore Au e Ngaro, He Kākano i Ruia mai i Rangiātea (I Will Never Be Lost, I Am a Seed Sown from Rangiātea): Te Wānanga o Raukawa as an Example of Educating for Indigenous Futures" presents a case study from a Māori tertiary education institute in Aotearoa/New Zealand. Author Kim McBreen (Waitaha, Kāti Mamoe, Ngāi Tahu) explains that this story must be considered within the broader context of the massive developments in Māori educational institutions and situated within the larger movement for treaty rights and decolonization. Te Wānanga o Raukawa is one of three wānanga, which are higher education institutions based on Māori practices and philosophies and offering a range of programs from vocational training to certificates, to diplomas, to bachelor and postgraduate degrees. Chapter 11 details the history and principles of Te Wānanga o Raukawa as part of this larger four-decades-long effort to reverse Māori linguistic and cultural extinction.

In "Designing Futures of Identity: Navigating Agenda Collisions in Pacific Disability," Catherine Picton and Rasela Tufue-Dolgoy consider how disability policy in Samoa is formed at the collisions of multiple ideological and cultural conceptualizations of disability. For Picton and Tufue-Dolgoy, these collisions occur both between and within colonial disability discourses, contemporary global ones, and Fa'asamoa (the Samoan way). Chapter 12 argues that existing policy has not accounted for the dynamic ways that community ideologies of disability are shaped and reshaped. They propose the Samoan concept of Tutusa (to be the same, equal) as a framework for honoring the many voices in disability, and as a tool for navigating the competing discourses in Samoan disability policy.

In "Decolonizing Education through Transdisciplinary Approaches to Climate Change Education," Teresa Newberry and Octaviana V. Trujillo (Yaqui) discuss their curricular and pedagogical practices at Tohono O'odham Community College, which is a tribally controlled college and the institution of higher education of the Tohono O'odham Nation. Transdisciplinary approaches are an important antidote to STEM-centric treatments of climate by incorporating traditional ecological knowledge (TEK) or Indigenous knowledges (IK). Newberry and Trujillo are particularly attentive to the question of pedagogical efficacy for Indigenous students in their work on climate change education. Transdisciplinary approaches that incorporate Indigenous knowledges are not only better research, but also better educational practice in supporting the educational success of Indigenous students. Such approaches offer high-context emphasis on community, place, specificity; and examples of problem-based learning meant to address Indigenous global and community problems. The authors share directly from their pedagogical practices—including models for incorporating elder input, science input, and policy input into climate change problem-solving.

In Chapter 14, "With Roots in the Water: Revitalizing Straits Salish Reef Net Fishing as Education for Well-Being and Sustainability," Nicholas XEMŦOLTW̱ Claxton (Tsawout) and Carmen Rodríguez de France (Kickapoo) guide us through the revitalization of the SX̱OLE, or Reef Net Fishery, in the territory of the W̱SÁNEĆ People, on Southern Vancouver Island in British Columbia. The Reef Net is an ancient fishing technology developed by the Straits Salish people to fish for Pacific Salmon. This chapter describes the history, context, and specific efforts to restore the fishery. A holistic decolonizing/revitalizing approach connects a tribal school with the restoration of the Reef Net and its practices. Indeed, the SX̱OLE is already a school of sorts—"the W̱SÁNEĆ traditional educational system or way, which fostered a deep knowledge, connection, beliefs of the people to the salmon and to the lands and Waters." As detailed in the chapter, its revitalization necessarily confronts multiple layers of colonization including settler law, schooling, diet, religion, economy, and environment. It offers a clear case of active decolonization of the education system.

This book would be incomplete without Chapter 15, a discussion of Indigenous language revitalization efforts. chuutsqa Layla Rorick (Hesquiaht) in "Waɫyaʕasukʔi Naananiqsakqin: At the Home of our Ancestors: Ancestral Continuity in Indigenous Land-Based Language Immersion" describes the Hooksum Outdoor School, a Hesquiaht-centered language immersion program. With an engaging approach, Rorick stories her own language journey as a literal calling from the land and from the ancestors. Her writing brings to life the re-membering of language as a restorative practice to counter the *dismemberment* or disembodiment enacted by residential schools and the reserve system. Rorick not only details the ways in which her Language Nest makes use of physical areas as curricula (place names, etc.) but even how re-membering operates at the level of grammar—because "our language integrates location information that directly connects speech to place." Given the diversity of Indigenous languages and their health as spoken languages, it is hard to generalize practices of language revitalization. However, what might be resonant with readers are the pedagogies of land-based language education that triangulate stories, ontologies, and place with Indigenous language.

The afterword, "Meeting the Land(s) Where They Are At," is written with loving humor, urgency, and patience. This is a story-sharing conversation between Erin Marie Konsmo (Métis) and Karyn Recollet (urban Cree) about meeting Indigenous Peoples and Lands "where they're at," namely meeting them in their disabled and "impure" realities. The authors share insights that are accessible yet profound, such as the acknowledgment that lands and waters are polluted everywhere, and so to treat some waters as "pure" and sacred and others as impure is against Indigenous callings for defending the water. Likewise, to treat normative bodies as capable and pure enough to be defenders of the waters, and others as too ill, too contaminated, too disconnected, is a form of ableism and queer-phobia. To meet lands and peoples where they're at is to engage with waters/bodies as they are. Considering how we nurture people not yet within reach of the water, Konsmo and Recollet discuss "the choreographies, the practices that we can employ 'at the water's edge' so that we can make sure that no one gets left behind." These practices may not be free of colonial contamination, but they are practices of harm reduction, of healing.

The Futurities of Indigenous and Decolonizing Studies in Education

This is a book about and written as Indigenous epistemologies and methodologies. As such, we are emphasizing land, water, and the more-than-human world, emphasizing relations as accountability, emphasizing a past-present-future that exceeds any nation-state or modern imperial formation. The chapters were all composed for the purpose of showing the edges, the hesitations, the bold futures of Indigenous and decolonizing studies in education. Here is what is remarkable: each of the chapters understands that the 21st century will be one of regeneration. The horrors of settler colonialism, of capitalism will not be the end chapter of the human story. It is powerful to write from this notion as a given. It is powerful to consider, as a baseline, that this millennium will be one of decolonization.

While powerful, it isn't easy to write as though this is a given. Settler governments and presidents, universities, schools, extractive infrastructures, the carceral system can seem very total, very permanent. Still, this book persists in wanting more, in wanting another kind of future. We can use the word future to describe a time that comes after now, a time that we will come to inevitably. We can also use the word *futurity*, a word that imbibes the future with what we are doing now to bring about different futures. The authors in this book attend to what we are doing now to bring about the futures we can't even fully imagine yet. This is because as Indigenous peoples and decolonizing educators, we have responsibilities that require/urge/direct/instruct us to be good ancestors to future generations of human and non-human entities, to the earth and sky, to land and water, to the stars and the molten crevices of the earth, to the past and the future. Our learnings and teachings have incorporated decolonizing strategies partly to protect us from what has happened under settler colonialism, partly to recover and revitalize those aspects of our knowledge we still need, and partly to ensure we are critically reflexive in our engagement with concepts such as education.

We hope that this book, a "first" in some ways, simply the "next" in so many more, can inspire conversations and works across many colonized territories, so that revitalization is more within reach, more inevitable. For those of you who, like us, have so far only found a place for these conversations in the edges of the scene, we hope that this book and the book series it opens can bring the ideas that matter to you out of the footnotes and into the body of the work.

This is a home for you, if you have only found a home so far in the footnotes.

References

Hunt, S. (2013). Ontologies of indigeneity: The politics of embodying a concept. *Cultural Geographies, 0*(0), 1–6.

Konsmo, E. M. (2017, September 24). *Water is life (But many can't drink it).* Toronto, ON: Response to lecture by Winona LaDuke at the University of Toronto Press.

Shotton, H. J., Lowe, S. C., & Waterman, S. J. (2013). *Beyond the asterisk: Understanding native students in higher education.* Sterling, VA: Stylus Publishing, LLC.

Simpson, L. (2016). Indigenous resurgence and co-resistance. *Journal of the Critical Ethnic Studies Association, 2*(2), 19–34.

Styres, S. D. (2011). Land as first teacher: A philosophical journeying. *Reflective Practice: International and Multidisciplinary Perspectives, 12*(6), 717–731.

Tuck, E. (2009). Suspending damage: A letter to communities. *Harvard Educational Review, 79*(3), 409–428.

Tuck, E., & McKenzie, M. (2015). *Place in research: Theory, methodology, and methods.* New York, NY: Routledge.

Tuck, E., & Yang, K. W. (2012). Decolonization is not a metaphor. *Decolonization: Indigeneity, Education & Society, 1*(1), 1–40.

Tuhiwai Smith, L. (1999). *Decolonizing methodologies: Research and indigenous peoples.* London, UK: Zed Books.

Wilson, S. (2001). What is indigenous research methodology? *Canadian Journal of Native Education, 25*(2), 175–180.

Wilson, S. (2008). *Research is ceremony: Indigenous research methods.* Black Point, NS: Fernwood Publishing.

1

LITERACIES OF LAND

Decolonizing Narratives, Storying, and Literature

Sandra Styres (Kanien'kehá:ka)

Introduction

Indigeneity[1] and working within Indigenous contexts is first and foremost about reciprocity and relationships. These relationships involve an acknowledgment and understanding of cultural positionalities and relations of place.[2] It is important that I locate myself both in terms of recognizing the traditional lands on which I stand and do this work as well as the background informing my perspectives. The land on which this paper was written is the shared territories of the Mississaugas of the New Credit First Nations and the Six Nations Confederacy (Mohawk, Oneida, Onondaga, Cayuga, Seneca, and Tuscarora) on A'nó:wara Tsi Kawè:note (Turtle Island), and more specifically on what is now known as Oniatari:io (Ontario). As an academic who is of Kanien'kehá:ka (Mohawk), English, and French ancestry, I reside on Six Nations of the Grand River Territory, a First Nations community located in Oniatari:io. Further, it is also important to acknowledge the complex and tangled histories of those on whose traditional lands the mainstream educational institution where I teach my courses is located—the Ouendat (Wyandot-Huron), Chonnonton (Neutral), Onondowahgah (Seneca-Hodenosaunee), and the Misi-zaagiing (Mississaugas-Anishinaabek) nations. It is the philosophies embedded in our places where land, learning, identity, and education intersect. Kovach (2009) writes that "we know what we know from where we stand" (p. 7).

Drawing upon instructor and student experiences from several courses but more particularly from a course I developed and taught over several terms called Literacies of Land: Narratives, Storying and Literature, this chapter focuses on the ways literacies of Land (capital "L") are rooted in and informed by understandings of Land and self-in-relationship that open opportunities for decolonizing frameworks and praxis that critically trouble and disrupt colonial myths and stereotypical representations embedded in normalizing, hegemonic discourses and relations of power and privilege while exploring diverse Indigenous literacy contexts. I hope to offer some insights and practical examples of the ways decolonizing praxis can be actively incorporated into pedagogical practices to engage critical reflection and mindfully and purposefully explore the various tensions, challenges, and resistances of locating and positioning Land with a capital "L" within classrooms. Using First Voices in culturally aligned and place-conscious texts, stories, oral traditions, and symbolically rich themes that support literacies of Land as living and emergent, in this chapter I explore the ways these literacies can inform decolonizing frameworks for exploring the importance of understanding and acknowledging place in literacy education (having implications across all educational contexts) for the benefit of all learners. Emphasis is placed on the philosophical nature of Land in relation to critical literacies that include narratives, storying, and literature together with constructions of self in relation to educational contexts. Storying refers to the ways we describe, by means of stories, our experiences through personal, community, national, and global narratives. Both storying and literacy are social constructions combining orality and narratives to communicate not only among individuals but also between human beings and their world.

As we well know language is never neutral—it can teach us, inform us, entertain us, persuade us, and manipulate us—it can misguide and misdirect truths, thereby perpetuating colonial myths and stereotypical representations, or it can disrupt normalizing and hegemonic dominant discourses and liberate critical thought. Critical literacy encourages students to actively analyze and engage with meaning-making through a variety of texts, media, and popular culture looking for and exploring underlying messages and symbolic representations—in this case the ways Land is an articulation of ancient knowledges grounded in the experiences of self-in-relationship to place. Indigenous literacy is based on reading the cosmos—it is about reading all the things around us that are not necessarily the written word but nevertheless contain valuable information. Peter Kulchyski (2005) tells us that

> land is a space that is somehow meaningfully organized and on the very point of speech, a kind of articulated thinking that fails to reach its ultimate translation in proposition or concepts, in messages . . . the various landscapes, from frozen inland wastes to the river and the coast itself, speak multiple languages . . . and emit a remarkable range of articulated messages.
>
> *(p. 189)*

Armstrong (1998) tells us that,

> all my Elders say that it is land that holds all knowledge of life and death and is a constant teacher . . . the land constantly speaks. It is constantly

communicating. We survived and thrived by listening to its teachings—to its language—and then inventing human words to retell its stories to our succeeding generation.

(p. 178)

Musqua tells us that "everything in the universe is speaking to us. It's a literacy in itself" (as cited in George, 2010, p. 4). Similarly, Hawaiian scholar Goodyear-Ka'ōpua uses the term aloha'āina to describe what she calls land-centered literacies that extend beyond the mainstream definition of literacies that focus solely on linguistic and social practices related to printed text. Aloha'āina literally means to love and respect the land and is a central tenet of ancient Hawaiian thought. Aloha'āina critically engages observational, interpretive, and expressive skills that read the cosmos, conduct and participate in ceremonies, as well as listen for and find meaning in the responses from their places (wind, rains, animals, trees, waterways, etc.)—aloha'āina is about "writing themselves into the landscape" (2013, p. 34).

One of the main goals of critical literacy is to open up opportunities for learners to understand themselves first and, through critical self-reflection and to gain a better understanding of each other and the ways power, privilege, and colonial relations continue to inform our ways of knowing and being in the world. The concept of Land as a philosophical underpinning along with understandings of self-in-relationship draw upon deeply intimate, sacred, and ancient knowledges, thereby centering, legitimizing, and grounding teaching and learning within Land as the primary foundation of all our teachings. Ancient knowledges are (re)membered experiences that form deeply intimate and spiritual expressions of our connections to Land.

Land With a Capital "L"

Before attempting to articulate any understandings of Land (capital "L"), it is important to begin by examining some of the complex ideologies relating to space and place, as well as to explore some of the ways space and place may be connected to but are very specifically distinct from my conceptualizations of Land.

Space is a continuous area or expanse that is free, available, or unoccupied (Styres, 2017, p. 45). Space is empty and abstract, whereas place is concrete, sensed, and grounded in lived experiences and realities. Space, in its formal context, is primary, absolute, infinite, and empty, and place-making emerges from the vastness and existence of space (Styres, 2017, p. 46). Space requires the substance of culture and stories to render it placeful. Spatial scholars such as Bachelard (1994), Casey (1996), and Lefebvre (1991) assert that places "gather experiences and histories, even languages and thoughts . . . and the trajectories of inanimate things" (Casey, 1996, p. 24, 26). Feld's (1996) notion of inter-sensory perception allows a culture-sharing group to "turn over" the surface to look "underneath or inside," thereby revealing the subtleties, the "resonant depth" of meaning captured in place names, stories, songs, teachings (p. 98, 99)—ancient knowledges that are (re)membered and embodied experiences forming deeply intimate and spiritual expressions of our connections to Land. In this context, inter-sensory perception is essentially the study of the ways information from our various senses (sight, sound, touch, smell, self-motion [embodiment] and taste), are integrated by the nervous system. Inter-sensory perception enables us to have meaningful perceptual and embodied experiences of our places. Embodied or emplaced spaces, while always intimate, are never neutral.

Casey (1996) writes that we are never without "emplaced experiences . . . we are not only *in* places but *of* them" (p. 19). In other words we find our existence in the intimate and embodied expressions of place. Such knowledges are highly contextualized, soulful, (re)membered, and experienced. Soulfulness is deeply intense and emotional expressions of feeling; as such, place is storied, relational, and intimate. In this way we are in place as much as it is in us—every experience and expression of place is replete with multiple layers of memories, each inform-ing the other in diverse and entangled ways (see also Styres, 2017, p. 47). These memories can be (re)membered through the (re)telling of stories and experi-ences of and in place. Space, then, is an empty generality (see also Styres, 2017, p. 47). By inhabiting spaces—by being present in those spaces, to occupy those spaces, to story those spaces, to (re)member and (re)cognize those spaces—they become place*ful*.

Place refers to physical geographic space and is defined by everything that is included in that space—also referred to as landscape, ecology, and/or environment—and is denoted as land (lower case "l"). Connected but distinct, Land (capital "L") is more than physical geographic space. Land expresses a dual-ity that refers not only to place as a physical geographic space but also to the underlying conceptual principles, philosophies, and ontologies of that space. This duality is not to be construed as dichotomous, oppositional, or binarial but rather expresses the ways Land embodies two simultaneously interconnected and inter-dependent conceptualizations. Land as an Indigenous philosophical construct is both space (abstract) and place/land (concrete); it is also conceptual, experiential, relational, and embodied (see also Styres, 2017, p. 49). Placefulness is not some-thing independent from Land but exists *within* the nuanced contexts of Land. Land reaches boundaries of place by embodying the principles, philosophies, and ontologies that transcend the material geography of land and the making of place or placefulness.

With this understanding in mind, Land is more than the diaphanousness of inhabited memories; Land *is* spiritual, emotional, and relational; Land *is* experien-tial, (re)membered, and storied; Land *is* consciousness—Land *is* sentient (see also Styres, 2017, p. 93). Land refers to the ways we honor and respect her as a sentient and conscious being. Therefore, in acknowledgment of the fundamental being of Land I always capitalize Land. I have come to know Land both as a fundamental sentient being and as a philosophical construct (see Styres, 2017, p. 183).

Land, as a theoretical and philosophical concept, comprises storied and jour-neyed connections of self-in-relationship—to each other, to our places, and to all of creation—as a central model for interpretation and meaning-making.

Journeying Through Storied Landscapes

Storying is essentially the ways we narratively describe *ourselves* as Indigenous peoples locally, nationally, and globally. Land is at once storied and relational informing the social, spiritual, and systemic norms and practices of a particular culture-sharing group in relationship to their places. LaDuke (1999) writes that, as Indigenous people, "our leadership and direction emerge from the land up—our commitment and tenacity spring from our deep connection to the land" (p. 4). Indigenous people exist in deeply intimate and sacred relationships with Land—it is the relationship that comes before all else. Our first environment was water— we are born of water—water is the lifeblood of mother earth (Styres, 2017, p. 59). There is a Haida teaching that states "we do not inherit the land from our ancestors—we borrow it from our children."

From the time we are born our stories intersect and connect with other stories as we walk this earth. The tracks of all our ancestors can be traced at varying levels, with the most recent ones evident on and near the surface of this land. Buried deeply are the first tracks—those of Indigenous people who have and continue to exist on this land since time immemorial; in other words, time before we can imagine time. Since those first tracks were made, there were many other tracks of those who walked at various times—overlapping—layers upon layers.

Storied Landscapes form spatial and temporal tracks left by our ancestors that can be *read* "with as much care as one reads the narratives of classical history" (Kulchyski, 2005, p. 18). Traditional knowledges were and continue to be trans-mitted through storying; shared values and beliefs; as well as land-centered activi-ties, reflections, and observations—they are woven out of individual and collective experiences. Many Indigenous philosophers both across Turtle Island as well as across the great waters tell us that traditional knowledges are based on storying and ancestral teachings grounded in Land, the ideologies of rational thought, and the principles embedded in our sacred stories. Silko (1977) writes, "as long as you remember what you have seen, then nothing is gone. As long as you remember, it is part of this story we have together. *Remember*, she said, *remember* everything" (p. 231, 235). Storying through remembered and recognized knowledges are one of the ways that oral traditions may serve to disrupt dominant Western conceptu-alizations and re-tellings of the tangled histories of colonial relations.

Whether someone chooses to acknowledge it or not, we all exist in rela-tionship to each other and to this land—a land that has and still does exist first and foremost in relationship to Indigenous people. Having said that, anyone can and should live in a reflexive relationship to their places, and they often do so without ever understanding or acknowledging the fundamental being and philosophical nature of Land or with the deeply intimate sacredness of the relationships Indigenous peoples have, not only with their places but also to Land. For those who want to live in deeply sacred and intimate relationship to Land must understand that it first and foremost requires a respectful and consistent acknowledgment of whose traditional lands we are on, a commitment to journeying—a seeking out and coming to an understanding of the stories and knowledges embedded in those lands, a conscious choosing to live in intimate, sacred, and storied relationships with those lands and not the least of which is an acknowledgment of the ways one is implicated in the networks and relations of power that comprise the tangled colonial history of the lands one is upon (see also Styres, 2017, p. 55).

Journeying is a process of coming to know. It is essentially learning through the chaos of moving from the familiar through to the unfamiliar while maintaining and observing a reflective frame of mind. It is as if the learner is on the bank of one side of a river—the side s/he is on is familiar and the learner feels comfortable there. However, the learner has to come to the edge of what s/he knows and what is familiar. A choice must be made—either the learner goes back the way s/he came or s/he sets out across these very treacherous-looking rapids and turbulent waters to reach the other side of knowing. Fear, anxiety, and uncertainty creep into the confidence the learner has previously placed in their knowing and is reflective of a very chaotic transitional period. Senses are overloaded with unfamiliar knowledges, thoughts, and reflections that disrupt a familiar and comfortable sense of being and knowing, but once in the middle we must press on through to the other side or be carried away by fear—the fear of myths and stereotypes that have, until now, informed how we have come to know. Trusting in the sacredness of the journeying process ensures that we will traverse the uncertain waters and arrive safely to the other side where we will find that what was once unfamiliar and uncertain territory is now filled with all that we can now know and connect to that serve to make this new place familiar to us. It is a place enriched with new knowledges and greater awareness and understandings because of this learning experience. Journeying is a place where our stories intersect and become interconnected with other stories—layers upon layers.

Mindful and purposeful praxis and course content is key to assisting learners in their individual and collective learning journeys across the turbulent waters to arrive unsettled and shaken up but safe on the storied landscape of Land. Land as a decolonizing praxis informs pedagogy through storied relationships. These stories are etched into the essence of every rock, tree, animal, pathway, and waterway (whether in urban or rural/natural or built environments[3]) in relation to the Indigenous people who have existed on the land since time immemorial. Therefore storied Landscapes refers to Indigenous stories and narratives of place—literacies of Land.

Decolonizing Narratives and Storying

The current context of colonialism is that the histories and contemporary realities of Indigenous peoples and colonial settlers within Canada, and indeed across Turtle Island, are now inextricably connected (see also Styres, 2017, p. 36). Smith (2012) writes that decolonization in contemporary understandings "is recognized as a long-term process involving the bureaucratic, cultural, linguistic and psychological divesting of colonial power" (p. 101). Alfred (2005) and Kuokkanen (2007) both assert that decolonization refers to the "present struggle for political, intellectual, economic and cultural self-determination" (Kuokkanen, 2007, p. 143). In this way decolonizing is at the heart of social and political sovereignty. Many scholars involved in decolonizing pedagogies and praxis consider resistances in engaging in decolonization as acts of denial, deflection, and a defense of the status quo, which serves to reinforce relations of power and privilege. Tuck and Yang (2012) write that "decolonization is not a swappable term for other things we want to do to improve our societies and schools" (p. 3)—it is not a metaphor—it is not a figure of speech or a symbolic representation of something else. There is a general unwillingness to engage in the uncomfortable process of decolonization because decolonizing is an unsettling process of shifting and unraveling the tangled colonial relations of power and privilege. There is also an issue of widespread purposeful ignorance relating to the history of colonization and the issues of pressing concern to Indigenous people across Turtle Island. At the close of the September 2009 G20 Summit, an international forum that brings together the world's leading industrialized and emerging economies, former Prime Minister Stephen Harper proclaimed: "Canada has no history of colonialism." This statement was made 15 months after the June 2008 Federal Government apology. Alfred (2009) writes that

> real change will happen only when settlers are forced into a reckoning of who they are, what they have done, and what they have inherited; then they will be unable to function as colonials and begin instead to engage other peoples as respectful human beings.
>
> (p. 184)

It is within this context of colonialism that terms such as *white* and *settler* garner much resistance and angst in class discussions. Students have said that they had gotten angry when they encountered terms such as white or settler in their readings—that they had stopped reading and could go no further—as if they hit a wall. They stated that they felt racialized and othered—which is itself very interesting when doing this work. It becomes very important that we unpack and explore these terms within the larger class discussions and that students come to a critical understanding of what these terms mean, how they are used, and an acknowledgment of the ways they are implicated in and informed by these understandings. Barker (2009) tells us that

> it is not enough to simply state that Settler people are "non-Indigenous," as is often done; this ignores the complexity of Settler society and culture itself and normalizes non-Indigenous society . . . settlers are those peoples who occupy lands previously stolen or in the process of being taken from their Indigenous inhabitants or who are otherwise members of the "Settler society," which is founded on co-opted lands and resources.
>
> *(p. 328)*

The term settler serves to make the necessary distinction between the Indigenous peoples of a particular place and those whose roots originate elsewhere—often Europe, but it can also refer to anyone seeking to live on Indigenous peoples' traditional territories and who benefit from the privileges of colonial relationships.

Likewise, not all settlers are "white"—nor would they identify themselves as white. Whiteness is not about racial profiling based on identity and skin color but rather relates to whiteness as a structural-cultural positioning of relations of power and privilege. It is not about *who* is whiteness but rather *how* whiteness is perpetuated and maintained through networks and relations of power and privilege within and across societies and—in this case—within educational contexts. Concepts of settler and whiteness are rooted in the myth of meritocracy, relations of power and privilege, and an assumption that everyone has access to the same resources, is working from the same starting line, and is on the same level playing field. In other words, that equal opportunities exist for everyone across all platforms that include, but are not limited to: race, society, sex, gender, religion, politics, and culture. Relations of power and privilege and the networks that sustain them are always striving to maintain the status quo and recenter whiteness and settler colonial relations.

I agree with Alfred (2005) that we cannot allow the ideologies of colonialism to become the story of our existence—as it is a discourse that continues to center colonial relations of power and privilege that hinders our ability to move forward by continuously reinforcing victimizing constructs of reality. However, to blindly let these discourses go unchallenged is to perpetuate the myth that Canada has no history of colonialism and, further, that we have all arrived unscathed by this colonial legacy. I would also say that none of us who reside within Turtle Island or indeed any colonized land can erase colonial relations from our narratives—it is inextricably woven into our stories of struggle, resistance, assertions of sovereignty, and the reclamation of inherent rights embedded in our places (see also Styres, 2017, p. 37).

Decolonizing storying through narratives of place trouble and challenge colonial myths and stereotypical representations, as well as disrupt and problematize normalizing and hegemonic dominant discourses while opening spaces that liberate critical thought, questioning, and sense-making. We all come from places—some here locally or from somewhere else on Turtle Island (North America) or across the great waters. The tracks of all our ancestors can be traced at varying levels with the most recent ones evident on and near the surface of this land. Buried deeply are the first tracks—those of Indigenous people who have and continue to exist on this land since time immemorial. Since those first tracks were made, there were many other tracks of those who walked at various times—overlapping—layers upon layers (Styres, Haig-Brown & Blinkie, 2013, p. 199). Now all our tracks lie on what was and still is First Nations Territories and whether we chose to acknowledge it or not, we now exist in relationship to each other and to this land. A land that has and still does exist first and foremost in relationship to Indigenous people. To be in good relationship with one another requires a critical conscious awareness and an acknowledgment of whose traditional lands we are now on as well as the historical and contemporary realities of those relationships.

Decolonizing Praxis

Decolonizing requires developing a critical consciousness about the realities of oppression and social inequities for minoritized peoples. Developing critical consciousness begins to trouble the ways purposeful ignorance twists the historical realities and the ways colonialist ideologies become normalized within national discourses and internalized among minoritized peoples. We, all of us, must develop a critical discourse that explores the ways colonial relations are and continue to be perpetuated and maintained through relations of power and privilege.

Praxis as is defined in an educational context generally refers to the practical application of the art and science of teaching—in other words moving from the theoretical into a practical application of the theory behind how what we do is enacted or embodied experientially in the classroom. Decolonizing praxis, by its very nature, resists mainstream approaches to teaching and learning as well as challenging taken-for-granted assumptions embedded in the hidden curriculum within classroom practices. In the classroom, decolonizing praxis challenges colonial relations of power and privilege that are systemically embedded in academia. When decolonizing praxis is introduced into the classroom context, it discomforts and challenges taken-for-granted biases and assumptions. This unsettling provokes many nuanced emotional responses from students, particularly mainstream students, that can range from guilt and shame to denial and resistance. These emotional responses are neither positive or negative but rather result in resistances that need to be unpacked and explored and as such are important sources of learning. Tuck and Yang (2012) write that "resistances by settler-participants to the aspiration of decolonization illustrate the reluctance of some settlers to engage the prospect of decolonization beyond the metaphorical or figurative level" (p. 26). Decolonizing praxis actively engages with colonial relations of power and privilege in order to unsettle and disrupt the status quo within educational contexts. Marie Battiste (2013) writes that "in order to effect change, educators must help students understand the Eurocentric assumptions of superiority within the context of history and to recognize the continued dominance of these assumptions in all forms of contemporary knowledge" (p. 186).

It is important to take seriously the responsibility for mindfully and purposefully introducing decolonizing praxis and strategies for engaging multiple resistances in the classroom that arise from nuanced emotional responses to provocative course content that challenge the strongly cherished and largely unexamined mythology of *Canada the good and benevolent nation*. Decolonizing pedagogies and practices open up spaces with the learning environment where students can question their own positionalities, prior knowledge, biases, and taken-for-granted assumptions together with the ways they are implicated in and/or affected by colonial relations of power and privilege. This work is not easily accomplished, as instructors who choose to engage in this work are often teaching challenging and provocative course content that frequently has at its core key elements related to social justice issues. This type of inquiry can only take place when students are positioned to engage in critical conversations that explore the spaces between worldviews that take into consideration words and the ways we use language to racialize, compartmentalize, and label *others*, particularly in a socio-political context; biases, assumptions, and strongly held beliefs and perceptions concerning the issues of pressing concern to all minoritized peoples, but particularly in this case to Indigenous people across Canada; deficit theorizing models of education; and the understanding of *whiteness* in terms of colonial relations of power and privilege through carefully mediated dialogue and deep critical inquiry. Students often express these spaces as places of tension and contestation along with messy ambiguity as their emergent understandings of what they know and how they came to know it comes into question.

One of the challenges for instructors is that they bring their own sociocultural identities into classrooms while attempting to manage the challenging and provocative course material. Another challenge that instructors face is confronting their own biases and assumptions that are both known and those that may be uncovered unexpectedly while simultaneously managing student resistances and tensions to the provocative course content. Instructors must also be aware of their own triggers and operate at multiple levels while being present and facilitating the process in the moment. This is also particularly important for teacher education where we are training teachers how to be teachers. Building upon their own deep critical self-reflection, instructors can begin engaging students in critical conversations. It is important to give great care to pedagogical choices and the ways those choices impact the use of decolonizing praxis within the classroom and beyond. Decolonizing praxis opens up possibilities for students to critically immerse themselves in an experiential engagement with course content, allowing students to shift toward a deeper, more critical consciousness.

Transcending Classroom Walls

So what does all of this look like in the classroom? The courses I teach are all based on a lecture-light and highly reflective format that opens spaces for inquiry and experiential approaches to course content. This approach de-centers the focus on the instructor as the fount of all knowledge and pushes students to consider their own prior knowledge, positionalities, and the resulting implications of what they have learned from course material by considering the ways they may balance and harmonize this new knowledge. In effect, addressing a question I often ask them: Now that you know what you know, how will you use it to inform your personal and professional practices?" It is important to make mindful and purposeful choices in course content that provoke critical conversations and resistances that unsettle, disrupt, and hopefully shift consciously and unconsciously long-held beliefs and understandings, treasured myths, and taken-for-granted assumptions concerning Indigeneity and Canada's 500-plus-year relationship with the host peoples of this land. In this way the classroom becomes contested space.

In Literacies of Land, students are introduced to challenging and provocative topics and issues that they explore through various First Voices in relation to their places through the use of literary texts, media, and oral stories. The reason First Voices are so critical is captured in the words of Jeanette Armstrong, wherein she so eloquently states that

> through my language I understand that I am being spoken to, I'm not the one speaking. The words are coming from many tongues and mouths of the Okanagan people and the land around them. I am a listener to the language's stories, and when my words form I am merely retelling the same stories in different patterns.
>
> (as cited in King, 2003, p. 2)

Throughout the Literacies of Land course we explore issues such as: a curriculum of place and the ways land is the primary teacher; issues around contestation and appropriation; narratives of the body in relation to land; treaties as literacies; storywork, trickster tales, and understanding the world through stories. Thomas King (2003) tells us that "the truth about stories is that that's all we are. You can't understand the world without telling a story. There isn't any centre to the world but a story" (p. 32). Imagine if we could peel back the layers of concrete and earth upon which we are currently located—students are asked to think about what they would see? What stories still exist and persist? Students are asked to engage in thinking about and responding to their story concerning their relationship to this land: Whose traditional lands are they on at this moment? How have they come to be in this place? What is their relationship to the land they are on right now—perhaps in relation to the places they have come from? Finally, what do these questions mean to them? Land is positioned within the Literacies of Land classroom by exploring these questions in relation to the course content and exploring the issues of pressing concern to Indigenous people and their communities. Land is consistently informing decolonizing pedagogies and praxis through storied relationships. And as previously stated, these stories are etched into the essence of Land since time immemorial.

Educators have an important role in helping students examine their worlds in critically thoughtful ways—to take the time in class and ask and unpack the risky and tough questions. In an interview Jeanette Armstrong (2002) stated that: "we need to decolonize ourselves (all of Canada) by deconstructing colonial myths—this translates into resistance and advocacy—be an advocate of your own thinking" (p. 299). To journey beyond the boundaries of dominant Eurocentric[4] impositions of colonial ideologies to find new ways of articulating understandings of self-in-relation to Land. Representations in literature can help students to understand their world by engaging with, in the case of teachers in classrooms, age-appropriate complex understandings of their everyday realities, as well as to begin engaging with the complex issues of concern to Indigenous peoples, their knowledges, and cultural histories. Literatures that simply appropriate and misrepresent Indigenous knowledges within a mainstream retelling reinforce stereotypes and promote cultural theft. It is important for students to look beyond the "quaint" or "romanticized" notion of Indigenous stories in order to see them as providing complex information about our world and the ways to appropriately be in relation with that world. Courtland et al. (2009) write that we need to move beyond texts that romanticize Indigenous people and portray them as people who lived in a distant past—a people of folktales rather than vital contributing human beings within a contemporary Canadian context. Stories and counter-stories are key in disrupting dominant normative discourses. Indigenous narratives call into question relations of power and privilege that inform dominant representations and legitimization of truth and notions of authenticity. Indigenous narratives can open opportunities for engaging with learning through the process of inquiry and critical self-reflection. Louis Castenell and William Pinar (1993) write that:

> we are what we know. We are, however, also what we do not know. If what we know about ourselves—our history, our culture, our national identity— is deformed by absences, denials, and incompleteness, then our identity is fragmented. Such a self lacks access both to itself and to the world. Its sense of history, gender and politics is incomplete and distorted.
>
> *(p. 4)*

Generally speaking Canadians, in purposeful ignorance, believe that everyone pursues and upholds social justice—particularly as it relates to education . . . and only so long as it is not too uncomfortable.

Notes

1 Indigeneity refers to the quality and state of being Indigenous. Quality of being refers to the characteristics of being Indigenous such as genuineness, experiences, and authenticity; similar but distinct, state of being refers to the ways one exists in relationship to his/her world.
2 Relations of place refers to the intricate and complex relationships people have to their places.
3 Built in this context refers to human-made rather than anything made out of or from the natural world.
4 In this context Eurocentric refers to the privileging of dominant Euro-centered cultural values and beliefs in education, scholarship, knowledge production, the legitimization of intellectual capital, and networks and systems of power. It is a way to articulate a particular world view—*dominant* Western ideology.

References

Alfred, T. (2005). *Wasáse: Indigenous pathways of action and freedom*. Peterborough, ON: Broadview Press.

Alfred, T. (2009). Restitution is the real pathway to justice for Indigenous peoples. In *Responsibility and renewal: Canada's truth and reconciliation journey* (pp. 179–187). Ottawa, ON: Aboriginal Healing Foundation.

Armstrong, J. (1998). Land speaking. In S. Ortiz (Ed.), *Speaking for the generations: Native Writers on writing* (pp. 175–194). Tucson, AZ: University of Arizona Press.

Armstrong, J. (2002). Jeanette Armstrong. In D. Jensen (Ed.), *Listening to the land: Conversations about nature, culture and Eros* (pp. 282–299). White River Junction, VT: Chelsea Green Publishing Company.

Bachelard, G. (1994). *The poetics of space: The classic look at how we experience intimate places.* (M. Jolas, Trans.). Boston, MA: Beacon Press. (Original work published 1958).

Barker, A. (2009). The contemporary reality of Canadian imperialism: Settler colonialism and the hybrid colonial state. *The American Indian Quarterly, 33*(3), 325–351.

Battiste, M. (2013). *Decolonizing education: Nourishing the learning spirit*. Saskatoon, SK: Purich Publishing Ltd.

Casey, E. S. (1996). How to get from space to place in a fairly short stretch of time: Phenomenological prolegomena. In S. Feld & K. Basso (Eds.), *Senses of place* (pp. 13–52). Santa Fe, MN: School of American Research Press.

Castenell, L., & Pinar, W. (1993). Introduction. In L. Castenell & W. Pinar (Eds.), *Understanding curriculum as a racial text: Representations of identity and difference in text* (pp. 1–28). New York, NY: State University of New York Press.

Courtland, M., Hammett, R., Strong-Wilson, T., Bainbridge, J., Johnston, I., Burke, A., . . . Shariff, F. (2009). Curricula landscapes: Preservice teachers' perceptions of place and identity in Canadian multicultural picture books. *Journal of the Canadian Association for Curriculum Studies, 7*(1), 135–159.

Feld, S. (1996). Waterfalls of song: An acoustemology of place resounding in Bosavi, Paupa New Guinea. In S. Feld & K. Basso (Eds.), *Senses of place* (pp. 91–135). Santa Fe, NM: School of American Research Advanced Seminar Series.

George, N. (2010). *A new vision guiding boriginal literacy*. Southampton, ON: Ningwakwe Learning Press.

Goodyear-Ka'ōpua, N. (2013). *The seeds we planted: Portraits of a native Hawaiian charter school*. Minneapolis, MN: University of Minnesota Press.

King, T. (2003). *The truth about stories: A native narrative.* Toronto, ON: House of Anansi Press Inc.

Kovach, M. E. (2009). *Indigenous methodologies: Characteristics, conversations, and contexts.* Toronto, ON: University of Toronto Press.

Kulchyski, P. (2005). *Like the sound of a drum: Aboriginal cultural politics in Denendeh and Nunavut.* Winnipeg, MB: University of Manitoba Press.

Kuokkanen, R. (2007). *Reshaping the university: Responsibility, indigenous epistemes, and the logic of the gift.* Vancouver, TO: UBC Press.

LaDuke, W. (1999). *All our relations: Native struggle for land and life.* Cambridge, MA: South End Press.

Lefebvre, H. (1991). *The production of space.* (D. Nicholson-Smith, Trans.). Malden, MA: Blackwell Publishing. (Original work published 1974).

Silko, L. M. (1977). *Ceremony.* New York, NY: Penguin Books.

Smith, L. T. (2012). *Decolonizing methodologies: Research and indigenous peoples* (2nd ed.). New York, NY: Zed Books.

Styres, S. Haig-Brown, C. & Blimkie, M. (2013). Toward a Pedagogy of Land. *Canadian Journal of Education 36*(2): 188–221.

Styres, S. (2017). *Pathways for remembering and recognizing Indigenous thought in education: Philosophies of Iethi'nihsténha Ohwentsia'kékha.* Toronto, ON: University of Toronto Press.

Tuck, E., & Yang, E. W. (2012). Decolonization is not a metaphor. *Decolonization: Indigeneity, Education & Society, 1*(1), 1–40.

2

HAA SHAGEINYAA

"Point Your Canoe Downstream and Keep Your Head Up!"

*Naadli Todd Lee Ormiston
(Northern Tutchone, Tlingit)*

> *"The Journey Within"*
> *All that I ever do*
> *Is seen in the currents of the river*
> *All that I would ever be*
> *Moves quickly to the sea*
> *When I've had too much of it I rest*
> *Turn to the old people who know*
> *Their strength and courage flow*
> *Then I rise to the surge of the river again*
> *The teachings fill my mind*
> *Touching the water emancipates my spirit*
> *The land is speaking, the smooth waters wind*
> *And I launch the canoe on the river again*
> *I cherish the gifts from the journey*
> *Respect, sharing and haa shageinyaa*[1]
> *And the river becomes a part of me*
> *I have become part of the river*
> *All that I ever do*
> *Is seen in the currents of the river*
> *And all that I would ever be*
> *Moves quickly to the sea*

(Naadli)

Haa Shageinyaa: Point Your Canoe Downstream, Paddle and Keep Your Head Up!

I have been on many canoe journeys over the past 30 years throughout the land of my people. Specifically, I share teachings[2] I have received on one of those trips with my brother (a 55-day, 850-mile journey in the early 1990s) on the Eagle, Bell, Porcupine and Yukon rivers. This journey would span the North West Territories, Yukon and Alaska—all of which are our traditional territories. For me, it was a journey of new beginnings, survival, "coming-to-know" and transformation. I am fortunate to have retained memories from my journal through this time, which are intertwined throughout this story. Journaling for me is an ongoing way of preserving my thoughts, feelings, memories and stories of my land-based experiences—not usually shared with others. I would like to honor my brother Rolly who joined me on this journey, as he spent much of his life in the bush, while I spent much of my life in the city. We re-connected in 1985 in Whitehorse, Yukon. Both of us had been on several canoe journeys together in the Yukon and NWT prior to this trip, but not as long as this one. My intent in sharing part of my story on this journey is to demonstrate how paddling is pedagogy and how it can help guide us in the future toward Yan gaa duuneek, a Tlingit word which means to walk with dignity. More specifically, this story explores the ways in which the various elements of the Canoe Journey narrative can offer a framework for thinking about and living decolonization, and it provides an opportunity to consider the power of traditional teachings for their epistemic range and the hope for creating change. Welcome to a portion of our journey.

> The Canoe Journey teaches me that, as Indigenous peoples, our life histories are disparate and not homogenous. For transformation to be possible, we must nurture a collaborative journey among each other, while being attuned to the specificities and variances of life narratives.

FIGURE 2.1 Teaching and Learning: Nurturing Individual and Collective Approaches

Preparing for this 55-day Canoe Journey began in June 1990 with a series of smudges that includes a mixture of sage, tobacco and cedar, and a two-day fast at one of our elders' homes—Pat's cabin in Dawson City, Yukon. Pat is from the Tr'ondek Hwech'in First Nation and worked many years at the local radio station. Over the years, he became a close friend and a spiritual advisor to me. Pat drove us and our canoe in his old Jeep Cherokee from Dawson City to Eagle Plains, North West Territories (NWT). Eagle Plains is located half way to Inuvik, NWT on the Dempster Highway. This curvy, isolated and endless highway is the most northern highway in Canada. Aside from a lodge in the area, the terrain is noticeably barren, with the Ogilvie Mountains in the far distance to the west and to the north, sprawling tundra which is often referred to as the "last frontier." We set out on our journey at Eagle Plains and this journey took us from Eagle Plains NWT through the Eagle and Bell rivers, to Old Crow, Yukon and down the Porcupine River into the Yukon River and Fort Yukon, Alaska. Our journey ended in Tanana Alaska in August. We chose to stop and spend time in the various communities that we journeyed through—communities that are only accessible by air or water.[3] When I set out on this journey, I had very little understanding of the lasting effects this would have on who I am today and where I hope to be in the future. Today I think of the power of metaphors and one of the elders, Edith Josie, who said . . . *Point your canoe downstream, keep your head up, listen to the land and paddle with a purpose!* I use her words as a metaphor and as means to keep myself focused, and to be attentive to all that is around me no matter where I am or what I am doing.

Our canoe was a 17-foot cedar/fiberglass, which we purchased from Pat in Dawson City. We knew about the importance of packing no more than 50 pounds of gear so that we could still comfortably maneuver the canoe through the fast-moving, unsettled waters we were to face. We brought most of the gear in White-horse,[4] which included the typical camping gear to survive the elements: sleeping bags, a tent, a two-burner stove, camping fuel, matches, rope, plastic, a compass, bug dope, candles, a first aid kit, bear horns, rain gear and a couple changes of clothes. Packing minimal food was a little trickier, as we expected to live off the land, but we carried enough food for about 30 days. Typical meals included lentils, beans, pasta, dried fruit, rice, powdered milk, sugar and oatmeal. We also packed lard, onions, garlic, and flour, as these were essential to prepare the fish and wildlife we gathered along our route. We carried with us a .22-caliber rifle and a compound crossbow for hunting, along with two fishing rods and several skinning knives. Our regular diet on this trip consisted of porcupine, beaver, geese, arctic grayling, dolly varden and northern pike. The way we saw it at the time, our simple existence within the canoe was in the hands of the land and the Creator.

> The Canoe Journey teaches me that preparation is about honoring the pedagogical, epistemic, ontological, and affective needs of the medicine wheel teachings. To prepare only for one specific need is to prepare inadequately for the complex dimensions and forces that comprise the four directions of the wheel.

FIGURE 2.2   Teaching and Learning: Total Preparation

There was an overwhelming rush of joy and happiness the moment we pushed off shore at Eagle Plains, knowing that we were embarking on a journey that had no time constraints and our primary commitments were to our relations—with our surroundings and to each other. I wrote in my journal on day three of the trip: "I don't know if there is anything like being on the water first thing in the morning at sunrise where the flow of the river and the sun's light off the water and the feeling of tranquility are so surreal" (journal, June 1990). You feel that serenity after days on the river: it is exhilarating, and it got me wondering about what it might have meant for our ancestors that this canoe journey was their only mode of transportation back and forth to the different communities up North.

> The Canoe Journey teaches me that in the silence, there is memory, experience, and a place for bearing witness. The journey teaches me that in the silence is a spirit, recorded history, and, as human beings, we must prepare for accountable listening to hear the stories that silence offers.

FIGURE 2.3 Teaching and Learning: The Gift and Power of Silence

An average day on our journey would consist of seven to nine hours of paddling. This journey was all downstream, including one set of rapids and one portage.[5] Because the sun never sets in the far north during the short summer months (June, July and the first part of August), it was not unusual for us to paddle some days for 12 to 14 hours. In fact, even though Rolly had a watch, it broke early in the course of our journey, and we were forced to tell time by the positioning of the sun in the sky as it circled the sky. Time really began to have no relevance for us in a Western linear manner on this journey. I pondered how circular cycles of time provided a shared sense of identity and history, of doing things when they were meant to be done and lasting for as long as they were meant to last. There were also stretches of seven to nine days on this journey where we saw no other human beings. Finding a place to set up camp some evenings could be an adventure, especially when windy, as the fast-flowing river required quick, careful maneuvering from both the bow and the stern of the canoe to get to shore while ensuring we did not tip over with our supplies.

Traplines are a route along which a trapper/hunter sets traps for his or her game and there are many in our traditional territories in the Yukon, NWT and Alaska. They formed the basis for the "mapping" of our traditional territories as we respected where our family's traplines ended and where others began. Historically, canoe journeys (dog sleds and snowshoes in the winter) provided the mode of transportation to and from our family traplines. It was common to find old abandoned or unused trapline cabins on this journey. These small log cabins were an appropriate shelter for traditional hunters/trappers in the old days.

Elder Ray told us long ago that trapline cabins could be used as shelter and to prepare our food as long as we showed respect for the people (the ancestors) whose territory and spirits we were squatting on. This meant that we were to leave everything as it was when we arrived: water needed to be emptied, dishes washed and the garbage taken out to be buried or burned. We were not to take anything that belonged to the keepers of cabins and we should leave something behind, an offering, even if just a letter expressing our thanks with an introduction to who we are and where we are from. We stayed in various trappers' cabins for up to eight nights during the course of our journey. Most of these were located on the Bell and Porcupine rivers, and they were a welcome retreat for us from the elements.

> The Canoe Journey teaches me that, similar to spirit, land, animal and water relations, humans can never forget the lessons we are taught of responsibility, accountability and reciprocity. The Canoe Journey shows me how these aspects are necessary not just as hospitality, but as survival.

FIGURE 2.4 Teaching and Learning: Practicing Teaching

We faced our only rapids early in the trip. On this morning, as we arose, we saw a couple elders near the mouth of the Little Bell River. We paddled over to where we met the two elders from Old Crow, John and Peter, hauling in their fish nets. After introductions, we spent over half the day with them, assisting in hauling in their catch and cleaning and gutting close to 100 chinook salmon. The men had traplines and a cabin close to where the Little Bell River and the Bell River meet, and they fed us there, shared some stories before sending us off after lunch with a fresh chinook. They warned us to observe the rapids carefully before entering their course. These particular rapids were approximately 50-meters long and had two channels to choose from. The channel on the right was the safest, although we needed to climb the riverbank to see just how fast flowing the river was because, if it was too fast, we would need to stay clear of the right wall; too far right and we would meet a rather nasty eddy line that could capsize us. They are considered "class three rapids.[6]" In the late afternoon, we walked down the path on the riverbank beside the rapids while Rolly spoke to the river. From our vantage point, we could observe the movement of the river, and this helped us navigate a pathway through the rapids. Over the years, I had come to realize how an eddy of stagnant water or a spray of water turning back on itself could expose where the rocks, currents and ledges were lying, just under the surface of the water. I knew that we would have to avoid these areas.

We walked back to where our canoe was moored and began to paddle toward the rapids. Our practice was to switch roles every few days, and that day I was the stern paddler. As the stern paddler, I was responsible for navigating the path of the canoe while working with my brother to help direct the path and listening to him calling from the bow to indicate any potential upcoming obstacles. During a Canoe Journey, it is essential that we work in collaboration; when paddling into rapids, our need to work co-operatively was imperative.

The Canoe Journey teaches me that collaboration is not an abstract term that we merely talk about; collaborative relationships based on trust and mutuality are the vanguards of survival.

FIGURE 2.5   Teaching and Learning: Collaboration for Survival

In the far North, the mating season for geese is from late June and into July. This is the time when the geese fly low in small flocks of five to seven, so it is a good time to shoot one. Rolly and I bagged three geese during this trip, all on the Porcupine and Bell Rivers during the 10-day passage between Eagle Plains and Old Crow, Yukon. I shot the first one from the canoe at about a 20-yard distance into the air to the right of us. I aimed for its belly but got him in the wing. He landed in the woods to the north of us—about 30 yards away. We landmarked the spot, paddled over to the bank of the river and rustled through the bush for what seemed like an eternity. As described in my journal:

> When we finally got to the goose in an opening of the bush, it was flapping its wings in frenzy but couldn't move from its location; my brother told me to break its neck. I tried to do it but I had never done this with a goose, only a duck. I could not twist its long neck in three tries. Finally my brother came over, told me to hold the feet and let the goose's head dangle towards the ground; Rolly slit its throat with his buck knife. Plenty of blood surged through its neck to the ground and I felt somewhat embarrassed, but my brother smiled and told me not to worry, and just to watch him next time. He also reminded me I should keep my knife ready as a back-up plan in case things don't go as planned. I skinned the goose and gutted it before bringing it back to the boat, where we put it into a large plastic bag half filled with river water until we made camp a couple hours later. We buried most of the guts where we skinned the goose and left sage as an offering. While sitting by the campfire tonight, I talked again with Rolly about how I felt bad about not being able to kill that goose. He just smiled again and said, "That's good because if an animal gives itself to you, that is a gift you must respect. That means you must not let it suffer more than it needs to. If you don't treat it right, it may not give its life to you in the future." Good teaching today. Goodnight.
>
> *(Naadli, journal, 1990)*

The Canoe Journey teaches me that trust involves being continuously open to learning, to knowing when you don't know, and knowing when to trust others to show you how to learn.

FIGURE 2.6   Teaching and Learning: Trust to Learn from Others

On this trip, we shot two other geese and I did snap one of their necks, after observing Rolly a second time. I remember thinking how we could have shot more geese, but we had an abundance of other animals to eat. We feasted on several beavers, porcupines and grouse on this journey. The late afternoons and evenings were opportune for dropping our lines in the water; we usually found the best fishing spots were where the endless creeks flowed into the rivers. We enjoyed northern pike, grayling, dolly varden, and Arctic char. On one particular night of this journey, we came across a grizzly bear. I was sleeping, as I occasionally did, under our canoe while Rolly was about 25 feet from me in the tent. We had become accustomed to keeping our food supplies in the bush, well away from our camp, so as to not attract animals to us. I remember hearing the bushes near us rustling and thought a moose or caribou was close by. As stated in my journal:

> I awoke to the sound of something last night nearby. I lay still until I looked out from my sleeping bag and saw what appeared to be a bear walk out around the tent towards the fire pit. It was a light brown bear and appeared to be quite full grown. I was not sure how to react; I thought about what options were available to me. The bear horn was near the tent, but the cross bow was on the ground near the stern of my canoe. I thought for a second about reaching for it but knew it would be risky as I would have to maneuver to it while in my sleeping bag. I simply froze, partly in fear and partly in awe. I observed the grizzly going towards the fire pit and poked its nose towards one of our canteens, and then looked across and straight at me. He walked to within four feet of me, sniffing around for my scent. I remember thinking/praying "I am not here to harm you; please don't harm me." Even though the words never reached my lips, I did move, whether accidentally or on purpose, I cannot be certain. The bear looked right at me with its distant brown eyes, and he seemed to be checking me out. He moved his snout back and forth repeatedly and I knew he knew I was there. The grizzly then stood straight up on its hind legs which looked to be about ten feet high, front paws extended and let out one large growl. He returned back to all fours and wandered off into the bush. I heard the tent unzip and Rolly was beside me, wide eyed, asking if I was okay. We never slept last night at all. I never told Rolly about my fear of that grizzly . . . or that my bladder had almost burst when that grizzly was walking away.
>
> (Naadli, journal, 1990)

Disembarking from our canoes and spending time in each of the three communities[7] we chose to visit along this journey was most memorable. Today, I reflect on Shawn Wilson (2008) and his book, *Research as Ceremony: Indigenous Research Methods*, where he uses the term "relational accountability" and speaks to principles of authenticity, credibility and reciprocity as being foundations of an Indigenous research methodology rather than goals of validity or reliability (p. 101).

On this Canoe Journey, I am left to ponder the realization that Tlingit values of respect, haa shageinyaa and reciprocity structure the social relations
between people, they also structure and maintain relations between humans
and animals. Our lineages attest to this. As a member of the wolf clan, I am a
part of the wolf and he is a part of me. As such, I carry the traits and responsibilities of the wolf.

FIGURE 2.7 Teaching and Learning: Our Connection to Animals

These terms really are universal; they serve as the basis of living a good life, so
I now reflect on the power of these relations through my stopovers on this journey. I learned about respecting the people/communities that we were in, and that
I should not ask for things, including knowledge, but wait to have things shared
with me when they were meant to be. The people shared many stories with us in
each of the communities. Taking the time to listen to those stories was important
and it reminded me that this is how we as Indigenous peoples have always come
to know. Mindful observation and reflection are important aspects for learning
and building connections.

The Canoe Journey teaches me that paying attention to the linkages between
Nations, territories, histories and identities is about forging continuity, communal resilience and collective identity between Indigenous communities.

FIGURE 2.8 Teaching and Learning: Community Linkages

That first night we arrived in Old Crow, we were invited to the community
dance at the hall where elders, parents and youth came together to honor one of
the young graduates who had recently returned from F.H. Collins High School
in Whitehorse. The night was highlighted by fiddling and "jig" dancing. A young
man introduced us as visitors to their community and we received gifts from some
of the community members in the form of dry moose meat, lard and blankets
to take with us on the rest of our journey. Protocol required that we formally
introduce ourselves and share stories about our journey and what we discovered
on the rivers thus far. We were asked mainly about any caribou migration patterns
we had witnessed and whether there were any settlers hunting them on the river.
For the people of Old Crow, one of the highlights on this night was watching
Rolly and I dance to the fiddle in the community hall. While dancing the jig is
customary for Gwitchin people, it was the first, but not likely the last time I will
do that! My feet simply could not keep up with the speed of the fiddles, no matter

how much the people clapped along . . . eating, humor and dancing is customary though, and this was a fun evening for all!

The next evening we spent time with some of the elders. One of the most memorable meetings was with elder Edith, who was the most remarkable woman I met on this journey. I used to read her stories about life in Old Crow in the *Whitehorse Star* newspaper in which she had a weekly column entitled "Here are the news." On this particular night, she spoke of the old days. She recounted how, when the store was built in the current locale of Old Crow in 1950, this meant the whole village moved from Old Rampart House, the former village of the people. She spoke of how that day many of the old people had never eaten store-bought meat in their lives. Edith also spoke of the creation stories, and I realize how these stories speak to the importance of how the Gwitchin people and the caribou are related. I also recall how passionate she was when speaking to the importance of hunting and trapping muskrats and actually invited us to go with Alfred to pick up supplies at his camp in Old Crow Flats.

Alfred invited us to his camp north in Old Crow flats, which is about a hundred kilometers south of the Beaufort Sea—the world's most northern sea. We left for the overnight trip on the fourth day of our stay in Old Crow. Old Crow Flats is about a four-hour boat ride, using a small 25 hp engine, from the community. It is where the Vuntut Gwitchin First Nations gather from mid-April until mid-June every year for muskrat trapping season. Old Crow Flats is located on a plain, and the flats encompass a multitude of lakes with rivers running through them. The people hunt muskrats in April and May when ice covers the lakes. Although we missed the opportunity to participate in trapping, we were honored to help Alfred and his son gather some of their gear, stay overnight and bring supplies back from his camp to Old Crow. Alfred spoke of how muskrats are one of their main sources of fresh meat until the caribou travel through on their summer migration to the calving grounds each year. Each family in Old Crow has their own trapping area in Crow Flats, which is passed down from generation to generation. I saw the remnants of camps where the people had resided for up to two months during "muskrat" season. That night we slept in wall tents that were still up at the camp for Alfred's family; the tents and their floors were lined with spruce boughs. We heard many stories of trapping and hunting in the area, ate muskrat around the fire and slept soundly that night.

> The Canoe Journey teaches me that our everyday lives contain an archive that documents our philosophies, our laws, our customs, values, and practices. I learn that working on the land is a powerful site of pedagogical instruction and identity formation.

FIGURE 2.9 Teaching and Learning: The Power of the Land

Today, the Vuntut Gwitchin First Nation in Old Crow is home to almost 300 First Nations. You still can only get there by air or water—except for winter ice roads which run from where we began our canoe trip in Eagle Plains to Old Crow. The elders speak of global greed (warming) and how the winter roads are less and less accessible each year because the waters are not freezing. The migration of the caribou has also been affected through climate change and the renewed threat of Alaska oil and pipeline companies that want to explore in the Arctic National Wildlife Refuge area. One of the internal struggles of this small community, which is indicative of other Indigenous communities, is that many of the children have to leave the community after grade nine if they are to maintain their mainstream or Westernized education. This is not an easy decision for some families because like so many of us, they are taken away from the culture and traditions of their Nations at a young age and many do not return.

This Canoe Journey gifted me with an important teaching from a community member in Old Crow who, before we left said, "point your canoe downstream, keep your head up, listen to the land and paddle with a purpose!" A teaching taken from this experience has shown me the importance of understanding my surroundings, of moving through challenges, and importantly, not giving up. Although the community member's teaching was said to me in a disciplinary manner, I remember her words: today they resonate for me as a way to emphasize the importance of how to walk in a good way.

FIGURE 2.10 Teaching and Learning: Never Giving Up

From Old Crow, we continued our journey to Fort Yukon, Alaska; this part of the journey lasted 15 days. The relentless rain on this leg of the journey had me feeling somewhat depressed as I wrote in my journal one morning while contemplating embarking back on the river again:

It rained with a hard wind most the night, hard to sleep, everything is dripping wet, and the sky still looks gray and threatening today. Even if it doesn't rain, today I just don't feel like paddling. I am lonely now, thinking about my warm bed, my relatives, my friends. What would they think of me not wanting to go on? Shit, I got no choice anyways. Rain or shine, we could light the fire later; Rolly can play guitar and we could sing our hearts out. I asked Rolly if he wanted to stay here today and he just said "cool." Both of us are writing now in the tent with the sound of the rain pelting on our tent. We are family, we are so compatible together, and it makes the trip feel good . . . it's hard being out here some days . . .

(Naadli, journal, 1990)

There were occasions throughout our journey where we chose not to canoe and kept our camp in one locale for several days at a time and simply read, hunted, swam and wrote in our journals.

The Canoe Journey teaches me that loneliness, sorrow and solitariness are a necessary part of learning, teaching and leadership. I learn that loneliness, sorrow and solitariness are critical parts of the journey that allow space for introspection, reflection and recharging ourselves.

FIGURE 2.11 Teaching and Learning: Appreciating Loneliness, Sorrow, and Solitariness

We continued to hunt small game along the way: ptarmigan, beavers and porcupines. One of the most repulsive sights we saw was close to Fort Yukon, Alaska. We saw an animal lying on the riverbank, brought our canoe ashore and approached a dead caribou that had been shot many times at close range; we knew that a shotgun was used because of the bullet patterns in the caribou. Lead had repeatedly pierced the carcass in its head, belly and hind leg. Mosquitoes and flies were feasting on the carcass, but there were no signs of natural decay. The belly was still moderately warm. I felt the people who did this could be only a day or two ahead of us. Clearly, this was a form of trophy hunting or a pleasure kill where the pleasure comes only from shooting and the animal is left to die for no reason. We took photos of the caribou, provided an offering and paddled on. When we got to Fort Yukon, we shared our findings regarding the carcass upriver with the people. The next day I was asked to join several community members and the local conservation officer on a search for the hunters downriver in their boat. Although we spent most of the morning on the water, we never spotted anyone. Several days later Rolly and I heard they had caught two German men near Stevens Village, which is further downstream.

The Canoe Journey teaches me that we must continue in the history of the people by resisting the ongoing assault on our traditions and beliefs. The Canoe Journey teaches me that, as leaders, we must exercise vigilance in order to safeguard our land, our resources and all living beings.

FIGURE 2.12 Teaching and Learning: Vigilance

Our journey quietly ended in Tanana, Alaska, on August 11, within our ancestors' territory. Tanana is positioned where the Yukon and Tanana Rivers meet. The village is known as Nucha'la'woy'ya, meaning where the two rivers meet.

We stayed for two nights in Tanana, which is even smaller than Old Crow. There are about 200 people there. Hillary and her husband Paul put us up for those two nights and we sold our canoe to them for 200 dollars. We gave them many of our leftover foods and our old two-burner camp stove. They gifted us with two moose hide medicine bags; I still carry mine with me today. The money we got for that canoe paid for our flight to Fairbanks, Alaska which was only 125 miles from where we ended this Canoe Journey. Our 850-mile journey was over.

Reflecting back, this trip, for me personally, was about reconnecting with my identity and being able to find connection to people and places. You know, these connections were the most important thing to me. I grew up fast through these journeys too. In many ways, I transformed from a child into an adult through my Canoe Journeys. I learned how to survive with the elements, how the land has everything we need for survival, how solitude is needed in our lives, but how relationships are just as important: really it is about balance. I felt so healthy on these trips too; we ate well and there were no drugs or any alcohol on these journeys. They are truly journeys of "coming to know" the importance of place, identity and spirituality. Gunalchéesh.

Notes

1 Tlingit word signifying reverence for the spirit world
2 The key teachings are shown as figures framed in a box.
3 In the winter time, there are various ice roads between communities.
4 The city we were living in is located approximately 450 kilometers south of Dawson City, Yukon.
5 Portage refers to carrying supplies and canoe from one river to another. This was a three-kilometer portage due to getting lost on a subsidiary river.
6 This refers to rapids with moderate, irregular waves that may be difficult to avoid and that can swamp an open canoe.
7 Old Crow, Fort Yukon and Tanana.

Reference

Wilson, S. (2008). *Research is ceremony: Indigenous research methods*. Winnipeg, MB: Fernwood Publishing.

3

REZ PONIES AND CONFRONTING SACRED JUNCTURES IN DECOLONIZING AND INDIGENOUS EDUCATION

Kelsey Dayle John (Diné)

Yá'át'ééh! Biliganna nishłį́. Tł ááshchi'i báshíshchíín. Biliganna dashicheii. Bit'ahnii dashinálí. Kelsey Dayle John yinishyé. Teec Nos Pos dę́ę́' naashá. (Hello, I am white, born for the Red Bottom clan, my maternal grandfather is white, and my paternal grandfather's clan is Under His Cover Clan. I'm originally from Teec Nos Pos). I'm a doctoral candidate at Syracuse University and a National Science Foundation Graduate Research Fellow. My dissertation is on the Navajo horse. Currently, I live in Farmington, NM and work with a Navajo Tribal University. When I'm not working I run with my dog Junebug and spend as much time on horses and with my family as I can. Alongside my research, I'm learning Diné Bizaad (the Navajo language).

Only one semester into my doctoral program, I realized I was forced to "take a side" even though every physical and spiritual part of myself was not accustomed to this move. It's a move so embodied, so intellectual, and so spiritual, it can make someone who has never felt it before freeze. I later learned that feeling was my spiritual confrontation with a colonial system that forces separations into every point of academic training—like how thin wood splinters when you drive a nail through it. In the early days of my doctoral program, I'd let my mind wander back to what felt concrete to me—most notably the horses I'd grown up with. Little did I know that these mysterious and beautiful creatures would get me through my Ph.D., with a sense of purpose and joy, and would teach me more than I have ever learned in any classroom.

This chapter centers łį́į́' (the Navajo horse) alongside my experiences with some of the current conversations in Indigenous and decolonizing education. It is performative and draws on Indigenous/decolonizing methodologies (Denzin, Lincoln, & Smith, 2008; Kovach, 2010; Smith, 2012) to narrate what I call the *ontology of horses* for Diné[1] (the people), and the embodied, material, spiritual, and linguistic lessons horses teach about Indigenous and decolonial praxis in educational studies. I weave in and out of reflective story and stretch existent theory by mapping some productive tensions (Goeman, 2013).

Like my Diné identity, horses were woven into my existence even before I existed. My dad, my grandpa, and my grandpa's dad were all excellent horsemen. My mom also comes from a long line of people who are brilliant with horses. I don't remember the first time I rode a horse. My mom says I was probably about 1-year-old riding on my aunt's lap and just laughing. Horses are such a part of my family that neither me, my sister, my mom, nor my dad can remember the first time each of us rode a horse. I learned basic riding skills with a couple of quarter horses we had growing up. They were given to us by my grandpa on my mom's side who owned a cattle ranch in Colorado. My memories of horses consist of their individual personalities and how I learned to conduct myself according to each unique relationship.

The first horse I called my own is named Rusty; he is a little mustang pony no taller than 14-hands. Though he lived with us in Oklahoma a long time before I knew his whole story, he has motivated me during my dissertation. His story goes like this: around the time when there were wild horse round-ups on the Navajo reservation, a little mustang colt was left behind and showed up at my n1lí's (paternal grandfather) place, tse'tah (between the rocks), for food and water. My grandpa—who felt sorry for him—opened up the coral gate so he could get a drink and decided to keep him because he's a red roan, which he says in the Navajo way he's one of the hardest horses to find. My grandpa later told me everyone wanted Rusty, but he was not willing to part with such a unique gift. Instead, my grandpa gave him to his only son and he lived with my family in Oklahoma. My dad trained him, and as I entered into the final years of my doctoral program, I started riding him because he is the gentlest of all our horses. With a calm, collected, and good-natured disposition, he doesn't look particularly grand but has the kind of stamina only a mustang can have. Like most mustangs, he is stocky, with a long mane that hangs over his eyes and rugged, thick hooves. His coat changes from strawberry to almost white depending on the season. He stands almost a head lower than all our quarter horses but has the smoothest gait and the most endurance. My family is always surprised by how little water he drinks.

Western ways of knowing in education have worked to erase Indigenous peoples and worldviews and replace them with a colonial ideology present in every aspect of education—especially research (Smith, 2012). Indigenous and decolonizing methodologies are two emerging bodies of work where Indigenous scholars interrupt colonial or non-Indigenous knowledge systems. These methodologies both challenge and align with conventional qualitative research frameworks, while simultaneously negotiating the contradictions inherent in projects of decolonization. Interventions from Indigenous and decolonizing methodologies center Indigenous worldviews and connect education, policy, research, and Native communities. Only recently have Indigenous scholars started to have a large presence in the field of education, and even more recently have they begun to articulate the importance of attending to settler colonialism for decolonizing education (Tuck & McKenzie, 2015; Tuck & Yang, 2012).

Settler colonial studies troubles the practices and ideologies of a settler colonial nation: a settler nation is founded on the acquisition of Indigenous lands from Indigenous peoples through various acts of extermination (Tuck & Yang, 2012). Veracini (2013) writes that settler colonialism is distinct from colonialism because the mentality is "go away" rather than "work for me," respectively (p. 2). Attending to settler colonialism in education poses a new set of questions for decolonial praxis. These questions center land, materiality, and embodiment within epistemology, ontology, and methodology, as well as aim to point out the concrete settler logics that continue to destroy Indigenous peoples, lands, and worldviews. Indigenous methodologies, decolonizing methodologies, and settler colonial studies align and deviate, but I pull the fields together in this chapter to draw from the contributions in each camp utilizing both the alignments and contradictions.

In decolonizing education, settler colonial studies directs scholars' interests toward the material, the embodied, and the visceral lived realities through which colonization persists, but more importantly, it gives space to center the embodied realities through which Indigenous peoples resist. Tuck and Yang (2012) write, "within settler colonialism, the most important concern is land/water/air/subterranean earth (land, for shorthand, in this article.) Land is what is most valuable, contested, required" (p. 5).

Diné scholar Larry W. Emerson (2014) writes that decolonization is various resistances to a colonial worldview, but that "Diné peoples do not know about this history" (p. 57), meaning the academic language of *decolonization* and *settler colonialism*. Instead, he argues that Diné resist, or decolonize, in an embodied way. Even though many Diné are not familiar with the language or literature of decolonization, they live the reality of it already, on their own, every day. By centering the horse, I foreground non-academic and informal education common among Diné and their livestock. For the Navajo, the horse is everything. It's central to the Navajo creation story, land management, entertainment, work, and k'e (family and clanship systems). To talk about the horse, I don't translate academic language from the top down; rather I push my writing to reframe, re-visit, or re-view academic languages so that they might be able to accommodate the brilliance of łį́į́' (the horse).

When I sit atop a horse, I see the world a little bit differently. The same pasture or grouping of trees I pass daily suddenly takes on a new angle and a different meaning. I noticed this a couple months ago while riding at my grandpa's place near Teec Nos Pos. My family and I covered about ten miles of ground on our horses, and as we approached a steep ascent up the mesa, I felt scared of the unstable sliding rock, but Rusty and I pushed forward together up the slippery trail. As he started galloping at what felt like a right angle, I shifted my thoughts to trust him. From the top of the mesa, I viewed the area where I'd played as a child from a new perspective. Rocks that have stayed in one place for decades looked and felt different. Before seeing this familiar place from this angle, I had to trust my horse to let me see it differently.

And I remember thinking the phrase, "places you can only get to by horse."

When I look through the ears of my horse, both metaphorically and literally, I've found that I re-view meanings and patterns that seemed familiar to me. Re-viewing with the horse is not just something for riding on the Navajo Nation but has also helped me re-view what it means to be educated. In this chapter, I re-view three aspects of decolonizing education related to the Navajo horse—the sacred, land, and communication. These three themes also connect settler colonial studies to education. The sacred, land, and communication all sit at an intersection of literature from Indigenous, decolonizing, Indigenous feminist, and settler colonial studies. Though I write about them individually, they are connected and weave in and out of one another the same way that my memories and their meanings tumble together.

Horses, like Indigenous peoples, bring up a set of contradictions—similar to the contradictions we face as Indigenous and decolonizing educators. Horses, though powerfully magnificent, have the capability to be gentle, to heal, and to connect. They frighten us and they give us hope by occupying, with beauty, an intersecting slew of contradictions. The Navajo horse is itself a meaningful nuance that highlights more meaningful tensions for any Indigenous educators working toward decolonization.

More importantly, centering these three tensions also centers communal and traditional knowledges that Diné use to naturally navigate contradictions without academic theory or theoretical jargon. This does not mean that theory is irrelevant; rather it reframes the conversation and expands what can be "decolonial" by opening up space for the lived, material reality and the presence of the sacred both at the same time. To do this, I'll tell a narrative of łíį' (or the Navajo horse) after each section as a form of translation. Each story shows how horses taught me about decolonizing education. My story, like many Navajo stories, is one that resists settler colonialism in daily life—to do this, I must open up space to allow for stories, horses, and contradictions to be together.

The Sacred

> *They say,*
> *ride a horse when something is wrong,*
> *After you're done, unsaddle your horse*
> *Let him loose in the pasture,*
> *Watch him role*
> *And when he roles,*
> *Your problems role off his back too*

The origin of the Navajo horse is nuanced, perhaps even contradictory to some. Yet, Diné relationships with horses hinge upon ontological beliefs about origin,

creation, and the living world. Therefore, scholars must often sit with uncomfortable, contradictory "histories" about the horse's beginning. Anthropologists
claim that horses were introduced through Spanish colonization in the late 1700s.
However, horses are significantly present in Diné creation stories. More recently,
paleontologists have found evidence of horse-like fossils in areas of Wyoming
(Williams, 2015); scientists attribute this to the evolution of horses on the North
American continent millions of years before humans. This is complicated because
the connection between the land, the sacred/traditional ways, and the knowledge
that horses bring are all found in the sacred.

I am not an expert on Diné traditional knowledge and worldview; I'm just
starting to learn more. Additionally, I am not interested in sharing sacred knowledge outside its proper context. Therefore, my discussion of the sacred does not
speak for all Diné and is both limited and incomplete. Rather, I engage a discussion about why origin stories and horses are important for educational studies and
do so by speaking about the presence of horses in my life.

I know about horses and the Navajo way from the transmission of knowledge
between family members and friends in my community. When young people
learn about horses, they learn, like I did, that they are sacred by watching, listening, and interacting with them. This transmission of knowledge is not necessarily
passed down by telling young people that horses are sacred. Rather, young people
observe embodied interactions that communicate foundational beliefs about the
world in which they live. These interactions reflect Diné spiritual and physical
understandings about horses. In this respect, horses are a pathway through which
Navajo people learn, practice, and communicate their worldview.

Vine Deloria Jr. (1998) once wrote, "the major difference between American Indian views of the physical world and Western science lies in the premise
accepted by Indians and rejected by scientists: the world in which we live is alive"
(p. 40). In other words, both matter and humans live and are in a living relationship with one another. The way I was taught, Diné call this hózhǫ which means
beauty, balance, harmony, and walking in beauty. Part of balance is k'e, or our
relationship and clan system. In the Navajo way, animals are relatives or kin, and
we must respect them the way we respect ourselves.

Weirto (2014) describes how she learned that hózhǫ involves a relationship
between the four cardinal directions, where Diné receive instructions for walking in beauty from each characteristic associated with each direction. Part of the
instructions include holistic harmony with the natural world. In our instructions,
there is also a horse for each direction. Each time I ask an elder about horses, they
always remind me that they are as foundational as the four directions in Diné
thought and worldview.

Revisiting the sacred for educational studies requires re-viewing the long-
standing contradictions in the sacred/secular binary that continue to separate
spiritual or Indigenous ontologies from education. Vine Deloria's (1992, 1998,
1999, 2003) entire body of work pointed to the urgency of confronting religious/

spiritual questions in Indigenous/decolonial education. In Deloria's late writing, he urges future scholars to take on the project of reconciling the sacred/secular binary. But I caution, this is not a project of comfort or reason. It's a project that, like the horse, may bring more questions than answers.

Before one can truly understand horses on Diné Bikeyah, they must re-view foundational epistemologies that have separated mind/matter[2] and sacred/secular because instructions for horses exist in Diné creation stories and in the philosophy for walking in beauty—both of which are clearest in Diné Bizaad (the Navajo language). Many Indigenous scholars have done work to break down binaries in academic thought (Grande, 2004; Kovach, 2010; Smith, 2012) and more specifically Diné scholars in education (Benally, 1992; Kulago, 2011, 2016; Lee, 2014). But centering Indigenous languages is still a major project for decolonization to undertake. For young Diné men and women who, like myself, still have a lot to learn, we can find an entry point on the back of a horse.

Horses are intertwined with settler colonialism on Diné Bikeyah alongside Navajo people. Together Diné and łį́į́' resist dichotomies between mind and matter because horses are neither the same as humans, nor inferior to humans. They are a gift and entered the Diné world with a set of instructions—including ceremony, song, and husbandry (Clark, 1966). Horses bring healing, knowledge, and responsibility as their material and spiritual gifts from the Diyin Dine'é (Holy people). Only from this fundamental understanding can one begin to see what horses can teach us. To believe a horse is sacred is not easy. For those who did not grow up watching this belief lived out spiritually and physically, it requires a shift in worldview and values, as well as forces one to take a critical look inward and outward. It is as challenging to believe horses are sacred as it is to learn a new language.

Land

Wild horses run the Navajo range in every agency. Herds are scattered against the backdrop of Diné Bikeyah, highlighting the pastels that blend land with sky. It is easy to see they're sacred by the way they move across the brush. If you're new to the reservation, you'd say they're beautiful. But, their history in the context of settler colonialism makes this painted picture an example of something much more complicated. The history of settler colonialism messes with this image, twisting the pieces like a mis-matched puzzle, making it hard to enjoy.

On my way to visit my grandparents one afternoon, I see these horses and want so bad to only see their beauty. I pretend they're not uncared for and that it's OK for them to be running like this. I stop for them to cross the dirt road in front of me. I lose my critical edge and just notice their colors and the way the breeze gently lifts their manes. Then as the last set of hooves kick up dust near my tires, I remember the destruction that the sacred brings when it's not kept sacred. I think about all the people who have died when their cars hit wild horses on the highways and about the starving ribs that protruded on young colts. . . .

I hold both in tension loving these out-of-place creatures that are, strangely, exactly where they ought to be at the same time.

Like Indigenous peoples, horses are in relationship with the land. Horses, humans, and land merge together in a cyclical dance and, when one is disrupted, all are disrupted. Re-viewing how livestock relate to land provides a window for understanding Diné relationships with land, and in turn the worldviews that characterize the connection between both. Studying the horse on Navajo land also provides a vehicle for re-viewing the junctures where settler ideologies interrupt and lead to epistemic violence carried out in the implementation of destructive policies. To illustrate this, I provide one example: the livestock reductions of the 1930s and 1940s. These policies show the material reality of settler colonial logics and their destruction for both Diné and their livestock.

As mentioned earlier, anthropologists write that the horse was introduced through Spanish colonization in the late 1700s; however the horse exists in Diné creation stories. In the commonly written phrase, "the horse was brought over by the Spanish," Diné face a very subtle form of epistemic violence—one that delegitimizes Diné creation stories where the horse was present from the start. This commonly accepted horse origin story positions the horse as a non-"Indigenous" newcomer to the Americas and, thus, undermines the sacred relationship between Diné peoples, horses, and land. If the horse is new, then Diné's relationship to the horse is also new and all practices of caring for livestock are also characterized as *new* (read primitive).

Voyles (2015) writes about this concept in depth describing how the reservation system restricted traditional livestock practices. Instead of thinking "the area is too small," the logic was "Diné and their livestock are too many." In this version, only settlers are capable of "domestication" and good agricultural practices. Additionally, knowledge acquired through sacred practices isn't respected as true "knowledge"; instead, scientific knowledge dominates. This move positions one narrative as "right" and the other as "wrong." Deloria (2003) describes this move as the incessant need of settlers to position their narrative as "right" above any other.

Additionally, Henderson (1989) highlights that these policies did not account for the changes brought about by ranches, the implementation of reservation lands, and economic shifts. Henderson suggests that "overgrazing" was due in part to ranchers and patchwork land ownership.

When carried out, this underlying assumption prompted research conducted by non-Indigenous paleontologists, environmentalists, and other specialists who intervened in land management and policy. These specialists viewed the Indigenous world through a settler lens and instituted destructive grazing management plans (Henderson, 1989; Voyes, 2015; Weisiger, 2007, 2009). Prior to policy implementation, non-Indigenous researchers characterized Navajos as poor stewards of their lands because too many livestock (including horses) were overgrazing the range. Weisiger writes, "soil conservationists believed that the Navajos owned far more horses than they needed, and many were all but feral" (p. 29).

The policy aimed to correct "overgrazing" through forced livestock reductions in the 1930s to 1940s (Henderson, 1989). The policies required a cap on the amount of livestock a family could own and the limit was developed by non-Navajo researchers who were ignorant about the social, familial, and economic knowledge embedded in traditional pastoral practices (Henderson, 1989). The social roles in Diné society hinged on the exchange and possession of livestock. Henderson (1989) writes, "Navajo kinship and social organization were important in determining the nature of relations with neighboring groups" (p. 380).

Wesigner (2009) provides two aspects of social life that were not taken into account for horse limits: marriage and transportation. In a traditional marriage ceremony, the exchange of horses is customary from the man's to the woman's family. Men who have large amounts of livestock are considered masculine or capable of being responsible for family members. Horses exchanged to the woman's family were given to replace her absence after marriage. For transportation, horses were Navajos' primary mode of transportation and livestock limits did not allocate the correct number of horses needed for travel on the land (Wesigner, 2009, p. 214). Neither practice was considered when the policies implemented limits on livestock ownership.

As Diné navigated settler colonial intrusions upon their land accompanied by ideological and economic changes, livestock was their primary source of wealth and currency. Wealth in these terms was not only currency, or assets; rather, horse ownership marked responsibility and care, and was associated with traditions of raiding and racing (Weisigner, 2009). Horses are more than currency to Navajos; they are icons of intellectual and traditional wealth, healers and gifts to be used. Economically, slaughtering livestock destroyed the Navajo's potential for economic exchange with non-Navajos (Henderson, 1989). Overall, reduction policies ignored the context of settler colonialism and disregarded traditional pastoral social practices. These policies destroyed, rather than saved, the range (Weisiger, 2009) and, in turn, aimed to destroy aspects of worldview and Diné.

The problem, therein, lies in policies that elect slaughter as an appropriate form of land management. Even though the policy did not directly assault the bodies of Diné people, slaughtering livestock deeply affected Diné and their way of life. Even worse, slaughtering livestock was a second offense. When Diné were forcibly removed from their lands nearly a century earlier by Kit Carson, their livestock were slaughtered as a form of conquest (Locke, 2005; Voyles, 2015).

Alongside the slaughter of horses and other livestock, Diné continue to maintain strong ties with the horse and the two persist in survival alongside one another. The potential, therein, lies in re-viewing a Diné worldview communicated through and with the horse. "Where did the horse come from? Or at what time?" are not the only relevant questions, but we must also ask: "How have Diné built a *relationship* with the horse and used it as a tool to preserve a distinctly Diné economy, family, spiritual life, and worldview?" Marking the specific entrance of the horse into Diné life using science tends to dominate conversations on horse history. However, I argue this is a settler project because it's developed from the logic of naming and claiming authority over land and, in turn, policing the stories that the land and its people get to tell. Traditional Diné know the horse has been with us from the beginning and is a tool for decolonization, but even those who disregard Diné creation stories can still see how Diné have developed and maintained a relationship with the horse that has allowed them to prosper (LaVerne, 1966).

In a settler logic, science and Western stories are linear and always correct, making any other view crooked and illegitimate (Smith, 2012). Using this logic, slaughter of livestock can be justified to "save the range." When outside researchers conduct interventions and utilize a research lens that does not account for the worldview underlying peoples' relationship with land and livestock, slaughter becomes a solution. When policies created to preserve and restore the land are decided without the community's input, Weisigner (2007) calls it environmental racism. I call it settler colonialism because there was no critique of reservation lands and the effects that decreased space might have on traditional pastoral practices.

Language

If I could spend my time learning Diné Bizaad and riding horses out on the Navajo Nation, I would. All the decolonization literature in the world could never capture the feeling of running with a horse through the brush. Riding horses is like learning a language; some things you can only learn when you're young and not from any formal lessons. When people say they "took riding lessons," it always seems like a manufactured form of schooling rather than education. Growing up, I watched and acted, without too much instruction. I can still hear my dad's guiding phrases—his gentle suggestions about how the bridle fits into the horse's mouth, and to pull the synch through the buckle, and never let the horse go without brushing it. Perhaps these practices can be learned later in life, but what cannot be taught in any lesson is how to genuinely embody comfort around horses.

Like a language, my relationship to horses is living and can never end. I spent considerable time away from them throughout my teenage years and in college. But when I returned from graduate school one winter for Christmas break, I went riding with my parents. I hadn't run with a horse in a few years and remembered how much practice it took to move with the horse instead of against it. I thought maybe I'd lost it, but as we began to run, it felt natural. When I made a full circle, I felt relieved to hear my dad say, "You look good out there."

Preserving Diné Bizaad (the Navajo language) is central to both communities and schools on the Navajo Nation. In addition to spoken language, learning to be around horses is a very particular embodied language for Diné people. Horsemanship connects to each part of life as much as the spoken word. Without livestock, Diné people's relationship to the land would fundamentally change. Like speaking

Diné Bizaad, the Navajo worldview lives in the postures taken with horses. Horses, as well as other animals, help Navajos navigate linguistic, familial, and social networks using traditional knowledge to communicate with horses and, more importantly, to horses, as well as bring Navajos back to the Navajo creation stories.

Many families on the Navajo reservation have horses. Kids as young as 4 and 5 start riding, learning how to care for horses, how to feed, saddle, and train them. Most Navajo men and women on the reservation have their own horses if not family with horses. Diné say one must speak the language to learn the worldview; the same is true for Navajo horsemanship. One must learn the worldview to speak the language of horsemanship. Some people have it, others don't, and it's as obvious as a fluent speaker of Diné Bizaad.

The ontology of horses is acquired by observation rather than direct communication. I call it ontology because it incorporates the aforementioned sections—language, the sacred, and land. They all work in connection to form a way of being around a horse that goes beyond colloquial understanding of horsemanship. It's a language of movement, touch, and most importantly mental and spiritual disposition. This language, because it's embodied, needs both time and space to flourish.

Horses are a gift of freedom and navigation for the traditional ways that incorporate the environment and the lifestyle of living with the land. Young Diné men and women learn about the responsibility of caring for animals throughout their life. Feeding and watering are two practices. Due to limited access of water on the Navajo Nation, many people haul water and hay for their livestock over miles of land several times a week. Movements across Diné Bikeyah, either by vehicle or horse, characterize one aspect of living with horses. These movements facilitate a unique relationship to Diné land, and young Diné men and women learn the sacredness of water by having to haul it multiple times a week.

Alongside caring for animals, Diné people learn the ontology of horses, meaning how to be, spiritually and physically, around them. Much like native speakers of a language, it's easy to tell who has learned this language early in life; the same can be identified by the way that a person conducts themselves around horses. The ontology is communicated through an interactive language that reflects some distinct nuances about Diné worldview. Navajos use traditional knowledge to communicate with horses, such as the horse songs. More importantly, what makes Diné excellent horsemen are their traditional embodiments transmitted from Diné knowledge and worldview.

One characteristic is communication, or understanding their personalities, through time spent with them. Living on the land and building a relationship takes time, space, and worldview. It takes the land to know the horses, and the horses to know the land; additionally, it takes the worldview and the language to know the land and to communicate with the horses. Each body part of a horse represents a part of the land. This shows how all work together, balancing one another. Additionally, there are many plants and herbs indigenous to Diné Bikeyah that are used for horse husbandry and healing cuts, wounds, and sicknesses. These knowledges connect land, horse, and human.

My dad is one of the only people I know who can stay calm when a horse bucks him off and then climb back on again, sticking with the horse like a friend until they move together instead of against. I see now that I learned about being Diné by watching my dad interact with horses. Before school, I never would have named this "Diné," "Indigenous," or "decolonial" because when you are Indigenous or Navajo you don't generally call it that—you just are that. It's in the way that one lives their life; I never named it Native, it just was my dad. He loves the earth. He loves animals. Some may call him a "horse whisperer," but this isn't a phrase used in Diné communities. Horse training, loving land, and Nativeness gets idealized in movies and books—even in the academy—but his embodied example is concrete in actions, not words.

The horse, beyond an icon of knowledge and connection, represents Diné relationships with livestock and provides a glimpse into one part of the Diné worldview—one that I'm still learning from my horses and my family. Turning to the horse positions traditional and community knowledge as expert knowledge and points to both the violences of settler colonialism and the ways in which Diné resist through relationships that embody their traditional worldview. Decolonizing education, for Indigenous scholars, is an interdisciplinary project that intertwines science, gender, language, and religion. Similarly, the horse is also a gift that connects many parts of Navajo and non-Navajo life.

Horses are a gift that will continue teaching and connecting us. Horses are my gift as I finish my dissertation. Reflecting on them and being around them during this process gives me life and meaning.

Notes

1 Diné is what Navajo people call themselves. The literal translation is "the people." In this chapter, I use both Navajo and Diné interchangeably.
2 Many Indigenous scholars have critiqued traditional Western scholarship for maintaining a separation between mind/matter, otherwise known as the Cartesian Dualism (Descartes, 2008).

References

Benally, H. J. (1992). Spiritual knowledge for a secular society: Traditional Navajo spirituality offers lessons for the nation. *Tribal College, 3*(4), 19.

Clark, L. V. H. (1966). *They sang for horses: The impact of the horse on Navajo and Apache folklore.* Tucson, AZ: University of Arizona Press.

Deloria, V. (Ed.). (1992). *American Indian Policy in the Twentieth Century.* Norman: University of Oklahoma Press.

Deloria, V. (1998). *Red Earth white lies: Native Americans and the myth of scientific fact.* Golden, CO: Fulcrum Publishing.

Deloria, V. (1999). *For this land: Writings on religion in America.* New York, NY: Routledge.

Deloria, V. (2003). *God is red: A native view of religion.* Golden, CO: Fulcrum Publishing.

Denzin, N. K., Lincoln, Y. S., & Smith, L. T. (Eds.). (2008). *Handbook of critical and indigenous methodologies.* Thousand Oaks, CA: Sage Publications, Inc. doi:http://dx.doi.org/10.4135/9781483385686

Descartes, R. (2008). *A discourse on method*. (I. Maclean, Trans.). Oxford: Oxford University Press. (Original work published 1637).

Emerson, L. W. (2014). Diné culture, decolonization, and the politics of hózhǫ́. In L. L. Lee (Ed.), *Diné perspectives: Revitalizing and reclaiming Navajo thought* (pp. 49–67). Tucson, AZ: University of Arizona Press.

Goeman, M. (2013). *Mark my words: Native women mapping our nations*. Minneapolis, MN: University of Minnesota Press.

Grande, S. (2004). *Red pedagogy: Native American social and political thought*. Lanham, MD: Rowman & Littlefield.

Henderson, E. (1989). Navajo livestock wealth and the effects of the stock reduction program of the 1930s. *Journal of Anthropological Research, 45*(4), 379–403.

Kovach, M. E. (2010). *Indigenous methodologies: Characteristics, conversations, and contexts*. Toronto, ON: University of Toronto Press.

Kulago, H. A. (2011). *Diné youth define community: Finding routes to school and community partnerships*. (Order No. 3481058). Available from ProQuest Central; ProQuest Dissertations & Theses Global. (904661838). Retrieved from http://search.proquest.com/docview/904661838?accountid=14214

Kulago, H. A. (2016). Dewey called them Utopians, I call them ancestors. *Educational Philosophy and Theory*, 1–9.

LaVerne, H. C. (1966). *They sang for horses: The impact of the horse on Navajo and Apache folklore*. Tuson, AZ: University of Arizona Press.

Lee, L. L. (Ed.). (2014). *Diné perspectives revitalizing and reclaiming Navajo thought*. Tucson: The University of Arizona Press.

Locke, R. F. (2005). *The book of the Navajo*. Los Angeles, CA: Mankind Publishing Company.

Smith, L. T. (2012). *Decolonizing methodologies: Research and indigenous peoples*. London, UK: Zed Books.

Tuck, E., & Mckenzie, M. (2015). Relational validity and the "where" of validity: Place and land in qualitative research. *Qualitative Inquiry*, 1–6. doi:10.1177/1077800414563809

Tuck, E., & Yang, K. W. (2012). Decolonization is not a metaphor: Decolonization. *Indigeneity, Education and Society, 1*(1), 1–40.

Veracini, L. (2013). Introducing settler colonial studies. *Settler Colonial Studies, 1*(1), 1–12.

Voyles, T. (2015). *Wastelanding: Legacies of uranium mining in Navajo country*. Minneapolis, MN: University of Minnesota Press.

Weisiger, M. (2007). Gendered injustice: Navajo livestock reduction in the New Deal Era. *Western Historical Quarterly, 38*(4), 437–455.

Weisiger, M. (2009). *Dreaming of sheep in Navajo country*. Seattle, WA: University of Washington Press.

Werito, V. (2014). Understanding hózhǫ to achieve critical consciousness: A contemporary Diné interpretation of the philosophical practices of hózhǫ. In L. L. Lee (Ed.), *Diné perspectives: Revitalizing and reclaiming Navajo thought* (pp. 25–38). Tucson, AZ: The University of Arizona Press.

Williams, W. (2015). *The horse: The epic history of our noble companion*. New York, NY: Scientific American/Farrar, Straus and Giroux.

4

RIVER AS LIFEBLOOD, RIVER AS BORDER

The Irreconcilable Discrepancies of Colonial Occupation From/With/On/Of the Frontera

Marissa Muñoz (Xicana Tejana)

On one side: A 20-minute walk from my grandmother's house will take you to the banks of the Rio Grande/Rio Bravo dividing Laredo, Texas, from Nuevo Laredo, Tamaulipas. Ten more minutes of walking, and you reach the Paso del Indio. Historically, this is the place where the river bends, and if you know the seasonal timing, crossing between the countries means wading through shallow waters, rather than the treacherous undercurrents that gave the river its name. It is a hidden place, encoded in the deep-time relationships between beings there. A few miles downstream are the largest naturally growing peyote gardens in North America. Within our community, there are knowledge keepers who know the songs, practice the ceremonies, and read the rock art that connects the star people to the sacred springs, to the medicine gardens. People from all over Turtle Island journey to these sacred ecologies nurtured by the Rio Grande/Rio Bravo.

On the other: Laredo, Texas, is also home of the Princess Pocahontas Pageant, which takes place every year during the month-long George Washington Birthday Celebration. Debutantes are feted all year and presented to society at a formal ball, each with her own Indian name, color theme, and elaborate Native-ish costume, complete with ultra suede gown, headdress, and intricate sparkling glass beadwork. Originally, the pageant was enacted in 1898 to tell the story of how Pocahontas saved the city of Laredo from an Indian ambush (Dennis, 1997; Young, 1998). The colonial mythology is re-enacted each year, to *honor* our collective, pan-Indian-ish ancestors.

In this chapter, I trouble some of the irreconcilable discrepancies around identity, collective memory, and public pedagogies of my borderland community. I will play the part of tour guide, to walk you along our river and share stories from the frontera, recorded in practices, the bodies, and landscapes (Riaño-Alcala & Baines, 2011) of those who remember. I draw from serpentine conocimiento

(Lara, 2014), critical practices of writing home (Asher, 2009), and red pedagogy (Grande, 2008) to guide my responsibilities as a knowledge keeper, mother, and Xicana activist scholar educator.

Introduction

I was taught to begin with the ancestral language so that the land understands when we call it by name. In the Carrizo/Comecrudo language, the land is named Somi' Sek (Mancias, 2015). Today, we call most of the territory Texas. This study grows out of a Xicanx[1] Tejana[2] epistemology that prioritizes Indigenous land- and river-based ways of knowing and being within a borderland context of multiple, overlapping, and ongoing violences against the land and people. More specifically, these concepts have emerged with a return to my own ancestral territory, as a practice of decolonial/anticolonial thinking about the irreconcilable discrepancies of Indigeneity and colonial occupation about/on/of/from the frontera, my home. Working from tacit, place-based knowledge of Laredo, Texas, this chapter will draw from the embodied and emplaced stories of collective memory to disrupt imposed narratives of Indigeneity and life along the Rio Grande/Rio Bravo.

The borderlands are not a metaphor. For the millions of people who make a life along the nearly 2000-mile line the separates the US from Mexico, the borderlands are real, live people, living in real, tangible places. The borderlands is home. The borderlands are diverse geographies of distinct places, cultural interfaces, histories, ecologies, and perspectives that have been continuously traversed and settled since time immemorial. When we limit our thinking to metaphors of the border in the context of settler colonialism, we perpetuate an erasure of the history, place-based knowledge, and material reality of border residents, resulting in intellectual colonialism (Castillo & Tabuenca-Cordoba, 2002). Further, we displace the original peoples who have resisted, survived, and continue to challenge colonial occupation of their ancestral territories, drawing from intergenerational collective memory that predates the invention of the colonial border. There are an infinite number of ways that people make meaning with/in/through the river, and separately, how we make meaning at/on/through the US-Mexico border. Furthermore, not only do borderlands, as objects of study, shift and change meaning as contexts change, they also shift with differences in positionality of those who study them. In other words, perspective is everything.

Restor(y)ing From the Community

Indigenous knowledge and traditions have survived colonization in the stories and collective memory of intergenerational survivors. In most communities with ancestral ties to land, evidence of such knowledge is observed in the daily practices, on the bodies of survivors, and across the landscapes (Riaño-Alcala & Baines, 2011), in spite of efforts to decimate, replace, and forget. Due to the fraught nature of the borderland contexts in particular and the ever-present danger of erasure, this study moves toward holistic, embodied,[3] and emplaced[4] approaches for understanding. Stories serve as decolonizing approaches that bear witness, revitalize, and remember the pre-border relationships between the river, the land, and the people that have survived in the collective memory of the community. My personal long-term commitment is to engage a process of restorying (Corntassel, 2009), using oral history and testimonios to restore and restory my community in order to remember who we were before our river became an occupied, armed, international border.

On the surface, my role as author is that of local tour guide, bringing you, dear readers, along the rivered land- and memory-scapes, calling attention to particulars of place from an insider perspective. My compass is serpentine conocimiento (Lara, 2014), drawing from Mexican Indigenous teachings that all life is connected to both earthly and spiritual realms, emphasizing duality, intuition, and fluidity. Some details I know from having lived (t)here, walking the land with my folks. Some details I know from sitting around the kitchen table after the dishes have been cleared and listening into the conversations of friends and family. Some details come from inside my cells, a deep way of knowing and being. I am speaking as a Xicana fronteriza mother/daughter/granddaughter activist educator scholar. Thus, intentionally, I'll narrate as I would when I'm home, a think-aloud on paper, from home and memories of home, with bits of Indigenous scholarship, read and remembered, cited along our way.

Our goal is to take a walking tour along the Rio Grande/Rio Bravo wearing our all-terrain huaraches and critical borderland eyeglasses to practice critical borderland thinking and epistemic disobedience (Mignolo, 2011). While decolonization is a massive multi-layered undertaking, working to uproot the settler colonial systems of racist heteropatriarchy, unsettling everyone by intentionally honoring land as knowledge (Tuck & Yang, 2012), our only task today is to take a walk along the river and break all of the academic rules of formal writing by platicando y andando the way locals do.[5]

We will talk about what we see, what we don't see, and what we imagine, free from an obligation to respond to colonial structures (Monture-Angus, 1999), including colonial structures of thought.[6] Our tour will begin with some borderland context, move on to two distinct learning moments, and work to shift our language toward processes of becoming, rather than imposing outcomes, expectations, or singular conclusions. And, as my dad says, "We will get there when we get there . . . when we get there" (Oscar Muñoz, oral communication, almost every day), wherever our "there" happens to be today.

Bienvenidos a Los Dos Laredos[7]

Welcome! Laredo, Texas, is my hometown. It is a community older than the border, with a river twisting and meandering through the bisected city halves. The

Rio Grande/Rio Bravo[8] splits the two Laredos between two different countries, (at least) two different languages, and (at least) two very different worldviews. Locals are (mostly) fluent in both. While you may hear the local dialect and think we are pocho, please remember that frontera residents are not only speaking in the confluence of two different languages but are also thinking in the convergence of different epistemologies.

Around here, in the frontera, the dominant US whitestream (Grande, 2008) hegemony is not the default frame for understanding knowledge or life. So, our fronteriza ontology is not a double consciousness in a du Bois-ian sense (du Bois, 1903) of an outer versus inner understanding of border thinking (Mignolo & Tlostanova, 2006), but a constant polyvocal argument between the two dominant voices from each side of the border, and the multiple voices of resistance (Castillo & Tabuenca-Córdoba, 2002). The dynamic local cultural interface is nuanced, allowing simultaneous, juxtaposed, irreconcilable cultural realities (Anzaldúa, 1999). For this reason, the concept of serpentine movement and land-based ways of knowing accurately captures fronterizx[9] knowledge of, and ability to navigate the complex, fraught terrain of the frontera.

It is often said that the sister cities of the US-Mexico border are more alike to each other than to their respective countries, due in large part to the mutually responsive linguistic, social, and cultural influences. We were the only sister cities split by the border who opted to share the same name of Laredo/Nuevo Laredo. For many generations, the line that divides has been arbitrary: life on both sides is dictated by the scorching heat and thorny brushlands common to the greater bioregion. Local populations are fluid, as many people commute across the river in each direction on a regular basis, with family, friends, work commitments, and business interests on both sides. Crossing the river/border used to be as mundane as crossing the street, but everything has changed in the last 25 years or so, which genealogically speaking is considered one generation. The river nurtures both cities as it always has and, in spite of the hypervisible border, we are one community.

This is my grandmother's home on Main Street. I asked you to meet me here as a starting place for today's adventure because it is one of the older parts of town, shaped by multiple generations of embodied and emplaced knowledge. Notice the way cultural knowledge marks the landscape, the homes, the shared public spaces. Some of the older homes preserve the original adobe brickwork from the early 1800s, while others have been updated by each subsequent generation of the family who live in the home, much like rings of a tree mark growing seasons.

Notice also our timing today. We are meeting at dawn the way the elders do, knowing that dawn and dusk are the only times to be outside without suffering the scorching 100-plus degrees Fahrenheit heat that bakes the landscape from mid-March until late-September. Awareness of timing and the climate is one of the primary land-based knowledges locals need to make a happy life in our part of the frontera. Many locals cultivate the sensitivity and can feel changes coming in their bodies even before the weather forecaster tells of upcoming weather events.

Let's take a moment to unsettle what we think we know about the river. Erase the border. Just focus on being human, on being here on the land, near the river. Start by looking up at the sky. Most of the borderland sky is enormous, uninterrupted by tall trees or buildings, the vast expanse of atmosphere and constellations always within reach. In this flat terrain with few visual landmarks, the ones-that-came-before navigated by looking up.

Upstream, Look Back in Time

The history of the land begins with Native peoples and our relationships to the land. We begin our walk working from the land- and memory-scapes of the widest perspective, from the creation story of centeotzintli (corn) and its subsequent spread across the continent. The movement of corn and peoples can be traced over 7000 years, and as each generation of corn germination requires human intervention, many creation stories include the co-creation of humans and corn as interdependent siblings (Rodriguez, 2014). The land holds a much longer memory of our people than we do of the land.

Similarly, the river has a long memory. We won't get there today, but upriver from here a few hundred miles, the ancestors left stories along the river, where they knew it would be found, at the confluence of the Pecos River and Rio Grande/Rio Bravo. The White Shaman Panel (named by archeologists) is a set of rock paintings that are around 3000 years old (Maestas, 2003), telling a creation story linking the land, the four local sacred waters, and constellations in a mapped timeline spanning approximately 9000 years (G. Perez, oral communication, October, 2, 2014). The panel is located on private land and not easily accessible to a curious public, but one of many sites of significance along the rivered landscape. Be warned—as we walk, the vistas may stir you to settle into old colonial tropes of *untouched wilderness*, but look deeper; think more thoroughly. The land and Rio Grande/Rio Bravo are full of memories. Please watch your step; everything has thorns.

From here, we will walk down Jefferson toward what is now the Water Treatment Plant, where many of the older generation in town learned how to swim. My great aunties tell stories of how a few generations ago, the children used to swim races back and forth there, able to read the water's temperament. It was never completely safe or benign, but as children, they were fluent in the river's language of temperature, color, current, and surface turbulence, in ways that today we are not. They could read the Rio Grande.

Texas has scrub-lands bounded by the Great Plains to the north, the Gulf Coast and piney forests to the east, the Sierra Madre Occidental mountains to the south, and to the Chihuahuan desert to the west. These particular eco-regions dictated the small-group, nomadic, hunter-gatherer lifestyle of the many Indigenous peoples, who strategically migrated according to seasonal pressures (Maestas, 2003;

Swanton, 1940; Galindo, 2003). To be clear, this is not a description of primitive peoples, or a version of the noble savage trope, but the material necessity for minimalism in this particular landscape, supported by deep-time land knowledge and extensive networks of relatives across the territory.

For first peoples, a relationship with the land serves as the foundation for all knowledge. Indigenous ancestral languages emerged from the relationships to land (Armstrong, 1998) based on the specific ecologies communities lived in relation to. Within each Indigenous language is the specific, nuanced understanding of how all life is related within their specific ecology. In Texas, there were hundreds of distinct, autonomous groups that lived across the watershed of the Rio Grande/Rio Bravo, who had distinct languages, cultures, and worldviews, yet also spoke common languages such as Coahuilteco. Familial groups relied on ancient, well-organized trade networks, inherited from the many centuries of peoples before them, moving back and forth across the greater territory much the way we do now. Strategically, family groups could be absorbed into neighboring communities or dispersed into smaller groups across the landscape, as needed. All life revolved around the land and rivers.

Coahuilteco was one of the most widespread languages spoken by Texas' first peoples. While some early historians argue that speakers belonged to a single cultural group, we now understand it to be a pidgin language, shared by many different peoples across the region (Swanton, 1940; Macias, 2015). By the 1600s, Coahuiltecan-speaking peoples built a flourishing network of over 200 smaller affiliated tribes and bands (Adams, 2008). The language, much like the cultural practices of the people, were a combination of specific land-based knowledges of the greater region, with notable linguistic similarities to other Hokan languages) including Comecrudo, Cotoname, Karankawa, and Tamaulipecan dialects) and distinct from the Athapascan or Uto-Aztecan languages (Swanton, 1940). Whereas anthropologists tend to name peoples by the linguistic connections, the people of the Lower Rio Grande Valley between 1790 and 1818 called themselves the Malagueros, Garzas, Zalayas, Aguichacas, Anda el Camino, Chinitos, Cotonames, Cueros Quemados, Pajaritos, the Eastern and Western Carrizos, and Guajolotes (Galindo, 2003). These are just a few of the many Indigenous peoples from the region, in a snapshot of a territory that has been continuously inhabited for centuries. The records that survived colonization are those of the colonizers, who were quick to decimate Indigenous libraries and intellectual traditions. Today, anthropologists and linguists study word lists compiled by the proselytizing Spanish-speaking mission friars from a few hundred years ago. Some may not be the most accurate sources for ancestral languages, but in many cases, these are the only written records we have. Like everything else around here, if you know where to look, you could find everything you need . . . even a few local elders who still speak their ancestral languages of Carrizo or Coahuilteco. The ancestral intellectual traditions of the land have survived in the living archives we call elders. Yet, to the settler power structure, once they destroyed the written records, these languages were considered extinct.

Colonial frames of reference often limit and cloud our understanding, much like looking through someone else's prescription eyeglasses distorts our visual perception, limiting, what we notice. Textbooks suggest that the Texas Indigenous history is a succession of less advanced, primitive cultures that left no traces of significance. Without any records, it became easy to characterize the Indigenous peoples as sub-human, justifying the atrocities of colonizing the land and peoples. However, our trusty critical borderland lenses help us to see that the local peoples were particularly adept at responding to the rugged, volatile environment, and strategically made themselves invisible to the waves of colonizers. Survival depended on adaptation and our ancestors were masterful shapeshifters, with thousands of years of Indigenous intellectual traditions that supported life on these lands.

Here we are, on the banks of the river. Standing here, you can see that the river is not a border. Since time immemorial, the river has been a map of Yanaguana, or Yanawena (depending whom you ask), which in the Carrizo/Comecrudo language means *place where I rest*. Indigenous peoples from different nations have retraced the steps of our creation story on their pilgrimages to collect the sacred plant medicine, Paxe.[10] Wherever the peyote medicine has traveled, it carries Carrizo/Comecrudo and Coahuilteco, and the ancestral languages of Texas with it, in the form of song and ceremony. The songs call the spirits of Yanaguana, honoring the spirit waters, and remind us of our responsibilities for mutual nurturance. Hikuri[11] is also a sacred plant medicine for my relatives from the south, the Wixairika peoples, and interestingly, the plants there speak Wixairika, the language that emerged from Wirikuta, the place of creation (Matsuva, oral communication, March, 2006). In each place, the land and river tell the stories of emergence, connecting the peoples, languages, and knowledges.

Our stories map of a different understanding of the universe. In the old way of thinking, the river used to bring relatives from all directions together at/in/of/on/through/across/with the water. Today, the border creates a semi-permeable boundary, tightly controlling the flow of bodies and ideas[12] over several bridges that moves over the waterway. For most border-crossers, the river and water are untouchable, merely sights along the road.

The next stop is the Paso del Indio Nature Trail, located on the Laredo Community College Campus. If we were restricted to staying on land, we'd have to go back toward town, as there is no longer access to walk along the river in this direction. Luckily for us, we have our canoes, permits, IDs, and the names of several local well-regarded gatekeepers ready. We will follow the river downstream, the direction our bird relatives are traveling, to see what we can see by canoe.

Please keep your whole self in the canoe, our river may look very peaceful, but it hides dangerous undercurrents and has earned the reputation as un traidor, or traitor, quietly pulling people under the murky waters. Occasionally, cows or other wildlife become international creatures and may swim across, but they don't bother folks too much. The multiple agents, officers, troops, and fringe militia groups patrolling the regions are only interested in hunting down brown people.

Seven Flags of Settler Colonialism

On that note, let's revisit Texas history. The phrase *six flags of Texas* refers to six different eras of colonial occupation, during which all parts of the state we know today were claimed by a colonial empire, with some back and forth between Spain and France. Laredo/Nuevo Laredo has a unique history of seven flags, as the only community in the greater region that also attempted independence as a republic.

This is usually how history begins, as though colonization were the beginning of all creation. However, we know that the colonizers would never have survived without the Indigenous knowledge of the land. So, as we get closer to our next rest stop, consider our particular location and context as an example. At the time of its founding, Laredo was part of the Mexican territory called Coahuila y Tejas, under the second of its seven flags. Although *officially* founded in 1755 by Don Tomas Sanchez de la Barrera, the location of Laredo along the Rio was chosen for its proximity to the Paso de los Indios,[13] because the bend in the river created a low-water seasonal passage across the river (Adams, 2008). This particular location was well known and used by Indigenous peoples long before being *rediscovered* by Spanish patrols, who learned to live in the area from the local Indio experts. The colonial community grew around the Paso de los Indios the same way it grew around los Indios. In response, fronterizxs shapeshifted as they (we) have for centuries, integrating without assimilating, and surviving colonial encounter after colonial encounter.

In 1848, the Treaty of Guadalupe Hidalgo was signed to end the Mexican-American War, costing Mexico almost one million square miles of territory, including California, Arizona, New Mexico, as well as parts of Colorado, Utah, and Nevada. In Texas, this treaty shifted the international border from the Nueces River south to the Rio Grande/Rio Bravo, in effect causing the border to jump over thousands of Indigenous, Mexican and Tejano families. In its original form, the treaty was written with provisions to protect these families as *Mexican citizens* residing in the territory, consisting primarily of "pueblos de indios, genizaros . . . and mestizos"[14] (Urrieta, 2003, p. 160), to be granted American citizenship and to retain the title to their lands. However, President James Polk omitted these articles upon ratification (Hernandez, 2001) to re-classify the territory unclaimed, rendering Mexican- and Indigenous-descended peoples across the southwest landless exiles in their (our) own ancestral territories.

While the treaty is most known for dramatically increasing the geographic size of the US, it did so by dispossessing many thousands of families of their homelands and effectively normalizing the construction of a class of inferior non-citizens and lasting legacy of oppression and racial hatred (Hernandez, 2001). To this day, Eurocentric politicians and mainstream US media often parrot a race-based entitlement to what is now the US by conflating anyone of Mexican Indigenous ancestry with "illegal alien" immigration status. Rhetorical stereotypes repeated at the national level have served to flatten the real diversity of the borderlands, erasing the many people who always have been, and still remain, in these communities along the frontera.

Here we are at the Paso del Indio Nature Trail. We can disembark here and have a look around. Just take a minute. Really look around. Do you notice the embodied and emplaced details that give significance to this little patch of carrizo on the riverbank? Paso del Indio is just a name on some old maps, but when you are here, and you learn the history of this place, it's a different understanding to the river that comes from your mind understanding your body in this particular place and context. This is what it is to restory actual places along the Rio Grande/Rio Bravo.

Last month, all of this area was underwater due to the rain upstream in Eagle Pass/Piedras Negras. We didn't get any rain here, but the rainfall upstream caused flooding in several areas in town. Because Laredo sits slightly higher than Nuevo Laredo along the river, residents on that side with homes near the riverbanks saw quite a bit more damage to houses and roads. In previous generations, the community members from both sides of the river used to come together to help rebuild in times of crisis; however, all of that has changed in recent (military-occupied) times. Maestas reminds us that "human migration back and forth across the Rio Grande has been an important aspect of local Indigenous life for thousands of years" (2003, p. 1). Long before any colonial encounters, there was a rich diversity of Indigenous peoples for whom there were no colonial borders. While some families can trace their Indigenous genealogies, there are also traces of Indigenous culture and knowledges embedded in social history, the language, ceremonial observances, burial practices, storied sites, sacred medicines, and knowledge of natural springs that push us to understand south Texas as a Native sacred geography (Maestas, 2003). In spite of the shifting and fraught identities of the people, the Indigenous intellectual traditions, stories, and relationships survive in the collective memory of the people who continue to live in their ancestral places.

We've caught the attention of the Border Patrol now. They must have seen us make our way downstream in our canoes. They will likely make several passes with their big loud river-boats to intimidate us. Notice the machine guns welded to the sides? In any other context, such heavy artillery would seem out of place in a *public space*. Politicians have decided our borderland home is a warzone; hence, combat-grade weaponry in communities and public spaces is the new normal around here. Let's sit here under the shade of a tree and talk for a while until they go.

Historicized Mythologies

American history books describe a mythological Texas, full of tales of Davy Crockett, the Alamo, bloodthirsty Indians, and lazy Mexicans, told to justify colonization and naturalize the current social inequity. The same racist stereotypes have been repeated for so long that communities have come to accept what they must as true, falling into the trap of the resonance effect (Gross, 2003). Identity is fraught territory and has been for many generations, the dangers of which are borne unequally across a mixed population. Demographic data shifts depending on who is asking. Yet, around the kitchen table, friends and relatives share stories, the names, and cultural practices of our Indigenous heritage. Even that one relative who claims to be 100% Spanish has an Indigenous grandma or two.

Don't worry. The patrol boats will pass. They are on a schedule.

It was no accident that in the founding treaties and declarations of the US, the identity of the first peoples was never clearly articulated, much less articulated with the names they gave themselves. If the people are not acknowledged, there is no need to recognize their citizenship, their rights, or their humanity. Interestingly, the history of the census reveals the confusion of imposed identifiers, such as categories based on language, geography, and ethnic heritage, similar to the confusion of the Spanish missionaries upon first contact. Anzaldua suggests that the purpose for historicized mythologies is to further the colonial agenda:

> Gringos in the U.S. Southwest consider the inhabitants of the borderlands transgressors, aliens—whether they possess documents or not, whether they're Chicanos, Indians or Blacks. Do not enter trespassers will be raped, maimed, strangled, gassed, shot. The only "legitimate" inhabitants are those in power, the whites and those who align themselves with whites.
>
> *(1999, p. 26)*

The danger she alludes to is real. When the uniformed people with guns demand to know who you are, survival requires that we give the right answer in language they understand. Because the border is our home, it means daily interrogation from systems of power, demanding we choose a pre-selected category on their forms, none of which fits. Colonial structures "have forcibly supplanted traditional Indigenous ways of identifying the self in relation to the land and community, functioning discursively to naturalize colonial worldviews" (Lawrence, 2003, p. 3). Today, the imposed criteria defining Indigeneity often relegate Native peoples into two narrowly defined categories: either card-carrying tribal members registered with the US government or extinct. Other manifestations of Indigeneity are seemingly invisible and/or erased not only by policy, but also culturally, through the use of confusing identification categories that conflate race, ethnicity, and language. Along the southern borderlands, the anti-Mexican racism of the US is compounded with the anti-Indígena classism of Mexico, rendering thousands of mixed heritage Mexican American Indians (as well as Mexican Indian Americans), severed from their traditional cultures by historical amnesia, shame, and denial.

The Racist Wall

After a few generations of shapeshifting, it has become harder to remember who we were as people of the land. I know the DNA of my ancestors are in this soil.

Generations are made visible when bulldozers bore holes into the land, scooping pottery shards and bits of bone into big mounds, making way for the cement and steel of a border wall. To a trained eye, each hole is a potential archeological site, full of evidence of thousands of years of continuous habitation in the area (Tamez, oral communication, May 23, 2017). For the willfully uninformed, it's just dirt.

Laredo does not have a wall. Not yet. But just downriver, you can see how physically impractical the wall is. The meandering path of the old river and shifting sediments make for poor wall foundations; so, in many frontera communities, the wall was built inland, in straight lines, as though cutting the crusts off the bread. For some US citizens, home lies between the river and the international border, on the wrong side of the wall. The daily commute in their own communities to go to work, school, or the grocery store includes surveillance, armed patrols, and declarations of citizenship to get to the other side of the wall. Home has become an occupied, armed, tense place for brown-bodied Indigenous fronterizos.

Interestingly, the response from the community is the same as it has been through the centuries, similar to the response in the event of a natural disaster. Folks face the threat, stay safe, come back the next day and rebuild. Hurricanes can blow away all their trees, floods can wash away their houses, apartheid barriers are built through their front yards, but fronterizxs always come back to their land and rebuild board by board, brick by brick. It is in our nature.

Water

Ok, back in our canoes for another little float along the river. You'll notice the northside of the river to be thick with overgrown salt cedars and caña, two invasive species that have taken over after all the native species were burned away and removed with chemical defoliants.[15] Such aggressive plant management happens every 10 to 20 years or so, as decision-makers tend to be afflicted with long-term memory loss and low comprehension of ecological systems.

While Mexico has a less destructive approach to habitat management, each country has different policies governing each bank of the river. The right hand does not know what the left hand is doing. The Rio Grande/Rio Bravo is also home to a network of distinct wetland habitats, and the home of several critically endangered species found nowhere else in the world. While there are ecologically minded fronterizxs who monitor and study the river as a holistic ecosystem and distinct array of flora and fauna; conversations about ecological preservation are immediately eclipsed by the hysteria of Border Security.

I use the term *ecological* in a broad sense, to collectively refer to the flora and fauna of specific places, sharing the food and water in an area, but connected by much more than physical biological logistics. Kuokkanen (2007) writes the "self and the world are not separate entities" (p. 41) but are connected by a "response-ability— that is, an ability to respond, to remain attuned to the world beyond oneself" (p. 39). In this sense, traditional ecological knowledge is the accumulation of knowledge that develops from being in relation to the ecosystem, "founded on spiritual-cultural instructions from 'time immemorial' and on generations of careful observation within an ecosystem of continuous residence" (LaDuke, 1994, p. 127). Evidence of this can be seen in the way that creation stories include the co-creation of both land, the water, and people within the same story.

Everyone wants to talk about water, especially as we are sitting in our canoes in the river. There is simply not enough time or space on this short little journey to get into it with the attention it deserves. In short, it is over allocated, underappreciated, governed by a tangled mass of outdated international laws, and will reach a crisis tipping point soon. Someday, I will write a whole book of fronterizx water stories. But today, we are just practicing thinking thoroughly, moving along/in/with/through the source of all life in this territory.

Which is to say, water is not the substance that supports life. Water *is* life. The water of the Rio Grande/Rio Bravo *is alive* inside the bodies of every person, every plant, every creature across the landscape, physically and spiritually connecting us to the land. At the most basic levels, water is what connects the two Laredos in an unmistakable interdependence. The Rio Grande/Rio Bravo is our circulatory system, bringing life to this land.

We'll just pull our canoes over to the riverbank just past the bend in the river. This is another site of significance, where the Holding Institute once stood, but was washed away by the flood of 1954. It is a site of forgetting and failed development experiments, one after another. Here comes another Border Patrol airboat.

You know, there used to be public parks along the river, with playgrounds, picnic tables and basketball courts, but with increases in Homeland Security, these spaces have become desolate and unused. My gran-tía Concha has lived in Laredo her whole life. She complains "What are they securing? I am no longer free to enjoy the river." It's interesting how quickly the community forgets the meanings of places, from one generation to the next. Today's youth may never know those freedoms.

. . . And Then There Is Pocahontas

The story goes something like this: On February 22, 1898, local Indians and white settlers fought a vicious battle for control of Laredo, Texas. The settlers gave up and presented Great Chief Sachem the key to the city, which he, in turn, presented to Princess Pocahontas, in return for her guidance and protection. Everyone celebrated for two days, then decided to re-enact the Boston Tea Party (Young, 1998; Who are the Red men? 1998). It was believed that George Washington allegedly used the name Great Chief Sachem as an alias to conduct military maneuvers. At some point, due to some creative imaginings, the name Great Chief Sachem of the story must have been a reference to George Washington having spent time in Laredo (History, 2017). Thus, it was George Washington who presented Princess Pocahontas a key to the city of Laredo.

The originators of the story included several prominent Laredoans involved with the Improved Order of the Red Men and the local chapter of Yaqui Tribe #59, neither of which are Indigenous organizations, but are fraternal organizations loosely patterned after the Great Iroquois Confederacy, freely borrowing names, vocabulary, and customs from assorted Native peoples (Young, 1998; Who are the Red men? 1998). Historical accuracy was clearly not their priority, as Pocahontas lived in Jamestown in the 1600s, George Washington in the late 1700s, and the Laredo battle is set in 1898 (Maximilliano, 2011), yet this convoluted story remains firmly rooted as the basis for one of Laredo's biggest community celebrations.

Every February, Laredo celebrates the George Washington Birthday Celebration (GWBC) as a month-long calendar of galas, parades, and community celebrations in a show of patriotic assimilation. In addition to the George and Martha Washington Debutant Pageant, there is also a Princess Pocahontas Pageant, organized and populated by Laredo's wealthy and powerful families. As Nathan (1999) so accurately describes the portrayal, "Think of a new doll: North American Indian Princess Barbie. Glossy, dark hair, perfect makeup. Vegas-plumed headgear, ermine white leather, gossamer silk, fur, pound upon pound of hand-sewn bugle beads, designer moccasins." The Princess Pocahontas Pageant stays true to its mythological roots, complete with Native-ish names, flute music, extravagant costumes, and grossly inaccurate stereotypes, woven into a non-threatening narrative of unity and benign kindness to the settlers.

> "As blue white smoke fills the stage, a revolving door hidden within a rocky ridge-like set turns and reveals a very stylized representation of Pocahontas. She is elaborately clad, from her white feather headdress to a rich, adorned and tassled costume that looks like an Indianized version of Dale Evans's cowgirl. Turning to the audience, she begins singing as if the production was a 1950s musical:
>
> *(Admist much applause)*
>
> "Here I am, It is I. I have come to serve my people As I walk for Mankind, I ask Please be giving, Be kind.
>
> *(Refrain:)*
>
> Because people everywhere have needs and loves to give Because people everywhere need hope and love to live . . ."
>
> *(Pocahontas' opening number, Pocahontas Pageant, February 22, 1996).*
> *(Dennis, 1997)*
> *(Reprinted with the permission of Marilouise and Arthur Kroker, editors CTheory)*

Nothing about the Princess Pocahontas Pageant is in any way authentic or accurate, or representative of the Indigenous ancestry of a majority of the south Texas population. The ostentatious display of wealth required for the costuming and conspicuous casting according to whom each debutant is related to, both genealogically and socially, offers many options for interesting critical analysis. Previous scholarship includes the work of Dennis (1997), who examined the pageantry as a cultural production that reinforces white racial superiority, and Young (1998), who examined the racial dynamics of south Texas during the formative years of the pageant, suggesting conspicuous demonstrations of wealth as "whiteness." More recent work by Peña (2006) suggests that US colonial mythologies de-politicize border spaces, while Cantu (2011), a Laredoan, offers an analysis of different examples of Indigenous cultural production in Laredo, including the performance of real and imagined Indigenous identity. However, for a huge portion of population, none of the analysis matters. Community members are dazzled, excited by the spectacle, and relish the escapism, unaware of the colonial narrative shaping our collective sense of identity.

In this place, at the bend in the river, sediment collects. If the land could talk, it would remember the Holding Institute Building that is no longer here, a pecan tree orchard that is no longer here, and countless other attempts to alter the meanings and purpose of this little landform shaped by the river. As people of the land, how do we remember our Indigenous roots that may have been forgotten, washed away, or buried under colonization? How do we remember ourselves as belonging to the river?

Let's head back to the canoes and let the Rio Grande/Rio Bravo guide our thinking. The path ahead is slow and undulating, meandering across the landscape. Intentionally, we'll (un)settle ourselves back into the canoes and think thoroughly as the water carries us along (careful to stay on the US side of the water). Let's activate our serpentine conocimiento and trust the water-, land-, and memory-scapes as archives of knowledge to inform our thinking practice.

Unsettled Geographies of Colonization

Let's begin with the land. We know that colonization is a social structure rather than an event (Wolfe, 2006), premised on racism and white supremacy, occurring without any further energy or investment from the colonizers (Monture-Angus, 1999). To understand colonization as a geography of race, Nayak suggests, "Many forms of racism have an explicitly territorial dimension that requires us to examine the complex interweaving of social relations and spatial structures" (2011, p. 551). Nayak argues that racism cannot simply be quantified or measured as an object, but instead is more accurately understood as embodied experiences that invoke emotional responses.

By extension, colonization can also be understood as our embodied experiences navigating hegemonic colonized/colonizing spaces. A geography of colonization in/of the frontera may map how racism and white supremacy are imposed onto spaces on the land, allowing an analysis of how Indigenous fronterizxs navigate the places we inhabit. Similarly, incorporating embodied geographies of colonization in the frontera would recognize the various ways racial dynamics are internalized by border residents.

Oftentimes, the hegemonic assumptions of white supremacy cause settlers to misunderstand the Indigenous responses to occupation. In the collective memory of the frontera community, the American wave of colonial violence was not the first encounter but, in some cases, the sixth and seventh episode of settler occupation and efforts to displace Indigenous peoples and knowledges (intentionally plural) from the land. Let's consider the strategies of survival that have been known and practiced in the frontera for many generations, as we think through what it means to simultaneously hold space for Paxe/Hikuri/peyote and Princess Pocahontas in the emplaced communities of Laredo/Nuevo Laredo.

Misunderstanding Benign Diversions

> "*Totatzine ipan in ilhuicac,*
> Our Father, who art in heaven,
> *ma titechmactilia in totaxcal,*
> give us our tortilla . . ."
> Don Pedro, conservative Nahua that he was, heard in this what was common-
> sense to every Nahua: one prays to the sun for maize.
>
> (Haly, 1996, p. 541)

In this example, we can see how the Lord's Prayer, when recited by an Indigenous person, may sound like an example of assimilation, yet when the words are transliterated back from Nahuatl to English, they reveal a Nahua cosmology. It is an example of shapeshifting, camouflaging Indigenous knowledge beneath the veneer of religious assimilation for the purpose of survival.

Consider the possibility of a similar mechanism at play in Laredo/Nuevo Laredo. For the casual visitor, Princess Pocahontas provides a veneer of Indigeneity, a tasty Other (hooks, 1992), that is available for public consumption. She represents a recognizable trope, familiar and benign to structures of colonization. Unintentionally, she is also a benign diversion, distracting attention away from the land-based Indigenous knowledge and peoples of the frontera. In this way, the colonial mythology of *a vanished race* remains uninterrupted in spite of the continued ceremonial practice across the region. (For the time being) Hikuri is not *vanished*. It is unfamiliar, unrecognized, and invisible to wearers of colonial lenses. While the concept of presenting a benign diversion may describe the Princess Pocahontas on the frontera, as the attention-grabbing spectacle, there is also a converse mechanism at work.

Silence as Protection

When we are thinking about decolonization, is it easy to fall into the habit of associating particular words with particular concepts. The word *silence*, in association with colonization, implies an *imposed* silence, as in *when we are/were silenced*.

It implies a trauma of not being heard, not having a voice, of having the ability to speak taken by someone or something outside of oneself. However, I'd like to suggest that silence is also an intentional response, an act of defiance, a refusal to engage, and an action of resistance.

In a flat, wide-open landscape of the frontera, lacking mountains or gorges to mark space, where fraught territories may overlap, silence is a natural defense. Silence is not compliance or acquiescence. Silence is resilience, a manifestation of adaptability. If we re-orient our thinking to ask how Indigenous peoples, knowledge, and cultural practices have survived in such a contested and fraught territory, we can start to understand how silence protects.

One of the first protocols around the plant medicines is that you don't go looking for them. When you know the land, and spend time in quiet reflection, particular plant medicines will come to you. It's a matter of mutual respect and patience to develop the relationship with plant relatives that share the landscape.

Humans are not simply a brain transported by a body. Gonzales (2012) reminds us that "Knowledge is experienced with the whole of our being" (p. xvii). Cultivating a practice of silence shifts our attention from verbal and thinking ways of knowing toward multisensory, embodied ways of being and knowing on the land. In this way, silence is productive, prioritizing holistic ways of knowing and being that includes physical, emotional, intellectual, and spiritual knowledges. It would follow that, for land-based peoples, survival includes silence as an embodied source of creativity and as a strategy of protection around traditional ways of knowing and being.

A Practice of Perpetual Unsettling

Our last stop today is Los Dos Laredos Park. We'll pull the canoes up on the shore there, before we get to the international bridges or the traffic of downtown. Notice all the empty parking lots just beyond the park? During my childhood, folks would come park here, in the parking lots for River Drive Mall, and walk across the bridge or dinner or errands. The mall is now gone, the parking lots are now empty, and locals no longer enjoy what used to be a weekly excursion across. Everything changes along the banks of our river.

At first glance, the presence of Princess Pocahontas and Hikuri in the same overlapping, shared space on the frontera may seem to suggest a conflict. It could be argued that each is an entity created by particular dynamics in the landscape through a specific set of cultural practice. The Princess Pocahontas Pageant is a colonial/colonizing spectacle that reinforces power dynamics in the community. Hikuri is a decolonial/decolonizing ceremonial practice that connects fronterizxs to intellectual traditions of their ancestral territory. Each practice gives meaning to space to create places of significance across the community landscape. Community members move in and out of places, negotiating meaning, impacting those around us, and internalizing elements from the environment.

However, as we map the geography of colonization of the frontera, we can't allow ourselves to get stuck in oppositional or binary modes of thinking. This is a land of *and*'s, not *either/or*'s. The river is a place of confluence. A map of the places that reinforce concepts of identity would be useful not to prove a point or singular perspective, but to portray the rich, nuanced texture of life in the frontera. The reality is that, every year, the Princess Pocahontas Pageant and Hikuri ceremonies take place, sharing time, sharing space, and possibly sharing participants. We are reminded that different bodies move differently through places and can do so without significant interference. Our community, Laredo/Nuevo Laredo, is a place of convergence and, as such, irreconcilable discrepancies flourish here.

To think of/on the frontera means to be comfortable with the discomfort or perpetual unsettling, with the unresolved stories, with the choques (Anzaldua, 1999) that rattle our whole being. As a fronteriza, if something here does not make sense, I can make sure I'm not wearing my American eyeglasses and choose my Mexican[16] frames, or my Indigenous frames, or my critical borderland shades to immediately change what I see, and change how I think. In this way, Mignolo's epistemic disobedience (2011) is built in to the fronterizx perspective. Depending on my context, I can also change my shoes to change how I walk in the world, but for the time being these all-terrain critical frontera huaraches never let me down.

Thank you for joining me on this little tour and think-aloud. You know, as many times as I've done this, it's different every time as different stories seem to come forward and need to be shared with different peoples. Here, in my frontera, the process of storying and restorying helps to resist the ongoing colonization of the land, colonization of our bodies, colonization of our minds. I'll leave you with one of my favorite teachings about the power of sharing stories. "Storytellers create and re-create the cosmos, giving form and meaning to the moment. Stories are medicine, they are our connection to the sacred power that is in all things" (Beaucage, 2005, p. 139). Embodied and emplaced pedagogies (like this moving think-aloud) that are built on storytelling, collective memory, and land-based knowledge, are a means of healing ourselves, and our communities. Thank you for witnessing my own restorying of home.

Notes

1 A person of Mexican Indigenous ancestry living in the US, though this concept is evolving. Also written as Chicana/Chicano (to indicate gender specificity in Spanish), Xicana/Xicano, Xicanx (to specify gender neutrality in both English or Spanish).
2 A woman from Texas.
3 Embodied refers to the critical awareness, not only of our bodies in relation to other bodies, but also an awareness of the impact of our surroundings on our physical being.
4 Emplaced refers to specific locations and contexts in which events happen, directing our attention to the specific dynamics of space within particular ecologies. People are a part of the geography, as one aspect of the complex and dynamic system.
5 Talking and walking around. Part one of our epistemic disobedience practice being how we recognize, value, and take in new information (i.e., input).

6 Part two of our epistemic disobedience being how we process, question, assimilate, and respond with creativity to our journey (i.e., response).

7 Welcome to the Two Laredos.

8 The river is named differently on each side of the border; thus, Rio Grande/Rio Bravo is a typographical representation of the river split by the border line. For residents, the names are interchangeable. I write both to remind myself to think like a Laredoan.

9 Fronterizx refers to a border resident. Also written as fronteriza/o, I have updated the term to reflect gender inclusivity.

10 Coahuilteco name for peyote, written as a proper noun, named as we would a person.

11 The name I was taught for peyote is Hikuri, a Wixairika (Huichol) name.

12 Castillo and Tabuenca Cordoba (2002) remind us that most borderland theories and concepts are written from a US perspective and are thus limited to only representing the one side of the border. Concepts written by Mexican scholars of the borderlands do not gain traction with US audiences, pointing to the selective semi-permeability of the border.

13 Translates to *way of the Indians,* but really means *the route the locals use.*

14 Indian villages, detribalized Indians, and mixed-race Indians.

15 An appropriate visual metaphor for the way colonization manifested differently on each side of the river.

16 One of the best ways to explain this is the difference in storytelling between American and Mexican stories. In my opinion, American stories, as told in books and movies, tend to end with a tidy, everyone-is-accounted-for ending. Mexican stories, by contrast, tend to focus on portraying a moment or person or idea, and simply ending when the audience understands something about our subject. The expectations of the audience shape the narrative. More than just a difference in storytelling, the example points to a deep ontological and cultural difference.

References

Adams, J. A. (2008). *Conflict and commerce on the Rio Grande: Laredo, 1755–1955.* College Station, TX: Texas A&M University Press.

Anzaldua, G. (1999). *Borderlands, la frontera: The new mestiza.* San Francisco, CA: Aunt Lute Books.

Armstrong, J. A. (1998). Land speaking. In S. J. Ortiz (Ed.), *Speaking for the generations: Native writers on writing* (pp. 174–194). Tucson, AZ: University of Arizona.

Asher, N. (2009). Writing home/decolonizing text(s). *Discourse: Studies in the Cultural Politics of Education, 30*(1), 1–13.

Beaucage, M. (2005). Aboriginal voices: Entitlement through storytelling. In D. Claxton, M. Townsend, & S. Loft's (Eds.), *Transference, tradition, technology: Native new media exploring visual and digital culture* (pp. 138–151). Banff, BC: Walter Phillips Gallery Editions.

Cantu, N. E. (2011). Dos mundos [two worlds]: Two celebrations in Laredo, Texas—Los Matachines de la Santa Cruz and the Pocahontas Pageant of the George Washington's birthday celebration. In R. Blanco-Cano & R. E. Urquijo-Ruiz's (Eds.), *Global Mexican cultural productions* (pp. 61–74). New York, NY: Palgrave MacMillan.

Castillo, B., & Tabuenca Cordoba, M. S. (2002). *Border women: Writing from la frontera.* Minneapolis, MN: University of Minnesota Press.

Corntassel, J. (2009). Indigenous storytelling, truth-telling, and community approaches to reconciliation. *English Studies in Canada, 35*(1), 137–159.

Dennis, D. (1997, August). Washington's birthday on the Texas border. *CTheory,* 2–17. Retrieved from https://journals.uvic.ca/index.php/ctheory/article/view/14834/5705

Du Bois, W. E. B. (1903). *The souls of black folk: Essays and sketches.* Chicago, IL: A. A. McClurg & Co.

Galindo, M. J. (2003). *Con un pie en cada lado: Ethnicities and the archaeology of Spanish colonial ranching communities along the lower Rio Grande Valley.* (Doctoral dissertation, University of Texas at Austin). Retrieved from https://repositories.lib.utexas.edu/bitstream/handle/2152/589/galindomj039.pdf

Gonzales, P. (2012). *Red medicine: Traditional Indigenous rites of birthing and healing.* Tucson, AZ: University of Arizona Press.

Grande, S. (2008). Red pedagogy: The un-methodology. In N. K. Denzin, Y. S. Lincoln, & L. T. Smith (Eds.), *Handbook of critical and indigenous methodologies* (pp. 233–254). Los Angeles, CA: Sage Publications, Inc.

Gross, A. J. (2003). Texas Mexicans and the politics of Whiteness. *Law and History Review, 21*(1), 195–205.

Haly, R. (1996). "Upon this rock": Nahuas and national culture, a contest of appropriations. *American Indian Quarterly, 20*(3), 527–562.

Hernández, S. (2001). The legacy of the treaty of Guadalupe Hidalgo on Tejanos' land. *The Journal of Popular Culture, 35*(2), 101–109.

History. (2017). *120th Washington birthday celebration* [website]. Retrieved from www.wbcalaredo.org/about-us/history/

hooks, b. (1992). *Black looks: Race and representation.* New York, NY: Routledge.

Kuokkanen, R. (2007). *Reshaping the university: Responsibility, indigenous epistemes, and the logic of the gift.* Vancouver, BC: UBC Press.

LaDuke, W. (1994). Traditional ecological knowledge and environmental futures. *Colorado Journal of International Environmental Law and Policy, 5*(127), 127–148.

Lara, I. (2014). Sensing the serpent in the mother, Dando a luz la Madre Serpiente: Chicana spirituality, sexuality, and manhood. In E. Facio & I. Lara (Eds.), *Fleshing the spirit: Spirituality and activism in Chicana, Latina, and indigenous women's lives* (pp. 113–134). Tucson, AZ: University of Arizona Press.

Lawrence, B. (2003). Gender, race, and the regulation of native identity in Canada and the United States: An overview. *Hypatia, 18*(2), 3–31.

Maestas, E. (2003). *Culture and history of native American peoples of South Texas.* (Doctoral dissertation, The University of Texas at Austin). Retrieved from www.lib.utexas.edu/etd/d/2003/maestaseg032/maestaseg032.pdf

Mancias, J., & Torres, A. (2015, July 23). *The biggest tribe you never learned about in your Texas history books.* [Article written by tribal historians and knowledge keepers of the Estok' Gna and Tejones of Texas first peoples]. Retrieved from www.freepresshouston.com/the-biggest-tribe-you-never-learned-about-in-your-texas-history-books/

Matsuva. (2006, March). Oral communication.

Maximiliano. (2011, February 13). *Pocahontas council attempts to make itself relevant* [blog post]. Retrieved from http://laredotejas.blogspot.com/2011/02/pocahontas-council-attempts-to-make.html

Mignolo, W. D. (2011, Fall). Epistemic disobedience and the decolonial Option: A manifesto. *Transmodernity,* 44–66.

Mignolo, W. D., & Tlostanova, M. V. (2006). Theorizing from the borders: Shifting to geo- and body-politics of knowledge. *European Journal of Social Theory, 9*(2), 205–221.

Muñoz, O. (almost every day). Oral communication.

Monture Angus, P. (1999). Considering colonialism and oppression: Aboriginal women, justice and "theory" of decolonization. *Native Studies Review, 12*(1), 63–94.

Nathan, D. (1999, March 5). Pocahontas on the Rio Grande. *Texas Observer*. Retrieved from www.texasobserver.org/968-pocahontas-on-the-rio-grande/

Nayak, A. (2011). Geography, race and emotion: Social and cultural intersections. *Social and Cultural Geography, 12*(6), 548–562.

Peña, E. (2006, November (3.2)). De-politicizing border space. *E-mispherica: Borders: Hybrid Imaginaries/Fractured Geographies*. Retrieved from www.hemi.nyu.edu/journal/3.2/eng/en32_pg_pena.html

Perez, G. (2014, October 2). Oral communication.

Riano-Alcala, P., & Baines, E. (2011). The archive in the witness: Documentation in settings of chronic insecurity. *International Journal of Transitional Justice, 5*(3), 412–433.

Rodriguez, R. C. (2014). *Our sacred Maíz is our mother: Indigeneity and belonging in the Americas*. Tucson, AZ: University of Arizona Press.

Swanton, J. R. (1940). *Linguistic material from the tribes of southern Texas and northeastern Mexico*. Washington, DC: U.S. Government.

Tamez, M. (2017, May 23). Oral communication.

Tuck, E., & Yang, K. W. (2012). Decolonization is not a metaphor. *Decolonization: Indigeneity, Education, & Society, 1*(1), 1–40.

Urrieta, L. (2003). Las identidades tambien lloran, identities also cry: Exploring the human side of indigenous Latina/o identities. *Educational Studies, 34*(2), 147–168.

Who are the Red men? (1998). *The improved order of Red Men* [website]. Retrieved from www.redmen.org/redmen/info/

Wolfe, P. (2006). Settler colonialism and the elimination of the Native. *Journal of Genocide Research, 8*(4), 387–409.

Young, E. (1998). Red men, Princess Pocahontas, and George Washington: Harmonizing, race relations in Laredo at the turn of the century. *The Western Historical Quarterly, 29*(1), 48–85.

5

INDIGENOUS OCEANIC FUTURES

Challenging Settler Colonialisms and Militarization

Noelani Goodyear-Kaʻōpua (Kanaka Maoli)

How can Indigenous and settler peoples work together to unmake relations of settler colonialism and instead imagine and move urgently toward decolonial futures? What is the role education can play? How can we create educational spaces that allow people to practice such transformation?

When settler colonialisms are fundamentally about the expropriation of land, transforming settler colonial relations requires both the reconnection of Indigenous peoples to ancestral landbases and the transformation of systems that structure our relations with land and with one another. As Eve Tuck and Wayne Yang write, decolonization in settler colonial contexts "must involve the repatriation of land simultaneous to the recognition of how land and relations to land have always already been differently understood and enacted" (Tuck & Yang, 2012, p. 7). This chapter approaches such projects from the context of Oceania, also known as ka Moana Nui (the great, expansive ocean) in Hawaiian or as the Pacific in English. I suggest that looking to the ocean—or looking at lands from vantage points on the ocean—opens up visions for and practices of decolonial future-making.

Pacific Islands studies scholars and creatives have reminded us that Oceania is not an inert place that can be simply pointed to on a map, nor described and contained by colonial knowledge categories. Albert Wendt writes that Oceania is

> so vast, so fabulously varied a scatter of islands, nations, cultures, mythologies and myths, so dazzling a creature, Oceania deserves more than an attempt at mundane fact; only the imagination in free flight can hope—if not to contain her—to grasp some of her shape, plumage, and pain.
>
> *(Wendt, 1983, p. 71)*

The peoples of Oceania grow up being at home with the sea. Our fluency with fluidity can be useful in helping to reimagine settler colonial ways of structuring

human relationships to land. Writing of our ancestors who navigated and traversed this vast ocean, 'Epeli Hau'ofa says of Indigenous Pacific peoples' relationships to ka Moana Nui:

> They played in it as soon as they could walk steadily, they worked in it, they
> fought on it. . . . Theirs was a large world in which peoples and cultures
> moved and mingled unhindered by boundaries of the kind erected much
> later by imperial powers.
>
> *(Hauʻofa, 1993, p. 8)*

Imperial boundaries in Oceania have been sustained by foreign militaries, and the
complex currents of violent militarization that Oceanic peoples have navigated
cannot be understated or forgotten (Barker, 2012; Camacho, 2005; Genz et al.,
2016; Kajihiro, 2008; Niheu, Turbin, & Yamada, 2007; Osorio, 2014; Shigematsu &
Camacho, 2010; Teaiwa, 1994; Tengan, 2008).

Following Oceanian authors and educators, this chapter suggests that looking to the ocean provides important insights into remaking settler colonial relations through education. In undertaking this journey, I map three major streams
in futures-oriented Indigenous studies: Indigenous futurity, Indigenous futurisms
and Indigenous resurgence. I then draw upon Vicente Diaz's theorizing from the
Native Carolinian navigational practice of etak as a way to posit that our purposeful movement toward decolonial futures must attend to both directionality and
positionality at collective and individual levels (Diaz, 2015). Given the fundamental ways that imperialism and white supremacy have relied upon militarization
in Oceania, I argue that decolonizing and Indigenous education must consider
demilitarization as an important element of our collective directionality. How
do we *do* this in our classrooms and other educational spaces, giving participants practice in such transformation? In the last part of the chapter, I draw on
some of my own co-teaching experiences in demilitarizing education and trans-
Indigenous exchange to offer some points for thinking about the need to more
fully address (de)militarization in Indigenous and decolonizing studies in education. But first, a story.

Indigenous and Settler Future-Making: WWV and RIMPAC

In the summer of 2014, two distinctly different global projects of futurity were
launched from my home islands of Hawaiʻi. That is to say, each of these projects
(re)presents a different directionality for potential Oceanic and global futures.

In June 2014 my family and I were among the hundreds who gathered to
send the canoes Hōkūleʻa and Hikianalia off on their worldwide voyage (WWV).
Chants, songs and hula were offered in a day-long celebration of the resurgence
of Indigenous Pacific voyaging. These two double-hulled sailing canoes, modeled
on ancestral waʻa built for long-distance voyaging, set off with the goal of visiting

85 ports in 26 countries over three years. The throngs of people standing on the rocks near the oceans edge, snapping photos of the vessels being towed out of the harbor toward open ocean where their sails would be unfurled, we knew were part of a historic moment in the life of the Hawaiian people and a movement of cultural resurgence that started a generation earlier.

In 1976, Hōkūleʻa became an icon for the renewal of our faith in ancestral knowledges when she first sailed from Hawaiʻi to Tahiti in an effort to prove that Polynesians had purposefully navigated the largest ocean in the world. That first voyage was navigated not by a Native Hawaiian, but by a Micronesian master navigator from Satawal, Mau Piailug.[1] With the WWV that began in 2014, the practices of celestial, open-ocean navigation that began to be revived in the 1970s and 1980s were explicitly handed over to a new generation of navigators, many of whom were not even born when Hōkūleʻa first helped to catalyze the Hawaiian cultural renaissance.

Aiming to cover 47,000 nautical miles, the purpose of the WWV has been carried in its name: Mālama Honua (to care for the Earth). The explicit mission of the international, multi-crewed and multi-million-dollar voyage was to generate consciousness about how to "navigate toward a healthy and sustainable future . . . to mālama (care for) Island Earth—our natural environment, children and all humankind."[2] Its organizers intended the voyage to teach spectators and students to think like voyagers on a canoe with limited resources and to underscore the urgency of addressing environmental issues like coral bleaching and ocean acidification. Long-distance voyages make abundantly clear the ways that cooperative human relationships are necessary to ensure the survival of all. As master navigator Nainoa Thompson explained before the journey began: "*We're not going to change the world; we're going to build a network of people around the Earth who are going to change it.*"

That same summer, a second and wholly different kind of maritime project commenced at the end of June 2014, when the US Pacific Fleet launched its biennial Rim of the Pacific (RIMPAC) exercise in and around Hawaiian waters and shores. RIMPAC is the world's largest international military maritime training and display. Led by the US military and held every two years, RIMPAC exercises first began in 1971 bringing together invited military allies of the US forces. Twenty-three countries participated in the 24th round of RIMPAC, engaging 47 ships, six submarines, more than 200 aircraft and 25,000 personnel in water, air and land components.[3] The 2014 RIMPAC war games were led by a combined taskforce, headed by a US commander and assisted by Australian and Japanese admirals. Its theme of "Capable, Adaptive, Partners" resembled the WWV's promotional materials in some ways, emphasizing international and cross-cultural collaboration in maritime prowess. The US Pacific Fleet's website explains that RIMPAC "helps participants foster and sustain the cooperative relationships that are critical to ensuring the safety of sea lanes and security on the world's oceans."[4] But the rhetoric is, perhaps, where the similarities between the WWV and RIMPAC end.

Whereas the WWV focused first on island centers of the Pacific and on restoring ecosystems on which island peoples depend, RIMPAC emphasized the military and capitalist trade interests of the rim countries and the strategic value those larger countries place on accessing and crossing over the Pacific's center.[5] If the WWV was an attempt to bring Indigenous Oceanic futurities to a global audience, RIMPAC engaged participants and its audiences in settler futurity—an imperialist and heavily armed vision for Oceanic and world futures. This was a future in which "anti-submarine, counter-piracy and air defense operations" were the focus; in which gunnery, missiles and warships secure the Pacific for rim countries to have open access over the ocean. These resource-intensive exercises and the national security discourse that works to legitimize them fly in direct contrast to what Pacific Island leaders themselves deemed as the most pressing security threat in the Majuro declaration: fossil fuel-burning induced climate change (Pacific Islands Forum, 2013). In its own green-washing attempts, RIMPAC, 2014 was touted as utilizing green biofuels. But the extractive and exploitative nature of settler futurities cannot be green-washed so easily. As RIMPAC, 2014 was beginning, Native Hawaiian and Filipinx demilitarization organizers Shelley Muneoka and Kim Compoc asked: "What is the carbon footprint of RIMPAC's live-fire training, sunken ships, explosive ordnance disposal, and expended fuel?" (Compoc & Muneoka, 2014) But unlike the WWV, with its constant livestreamed and recorded updates from crew members and vast community outreach into schools, the RIMPAC exercises were barely visible from the ground in Hawai'i. The transparency, in terms of course, resources used, and individuals participating in each project were vastly different.

Both the WWV and RIMPAC are engaged in material, rhetorical and pedagogical projects of future-making. I open this chapter by juxtaposing these two global projects sited in Oceania for two reasons: to demonstrate why it is important that Indigenous and decolonial education provide analytical and creative tools for thinking about futures; and to illustrate why Indigenous and decolonial education must include more critique of and explicit alternatives to imperialist militarization.[6] In the next section, I map three major streams in futures-oriented Indigenous studies, which can and should be taken up in more educational contexts.

Indigenous and Settler Future-Making

One of the central insights of the intellectual field of futures studies is that all representations of the future are political. Futures studies scholars remind us that there is not a singular future, rather they call on us to consider the politics of various representations of "the future" and the multiple possible futures that are opened or foreclosed by our actions in the present. Three different streams within Indigenous studies are focusing explicitly on Indigenous future-making: Indigenous futurity, Indigenous futurisms and Indigenous resurgence. Each of these

three streams of Indigenous studies takes on the politics of Indigenous future(s)-making in distinct but synergistic ways.

Indigenous Futurities

Futurity is not just another way to say "the future." Futurities are ways that groups imagine and produce knowledge about futures (Baldwin, 2012; Recollet, 2016; Tuck & Gaztambide-Fernandez, 2013). Ben Anderson problematizes the linearity of Western liberal democratic understandings of temporality, as evidenced in the kind of anticipatory actions that are undertaken to "preempt" and "prepare" for particular futures (Anderson, 2010, p. 788). He offers an analytic for thinking about how futurities operate. They assemble:

1. *Styles* of thinking about the abstract category of "the future" and about inter-temporal relationships (such as between past, present and future);
2. *Practices* that give content to specific futures, such as creating forecasts or predictions that populate "the future"; and
3. *Logics*, ways of legitimizing or guiding present actions by martialing beliefs about the future, with the aim of preventing, mitigating, adapting to, preparing for or preempting specific futures.[7]

Tuck and Gaztambide-Fernandez extend the term further by differentiating between *settler futurity*, which requires the containment, removal and eradication of autochthonous peoples, and Indigenous futurity, which does not foreclose the inhabitation of Indigenous land by non-Indigenous peoples but does foreclose settler colonialism and settler epistemologies. That is to say that Indigenous futurity does not require the erasure of now-settlers in the ways that settler futurity requires Indigenous peoples (Tuck & Gaztambide-Fernandez, 2013, p. 80). Indigenous gender systems and feminized bodies have suffered particular kinds of erasures and violences in settler colonial contexts. When we have been denied futures or control of our own futures, it is particularly important that Indigenous feminist theorists, like Arvin, Tuck and Morrill, place importance on ideas of Indigenous futures and futurities that arise from "the experiences and intellectual contributions of Indigenous women . . . [who] have been an invisible presence in the center, hidden by the gendered logics of settler colonialism for over 500 years" (2013, p. 14).

Recollet (2016) suggests that futurities, particularly Indigenous futurities, are both temporal *and* spatial, resting on particular assumptions about the relationality and causality between emplaced pasts, presents and futures. We might think about Indigenous futurities in terms of the relations between living, passed and yet-to-come. In that context, Indigenous futurities are enactments of radical relationalities that transcend settler geographies and maps, temporalities and calendars, and/or other settler measures of time and space. Such settler scales often obscure the ways we humans are living in intergenerational rhythms that we cannot always fully see because they extend beyond the horizons of our individual lifespans. Indigenous futurities can offer forms of knowing and performance, such as sonics, smells, ceremonies, embodied movement and other ways of, in Harjo's terms, "jumping scale" (Recollet, 2016, p. 94). As styles of thinking, practices of living and logics of ordering knowledge, Indigenous futurities tend away from controlling and possessive modes of knowing. Instead they frequently include ways of relating that involve putting our bodies in motion with various kinds of non-human rhythms that engage multiple senses. I have written elsewhere that we might think about such practices as a multiplicity of land-centered literacies (Goodyear-Kaʻōpua, 2013).

Indigenous Resurgence

Scholars and activists theorizing *Indigenous resurgence* have offered more detailed pictures of what Indigenous futures can look like and what we can do to get there (Aikau, 2015; Alfred, 2005; Alfred & Corntassel, 2005; Corntassel, 2012; Martineau, 2015; Simpson, 2011). Whereas the analytic of futurity has primarily been deployed as a mode of critique, praxis is the imperative of Indigenous resurgence. Early articulations of an Indigenous resurgence framework did not explicitly name "futures" as a site of analysis, but work in this field has definitely opened space for the creation of Indigenous alternatives to settler- or state-directed futures, and tactics have included acts of "*renaming, reclaiming, and reoccupying*," especially lands.[8]

Indigenous resurgence has grown as a direct response to and refusal of state recognition frameworks that aim to incorporate and contain Indigenous nations within settler state sovereignty. In the First Nations Canadian context, Indigenous resurgence poses a challenge to reconciliation politics. In one of the early pieces outlining the politics of resurgence, Alfred and Corntassel offer five mantras for resurgent Indigenous movement:

1. Land is life. We should seek to reconnect with our territories.
2. Language is our power. We should revitalize Indigenous languages.
3. Freedom is the other side of fear. We have to confront colonial structures, including those we have internalized.
4. Decolonize your diet. Colonialism changes our relationships to our bodies, and we must reclaim healthy personal and collective lifestyles.
5. Change happens one warrior at a time. Mentorship/apprenticeship and face-to-face relationships of accountability are crucial to our movements and peoples.

(Alfred & Corntassel, 2005, p. 613)

With these mantras they aimed to move from a politics of demand to one that focuses on regenerating Indigenous lives and collectives beyond the state. Alfred and Corntassel have recently acknowledged the need to update these mantras; for instance to include a re-centering of Indigenous women's leadership.[9] Corntassel writes about the importance of "everyday acts of resurgence" that will allow our ancestors and our descendants to recognize us as Tsalagi, Kanaka Maoli, Hopi, Maori, Mohawk, etc. (Corntassel, 2012); and in so doing, he connects with a point that Indigenous feminists have long elaborated—that the personal and familial are political spaces that must be central to decolonizing and healing processes. The commonality is in calling Indigenous communities, families and individuals to build ourselves up from within, even while acts of resurgence will look different as they emerge within the diverse contexts and self-conscious traditions of various Indigenous nations and communities.

Indigenous feminist scholarship makes gender central to a theory and praxis of Indigenous resurgence.[10] In her first book, *Dancing On Our Turtle's Back: Stories of Nishnaabeg Re-creation, Resurgence and a New Emergence*, Leanne Simpson explained that resurgence means

> significantly re-investing in our own ways of being: regenerating our political and intellectual traditions; articulating and living our legal systems; language learning; ceremonial and spiritual pursuits; creating and using our artistic and performance-based traditions. All of these require us—as individuals and collectives—to diagnose, interrogate, and eviscerate the insidious nature of conquest, empire and imperial thought in every aspect of our lives.
> *(2011, pp. 17–18)*

For instance, Simpson utilizes metaphors that come from women's embodied experiences to envision different ways of thinking about treaty-making and going beyond reconciliation. In her subsequent work, Simpson has also explicitly elaborated the ways that colonial gender violence and gender binaries must be challenged and overcome if we are to take seriously the restoration of "land as pedagogy" and land as sets of relations, which provide the context for knowledge-generation and futures-creation (2014).

Kwakwaka'wakw scholar Sarah Hunt and Cindy Holmes draw on a long history of queer and two-spirit Indigenous people writing about "the necessity for anti-colonial struggles and queer rights to be investigated as inherently linked," and they connect everyday and intimate practices of allyship "to queer, Two-Spirit and trans solidarity, resistance to heteronormativity and cisnormativity, locating these intersections in practices of decolonizing and queering the intimate geographies of the family" (Hunt & Holmes, 2015). As Indigenous nations and communities regenerate ourselves by drawing from within, the resurgence of Indigenous practices of gender and sexuality must be central.

Similarly, art, as an act of creation, is centered in Indigenous resurgence movements. Martineau's breath-taking study on Indigenous hip hop and visual artists demonstrates the importance of art in the "creative negation" of settler colonial relations and the (re)generative practice of "embodied becoming." Martineau explains the importance of such creative work, saying:

> the art of resurgence seeks the recoherence of our fragmented existence in a dynamic return to presence, unity, and holism. Resurgence rests on an aesthetic axis of transformation that, by developing critical consciousness, undoing colonial fragmentation, and revitalizing our nationhood, restores strength and re-coherence to our lives and our communities.
>
> *(2015, p. 96)*

He sees Indigenous art as inherently political, and through his analysis we see that Indigenous creators/creatives both imagine decolonial futures and enact practices that change the assumed linearity of past-present-future relationships.

Indigenous Futurisms

The creative and imaginative, even fanciful and speculative, capacities of Indigenous people are absolutely central to the emergent field of Indigenous futurisms. The term was first used in print by Anishinaabe author, Grace Dillon, in the first anthology of Indigenous science fiction (sf), *Walking in the Clouds*. The term and field draw inspiration from Afrofuturisms, which not only claims space for Black and Indigenous voices amidst science fiction—a genre dominated by straight, white, male voices and implicated in the reproduction of colonial narratives of conquest and discovery—but also calls us to imagine times and spaces beyond white supremacy. Similarly, Indigenous futurisms claim sf as a means to assert Indigenous presence, "a valid way to renew, recover, and extend First Nations peoples voices and traditions" (Dillon, 2012, pp. 1–2).

As assertions of Indigenous presence in the pasts/presents/futures, the field of Indigenous futurisms is not limited to writing but also includes game-creation, digital art, graphic novels, and other forms of world-making. Creators in the field claim categories and territories typically monopolized by colonial desires—such as "technology" or "space," and elaborate visions of multiple possible futures in which Indigenous people thrive. In "The Space NDN's Star Map," Cornum explains the intentionality of emerging Indigenous futurisms to overcome "the settler death drive." Instead, Indigenous futurisms imagine:

> Different ways of relating to notions of progress and civilization. . . . Advanced technologies should foster and improve human relationships with the non-human world. In many indigenous science fiction tales of the futures, technology is presented as in dialogue with the long traditions of the past, rather than representing the past's overcoming. . . . Indigenous

futurism does not care for speed so much as sustainability, not so much for progress as balance, and not power but relation.

(Cornum, 2015)

Capitalism, the state and whiteness are not unmarked assumptions in Indigenous futurisms, as in much of mainstream sf. Instead, Indigenous futurisms push the conventional boundaries of sf as a genre, self-consciously exploring the ways that dynamic Indigenous cultural practices and traditions are their own forms of advanced technology.

Articulating a specifically Oceanic take on Indigenous futurisms, Kanaka Maoli futures scholar Kahala Johnson cites the work of famed Tongan author and Pacific studies theorist "ʻEpeli Hauʻofa to signal the importance of our vast ocean in shaping Pacific islanders" conceptions of the world and what is possible. Johnson explains:

> we are the ocean . . . we are connected rather than separated by the sea. Drawing upon [Hauʻofa's] work, and on Hawaiian/Pacific concepts of the "innumerable," we envision Oceanic futurisms as an interstellar Sky of Islands flowing with saltwater futurists, astronesian wayfinders, and excolonial constellations.

(2016, p. 2)

Here Johnson pushes us to see Indigenous futurisms as more than just recent creations that are responses to white-dominated sf. Rather, this is just the most recent context for the reemergence of old and deeply genealogical practices of wayfinding. Such futures-creation includes situating ourselves in time and space through referencing bodies, stories, constellations in our vast ocean and cosmos.

One of the central connections of these three streams of resurgence, futurity and futurism is the point that, as Bryan Kamaoli Kuwada writes of Indigenous peoples, "the future is a realm we have inhabited for thousands of years" (2015). When even our futures are colonized and claimed by colonial logics, it is imperative that Indigenous and decolonizing education give students the tools by which to critically analyze representations of futures, as well as engage them in self-conscious practices of future-making. In the next section, I return to the point that such pedagogical practices must pay attention to (de)militarization and engage students in challenging and creating alternatives to imperialist militarization and the extractivist practices militarization both relies upon and protects, and I launch this argument from the context of Oceania.

(De)militarizing Oceania

Like all regions, Oceania is not just a geographic location but a political project, an assemblage of social forces that shape relationships of people, lands, waters, plants and other beings. Oceania names both a place and different imaginaries, different futurities, about or of that place. Ka Moana Nui, our great ocean, its islands and peoples are dreamed, mapped and traversed differently in Indigenous and imperialist/settler futurities.

Militarization has been a central pillar of imperialist and settler colonial futurities in Oceania for over 350 years. Since the late 17th century, with early Spanish efforts to colonize Guåhan (Guam), Pacific Islands have been eyed and attacked by European and Asian imperial powers seeking to enhance their military and economic positions. For instance, Pacific islands and islanders have experienced foreign nuclear testing perhaps more than any other place or people. Since the end of World War II, nuclear testing by the US, Great Britain and France has taken place in the Marshall Islands, Johnston Atoll, Kiribati, Australia and French Polynesia, with acute and ongoing effects on peoples' bodies, fishing grounds, cultural practices and even languages (Genz et al., 2016). Contemporary militarization in Oceania is an extension of historical colonial and imperial exploitation. As Shigematsu and Camacho write, we need to "recognize militarism as a constitutive institution and ideology of empire," and more fully engage in a critique of the links between colonialism and militarism (2010, p. xxvii).

In the Hawaiian context, it has gone like this: The US military forcefully seized the national lands of the Hawaiian Kingdom in 1898, after supporting an illegal and armed coup by a small group of white business elites five years earlier. Militarized schooling then worked on Kanaka minds and bodies to erase Indigeneity, reinforcing a hierarchal structuring of US racial relations. This erasure works to normalize persistent racial inequality in Hawaiʻi and, in the context of that economic inequality, militarism presents itself as an opportunity for both Native Hawaiians and marginalized Pacific Islander settlers in Hawaiʻi to climb the ladder. Within systems of white supremacy and settler colonialism, militarization becomes seen as the road up, but never out, of an unjust and oppressive social order.

From Hawaiʻi, American Sāmoa, Guåhan, the Commonwealth of the Northern Mariana Islands (CNMI), the Marshall Islands, the Federated States of Micronesia (FSM) and Palau, young Pacific Islander men and women enlist in the US military at far higher rates than other groups. All active and reserve branches of the US military actively recruit in the islands. Military recruiters—often local, fellow Islanders—specifically target high school and college campuses. For instance, the White House Initiative on Asian Americans and Pacific Islanders reports that proportionally Native Hawaiians and Pacific Islanders are overrepresented in the US Army by 249%.[11] Furthermore, Pacific Islanders serving in the US military comprise one of the largest groups per capita to be casualties of war. For example, Guåhan's rate of troop deaths in Iraq and Afghanistan has been approximately five times the US national average of deaths per 100,000 inhabitants (Harden, 2008). USA Today reported in 2005 that the US-affiliated Pacific Islands of American Samoa, Guam, the Northern Mariana Islands, the Marshall Islands, the Federated

States of Micronesia and Palau had a casualty rate, as a percentage of their islands' populations, exceeding every US state and more than seven times that of the US national rate (Zoroy, 2005). The documentary, *Island Soldier*, released in 2017, powerfully tells the story of the Nena family of Kosrae in the Federated States of Micronesia, illustrating the ways many of Micronesian families and communities behind these numbers are impacted by the deaths of so many of their loved ones (Fitch, 2017).

At the same time as Pacific Islanders are beckoned to US military service, militarism provides an infrastructure that sustains hegemonic imperial presence. This can be seen in the ongoing occupation of the Hawaiian archipelago by the US. Approximately 25% of the most populated island, Oʻahu, is controlled by the US Department of Defense, for military bases, testing, recreation and other uses. And the US military is expanding its presence in other islands and archipelagoes within the region.

In the early 2010s, the "Pacific Pivot" initiated under US President Obama and Secretary of State Clinton shifted more US military capacity toward the region, augmenting US military hegemony over the lands and waters of Oceania. This included a significant proposed military expansion in the Mariana Islands including Guåhan and the CNMI. On Guåhan, where 27% of the island is already controlled by the US military, the expansion included the planned relocation of US troops and their dependents, projected to create a 45% population growth on the island over a four-year period. Known by CHamorus as "the build-up," the realignment also included plans for the mooring of nuclear-powered aircraft carriers, the creation of new live-fire ranges and an anticipated 6.1 million gallons per day shortfall of water for the civilian community (Camacho, 2013, p. 1). While the proposed buildup was temporarily halted and has been scaled back due to a lawsuit filed by the National Trust for Historic Preservation, the Guam Preservation Trust and We Are Guåhan, plans to move forward with realignment continue to move forward under the Trump administration.

Moreover, the buildup on Guåhan goes hand-in-hand with the US expansion of its existing Mariana Islands Range Complex, which already encompasses almost half a million square nautical miles for a live-fire training range in the waters around the Mariana archipelago. Approved by the DOD in 2015, the new Mariana Islands Training and Testing Area (MITT) would double the MIRC's size to 984,601 square nautical miles—an area larger than "the size of Washington, Oregon, California, Idaho, Nevada, Arizona, Montana and New Mexico combined" (Santos Perez, 2017). Together with the existing Hawaiian Islands Range Complex and the transit corridor between them, the new MITT opens America's largest training and weapons testing area in the world.[12] The MITT includes permits authorizing 12,580 detonations of various magnitudes per year for five years; 81,962 "takings" (or, more plainly, killings) of 26 different marine mammal species per year for five years; and damage or kill of over six square miles of endangered coral reefs plus an additional 20-square miles of coral reef by bombs.[13] As of this writing, the US military is also preparing a revised EIS for the CNMI Joint Military Training (CJMT) proposal, which would allow two-thirds of the island of Tinian and the entire island of Pagan to be used for live-fire bombing and weapons training (Santos Perez, 2014, 2015).[14]

US President Trump's combative style has only heightened tensions and the normalization of hypermilitarization in the Marianas. In particular, on August 8, 2017, Trump declared that if North Korea made any threats to the US, "they will be met with fire and the fury like the world has never seen" (Borger & McCurry, 2017). Within hours the North Korean government responded with consideration of a missile strike on Guam. In characteristically insensitive fashion, Trump assured Guam's governor that the media coverage due to the North Korean threats had made Guam "extremely famous" and would increase tourism "tenfold" (Caguran-gan, 2017). On October 3, 2017, CHamoru educator and poet Melvin Won Pat-Borja of Independent Guåhan spoke powerfully back to this pissing match, testifying to the UN Special Political and Decolonization committee:

> I do not find comfort in President Trump's threats of fire and fury. There is no solace in the promise of more violence. Retaliation will not resurrect our children back from the dead. . . . My people are being buried under the rhetoric.[15]

Positionality and Directionality in Indigenous Future-Making: Demilitarizing Education Through Trans-Indigenous Exchange

When militarization, racism and colonialism are as much about projecting futures as they are historical processes, transformative Indigenous future-making is necessary for building alternatives and counter-hegemonies. Native Pacific Cultural Studies scholar Vicente Diaz's work on Indigenous Oceanic voyaging practices, specifically the Native Carolinian navigational techniques of etak and pookof, can help us to think about how such cultural practices are forms of future-making, and they give us analytical tools for teaching and theorizing Indigenous futurities and futurisms.

Etak orients travelers at sea by triangulating the relationships between the island of departure, the desired destination and a third point of reference, while pookof provides "an inventory of creatures indigenous to a given island, as well as their travel habits and behaviors" (Diaz, 2011, p. 27). These places and beings are mapped in the navigator's mind by using relationships to celestial bodies overhead, as well as currents below and around the canoe. These relationships are further mapped through the passing of stories, chants and other narrative forms from generation to generation.

At the *Our Future, Our Way: Directions in Oceanic Ethnic Studies* conference, Diaz explained that the tools Native Carolinian navigators have used to traverse their Oceanic world help them to understand both *positionality* and *directionality*—where they are and where they are headed—in relation to where they came from and to other orienting bodies on the move (Diaz, 2015). Moreover, he underscored the *relationality* between finding one's position and determining which direction to head next. Explaining the relationship between etak, pookof and the Carolinian compass, paafu, Diaz refutes descriptions of the paafu that center cardinal directions. His is a call to reject universality and fixity, and rather, to look at how Indigenous Oceanic "techniques of position-gauging" orient us to a different view of worlds-in-motion. He asks us to similarly consider relationality between Ethnic studies and Native/Indigenous studies:

> It might be productive or useful to also view the interdisciplines and struggles of and for ethnic studies and native studies as fellow travelers in an academic world that still understands itself to provide cardinal directionality—the adjudicative compass—to the production of knowledge.
>
> *(Diaz, 2015, p. 7)*

To reject cardinal directionality is to always pay attention to positionality and to our directionality in relation to other bodies-on-the-move.

In his earlier writings on this issue, Diaz focuses on how the techniques of etak and pookof allow Indigenous islanders-in-travel to move through spatialities and subjectivities, through relational ways of perceiving the world. He also suggests how we might apply these concepts to temporal movement as well, since Carolinian and other Pacific islander voyaging traditions depend on a "temporal depth" of knowledge, centuries-long histories and genealogies of maritime travel that shape Indigenous Oceanic orientations to time/space (2011, p. 22). Diaz's work suggests that "grounding" oneself in a canoe and an oceanic culture that survives the generative and transformative histories of colonialism, as well as the politics they beget, offers a particularly deep, substantive and compelling vantage point with which to map and move what are after all the mobile coordinates of indigenous cultural and political consciousness (2011, pp. 21–22).

How might it look to use such analytics in Indigenous and decolonial education that engages participants in land- and ocean-based activities? I want to close this chapter by sharing one example from my own co-teaching experience in an ongoing partnership between the University of Hawaiʻi at Mānoa's Indigenous Politics program (where I teach) and the Indigenous Governance program at the University of Victoria. In the joint graduate-level exchanges we have co-taught annually or biennially since 2006 with Professors Taiaiake Alfred and Jeff Corntassel, we make trans-Indigenous crossings, purposefully putting our students and ourselves in situations where we confront the realities of what it means to restore land/ocean-based relationships in the presence of the settler state and its institutions, including its military (Aikau, Goodyear-Kaʻōpua, & Silva, 2016).

We stage the exchanges to allow students to engage in Indigenous political study and practice across positionalities, across national, regional, class, sexual and gender affiliations. Indigenous and settler students (including students who are Indigenous in their own homelands but, as graduate students, become settlers on others' lands) come together to read, think, talk about and practice negotiating the complexities of restoring Indigenous land/water-based relationships. Together, as a transient learning community, we ask: How do we ethically participate in the work of reconnecting Indigenous people to ancestral lands when we are on the move, and when we are settlers in others' homelands?

When we host these exchanges in Hawai'i, we have used the Hawaiian concept of kuleana to give our students and ourselves a walking stick with which to make these journeys. Often translated to English by combining words like "rights, responsibilities, and authority," the 'Ōiwi concept of kuleana fundamentally implies ancestry *and* place (Kamakau, 1991; Warner, 1999; Young, 2006). Historically, kuleana relationships enable Kanaka to have access to and residence on the land. Varied kuleana can be layered in the land and in society. On a wa'a (canoe), there are also very clear lines of kuleana that must all be tended to and coordinated in order for the vessel to move and for people to be safe.

The concept of kuleana allows us to think beyond neoliberal subjectivities nurtured within the corporatized academy because it insists that individuals who may be differentially positioned vis-à-vis land and ancestors be accountable based on those specific relationships (Coté, Day, & de Peuter, 2007). Such a recognition does not relieve anyone from kuleana but rather acknowledges our different social, genealogical and spatial locations. Educators and scholars can use guiding questions about kuleana to consider our own actions: What is my kuleana, in this place, to these people, to my own ancestors and history? Is this particular issue, place, problem or position of authority my kuleana? What is not my kuleana? As we engage students in practices of Indigenous future-making in various locations, reflecting on questions of kuleana and positionality is important in transforming colonial relations.

But where kuleana suggests a rootedness in particular lands, the ocean reminds us we are also routed in travel. And here is where Diaz's work is especially helpful since it is based on the assumption that islands (and people) are on the move and that they are always expanding and contracting in relation to others. Etak is a method for locating oneself, of figuring out exactly where you are in relation you where you've been, where you're going and to other neighbors in motion. In relation to etak, kuleana can be an ethical praxis that asks one to consider what responsibilities a person has given their positionality in a particular location and time. If kuleana might be thought of as a walking stick, connecting you to the ground upon which you are residing and traveling, etak might be thought of as what Papa Mau Piailug talked about as the stick that allows us to envision the bridges between islands and to traverse oceans.[16]

In our UHIP-IGOV exchanges, the lead faculty members typically set the overall directionality of the journey together. For instance, our 2010 exchange focused explicitly on militarization and demilitarizing youth initiatives. We chose this focus based on the understanding that the directionality of settler state militarization is incommensurable with transformative Indigenous future-making, since settler futurities work to erase Indigenous presence. In contrast, Indigenous resurgence (as future-making) means both a refusal of the directions we cannot accept and a search for clarity in the directions we will collectively and personally pursue as we live our lives in relationship with place(s). What we did not anticipate in the 2010 exchange was the ways that, while our students embraced the overall destination of the course, their different positionalities meant that there would be different paths toward that general direction.

The course started with a demilitarization tour, in which we were confronted with the saturation of US military presence, "hidden in plain sight," on Oʻahu (Ferguson & Turnbull, 1999). Midway through our two weeks together, we had planned to go hiking through the rainforest at Kuaokalā to the ridge overlooking Mākua, a 4000-acre valley on Oʻahu's west side. The US Army has used Mākua as a live-fire training ground since the 1920s. In addition to the damage to Native ecosystems and cultural sites, the Army's operations take place on lands seized from the Hawaiian Kingdom when the US began its prolonged occupation. In 1998, a grassroots organization called Mālama Mākua filed suit against the Army for their continued use of the valley without an environmental impact statement (EIS). As part of the settlement, the Army provided funding for the State of Hawaiʻi to hire researchers and conservationists, some of them Kanaka ʻŌiwi, to monitor, protect and restore Native species and habitats in the area.

Our journey to Kuaokalā was guided by Kaleo Wong, who also happens to be one of the new generation of navigators that led Hōkūleʻa's Worldwide Voyage. Kaleo offered to guide us up to Kuaokalā to view Mākua's injuries, to conduct simple ceremony, and to see and discuss the difficult work of revitalizing the Native forest in the context of a settler state bureaucratic and military apparatus. He would show us the cracks in these systems, cracks that allow some Kānaka to restore relationships with and physical/spiritual health to this place and themselves.

Since we were crossing into territory currently controlled by the US Army and the settler State of Hawaiʻi, we were required to sign two forms releasing these settler entities from liability and providing our addresses and phone numbers. As our group of about 20 gathered on the morning of the hike, three students refused and did not show up. The three women—one Hawaiian, one CHamoru from Guåhan, and one Latina settler from Chile—called to tell us kumu (teachers) they could not in good conscience sign these forms and thus they would not be attending the hike. Their decision caused discontent among some of our group, but we carried on, not yet knowing their reasons for non-participation.

Later that night the three women showed up at my house to process the whole affair:

> "We have been talking about this stuff every day for a week! Don't the others see the contradictions in consenting to the military's control over this place?" one of them asked.

The stakes of the hike were further heightened because of the US military's ramp-up to a major expansion in Guåhan and the rest of the Marianas. Public hearings about the proposed expansion were being held on Oʻahu at the Pacific Command headquarters (PACCOM) during the same time frame as our course. One of the three students who refused to sign over her information and consent to the US military's control over Mākua was a CHamoru demilitarization activist, Kisha Borja-Kicho'cho'. Only a few nights before our hike, she had testified at the hearings on the proposed expansion. Kisha had explained the situation to our seminar participants in one of her early discussion posts:

> As you all know, since I talk about it every day, my home island of Guåhan and the other islands of the Marianas (namely, Saʻipan, Luta, and Tiniʻan) are about to be re-occupied by the U.S. military. . . . When looking at the current map of what the military already owns, I see a cookie cutter landscape. It's as if the military has taken cookie cutters and took the lands that it wanted then left my people with the scraps of dough. With this proposed buildup, the U.S. seems to be taking what's left of our scraps, rolling out the dough, and placing more cookie cutters on what we have barely been able to hold onto. Consequently, we CHamorus will be left on the edges of our lands, barely touching them and barely seeing them.
>
> *(2010)*

That night sitting on my living room floor, Kisha explained to me that her decision not to enter into Kuaokalā was also, in part, about her positionality in relation to Hawaiian lands: "If most Kānaka Maoli don't get to visit this place, why should I have that privilege?" Additionally, the students did not feel safe giving their names and contact information to the US Army.

We sat on the floor, sorting and cleaning greenery the women had gathered on their own hike. So that they would not be seen as "cutting class," the Kanaka Maoli student among them had considered her positionality and her kuleana and decided to take her peers through a different mountain range with which she was more familiar. As they walked through the forest, she taught them about the process of respectful gathering and how lei-making can be a way to honor and bind relationships. She became our teacher and we sat on the floor together, weaving lei of healing, engaging in an everyday act of resurgence.

As educators, we must plan opportunities for our students to connect with lands, waters and other beings of our worlds. But we must also remember that reconnecting these landed and oceanic relationships is an intensely personal process, one that teachers cannot script out in advance. Particularly in the context of our historical and contemporary experiences with the violences of militarization, in Oceania and beyond, we must make room for dissent, even when students are resisting the plans that we as instructors have laid out. In this case, the students also taught me how important it is for educators to take the time outside the context of "class time" to talk story with students and to hear what motivates their dissent. Only in doing so was I able to see that they were not only thinking hard about demilitarization as the directionality of our collective learning but they were also initiating meaningful alternatives that took their positionalities into account in ways that my co-teachers and I could not do in our pre-course planning as we set the schedule and itinerary. They were practicing their own versions of etak and of futurity.

Our encounter reminded me that Indigenous futurities include deeply sited practices, reliant upon epistemologies that emerge from specific places, and yet our resurgent movements and everyday practices also need to help us cross oceans. In that sense, my students' riff off the itinerary that my co-teachers and I had set out might also be seen as an example of what Vicente Diaz has called "indigeneity as discursive flourish, of potentially infinite and even contradictory cultural and political possibilities that still insist on the specificity of Native time and place" (2016, p. 137). They would not be limited to the kinds of foreclosures that a syllabus planned out months in advance can create. Such flourishes and improvisations in education seem to me to be a necessary strategy for navigating imperialist currents and sailing toward demilitarized and decolonized futures.

Notes

1 Satawal is an atoll in the Western Pacific and is within the Federated States of Micronesia. Although more closely culturally related to the people of Chuuk, Satawal is politically a part of Yap State. Being relatively distant from neighboring islands, the people of Satawal have maintained traditional non-instrument navigational knowledge over generations, as a matter of practical survival as well as cultural importance.

2 http://hokulea.org/. Accessed June 16, 2014.

3 The 2014 exercises included forces from Australia, Brunei, Canada, Chile, Colombia, France, India, Indonesia, Japan, Malaysia, Mexico, Netherlands, New Zealand, Norway, People's Republic of China, Peru, the Republic of Korea, the Republic of the Philippines, Singapore, Thailand, Tonga, the UK and the US. This was the first time China, Norway and Brunei participated.

4 See www.cpf.navy.mil/rimpac/2014/. Accessed June 25, 2017.

5 It is important to note, however, that Hokule'a's WWV did not visit islands of Micronesia or Melanesia, thus perpetuating a Polynesian-centric view of Oceania.

6 Cynthia Enloe defines militarization as a "step-by-step process by which something becomes *controlled by, dependent on*, or *derives its value from* the military as an institution or militaristic criteria."

7 In his article, Anderson deals with precaution, preemption and preparedness as three logics of Western, liberal democratic futurity.

8 For example, see the Indigenous Nationhood Movement's "Statement of Principles" at https://unsettlingamerica.wordpress.com/2013/11/05/indigenous-nationhood-movement/ Accessed March 14, 2018.

9 Taiaiake Alfred invited an updating of these mantras in a lecture at the University of Hawai'i at Mānoa on December 6, 2016, as part of an exchange between the Indigenous Governance and Indigenous Politics programs. These exchanges are discussed later in this chapter.

10 While Arvin, Tuck, and Morrill (2013), in their article cited previously, were not engaging directly with the Indigenous resurgence literature, it is useful to read their five challenges to decolonize gender and women's studies, alongside Alfred's and Corntassel's five original mantras of resurgence. The five key challenges that they say Native feminist theories offer to feminist discourses are:

1. Problematize and theorize the intersections of settler colonialism, heteropatriarchy, and heteropaternalism;
2. Refuse the erasure of Indigenous women within gender and women's studies and reconsider the implications of the endgame of (only) inclusion;
3. Actively seek alliances in which differences are respected and issues of land and tribal belonging are not erased in order to create solidarity, but rather, relationships to settler colonialism are acknowledged as issues that are critical to social justice and political work that must be addressed;
4. Recognize the persistence of Indigenous concepts and epistemologies, or ways of knowing; and
5. Question how the discursive and material practices of gender and women's studies and the academy writ large may participate in the dispossession of Indigenous peoples' lands, livelihoods, and futures, and to then divest from these practices.

11 See "What You Should Know About Native Hawaiians and Pacific Islanders (NHPI'S)" at www2.ed.gov/about/inits/list/asian-americans-initiative/what-you-should-know.pdf. Accessed October 25, 2017.

12 See map prepared by Juan Wilson at www.islandbreath.org/2016Year/06/160618pivotbig.jpg. Accessed October 25, 2017.

13 See http://senatorterlaje.com/home/sample-page/. Accessed October 25, 2017.

14 U.S. Marine Corps, Pacific. "CNMI Joint Military Training EIS/OEIS" at www.cnmijointmilitarytrainingeis.com/. Accessed March 14, 2018.

15 Statement by Melvin Won Pat-Borja, representative of Independent Guåhan (Guam), at the United Nations Special Political and Decolonization committee (Fourth Committee), 3rd meeting - General Assembly, 72nd session, October 3, 2017.

16 This characterization of Piailug's insight is based on Captain Bonnie Kahape'a-Tanner's description of his teachings, which inspired the "Connecting oceanic pathways: walking the stick of our ancestors" project to connect Hawaiian and Micronesian islanders residing in Hawai'i. See www.youtube.com/watch?v=aVY6BDKBMUE#t=50. Accessed January 16, 2017.

References

Aikau, H. K. (2015). Following the Alaloa Kīpapa of our ancestors: A trans-indigenous futurity without the State (United States or otherwise). *American Quarterly*, 67(3), 653–661. Retrieved from https://doi.org/10.1353/aq.2015.0031

Aikau, H. K., Goodyear-Ka'ōpua, N., & Silva, N. K. (2016). The practice of Kuleana: Reflections on critical indigenous studies through trans-indigenous exchange. In

Critical indigenous studies in the first world: Deliberations, debates and dilemmas in theory and practice. Tucson: University of Arizona Press.

Alfred, T. (2005). *Wasáse: Indigenous pathways of action and freedom.* Toronto, ON: Broadview Press.

Alfred, T., & Corntassel, J. (2005). Being indigenous: Resurgences against contemporary colonialism. *Government and Opposition, 40*(4), 597–614.

Anderson, B. (2010). Preemption, precaution, preparedness: Anticipatory action and future geographies. *Progress in Human Geography, 34*(6), 777–798.

Arvin, M., Tuck, E., & Morrill, A. (2013). Decolonizing feminism: Challenging connections between settler colonialism and heteropatriarchy. *Feminist Formations, 25*(1), 8–34.

Baldwin, A. (2012). Whiteness and futurity: Towards a research agenda. *Progress in Human Geography, 36*(2), 172–187.

Barker, H. M. (2012). *Bravo for the Marshallese: Regaining control in a post-nuclear, post-colonial world* (2nd ed.). Belmont: Wadsworth Publishing.

Borger, J. & McCurry, J. (2017, August 9). Donald Trump vows to answer North Korea nuclear threats with 'Fire and Fury.'" *The Guardian.* Retrieved from http://www.theguardian.com/us-news/2017/aug/08/donald-trump-north-korea-missile-threats-fire-fury.

Bradford, J. (2016). U.S. Counter-piracy efforts in Southeast-Asia 2004–2015: Consistent, cooperative and supportive. In C. Liss & T. Biggs (Eds.), *Piracy in Southeast Asia: Trends, Hot Spots and Responses* (pp. 33–58). Oxford: Routledge.

Cagurangan, M. (2017, August 12). Trump to Guam Governor: North Korea threats will boost tourism 'Tenfold.'" *The New York Times.* Retrieved from https://www.nytimes.com/2017/08/12/world/asia/trump-guam-governor-phone-call.html.

Camacho, K. L. (2005). *Cultures of commemoration: The politics of war, memory and history in the Mariana Islands.* Honolulu: University of Hawaiʻi Press.

Camacho, L. (2013). Poison in our waters: A brief overview of the proposed militarization of Guam and the Commonwealth of the Northern Mariana Islands. *The Asia-Pacific Journal 11* (51): 1–7.

Compoc, K., & Muneoka, S. (2014, June 23). We need to ask hard questions about RIMPAC. *The Hawaii Independent.* Retrieved from http://hawaiiindependent.net/story/we-need-to-ask-hard-questions-about-rimpac

Corntassel, J. (2012). Re-envisioning resurgence: Indigenous pathways to decolonization and sustainable self-determination. *Decolonization: Indigeneity, Education & Society, 1*(1), 86–101.

Cornum, L. (2015, January 26). *The space NDN's star map.* Retrieved January 13, 2017, from http://thenewinquiry.com/essays/the-space-ndns-star-map/

Coté, M., Day, R., & de Peuter, G. (2007). Utopian pedagogy: Creating radical alternatives in the neoliberal age. *Review of Education, Pedagogy & Cultural Studies, 29*(4), 317–336.

Diaz, V. M. (2011). Voyaging for anti-colonial recovery: Austronesian seafaring, archipelagic rethinking, and the re-mapping of indigeneity. *Pacific Asia Inquiry, 2*(1), 21–32.

Diaz, V. M. (2015). *From 'one history, one way,' to 'our future, our way' (By way of a rant about star compasses).* Presented at the Our Future, Our Way: Directions in Oceanic Ethnic Studies conference, University of Hawaiʻi at Mānoa.

Diaz, V. M. (2016). In the wake of Matáʻpang's Canoe: The cultural and political possibilities of indigenous discursive flourish. In *Critical indigenous studies: Engagements in first world locations* (pp. 119–137). Tucson: University of Arizona Press.

Dillon, G. L. (Ed.). (2012). *Walking the clouds: An anthology of indigenous science fiction* (1st ed.). Tucson: University of Arizona Press.

Ferguson, K. E., & Turnbull, P. (1999). *Oh, say, can you see? The semiotics of the military in Hawai'i*. Minneapolis, MN: University of Minnesota Press.

Fitch, N. (2017). *Island Soldier*. [Documentary]. Retrieved from http://www.islandsoldiermovie.com/about-1/

Genz, J., Goodyear-Ka'ōpua, N., LaBriola, M., Mawyer, A., Morei, E., & Rosa, J. (2016). *Militarism and nuclear testing* (Vol. 1). Honolulu: Center for Pacific Islands Studies, University of Hawai'i at Mānoa.

Goodyear-Ka'ōpua, N. (2013). *The seeds we planted: Portraits of a native Hawaiian charter school*. Minneapolis, MN: University of Minnesota Press.

Harden, B. (2008, January 27). Guam's young, steeped in history, line up to enlist. *Washington Post*. Retrieved from www.washingtonpost.com/wp-dyn/content/article/2008/01/26/AR2008012602050.html?sid=ST20 08012602071

Hau'ofa, E. (1993). Our sea of Islands. In *A new Oceania: Rediscovering our sea of islands* (pp. 2–16). Suva: School of Social and Economic Development, The University of the South Pacific.

Hunt, S., & Holmes, C. (2015). Everyday decolonization: Living a decolonizing queer politics. *Journal of Lesbian Studies*, *19*(2), 154–172.

Johnson, K. (2016, December). *Indigenous futurisms*. Presented at the Decolonial Futures, University of Hawai'i at Mānoa.

Kajihiro, K. (2008). The militarizing of Hawai'i: Occupation, accommodation, and resistance. In *Asian settler colonialism: From local governance to the habits of everyday life in Hawai'i* (pp. 171–194). Honolulu: University of Hawai'i Press.

Kamakau, S. M. (1991). *Ka Po'e Kahiko: The people of old*. (M. K. Pukui, Trans.). Honolulu: Bishop Museum Press.

Kuwada, B. K. (2015, April 3). *We live in the future: Come join us*. Retrieved from https://hehiale.wordpress.com/2015/04/03/we-live-in-the-future-come-join-us/

Martineau, J. (2015). *Creative Combat: Indigenous art, resurgence, and decolonization*. (Ph.D. Dissertation in Indigenous Governance). University of Victoria, Victoria, British Columbia. Retrieved from https://dspace.library.uvic.ca//handle/1828/6702

Niheu, K., Turbin, L. M., & Yamada, S. (2007). The impact of the military presence in Hawai'i on the health of Nā Kānaka Maoli. *Pacific Health Dialog*, *14*(1), 205–212.

Osorio, J. K. (2014). Hawaiian souls: The movement to stop the U.S. military bombing of Kaho'olawe. In *A nation rising: Hawaiian movements for life, land and sovereignty*. Durham, NC: Duke University Press.

Pacific Islands Forum. (2013, September 5). *Majuro declaration for climate leadership*. Majuro. Retrieved July 1, 2016, from www.majurodeclaration.org/the_declaration

Recollet, K. (2016). Gesturing indigenous futurities through the remix. *Dance Research Journal*, *48*(1), 91–105. Santos Perez, C. (2014, June 6). Looking at the "Tip of the spear". *Hawai'i Independent*. Retrieved from http://hawaiiindependent.net/story/u.s.-military-r-r-ra pe-removal-in-guahan

Santos Perez, C. (2015, November 6). The trans-Pacific partnership, pivot, and pathway. *Hawai'i Independent*. Retrieved from http://hawaiiindependent.net/story/the-trans-pacificpartnership-pivot-and-pathway

Santos Perez, C. (2017, September 5). Battleship Guam. *Hawai'i Independent*. Retrieved from http://hawaiiindependent.net/story/battleship-guam.

Shigematsu, S., & Camacho, K. L. (Eds.). (2010). *Militarized currents: Toward a decolonized future in Asia and the Pacific*. Minneapolis, MN: University of Minnesota Press.

Simpson, L. B. (2011). *Dancing on our Turtle's back: Stories of Nishnaabeg re-creation, resurgence and a new emergence*. Winnipeg, MB: Arbeiter Ring Publishing.

Simpson, L. B. (2014). Land as pedagogy: Nishnaabeg intelligence and rebellious transformation. *Decolonization: Indigeneity, Education & Society*, *3*(3), 1–25.

Teaiwa, T. K. (1994). bikinis and other s/pacific n/oceans. *The Contemporary Pacific*, *6*(1), 87–109.

Tengan, T. P. K. (2008). Re-membering Panalāʻau: Masculinities, nation, and empire in Hawaiʻi and the Pacific. *The Contemporary Pacific*, *20*(1), 27–53.

Tuck, E., & Gaztambide-Fernandez, R. (2013). Curriculum, replacement, and settler futurity. *Journal of Curriculum Theorizing*, *29*(1), 72–89.

Tuck, E., & Yang, K. W. (2012). Decolonization is not a metaphor. *Decolonization: Indigeneity, Education & Society*, *1*(1), 1–40.

Warner, S. L. N. (1999). Kuleana: The right, responsibility, and authority of indigenous peoples to speak and make decisions for themselves in language and cultural revitalization. *Anthropology and Education Quarterly*, *30*(1), 68–93.

Wendt, A. (1983). Towards a new Oceania. *Seaweeds and Constructions*, (7), 71–85.

White House Initiative on Asian Americans and Pacific Islanders. Fact sheet: What you should know about Native Hawaiians and Pacific Islanders (NHPI's). Retrieved from http://www2.ed.gov/about/inits/list/asian-americans-initiative/what-you-should-know.pdf.

Young, K. (2006). Kuleana: Toward a historiography of Hawaiian national consciousness, 1780–2001. *Hawaiian Journal of Law and Politics*, *2*, 1–33. Zoroy, G. (2005, May 26). From Tiny Pacific Islands Comes Outsized Sacrifice. *USA Today*. Retrieved from https://usatoday30.usatoday.com/news/world/2005-05-26-samoa_x.htm.

6

THE IXIL UNIVERSITY AND THE DECOLONIZATION OF KNOWLEDGE

Giovanni Batz (K'iche' Maya)

Indigenous decolonization within the educational system has been a facet within decolonial studies, with much work focused on decolonizing academia and its methodologies. Academia is often considered a pillar of colonialism in monopolizing the production of knowledge, and there have been a range of critiques and proposed solutions to confront these problems and challenges to best rethink our roles and relationships as educators and researchers with the communities we work with. These proposals include decolonizing academia and critical indigenous methodologies (Harrison, 1991; Smith, 1999), pedagogies of the oppressed (Freire, 2000), activist anthropology (Hale, 2008), Black feminist thought (Collins, 1991), Chicano personal narratives, and storytelling (Aguirre, 2005), among others. At the same time, outside of the walls of the ivory tower, there are many efforts from Indigenous communities and marginalized groups to create their own forms and spaces of knowledge production and education. The Maya in the Ixil Region have been theorizing and debating these questions on the roles of education through the Ixil University, founded in 2011, which seeks to teach students Maya ways of knowing, values and tichajil (the good life/el buen vivir in Ixil).

The Ixil Region consists of the three Ixil-Maya municipalities of Chajul, Cotzal, and Nebaj, located in the western highlands of Guatemala. Recently, the arrival of megaprojects such as hydroelectric dams and mining in the Ixil Region has been referred to as the "new" or "fourth invasion" since these have created social divisions, violence, environmental degradation, and persecution of community leaders (Batz, 2017). The three previous invasions consisted of Spanish colonization, the creation of coffee plantations at the end of the 19th century and early 20th century, and the Guatemalan Civil War (1960–1996), respectively, and are characterized by foreign intervention, genocide, displacement, state-sponsored violence, and resistance (Batz, 2017). It is within this historical socio-political context that the Ixil created the Ixil University to empower their communities and defend their territory.

The curriculum of the Ixil University focuses on three objectives: 1) territorial development; 2) management of resources and environment preservation; and 3) Ixil history and culture. Much of the curriculum seeks to prepare students to recover their identity, culture, and history as well as prepare them to defend their community's natural resources and territories, especially with the arrival of megaprojects in the region. The Ixil University is an innovative initiative unprecedented in Guatemala that has received national and international media coverage and has inspired other Maya groups to create their own universities (Botón, 2015; Figueroa, 2013; Flores, 2015). In his opening remarks entitled "Pluriversidad, Decolonialidad y Constelación de Saberes" at the oral thesis defense of the first cohort of the Ixil University held in November 2013, then-Rector Vitalino Similox claimed:

> This academic exercise is meant to cultivate our own cosmovisions, wisdoms, technologies, values and principles, productive and economic models, cultural practices that do not form part of the classical, European, North American formal curriculums, nor with the idea of forming professionals for the free market, but instead to understand, transform the needs and demands of their communities. The participants of the Ixil University, with this process, forms and strengthens their own capacities and potential. They prepare to become entrepreneurs and not employees, managers and subjects of their own destinies and not the objects of destiny.
>
> *(author's translation)*

It is this vision of self-empowerment of students to serve their communities among other reasons that have inspired other communities in Guatemala and elsewhere to adopt this model. The Ixil University does not have state recognition, but it has the recognition of the ancestral authorities as well as other universities at the national and international level in the form of convenios (agreements). The Ixil University does not have a physical campus, but rather holds classes in different communities of the region.

The purpose of this chapter is to examine the origins of the Ixil University, the problems and criticisms it has encountered, and the hope that their example serves as a point of reflection for educators and researchers. To achieve these goals, I will first examine the colonial nature of state-based formal education and its critiques. Second, I will examine why the Ixil University was created, as well as its functions, goals, and the work being produced there.

The study is based on ethnographic fieldwork conducted between 2011 to 2015 with actors involved and not involved with the Ixil University such as teachers, students, municipal mayors, and ancestral authorities, among others. In addition, many of my observations also emerge from working for two years as a tutor and facilitator between October 2013 and November 2015 at the Ixil University. I find my position ironic and enriching since I am an anthropologist trained within US academia, and at the same time, I am a self-identified K'iche' Maya born in the US who also has the personal project of recovering my Indigenous roots, identity, and history. While I served as a tutor and facilitator, I also consider myself one of the Ixil University's students since I learned a lot about Maya worldviews, history, spirituality, culture, and ontology.

It is important to note that the Ixil University should not be viewed as an object of study and I hesitated to write this text, mainly because I wanted to avoid the risk of romanticizing and appropriating their work. But, I decided to do so after I was encouraged by various members of the Ixil University to write an analysis of their work. My goal is to provide a reflexive critique of academia and its colonial nature, as well as presenting the Ixil University as a space where we can all learn from. The Ixil University is an example of how Indigenous peoples are creating their own spaces, within their own territories, for the benefit of their communities (not individuals). They are not opposed to Western education, instead they are open to all forms of knowledge. It is the Western system that was designed under an extractivist colonial logic that marginalizes, appropriates, destroys, and attempts to delegitimize all other knowledge. My hope is that their example can aid us toward strengthening our efforts and providing us with another set of tools in decolonizing academia and knowledge.

Decolonizing Academia

Education in Guatemala has historically served to incorporate Indigenous peoples into a "national culture" and has served as a space of physical and epistemic violence that views Indigenous knowledge, culture, and history as backwards and irrelevant (Montejo, 2005). Many Indigenous communities in Guatemala tell the stories of abuelos (elders) whose parents hid them in the temazcal (sweat lodge) and other locations to avoid being taken to school by ladino (non-Indigenous person) truant officers created in 1929 to force and oblige all children to go to school (Carey, 2006, pp. 182–183). While some say the abuelos should have let their children study, others say that going to school was bad since that is where children learn to be lazy and not work. Others were critical of teachers who were almost always ladino, many who held racist attitudes toward Mayas. Classes were also all in Spanish and many were not allowed to speak in their Maya languages. For example, in the 1940s the Instituto Indígena Nacional (National Indigenous Institute) observed in many towns Kaqchikel parents unwilling to send their children to school based on social reasons. In Parramos, Chimaltenango, the Kaqchikels claimed that there was a need for well-trained teachers who were of Indigenous background since ladino teachers "only preoccupied themselves in teaching their own race" (Instituto Indígenista Nacional, 1948a, p. 47, translation mine). In San Juan Sacatepéquez, the Kaqchikel claimed that ladino teachers refused to adequately teach their children due to their "racial prejudice" and fear that if Indigenous children were educated they would no longer "conform to submission or be influenced" by the ladino (Instituto Indígenista Nacional, 1948b, p. 52, translation mine). These comments from Kaqchikels in the 1940s demonstrate perceptions of unjust practices based on racial biases within the educational system, which favored ladinos. Education in this form was not about intellectual growth and empowerment, but rather a system of control. This violence is not limited to school structures and buildings, but carried out by researchers, mainly from the "developed" "Western" world who become agents (willingly or unwillingly) of these repressive forces by reproducing hierarchies of knowledge that fuel violence, marginalization, and exclusion of "other" knowledges and worlds.

Linda Tuhiwai Smith's *Decolonizing Methodologies: Research and Indigenous Peoples* argues that "research" and Western academia is tied to European imperialism and colonialism, and thus is negatively viewed by Indigenous communities across the world (1999, p. 1). Research in these cases is not limited to academia and includes journalistic and amateur works. Furthermore, Smith claims that research questions can be "rude" and that at "a common sense level research was talked about both in terms of its absolute worthlessness to . . . the indigenous world, and its absolute usefulness to those who wielded it as an instrument" (1999, p. 3). Anthropologists are the most visible actors within these critiques due to the ethnographic nature of their research and anthropology's dark history as a discipline, which found its origins in dedicating itself to the study of non-European "Others" (Restrepo, 2007). Indigenous peoples have long critiqued the role of anthropologists in colonizing Indigenous knowledges, stealing artifacts, and contributing toward their oppression (Deloria, 1969).

While many works have been written about the Ixils and other Indigenous peoples across the world, the vast majority of Indigenous peoples have never read or are unfamiliar with these works. Despite calls to decolonize knowledge and make our research more accessible, the general sense I have from various communities and people in Guatemala, both in academic and non-academic spaces, is that this does not happen in practice. Books are expensive and inaccessible to people outside of urban spaces, and electronic versions of these works are not translated in the language where research was conducted and assumes people have access to the internet, a computer and electricity. Academic conferences continuously take place in very expensive hotels, in very expensive cities, in very expensive countries that require visas, and are mostly attended by academics. Over-theorizing concepts and events without providing solutions to problems is not useful on a practical and real-life level for people on the ground. This is not an anti-theory position, but rather another call to find balance in making our research not just more accessible but more applicable and useful. Many Indigenous peoples have pointed to how irrelevant academic research is to the real world and its extractivist nature. Some Ixil leaders have expressed the need for Ixils to conduct their own research and not rely on outsiders such as anthropologists to do this work who "solo sacan información, y se van" ("only take out information and leave"). Whether one agrees with these sentiments, it is an indicator to a very serious problem. It is this history of the educational system and critiques that contributed to the foundation of the Ixil University.

Origins of the Ixil University

The history of the Ixil Region tells us a lot about the problems that the Ixils recurrently confront such as threats to ancestral territories, natural resources, and the imposition of Western perspectives that devalue Ixil worldviews, identity, culture, territories, and cosmovision. The residents of the three municipalities are mainly Ixil with a small presence of K'iche', Q'anjob'al, and ladinos. The majority of people are agricultural workers, and people earn between 30 to 35 quetzals a day (approximately $3.98 to $4.65).

The Guatemalan Civil War suffered the worst violence against the Maya since Spanish colonization. Beginning with General Fernando Romeo Lucas García (1980–1982) and followed by General José Efraín Ríos Montt (1982–1983), the Guatemalan state carried out a counter-insurgency campaign meant to displace, massacre, and eliminate Maya communities that the military viewed as a safe-haven for the guerrilla. The Guatemalan Commission for Historical Clarification (CEH) reported 669 cases of massacres that left 200,000 dead, of which 83% were Indigenous and 1.5 million displaced (1999, p. 100). The same report found that the military was responsible for 93% of these deaths. The CEH found that the department of El Quiché suffered 344 massacres, 114 of them in the Ixil Region alone (p. 100).

The recent arrival of megaprojects to the area has also created further social divisions and conflict. Due to an increasing global demand for natural resources coupled with neoliberalization, there has been a significant growth in infrastructure and extractive industries that have negatively affected Indigenous communities. These demands for electricity and metals, often for the benefit of foreigners living in developed nations and people living outside of the affected communities, have also meant displacement and conflict for those living on the territories of these projects. At the moment, the Ixil Region has two hydroelectric dams operating (Hidro Xacbal in Chajul and Palo Viejo in Cotzal), another in construction (Xacbal Delta in Chajul), as well as three amparos (legal protection for constitutional individual or community rights) that were resolved in courts involving hydroelectric dams (all in Nebaj). An amparo in these cases prevents companies from building their projects until the legal matter of consultation has been resolved by the judicial system. Furthermore, there is a mining project to extract barite (mineral used in fracking) in Salquil Grande, Nebaj, which has generated tensions and potential conflicts (Roberts, 2014). Deforestation is also a serious problem and it was estimated by an official in the National Institute of

Forests that approximately 80% of the trees being cut down in the Ixil Region were from illegal activity.

Ixil Critiques of Education

One of the main reasons the Ixil University was created was the view that the educational system was failing to prepare future generations to confront new challenges and their detachment from their communities. The educational system is often viewed by marginalized communities as a form of social upward mobility and as a very prestigious endeavor in "making it." However, among the critiques that the Ixils make regarding state-based Western education are that there are no jobs upon graduating. Moreover, this education prepares students to learn knowledge that is not applicable to their daily realities. Instead, students sometimes become ashamed of their Indigenous and campesino (farmer) identity since the educational system teaches them that this is not the road to a better life. To be a professional brings you social upward mobility, status, and success. As a result, those who cannot find employment upon graduation sometimes refuse to return and work in the fields since it gives them vergüenza (shame) to do so. It was estimated that in Cotzal there were 800 unemployed professionals, such as nurses, teachers, and accountants. There is also a common expression to highlight this employment crisis: "100 teachers graduate, and only one job opening." Many of these posts are also offered as political patronage by municipal mayors and politicians. Moreover, Ixil and Indigenous students at times become alienated and feel detached from their communities as well as experience discrimination and racism from their ladino counterparts within universities.

Attending school is also very costly and leads to debt, which can make school more inaccessible. Since there are no jobs, the educational system is a big investment. At times parents are forced to sell their lands to provide an education to a limited number of usually male children, which excludes many women from attending school. Moreover, there is no public funding within the educational system and this impacts the quality of the school system. Corruption at all levels only exacerbates these problems and there are many instances of teachers not getting paid for months. One young Ixil teacher told me that he was instructed by the municipality to split half his paycheck with another teacher, and if he did not do so, he would be fired.

Western education is also viewed as providing individual benefits as opposed to community benefits in accordance to Ixil worldviews. I do not believe anyone questions one's dream of upward social mobility or providing a better livelihood for oneself and family, but there are complaints about university graduates who take advantage of their community and others whose services are unaffordable. For example, some have said that an Ixil that becomes a medical doctor charges an unaffordable amount to cure people. This is in comparison to a curandero or healer who views their role not as a way to make money, but rather as their "calling," "responsibility," and/or "cargo" (position/job). Traditionally, many healers could not charge people directly and accepted whatever people could afford to offer. To heal someone is a gift, to profit off it would be unethical. Many curanderos say that those who are born with the gift of healing become ill and could even die if they do not take on this responsibility. Another example is a lawyer who charges high fees for a signature, for paperwork, or to defend people in courts. For Ixils, a lawyer should not be exploiting their knowledge of laws to make money, rather they should use their knowledge of the legal system to defend the rights of people and communities. The need for expensive professional services such as lawyers in social movements is extremely important, particularly when community leaders are persecuted by foreign companies and the state, and threatened with arrest warrants.

According to many Ixil leaders, there are many youth (almost exclusively male) who refuse to provide community service in the form of cargos (unpaid civic positions, each with their own unique set of responsibilities) within their community. Among one of the most important roles that youth are needed in is the cargo of secretary who writes out actas (acts). After one is nominated to a cargo by consensus through a community assembly, they are then contacted to accept or decline. At times, many of these youth say they are not able to accept this position since they are too busy with work, or are considering migrating to Guatemala City or the US, so if they accept their position then they will not be able to fulfill their responsibilities. Many say that they understand the economic needs of youth since they need to find employment to buy land and build a house in order to start a family.

Another reason for the creation of the Ixil University was a need to strengthen, recover, heal, and restore a sense of dignity of being Ixil and campesino, as well as their history. According to one of the community leaders, young people today tend to look outside for their future and thus, not appreciating or valuing what they have at home. As mentioned, the civil war was extremely violent and severely damaged the social fabric of Ixil communities. Families were displaced, divided, separated, and destroyed in multiple ways. Some children grew up in broken families or separated from their communities. Strong links between youth and elders remained tumultuous and some youth joined gangs after the war, leading to delinquency that violated community norms.

Detachment from the community is also rooted in the belief that, within urban spaces and cities, there is better education. Teachers I spoke to also expressed similar experiences. A teacher in Nebaj says that he asks his students from Cotzal and Chajul why they are paying and traveling more to study in Nebaj. Some of their responses are usually something along the lines of, "it's because there is *nothing* in my community." This view of there being "nothing" in their community indicates the decreasing value placed on their homes, a belief inculcated by the educational system. The town center of Nebaj is viewed as the most "modern" place within the Ixil Region, which is reinforced by the presence of various commercial businesses, government institutions, NGOs, hotels, and foreign workers and tourists. Instead, the Ixil University decentralizes this power dynamic. Similox states the Ixil University is the only university that looks for students and goes to their communities. As a former facilitator and tutor, I remember walking and traveling for hours to other communities with other students and facilitators in order to have classes. These are lived realities. The students from the Ixil University take days off from work and organize their classes. The Ixil University views itself as contra-corriente (against the current) since they are trying to reverse and prevent the damages caused by formal education.

It was these problems and others that led to the creation of the Ixil University. For one year, community leaders, ancestral authorities, members of Fundamaya (an Ixil NGO), and youth discussed at multiple meetings about creating an educational space to confront the many problems the Ixil Region was facing. By 2011, the founders had their curriculum set and were able to recruit students to form the first class of the Ixil University.

Researching Their Own Communities and Histories

The first two years of the program is based on classes that meet twice a month in which a certain topic based on Ixil worldviews and tichajil is discussed such as water rights, agriculture, gender, and sacred places, accompanied with an assignment that the student must complete before next class. The students are responsible for organizing and finding a space for the classroom, which can take place in the community center, a school, or another location. The classes are mainly in Ixil, but if there are non-Ixil speakers like K'iche's or visitors from outside the area, then the classes are sometimes conducted in Spanish. The students enrolled in the Ixil University come from various backgrounds. The majority of students work in the fields, many who could not continue their education due to the lack of funds, and a few are currently studying at or graduated from another university.

Assignments are based on the students' community and are hands-on. For instance, previous assignments included knowing how many natural springs exist in the community, the borders of their community, the different flora and fauna, and the names and purposes of sacred sites in their community. The logic behind these types of assignments is if one is to defend their community, one needs to know everything about their community. Within this framework, emphasis and priority is taken away from the outside and shifted to knowing one's own community. Many of these assignments are to be completed with the assistance of community leaders with knowledge relevant to the topic, such as ancestral authorities, spiritual guides, and family members. This is meant to enhance relationships between youth and students with elders and community leaders. Sometimes there are divisions within the community due to various factors such as family conflict, religion, etc. For example, many evangelicals view spiritual guides and Ixil ceremonies as the devil's work or "brujería" ("witchcraft"). Assignments that require contact with spiritual guides help in creating tolerance and communication and improve relationships among different sectors of society.

During their third year in the program, students are required to write a thesis, which they are expected to defend publicly to the Council of Examiners comprised of Ixil University administrators, authorities, and leaders from the student's respective community, professionals, and academics. The Council of Examiners is meant to ensure transparency and academic rigor, as well as test the oral skills of students. If they are to be community leaders, students need to be able to transmit their ideas to others inside and outside the Ixil Region. The thesis defense is similar to a thesis defense within Western educational universities, but the difference is that community leaders, professionals, and academics are all involved in determining the quality of one's work. Within academia, it is nearly impossible to have a non-academic be an official signatory to anyone's thesis. The vara (authority staff) is not respected or honored within the ivory tower. Upon completion of their defense and approval of their projects, students are then awarded a degree as Technicians in Rural Community Development with specialization on Natural Resources. They then have the option of completing a licenciatura (similar to a bachelor's degree) and work on another final thesis project.

These projects range from their topics to the methods that they employ and are a source of innovation and creativity conducted in a rigorous and careful manner. They explore topics that many outsiders have limited access to. Thesis topics were based on issues such as privatization of water and natural resources, the uses of medicinal plants, violence against women, agricultural practices, international migration to the US, among others. The unique part of these theses is not only analyzing a problem, but also the requirement of developing solutions in collaboration with community leaders to this problem. This encourages the student to think critically and offer solutions to their community.

In total, there have been 33 theses defended and graduates in the first three years (2013–2015) of the program. I present two of the theses produced to demonstrate their richness. Magdalena Terraza Brito's thesis, entitled *Los Efectos de la Guerra desde la Perspectiva de una Niña de la CPR* (2015), is to my knowledge the first and only work written about growing up in Communities of the Population in Resistance (CPR). In this very powerful work, Magdalena shares her personal experiences growing up in the CPR during the war when her family was forced to flee the violence by finding refuge in the mountains, where the military continued to persecute them. She is also able to tie the violence during the war to the violence occurring today with the arrival of hydroelectric dams, corruption, and those who deny genocide. Magdalena's work shows how through the Ixil University, youth, and students can share their own stories and histories in their own words as well as making connections between the violence of the war to the current political and social situation. She makes a call for reparations to take place for victims of the war as well as justice for human rights violations that occurred during the war.

Another thesis is Santa Roselia de León Calel's *K'iche's en la Región Ixil* (2014), which explores the arrival of hundreds of K'iche's to the Ixil Region in the early 20th century. Roselia's topic emerges from her personal experience of being a K'iche' who was born and raised in Xolcuay, Chajul, and who felt that K'iche's were continued to be viewed as outsiders even though they have lived in the Ixil Region for over a century. Again, to my knowledge, Roselia is the first to research specifically on the K'iche's in the Ixil Region, a significant group that usually gets unmentioned in almost every other academic work on the area. Her work focuses on their arrival and the relationships between K'iche's and Ixils. Roselia writes:

> Even though we are in Ixil territory, I also want them to have knowledge of everything that emerges within our society and the main thing is the history of our people, the Maya K'iche' since it is a human right to have access to collective memory. Lastly, the motivation for this work is based on my personal life as a K'iche' living in the Ixil Region in the community of Xolcuay in Spanish, Xo'lk'uay in Ixil, and Xo'l k'uja in K'iche', names that mean "between the two caves."
>
> *(2014, p. 3, author's translation)*

The Ixil University is not exclusively for Ixils, as there are many K'iche's enrolled. As Roselia has demonstrated, they can produce work that recovers history for self-empowerment and that of her community.

The Politics of Recognition

In Guatemala, there are 14 private universities and one public university, all of them with their flagship campus in Guatemala City, some with satellite campuses throughout various cities of the country. The only public university is San Carlos University, which is provided with five percent of the Guatemalan national budget (Universidad de San Carlos de Guatemala, 2017). The remaining universities need to be approved and overlooked by the Consejo de Enseñanza Privada Superior (CEPS), which was founded in 1966 during the military dictatorship of Coronel Enrique Peralta Azurdia and forms part of the Ministry of Education. Six of these private universities are named after non-Indigenous men (ladinos, Europeans, and Catholic saints) such as Universidad Da Vinci de Guatemala, Universidad Galileo, and Universidad Mariano Gálvez. In the Ixil Region, there are various satellite campuses with almost all of them operating in Nebaj. In 2015, the first university began operating out of a school in Cotzal, and to my knowledge there have been none in Chajul. Depending on the university and location, registration fees vary, as well as non-academic costs such as transportation and housing, since many of these universities are in centralized locations in cities. Some attend classes offered during the weekends. For example, some students travel from Nebaj to Santa

Cruz Quiche (the Department capital) as early as 3 am to take classes all day and then return home on the same day, as late as 8 pm. To receive a university degree takes a lot of sacrifice and hard work and is no easy feat, and it continues to be inaccessible, expensive, and centralized in urban spaces.

The Ixil University enjoys legitimacy as an institution by the ancestral authorities of the Ixil Region. They were involved in its creation and continue to play an active part in assisting students with their works. In addition, the Ixil University has been able to sign both national and international convenios with various universities such as San Carlos University, University of Torino in Italy, Nicaraguan Evangelical University-Martin Luther King, and Misak University in Colombia, as well as collaborating with others such as the University of Texas at Austin. These agreements are a form of mutual recognition between educational institutions and producers of knowledge. The Ixil University through its example has inspired others to create their own community universities, such as the Kaqchikel University.

Some teachers, students, and others not associated with the Ixil University criticize it and say that it is not "real" since their degrees are not recognized by the state, and that they do not have infrastructure. In an interview in 2014, a local municipal mayor stated that the Ixil University is illegitimate and criticized its teachings. Many students in the Ixil University say that at times students drop out since they are ridiculed within their community who view it as a waste of time. One student from Nebaj says that teachers within the community openly spoke against the Ixil University. In other instances, the Ixil University is called the "university of the guerrillas" in an effort to delegitimize and discriminate against them. Students have said that when they speak on issues of land, territory, megaprojects, and Indigenous rights, they are discriminated against by some members of the community. Other critics state that learning about Ixil history and cultures is a step backwards and that we now live in a "modern" world that needs a "modern" educational model.

The Ixil Region continues to be plagued by internal divisions rooted in the civil war. While the founders of the Ixil University consisted of former guerrillas, it also comprised of ancestral authorities, youth, non-Ixils, among others from Chajul, Cotzal, and Nebaj. Thus, it was not just one sector that founded the Ixil University, but rather an Ixil-Maya project. To attempt to discredit them is a form of epistemic violence that tries to undermine Ixil knowledge production. At the face of these external pressures to stop attending the Ixil University, students believe and are committed to the goals and the educational and intellectual tools that they are receiving and contributing to. That figures such as the municipal mayor and teachers criticize the Ixil University demonstrates the on-the-ground challenges that students, facilitators, and the administration face.

The success of the Ixil University can be measured by the youth who have become actively involved in their communities and social movements. Recently, the Constitutional Court ruled in favor of the ancestral authorities the right to consultation, in various cases involving electrical towers and dams. Graduates from the Ixil University have been accompanying many of the meetings between the ancestral authorities, communities, and the Ministry of Mines and Energy to provide any technical and logistical support needed. Others have become involved in their communities as young leaders and have taken cargos. Those who learned about and recovered knowledge of medicinal medicine are now practicing these knowledges and some community members seek their help. Others are actively reforesting, diversifying their crops, and becoming more aware of the ill effects of megaprojects, the use of chemical fertilizers, and consumerism. The Ixil University in many of these cases is fulfilling the need to prepare students to recover their history and practices, as well as apply it to their realities for the betterment of their communities.

Conclusions

The Ixil University serves as an example of rethinking education and seeks to empower communities and moves away from the ivory tower's extractive colonial nature that centralizes and appropriates knowledges. The formal and state-based educational system continues to unapologetically privilege Western thinking, history, culture, and its agents. Many Indigenous peoples and marginalized groups are often co-opted by a repressive academic system that detaches us from our communities; some of us have forgotten our roots in our pursuit of achieving educational success. Those in the ivory tower are taught to believe that the more education we have, the more social upward mobility and *individual* economic success we are supposed to enjoy. The Ixil University challenges us through their example to reexamine our purpose as an educational system and our role as researchers and educators.

That the Ixil University has had success in operating since 2011 in promoting and recovering ancestral and community knowledges among youth without "official" recognition from the state is a testament to the power that Indigenous peoples hold. Despite the fact that this very article is a written work about the Ixil University, their experiences and lived realities are not limited to jargoned words about liberation, freedom, and decolonization. They are recreating and reimagining what knowledge should look like and what purposes they should serve.

Acknowledgment

I would like to thank the people and communities of the Ixil Region for allowing me to work with them and their support for my research. I also thank the students, founders, facilitators, and ancestral authorities of the Ixil University for serving as an example to the world, not through discourse, but through their actions and teachings that give hope for a different tomorrow.

References

Aguirre, J. A. (2005). The personal narrative as academic storytelling: A Chicano's search for presence and voice in academe. *International Journal of Qualitative Studies in Education, 18*(2), 147–163.

Batz, G. (2017). *The fourth invasion: Development, Ixil-Maya resistance, and the struggle against megaprojects in Guatemala.* (Unpublished doctoral dissertation). University of Texas at Austin.

Botón, S. (2015, March 9). Guatemala: Se levanta Universidad Ixil, sobre cenizas de la represión uerray. *Telesur.* Retrieved April 16, 2017, from www.telesurtv.net/opinion/ Guatemala-Se-levanta-Universidad-Ixil-sobre-cenizas-de-la-represion-militar-20150309-20150050.html

Carey, D. (2006). *Engendering Mayan history: Kaqchikel women as agents and conduits of the past, 1875–1970.* New York, NY: Routledge.

Collins, P. H. (1991). *Black feminist thought: Knowledge, consciousness, and the politics of empowerment.* New York, NY: Routledge.

Comisión para el Esclarecimiento Histórico. (1999). *Guatemala: memoria del silencio.* Guatemala: CEH.

De León Calel, S. R. (2014). *K'iche's en la Región Ixil.* Guatemala: Universidad Ixil.

Deloria, V. (1969). *Custer died for your sins: An Indian manifesto.* New York, NY: Macmillan Company.

Figueroa, Ó. (2013, November 23). Universidad Ixil forma nuevos líderes. *Prensa Libre.* Retrieved April 16, 2017, from www.prensalibre.com/quiche/Universidad-Ixil-forma-nuevos-lideres_0_1034896520.html

Flores, A. (2015, January 15). La uerra no pudo con la esperanza. *Plaza Publica.* Retrieved April 16, 2017, from www.plazapublica.com.gt/content/la-guerra-no-pudo-con-la-esperanza

Freire, P. (2000). *Pedagogy of the oppressed.* (M. Bergman Ramos, Trans.). 30th anniversary edition. New York, NY: Continuum.

Hale, C. R. (2008). *Engaging contradictions: Theory, politics, and methods of activist scholarship.* Berkeley, CA: University of California Press

Harrison, F. V. (1991). *Decolonizing anthropology: Moving further toward an anthropology for liberation.* Washington, DC: American Anthropological Association.

Instituto Indígenista Nacional. (1948a). *Parramos: Sintesis Socio-Economica de una Comunidad Indígena Guatemalteca.* Guatemala: Ministerio de Educación Publica.

Instituto Indígenista Nacional. (1948b). *San Juan Sacatepequez: Sintesis Socio-Economica de una Comunidad Indígena Guatemalteca.* Guatemala: Ministerio de Educación Publica.

Montejo, V. (2005). *Maya intellectual renaissance.* Austin, TX: University of Texas.

Restrepo, E. (2007). Coloniality y antropología. In S. Castro-Gómez & R. Grosfoguel (Eds.), *El Giro Decolonial: Reflexiones para una Diversidad Epistémica más allá del Capitalismo Global* (pp. 289–304). Bogota: Siglo del Hombre Editores.

Roberts, T. (2014, June 10). *The other side of fracking: Connecting the dots along the supply lines.* Retrieved January 11, 2017, from www.huffingtonpost.com/tobias-roberts/the-other-side-of-fracking_b_5476952.html

Smith, L. T. (1999). *Decolonizing methodologies: Research and indigenous peoples.* London, UK: Zed Books.

Terraza Brito, M. (2015). *Los Efectos de la Guerra desde la Perspectiva De una Niña de la CPR.* Guatemala: Universidad Ixil.

Universidad de San Carlos de Guatemala. (2017). *Desarrollo histórico de la USAC.* Retrieved August 27, 2017, from www.usac.edu.gt/historiaUSAC.php

7

DECOLONIZING INDIGENOUS EDUCATION IN THE POSTWAR CITY

Native Women's Activism from Southern California to the Motor City

Kyle T. Mays (Saginaw Chippewa) and Kevin Whalen

Introduction

Indigenous women in the postwar period cannot easily be identified by the broader white feminist movements of the time; nor can they be myopically placed within the emerging work of Indigenous feminism, which at present, suffers from two shortcomings. First, earlier iterations of Indigenous feminism, in their attempt to critically understand the role of Indigenous women in precolonial societies juxtaposed to Western feminism, utilized a nationalistic approach to explain Indigenous women's experiences (Trask, 1996; Tohoe, 2000). Using nationalism as a framework allowed some to ignore the patriarchy that actually exists in Indigenous communities, even as it may be a result of colonialism. Patriarchy exists and we should acknowledge it. Second, the scholarship, with few exceptions, has ignored cities and small urban communities, and Indigenous women's role in those places. More recently, scholars of Indigenous feminism have offered new analyses that extend the conversation to ethnic studies, and we rely on recent Indigenous feminist theories to frame our chapter (Ramirez, 2008; Hundorf & Suzack, 2010). In particular, we use Arvin et al. (2013), who advance Native feminist theories, which they argue makes connections "between settler colonialism and both heteropatriarchy and hetereopaternalism" as well as the "compound issues of gender, sexuality, race, indigeneity, and nation" (10). Here, we would add place. For places like Detroit and the Inland Empire both shape Indigenous women's experiences, and they also shape it; it becomes a part of their identity (Goeman, 2013). Native feminist theories are useful for understanding the activism of urban Indigenous women because they deal specifically with urban contexts, how class formations happen among urban Indigenous communities, as well as how issues of race—as in the case of Detroit Blackness—also shape the urban Indigenous experience.

Indeed the Indigenous experience in a city is different from a reservation or rural place and that should be acknowledged, especially in postwar US cities (Lobo, 2009; Krause & Howard, 2009).

Within the fields of education and urban Indigenous history, Native people remain on the margins. Yet scholars like Sandy Grande (2004) and Eve Tuck and Wayne Yang (2012) have challenged others to more carefully engage in decolonizing education, including understanding the importance of place in education (McCoy, Tuck, & McKenzie, 2016). Indeed scholars remind us that decolonization is not a metaphor and gender has to be a central component of any decolonization practices and theories, historically and today (Tuck & Yang, 2012; Simpson, 2015).

Similarly, historians writing about indigenous people in cities often borrow analytical frameworks from histories of non-Native immigration, which have often overlooked gender as a category of analysis (Danziger, 1991; Fixico, 2000; LaGrand, 2002). Meeting at the intersection of Indigenous education, Indigenous gender studies, and urban Indigenous history, we examine the role of Native women from Detroit and Southern California's Inland Empire, and how they engaged in a variety of decolonial educational efforts in postwar cities. Native women were actively engaged in culturally sustaining/revitalizing pedagogy (McCarty & Lee, 2014; Paris, 2012).

In Detroit, we examine the role of Judy Mays, a Saginaw Anishinaabe woman who was a key architect of Indigenous education in postwar Detroit. Influenced by her mother's activism in the city, we investigate two Native educational institutions—Detroit's Indian Educational and Cultural Center, founded in 1975, and Medicine Bear American Indian Academy, founded in 1994—and the role that Native women played in creating decolonial educational spaces for Native and non-Native youth in a predominantly Black American city.

In Southern California's Inland Empire, we examine roles of Native women who worked at Sherman Institute, a federal Indian boarding school in Riverside, California. Here, we give special attention to Lorene Sisquoc (Cahuilla/Apache), who has worked as a cultural traditions teacher at Sherman since the 1990s and helped to transform Sherman Institute from a place of dispossession into a hub for intertribal cultural survival.

We move in both time and space, from postwar Southern California to Detroit, in order to illustrate how Native women challenged colonialism and gender conventions through education. They were what we call urban Indigenous feminists (Arvin et al., 2013; Mays, 2015). These urban Indigenous feminists were specifically located in their particular place and, out of that experience, created and maintained Indigenous culture and education in their respective places. In this way, they often challenged the Indigenous male-dominated spaces in which they lived and helped foster a new generation of Indigenous youth, who were multiracial and multitribal, and almost exclusively products of urban environments.

Detroit's Indian Education and Cultural Center

A school for Detroit's Indigenous students had been an idea since at least early 1972. The North American Indian Association put out a poll for their readership in order to determine if the community supported such an effort (NAIA, 1972). However, though a community idea, Esther Mays's vision for creating an institution that would help sustain Indigeneity in the Motor City as well as transmit Indigenous cultures to students from their educational institution was a major part of Mays's vision of being Indigenous in postwar Detroit.

Esther Shawboose was born on May 3, 1924 to Westbrook Shawboose, a day laborer, and Elizabeth (Liza) Silas, a stay-at-home mother. She was born a month before President Calvin Coolidge signed into law the Indian Citizenship Act on June 2, 1924, which gave Indigenous people US citizenship. She was born neither a US citizen nor a member of the Saginaw Chippewa Tribe, which had not yet formed into a political unit (Benz, 2005). As an adolescent, she attended the Mt. Pleasant Industrial boarding school at an early age before the school closed in 1934. According to her children, she never discussed her tenure. Whatever her experience, it gave her motivation to make sure that Detroit's Indigenous youth did not have the experience that she had as a child.

In a city predicated on Blackness and whiteness, an institution that nurtured Indigenous identities was paramount. Thus, the Detroit Indian Educational and Cultural Center was created to serve those needs.

There are two important points that should be made about the DIECC. First, it was designed to meet the great diversity of Indigenous peoples living in Detroit. Second, it was an embrace of modernity— through education— for Indigenous peoples. By modernity I mean embracing something new, respecting the diversity of Indigenous America, and not being held down by what some may call "traditional." In other words, challenging how Indigenous peoples would be represented among their own community and society. Importantly, though, Indigenous parents understood that their children needed education to succeed in a rapidly changing postwar America.

From the beginning, parental involvement in the school was a desire of the co-chairpersons and the educational committee. The DIECC staff encouraged community involvement by institutionalizing it. The Detroit Indian Parent Advisory Council and the Detroit American Indian Parent Council, both of which kept Indigenous student concerns first, guided all decisions. Esther Mays and Walter Albert served as the chair-persons for each council. In addition, they held employment opportunities for at least 10 high school students to serve as mentors to younger students. They also encouraged the involvement of the elderly, who would serve as counselors to the young people, teaching them about Indigenous histories and cultures. The staff understood that they were dealing with a diverse Indigenous population throughout Detroit, even though the majority of their constituents were Anishinaabe.

Though Esther Mays was a co-founder of the DIECC, and herself also served on Michigan's Indian Educational Advisory Council, the major architect of the educational curriculum was her daughter, Judith (Judy) Mays. Judy was well qualified. She graduated with a bachelor's degree in education administration from Michigan State University, and she would later graduate with a master's degree in education administration and a bachelor's degree in business administration from Wayne State University. They met weekly on Saturdays, from 9 am to 3 pm.

The DIECC was a place for Indigenous people to come and interact and served as a broad cultural, social, and educational center for the community. The DIECC's educational component had two purposes. First, they wanted to reduce the high dropout rate that existed among Indigenous youth. Second, they desired to create an environment where both Indigenous and non-Indigenous students would be able to learn about the unique contributions of Native Americans in US history and in Detroit. They would do beadwork, go on trips to learn about plants, and even participate in some language classes (Anishinaabemowin).

The community was ecstatic. "Detroit's Native American children have a place to go now to be together and to learn singing, beadwork, legends, history and all the things it takes to keep Indian heritage alive in the young." Students also learned Indigenous drumming and singing (Native Sun, 1975). In addition to the "formal" schooling that would take place, members of the staff also provided emergency services, including optical and dental, as well as counseling for youth. Within three years, the DIECC served nearly 100 Detroit Public School students every Saturday throughout the school year (ibid).

A year after the DIECC's existence, Judy wrote a letter to the *Native Sun*, a local community newsletter published monthly, encouraging parents to get involved. "WE NOW HAVE OUR SCHOOL," wrote Judy. She followed that up with a rhetorical option rooted in the discourse of self-determination: "Can we sit back and let someone else do our work?" Realizing that only through community involvement could the DIECC reach its potential, Mays appealed to the parents, stating, "Indian parent interest and participation is the only way our school program can proceed as originally planned, for it is you who carry the Indian culture and traditions of your tribe in your hearts." Judy's point is important, for it reveals that Mays had a broad view of what it meant to be Indigenous in the postwar era, amidst the Red Power Movement. She also understood the notion that Indigeneity was not to be relegated to cultures of the past, but lived in the daily realities of Indigenous people. Children growing up in Detroit had to know that being Indigenous was not what they saw in popular culture. They would learn from their parents and elders who were shaped by a city and yet maintained their Indigenous identity. Indeed, the point of the DIECC's curriculum was to foster in students to "be more effective in [their] ability to understand [their self] and [be] better equipped to cope in a public school system that has not geared itself to meet his individual needs" (Ibid).

Mays believed that the DIECC staff could handle the teaching and tutoring of remedial subjects such as math, science, and social studies, but only Native peoples who understood certain types of knowledges could teach that to children. Indeed parents were situated to pass on certain types of knowledges not only to their own children but also to others. "We are of many tribes and these characteristics of the various tribes differ. Learning all these variations is more than our staff can absorb in a short time" (1975). The acceptance of Indigenous diversity among Detroit's Indigenous community was profound. It was not just that Mays was sensitive to the diversity within Indigenous Detroit, she also understood the politics of division that impacted the community; they did not want these rifts impacting students. They were also open to community criticisms and suggestions. The DIECC was important for cultivating an Indigenous identity in students, but Mays and the staff also understood that the broader public required a re-education.

Judy Mays continued working with the Detroit Indian Educational and Cultural Center throughout the 1980s. She did not stop trying to fulfill the dream of her mother: opening a full-time school for Native youth. Finally, in September 1994, after years of toil, Judy helped reclaim Indigeneity by inserting the most important manifestation of it in modern Detroit: Medicine Bear American Indian Academy, the nation's third-ever public school with an Indigenous-centered curriculum.

Each morning, before the school day began, students at Medicine Bear American Indian Academy would do a pledge of allegiance. This pledge of allegiance, however, was not a blind allegiance to the symbolic representation of US colonialism—the American flag. It was a pledge to themselves, to the community. The pledge was called the Indian Pledge of Allegiance:

I: I will always respect myself and others
N: Never fight or call others names
D: Don't do drugs
I: Improve in school
A: Always respect parents and teachers
N: Never be a dropout

The Indian pledge of allegiance fit the particular circumstances that students found themselves in: post 1980s Detroit, which was a particularly challenging time to be a young person growing up in the Motor City. But it was not just the Indigenous pledge of allegiance that was important; it was the space of hope and healing, designed for the postmodern Indigenous (and non-Indigenous) student, who would go on to hopefully be the future leaders in the Motor City. Medicine Bear American Indian Academy, the vision of an Indigenous mother, Esther Mays, was realized under her daughter in 1994.

Medicine Bear was open to all students in Detroit. Judy and the design team opened their doors with students from grades kindergarten through third, with the long-term goal of expanding into grades K-12. Judy wanted to go to K-12 so that the whole schooling experience of students, especially Indigenous students, was rooted in an Indigenous perspective, and so that their cultures could be celebrated and sustained. However, priority to the tune of 55% was reserved for students of Indigenous ancestry and those who lived within a one-mile radius of the school.

On March 20, 2000, Judy Mays received a letter from the Detroit Public School's Department of Human Resources. In the letter Mays was told that her contract as principal of Medicine bear would not be renewed because of nepotism. Mays was shocked. DPS sent her this notice because she hired her sister, Tracy Mays, to run the Detroit Indian Educational and Cultural Center in another building. The irony here is that a Mays family member had always been a part of DIECC. Nepotism is a difficult charge in this case. As Cree scholar Shawn Wilson (2008) argues, "in the dominant system, nepotism generally involves the use of friends and relations in a concerted effort to keep others out" (81). Detroit's Indigenous community was small and Judy was perhaps the most qualified Indigenous persons to make such a decision. Wilson continues, "In healthy Indigenous communities . . . the strength of established bonds between people can be used to help uplift others." Ironically, the DPS by-laws only outlawed nepotism among school board members.

A difficult question to grapple with is: What is the deep reason for closing Medicine Bear? Nepotism is a good excuse; perhaps not the best answer. Prior to the school closing, Judy and the staff held meetings with architects and DPS to discuss moving to a new building. "They promised us a new school. We looked at property, we had meetings about what it would look like. [DPS] hired an architect. The board never went through with it. I don't know if it was money or what." It was, in fact, money.

During 1999, the Detroit Public Schools was taken over by an Emergency Financial Manager. The District did not suffer from a deficit. Speculation suggests that DPS was one of the city's largest landowners and venture capitalists wanted to own the land.

After contacting Detroit's Native community, on June 14, 2000, Mays and nearly 100 supporters of Medicine Bear gathered to attend a rally in front of the Detroit Public Schools Center Building on Woodward Avenue, Detroit. Mays's sister, Tracy, took the microphone. In dramatic fashion, she wrapped her hands around her two long braids, looked at the crowd, pulled the braids together, raised an orange pair of scissors, and, one by one, cut each braid. The crowd gasped in uniform. The crowd erupted with moans and wailings; people cried. After moments of despair, Tracy handed each one of her clipped braids over to her children. She then went back to the podium and said, "I want (Detroit Public Schools [Superintendent] David Adamany to know why I cut my hair." "I am in mourning," she said, "for the loss of the city's only Native American principal, because it is like a death, and it is a part of our culture to cut our hair when we are in mourning" (Lewis, 2000).

The day after her contract was officially not renewed, on August 1, Judy Mays filed paperwork in the Wayne County Circuit Court suing DPS, charging them with "contract, and age, sex and race discrimination" (Lewis, 2000). I will end here. Judy did not win her case. Tracy left the position as director of DIECC. The Medicine Bear American Indian Academy, the vision of a mother, the lifework of a daughter, the outcome of their Urban Indigenous feminism, crumbled. Medicine Bear was closed officially by the school district after the 2001–2002 school year. Reflecting back on her time at Medicine Bear, a former student stated, "I'm not Native, but what it meant for me was a really very diverse and non-discriminatory school with a very tight-knit family feel. I really needed that type of environment as a kid."

Being fired from Medicine Bear was heartbreaking for Judy. Indigenous education largely vanished after she was gone. However, I do not want to end on such a negative note. In fact, after talking with family, many of them have thanked me for helping recall the important work that Judy did for Indigenous children and Detroit. When I asked her what the legacy of Medicine Bear was, she replied:

> We were the third [public] American Indian school in the country. I think they were in Minneapolis and Milwaukee. We were the third one. It was innovative to have a school like that. And the legacy is that we made it. It was a dream of my mother's—always to have a school for Native American children in Detroit. That was a legacy fulfilled through me by opening and being a part of her dream. To have it opened for kids, that would be the legacy—see someone's dreams come to fruition. [My mom] didn't get to see Medicine Bear. That's what drove me—I was driven by that. And since I had been in Indian education so long, it was just like an extension.
>
> *(interview with Mays, 2014)*

Although still stinging from the pain of being fired from her role as principal and fulfilling her mother's dream, she remained positive about the legacy:

> It was a very rewarding experience and am humbled to have had the opportunity to do some of the things I was able to do. Living on for my mom. Taking over for her, that was very gratifying. And I would do it again if I had the chance, in spite of the ending. I would still be at Medicine Bear. But since I left there, my life just went down—depression and all.
>
> *(Ibid)*

The Inland Empire and Sherman Institute

Lorene Sisquoc (Mountain Cahuilla/Fort Sill Apache) was born in Riverside, California, in 1960. A direct descendant of Mangas Coloradas, the last chief of the Mimbrenos Apaches, Chief Loco of the Warm Springs Apaches, and the

Mountain Cahuilla leader Net Manuel Largo, Sisquoc is the cultural traditions leader at Sherman Indian High School (formerly Sherman Institute). A lifetime activist, she has helped to transform Sherman Indian High School from a place of ethnocentrism and assimilation into a site of cultural regeneration for Indians in Southern California and beyond.

Federal Indian education was born out of the early Captain Richard Henry Pratt provided the prototype for federal off-reservation boarding schools in 1879 when he opened the Carlisle Industrial School in Carlisle, Pennsylvania, where he promoted a blend of academic and manual training would prepare young Indians to leave behind their peoples, lands, and cultures in favor of total assimilation into white, protestant America (Hoxie, 2001; Pratt, 1964; Adams, 1995). Sherman Institute opened its doors in 1902, a half century before the birth of Lorene Sisquoc. From the outset, the school operated on the assumption that Progressive Era conviction that Native American peoples could be "uplifted," that "savage" ways of thinking and acting could be completely abandoned in favor of the cultural characteristics of white, Protestant Americans ((Sakiestewa Gilbert, 2010; Keller, 2002).

Despite working to eradicate Indian identities, government boarding schools hired young Indians to work on their staffs. As early as 1898, just four years before Sherman opened its doors, Native Americans comprised 45% of the staff of the Bureau of Indian Affairs (BIA) Indian School Service. Sherman was no exception. From its inception, the school hired young Indians, many of them graduates of Sherman and other boarding schools, to work as teachers, disciplinarians, matrons, and general laborers. Indian employees quietly worked to subvert culturally harmful aspects of Indian School Service curricula. In this way, many Native students and their families made Sherman a key component of their family identities (Ahern, 1997).

In this way, Lorene Sisquoc's extended family became a vital part of the legacy of Native American employees at Sherman Institute. Sisquoc's grandmother, Ida Gooday-Largo (Warm Springs Apache) was born a prisoner of the US government at Fort Sill in 1903. She attended Chilocco, a government-run, non-reservation Indian boarding school in Oklahoma. Gooday-Largo arrived at Chilocco in the wake of family tragedy. The school provided much-needed care after the death of her mother, which left the Gooday family struggling to care for Ida and her siblings. Later, she transferred to Phoenix Indian School, another federal, off-reservation boarding school. After graduating there, Gooday-Largo earned a teaching certificate in 1927 from Haskell Indian School in Lawrence, Kansas (today known as Haskell Indian Nations University). Much like her granddaughter would, Gooday-Largo dedicated the remainder of her life to Indian education. She taught at Indian schools on the Pima, Hopi, Tohono O'odham, and Navajo reservations before arriving at Sherman Institute in the summer of 1951 (Laddy, 1993).

Like many employees at off-reservation boarding schools, Gooday-Largo lived and raised her family on the campus of Sherman Institute. Her daughter, Tonita

Largo-Glover, attended nearby public schools, but she came to identify deeply with the intertribal community of students and teachers at Sherman. After attending college and working as a nurse, she returned to the school in June of 1969 to work as a teaching assistant and dormitory supervisor. Largo-Glover brought her daughters, 9-year-old Lorene and 2-year-old Stephi, with her. She raised her family on campus, just as her mother did before her.

When Largo-Glover began working at Sherman, she saw traditional Indigenous spiritual and cultural traditions of Indian students virtually ignored. Indigenous languages, traditional prayers and songs, and sweat lodges remained taboo, and students who wanted to practice elements of their cultures had to do so within highly regulated settings: they could paint in art class or perform Native dances as demonstrations for public audiences. Students had few opportunities to engage in the traditional cultural and spiritual practices of their tribes. Throughout the 1980s, Largo-Glover worked quietly and behind the scenes, encouraging students to share with one another their traditional cultural and spiritual traditions outside of class. This discrete creation of spaces for Indigenous cultures took place at Sherman in the early 1980s, just as Largo-Glover's daughter, Lorene Sisquoc, returned to the school after a 10-year absence. Sisquoc would follow the tradition of cultural leadership that her mother and grandmother had set before her (Sisquoc interview with Whalen, 2010).

Sisquoc became active in the traditional community of Southern California Native Americans in 1973. That year, she spent her first of many summers at the Redwind Foundation in Topanga Canyon, California, a summer camp for young Native people. Trading songs, stories, histories, and traditions with Native Americans from across the US, Sisquoc saw common threads running through all the Native cultures and traditions she encountered. She took from her time there a determination to teach others to live responsibly as caretakers of the land, and to share with others the cultural traditions of her ancestors.

In 1982, Sisquoc returned to Sherman Indian High School to work as a dormitory staff member. Following the path set by her mother, Sisquoc used her time in the Sherman dormitories to encourage students to preserve and promote their cultural heritages. She spread a message passed down by elders, encouraging students to embrace their spiritual and cultural traditions as a means to resist the lures of drugs and alcohol. In the mid-1980s, the efforts of dedicated staff members like Sisquoc and her mother began to pay dividends as Native languages and cultures became increasingly visible on campus. A tangible marker of this progress came in 1986, when Tonita Largo-Glover co-coordinated the school's first-ever powwow.

After providing three years of guidance and supervision in the Sherman dormitories, Sisquoc began volunteering and training under the guidance of Ramona K. Bradley, the co-founder of the Sherman Indian Museum. Bradley instilled in Sisquoc a powerful belief in the importance of preserving the archival records of Sherman Institute and Indian High School and the cultural materials representing the students who had passed through Sherman and their peoples, whether in the form of traditional dress, creative art, or ceremonial objects.

In 1991, Sisquoc became the curator and manager of the museum. Faced with scant funding and no full-time staff, she worked tirelessly and on a volunteer basis to keep the museum's doors open. In her time as manager and curator, Sisquoc managed and expanded a substantial collection of Indian art. Once a space for ethnographic relics, the Museum now holds art that reflects important transformations that have taken place at Sherman Indian High School and across Native America. Works by activist artists such as Billy Soza Warsoldier reflect on critical themes, including tribal self-determination, control over and protection of natural resources, cultural and spiritual regeneration, and the stereotypical portrayals of Indians that plague American popular culture (ibid).

Sisquoc has also guided countless researchers through the museum's archives. A steady stream of visitors trickles through the doors of Sherman Indian Museum, looking for information about parents, grandparents, siblings, aunts, and uncles who attended Sherman Institute long ago. Sisquoc's efforts have helped relatives and descendants of Sherman students learn about their ancestry and culture. Moreover, Sisquoc's careful and culturally informed guidance has helped historians comb through the thousands of documents housed at Sherman Indian Museum. It is thanks to the guiding hand of Sisquoc that many scholarly books, articles, and dissertations have risen from the rich archival collections at Sherman Indian Museum. These works have helped to illuminate the experiences of students and teachers at Sherman, and to demonstrate the significance of the larger non-reservation boarding school system within the American and Native American experiences.

Early in her career, Sisquoc began working beyond Sherman Indian High School to preserve and continue Native American cultures. Along with Tongva Indian activist Cindy Alvitre, Sisquoc started the Mother Earth Culture Clan in 1986. Through the Mother Earth Clan, Sisquoc and Alvitre brought a positive message of cultural revitalization to urban Native American youth in Southern California. Impressed by her message, Sherman principal Don Sims asked Sisquoc to teach the cultural traditions of Southern California Native Americans to Sherman students. In the fall of 1985, Sims gave Sisquoc a budget, a classroom, and time away from the dormitories to begin a cultural education program at Sherman.

Where Native American cultural traditions had once been held to the peripheries of Sherman Institute, Lorene Sisquoc helped to make them a key component of the educational experience at Sherman Indian High School. The study of Native American histories, cultures, languages, and spiritual traditions became a part of the standardized curriculum at Sherman. Sisquoc taught all incoming freshmen about the cultural traditions of the Indigenous people of Southern California. Her cultural education program served two important functions: it taught students the cultural traditions of some of the Indigenous peoples of Southern California, and it encouraged students to explore their own cultural heritages in a similar way. Later, Sisquoc offered courses in traditional Native American basketry and museum studies, along with museum and cultural programming internships to students from Sherman Indian High School and the University of California, Riverside.

In 1991, Sisquoc moved outside the walls of the Sherman Indian Museum in order to honor the memories of Sherman Institute students who died while attending school. Like all non-reservation Indian boarding schools, a combination of close living quarters and a rudimentary understanding of contagious diseases meant that the student body at Sherman suffered from frequent illnesses, some of them epidemic. Many students contracted trachoma, a disease that caused scarring of the eyelids and blindness for some. Tuberculosis, smallpox, pneumonia, measles, influenza, diphtheria, and typhoid fever all attacked the Sherman community during its first 20 years, with trachoma and tuberculosis occurring most frequently. Unfortunately, the prevalence of these diseases meant that some children never returned home from Sherman Institute. Between 1902 and 1922 alone, 62 students died from accidents, illnesses, and epidemics. Tragically, many parents did not learn that their child was sick until after he or she had already died. When the families of deceased students could not be located or could not afford to have their children's bodies sent home, administrators interred students at an isolated school cemetery plot on the school farm, located on five miles west of Sherman Institute (Keller, 2002).

When Lorene Sisquoc arrived at Sherman in 1982, the cemetery had fallen into disrepair. Connected to the outside world by a small, uneven dirt road, the cemetery had become choked with weeds and empty beer cans. Small headstones had shifted and deteriorated from over a half century of neglect. Many of their names were no longer legible. Sisquoc received federal funding in 1994 to construct a wrought iron fence around the cemetery. Later, Sisquoc helped to guide historian Jean Keller through the archives of the Sherman Indian Museum as she researched a typhoid fever epidemic that killed 35 students during the 1904–1905 school year. As the two learned more about students who had lost their lives to disease while at Sherman, they became increasingly aware of the school cemetery and its dilapidated state. Determined to honor the memories of the children who perished at Sherman, Sisquoc and Keller raised community awareness of the cemetery. They wrote letters to the BIA and the Department of the Interior, contacted local news outlets, and informed families living near the cemetery of its history and significance. Later they used ground-penetrating radar in order to replace headstones above the bodies they marked. As community awareness of the Sherman Indian Cemetery grew, volunteers interested in maintaining or improving the once-neglected plot contacted Sisquoc and Keller. Sisquoc and Keller helped two local Eagle Scouts procure funds from the Pechanga Tribe for new headstones and students from a local college welded an arch to place above the cemetery entrance. Once forgotten, the Indian students laid to rest at the Sherman Cemetery received a steady stream of care and attention thanks to the efforts of Lorene Sisquoc and Jean Keller. In large part for her efforts with the cemetery, Sisquoc became one of five people ever to be granted the City of Riverside Martin Luther King, Jr. Visionary Award for community cultural awareness when she received the award in 1997 (Rasmussen, 2003; Riverside Press-Enterprise, 1997).

In 2001, Sisquoc played a key role in organizing the centennial celebration, marking 100 years of Indian education at Sherman. She designed a centennial rose garden to commemorate all Sherman alumni, designed a logo for a Sherman centennial coin, produced a centennial documentary on Indian education at Sherman Institute, and planned and coordinated a celebration to honor alumni. That same year, she co-organized and hosted the "Boarding School Blues" symposium with Clifford Trafzer, professor of history at the University of California, Riverside. The symposium brought renowned scholars of Indian education to Sherman Indian High School, where they shared their research with Sherman students and community members. Sisquoc, Keller, and Trafzer edited the papers to create *Boarding School Blues: Revisiting American Indian Educational Experiences*, an edited volume on the boarding school experience. Many of the articles included substantial input from current students at Sherman Indian High School. For her efforts in coordinating and implementing the centennial event, Sisquoc received a Star Award for service from the US Department of the Interior (Trafzer, Keller Sisquoc, 2005).

Finally, in fall of 2007, Sisquoc co-founded the Clark Culture Center along with Cultural Traditions assistant Josie Montes. Named in honor of Sherman graduate Dr. Frank Clarke, a 1939 graduate of Sherman, the center focuses on a holistic approach to healthy living through Native American traditional values. Sisquoc and Montes provide students with pride and awareness of their rich cultural traditions and values and how to apply them in their family and community lives. The Clarke Culture Center features traditional Indigenous herbs and medicines, information on Indigenous foods, and a cultural library. The center hosts cultural events on a nightly basis, where students engage in cultural activities including Native American arts, crafts, stories, songs, talking circles, and Indigenous language conversations (interview with Whalen, 2010).

Conclusion

In many ways, the stories of Judy Mays and Lorene Sisquoc are unique, rooted in their own places, institutions, and tribes. Put them side by side, though, and the two women demonstrate some clear possibilities for what Native feminist theory within Indigenous education has looked like for the past half century, and how it might move forward.

To be sure, much of the story lies in the similarities between the struggles faced Mays and Sisquoc and the programs they built. In the face of long odds and institutions that resisted decolonization, they created programs and curricula that finally made places for Indigenous students and their families, languages, and cultures. But beneath the nuts and bolts of their curricula lie important intellectual commonalities. As they worked to decolonize Indigenous education in Detroit and urban Southern California, Mays and Sisquoc engaged in deeply intellectual projects amidst challenging circumstances. They dove head-on into the complicated politics of Indigenous education within settler contexts, carefully deciding when to work subversively behind the scenes, and when to push their work above the surface in order to make institutional places for their brands of Indian education. They wove together programs and curricula flexible enough not just to *include* diverse Indigenous languages and cultures, but also to highlight each one in order to create a new, urban, intercultural fabric for Indigenous education. They showed that Indigenous cultures don't fade away under the bright lights of modernity and urbanity, but rather thrive and grow.

Finally, the Indigenous feminisms of Mays and Sisquoc suggest a reconsideration of gender and intellectual leadership within movements for decolonization. For too long, the story of Indigenous leadership in postwar decolonization movements has gone something like this: men came up with the important ideas and shared them with the world, while women did the day-to-day work that held Red Power together. The hard work of Mays, Sisquoc, and their mothers call this gendered division of labor into question by highlighting the intellectual contributions from those who practiced Indigenous feminisms. They engaged in the deeply intellectual work of forging intercultural curricula, placing Indigenous cultural values at the center of their pedagogies, and forging spaces within cities and schools that had resisted the acknowledgment of Indigeneity at every turn. For Mays and Sisquoc, Indigenous feminisms rested at the heart of decolonizing Indigenous education.

References

Adams, D. (1995). *Education for extinction: American Indians and the boarding school experience.* Lawrence, KS: University of Kansas Press.

Ahern, W. (1997). An experiment aborted: Returned Indian students in the Indian school service, 1881–1908. *Ethnohistory, 44*(2), 263–304.

Arvin, M., Tuck, E., & Morrill, A. (2013). Decolonizing feminism: Challenging connection between settler colonialism and heteropatriarchy. *Feminist Formations, 25*(1), 8–34.

Benz, C. M. (Ed.). (2005). *Diba Jimooyoung: Telling our story: A history of the Saginaw Anishinaabek.* Mt. Pleasant, Michigan: Saginaw Chippewa Tribe of Michigan.

Danziger, E. (1991). *Survival and regeneration: Detroit's American Indian community.* Detroit, MI: Wayne State University Press.

"Five Honored for Exemplifying King." (1997, January 26). *Riverside Press-Enterprise*, B8. Retrieved from www.newsbank.com.

Fixico, D. (2000). *The urban Indian experience in America.* Albuquerque, NM: University of New Mexico Press.

Goeman, M. (2013). *Mark my words: Native women mapping our nations.* Minneapolis, MN: University of Minnesota Press.

Grande, S. (2004). *Red pedagogy: Native American social and political thought*. Lanham, MD: Rowman & Littlefield Publishers, Inc.

Hoxie, F. (2001). *A final promise: The campaign to assimilate the Indians*. Lincoln: University of Nebraska Press.

Huhndorf, S., & Suzack, C. (2010). Indigenous feminism: Theorizing the issues. In C. Suzack, S. Huhndorf, J. Perreault, & J. Barman (Eds.), *Indigenous women and feminism: Politics, activism, culture* (pp. 1–17). Vancouver, British Columbia: University of British Columbia Press.

Keller, J. A. (2002). *Empty beds: Indian student health at Sherman institute, 1902–1922*. East Lansing: Michigan State University Press.

Krause, S. & Howard, H. (Eds.). (2009). *Keeping the Campfires Going: Native Women's Activism in Urban Communities*. Lincoln, Nebraska: University of Nebraska Press.

Laddy, T. (1993, July 10). Born a captive of government, oldest tribal survivor endures. *Riverside Press-Enterprise*. Retrieved from www.newsbank.com

LaGrand, J. (2002). *Indian metropolis: Native Americans in Chicago, 1945–1975*. Chicago, Urbana, IL: University of Illinois Press.

Lewis, S. (2000a, June 13). Parents support fired principal. *Detroit News*, 8.

Lewis, S. (2000b, August 15). Fired academy principal sues. *Detroit News*, 6.

Lobo, S. (2009). "Urban clan mothers: Key households in cities. In Krause, S. & Howard, H. (Eds.). *Keeping the campfires going: Urban Native Women's Activism in Urban Communities* (pp. 1-21). Lincoln, Nebraska: University of Nebraska Press.

Mays, K. (2015). *Indigenous Detroit: Indigeneity, Modernity, and Racial and Gender Formation in a Modern American City* (Unpublished doctoral dissertation). University of Illinois, Urbana-Champaign, Illinois, United States.

McCarty, T., & Lee, T. (2014). Critical culturally sustaining/revitalizing pedagogy and indigenous education sovereignty. *Harvard Educational Review*, *84*(1), 101–124.

McCoy, K., Tuck, E., & McKenzie, M. (Eds.). (2016). *Land education: Rethinking pedagogies of place from indigenous, postcolonial, and decolonizing perspectives* (1st ed.). London: Routledge.

Native Sun. Vol 5(6), (June 1975). Library of Michigan, Lansing, Michigan.

North American Indian Association News. Vol. 6(5) (1972, November). Library of Michigan, Lansing, Michigan. *North American Indian Association Newsletter*, *2*(11).

Paris, D. (2012). Culturally sustaining pedagogy: A needed change in stance, terminology, and practice. *Educational Researcher*, *41*(3), 93–97.

Pratt, R. H. (1964). *Battlefield and classroom: Four decades with the American Indian, 1867–1904*. New Haven, CT: University of Connecticut Press.

Ramirez, R. (2008). Learning across differences: Native and ethnic studies feminisms. *American Quarterly*, *60*(2), 303–307.

Rasmussen, C. (2003, February 23). Institute tried to drum civilization into Indian youth. *Los Angeles Times*. Retrieved from www.newsbank.com

Sakiestewa Gilbert, M. (2010). *Education beyond the Mesas: Hopi Students at Sherman Institute, 1902–1929*. Lincoln, Nebraska: University of Nebraska Press.

Simpson, L. (2015). Not Murdered and Not Missing: Rebelling Against Colonial Gender Violence. In Milstein, C. (Ed.). *Taking sides: Revolutionary Solidarity and the Poverty of Liberalism* (pp. 114-123). Chicago, Illinois: AK PressTohoe, L. (2000). There is no word for feminism in my language. *Wicazo Sa Review*, *15*(2), 103–110.

Tohoe, L. (2000). There is no word for feminism in my language. *Wicazo Sa Review*, *15*(2), 103–110.

Trafzer, C. (2005). *Boarding School Blues: Revisiting American Indian educational experience*. (J. Keller & L. Sisquoc, Eds.). Lincoln, Nebraska: University of Nebraska Press.

Trask, H-K. (1996). Feminism and indigenous Hawaiian nationalism. *Signs: Journal of Women and Culture in Society, 21*(4), 906–916.

Tuck, E., & Yang, K.W. (2012). Decolonization is not a metaphor. *Decolonization: Indigeneity, Education and Society, 1*(1), 1–40.

Wilson, S. (2008). *Research as ceremony: Indigenous research methods*. Halifax, Winnipeg, MB, Canada: Fernwood Publishing.

8

QUEERING INDIGENOUS EDUCATION

Alex Wilson (Opaskwayak Cree Nation) with Marie Laing (Kanyen'kehá:ka)

This chapter is based on a phone interview that took place between Alex Wilson (in Opaskwayak Cree Nation) and Marie Laing (in Toronto) on June 20, 2017. The conversation was based on a set of questions developed by Laing with assistance from Nisha Toomey. Here, we present a condensed and edited version of the conversation on community-driven research, Indigenous education, and two-spirit scholarship.

Dr. Alex Wilson, Opaskwayak Cree Nation, is a professor at the University of Saskatchewan. Her scholarship has greatly contributed to building and sharing knowledge about two-spirit identity, history and teachings, Indigenous research methodologies, and the prevention of violence in the lives of Indigenous peoples. Acknowledging that Western conventional ways of understanding LGBTQIA+ experiences do not describe well the everyday experiences of Indigenous peoples, her research led to development of the model of "Coming In" to describe individual and community empowered queer identities. She is one of many organizers with the Idle No More movement, integrating radical education movement work with grassroots interventions that prevent the destruction of land and water. She is particularly focused on educating about and protecting the Saskatchewan River Delta and supporting community land-based efforts.

Marie Laing: How did you come to the field of education?

Alex Wilson: My parents are both educators so the field has always been a familiar and comfortable place. When I first went to university, though, I was more interested in the hard sciences, beginning in a pre-med program and then moving into a general microbiology degree program. Midway through that, I took a long break from school to work, and when I returned I majored in psychology. It was not until graduate school that the focus shifted to education and psychology. I had not intended to teach at a university but in the end that's where I landed.

Laing: Can you speak a little bit about the relationships that you see between community organizing, activism, and the academy?

Wilson: Most Indigenous scholars I know are in the academy because there's work that needs to be done in our own communities. There is a need for Indigenous people not just to theorize but, more importantly, to apply their theory in ways that help our communities. In my own case, activism was what propelled me to higher education. In the last years of my undergraduate degree (which was completed at a California State University), I was co-facilitating an LGBTQIA+-identified youth rap group. After coming home for the summer and returning for the last semester that fall, all of the Native American kids who were in the group had committed suicide over the summer. That was both traumatic and eye-opening. Growing up in my home First Nation most of my experiences around sexual orientation and gender identity had been positive. There was tremendous support from family, from elders, and from community members. But, I know many others who did not have that same support. When finding out that those Indigenous youth in the rap group had committed suicide, I realized that there are intersecting factors in our lives that can be so overwhelming for some people that they do not feel safe in this world. That led to an unsuccessful hunt for published research on Indigenous LGBTQIA+ youth and suicide. I found nothing on this specific topic and as far as I could tell, up to that point, no one had done any kind of formal research that related to the broader topic of Indigenous LGBTQIA+ youth.

Of necessity, then, activism intersects with scholarship and propels the work we do. Many of the Indigenous scholars I know have similar stories. We've become academics because concerns or issues in our own lives or the lives of our families or communities made it seem necessary to position ourselves so that we can not only name them but also understand why they exist and, we hope, drive and implement change to address them. We know that, historically and still today, education has greatly failed Indigenous people and we hope that our work will help change that. Like many of my peers, I have a long history of activism, beginning as a youth involved in ACT UP, Queer Nation, and Indigenous land rights. I think most of us didn't even consider ourselves activists. We learned, out of necessity, that there were things we had to do to protect our families and friends and defend our lands and waters.

Restoring Relationships to Land

Laing: In your 2016 talk at the University of Winnipeg, "Coming In To Indigenous Sovereignty, Relationality, and Resurgence," you talked about land-based education as one route for us, as Indigenous peoples, to return to our own educational systems. Could you talk a little bit about that?

Wilson: With the possible exception of Indigenous Australians, Indigenous people in the Americas have lived continuously on our land for millennia. A lot of knowledge comes along with that relationship and connection to these lands and waters. We've also been impacted by different climatic and political forces. For example, the Cree language of my family includes terms that refer to both the last ice age and the ice age before that. We migrated when the ice came, returned here when it receded, and throughout maintained a very strong connection to and relationships with the lands and waters that we moved through, relied on, and lived with. Our education systems—that is, traditional ways of understanding and learning about the world around us—and the knowledge that we had accrued in the context of the places and spaces that we come from had remained intact for almost 100,000 years. Then suddenly, in the blink of an historic eye, all of that changed.

The term epistemicide is an accurate descriptor of the sustained effort to sever Indigenous peoples from traditional education and traditional knowledges. For Indigenous people in the Americas, epistemicide began with the colonization of our lands and waters and continues today. Most people who are familiar with the history and present-day experiences of Indigenous peoples have some awareness of the many ways in which, as part of the process of colonization, Indigenous people's bodies have been regulated, controlled, subjected to violence, and killed. Many who have learned about this history describe these activities as genocidal. Similarly, colonization, by displacing or removing Indigenous peoples from our traditional lands and waters, has cut our ties to critical sources of our traditional knowledges. I, along with many of my peers, recognize this as epistemicide.

In Canada, there have been many government policies that have disrupted our relationships with the land. In some cases, these policies were designed to separate us from our traditional lands and waters, and in others, this has occurred as an unintended result. Regardless, though, the impacts are the same. I live and work in the Saskatchewan River Delta, where the river itself and other waterways are regulated and controlled by corporate entities such as hydroelectric companies and Ducks Unlimited. This has impacts on the waterways and on all living creatures (including people) who rely on those waterways for food, transportation, and other resources. Reconnecting to land is critical for moving forward and trying to undo the legacies and ongoing impacts of colonization and land-based education is, at its core, an anti-oppressive form of education. Reclaiming or restating our relationship to our lands and waters is a starting point, and then nurturing that as an ongoing relationship reinforces the fact that we have the right to be there. It also reignites the continuity of energy that has existed for hundreds of thousands of years and that makes us human. It is part of our cosmology. I think once you get onto the land (and literally, you do not have to drive hundreds of miles—you can just walk outside or look at the sky), you ignite that energy.

It is really critical that, as we move forward as Indigenous people, we reclaim and nurture our relationship with the land and waters because you cannot really protect something you do not know much about. The more you learn about the land and waters, the more you realize that they determine everything. When you're on the land, all the socially constructed hierarchies around gender, around sexual orientation, around race, or around class disappear. The land engenders itself and we engender it.

Laing: In this framework, the connections between land sovereignty and body sovereignty are really strong.

Wilson: They are inseparable. Christianity and Western culture have really impacted our communities. Many of our people have internalized what Judeo-Christianity has taught them and adopted the pedagogy it uses to instill those teachings, that is, proselytization, a framework that employs rules, regulations, dogma, enforcement of laws, practices and institutions of social management. This includes people who say they are not Christian and practice, for example, traditional Cree spirituality but have internalized this framework and transported or transposed it onto our own spiritual traditions. So now, instead of ten commandments, we are directed to follow "teachings," which draw on the same ideas and generate the same outcomes you might find in a Christian church and impacts the bodies of Indigenous people in diverse and asymmetrical ways. It introduces a framework that is hierarchical and that benefits certain people and oppresses others, in particular, women and two-spirit people. It is a delicate topic to discuss because people have gone through so much. The last thing they want to face is that their beloved relation might have taught them or modeled oppressive practices. But, it has to be said otherwise the same people benefit while others are continually hurt and in the end the colonial agenda prevails.

Susan Faludi (1991) introduced the term "backlash" to describe how, within the women's movement, when (big or small) wins occur that move women closer to achieving equality with men, an anti-feminist backlash follows. Within Indigenous rights or sovereignty movements, we also find that when our actions generate positive change or we feel like we're making progress, something similar to Faludi's backlash often occurs. What's different about how this plays out in

Indigenous communities is that when that pushback occurs it typically most affects or impacts specific groups and, for that reason, I describe it as "whiplash" rather than backlash. Indigenous women and two-spirit people bear the brunt of colonial hierarchies and processes and we also bear the brunt of whiplash that occurs when colonial frameworks invade our own cosmology and are presented as "natural," as something that has always been a part of our traditional teachings. The impacts accumulate, undermining our sense of self-in-community, and I think that contributes to the horrifyingly high number of Indigenous women and two-spirit people who are missing or may have been murdered in North America. Within the context of colonialism, violence is highly gendered. While many Indigenous men are also missing or murdered, it is typically in circumstances and/or relates to factors that are very different than those of Indigenous women and two-spirit people.

Body sovereignty is inseparable from sovereignty over our lands and waters. It means that we are reclaiming and returning to traditional understandings of our bodies as connected to land. That does not mean assigning women to roles as child-keepers or keepers of the tipis. It does mean understanding that our traditional cosmology, like all aspects of creation, was not and is not fixed. It is fluid, flexible, and constantly recreating itself. Creation was not a single event—it is an ongoing state of being, and our creation stories do not end. We have a lot of work to do in our own communities. We need to talk with each other about the pervasive influences of Christianity and other Western or Eastern religions in our cultures, and the ways in which they have impacted our own spirituality, our bodies, and our body sovereignty.

Decolonization

I rarely use the term decolonization. It is a useful and valuable term that describes well what we are doing, but I avoid using it because I do not think we (or our struggles) should be defined by colonization. I am Nehinuw (Cree) and our people, like all Indigenous peoples or people of any culture, have a worldview that, over time, has not changed in some aspects and has changed significantly in other aspects. Those changes do not make our worldview any more or any less valid or less legitimately Nehinuw/"Cree." Rather, they signal that our worldview and our culture itself are responsive and dynamic—they are alive. If we describe ourselves as "decolonizers," it implies that colonization is what defines us, but my people were Cree before the colonizers arrived. While we have been impacted by colonization, our Cree identity and worldview have survived and have persisted. I rarely use the term decolonization because it gives colonization power. It also assumes that we do not change as Indigenous people, and we have always been changing.

Many people are familiar with the use of the iceberg analogy in discussions of culture. It's also useful as a way talk about knowledge systems (Wilson, 2016;

St. Denis, 2011).[1] As Indigenous people, our cultures are shaped by knowledge and ways of knowing that are connected to the land. Anyone who has access to Google can learn about material expressions of our cultures like our clothing or our food, but that is just the tip of the iceberg. What's visible is far less important or substantial than the 90% of the iceberg that is beneath the surface of the water. Similarly, the most critical aspects of our cultures are those that are not seen—our value systems, our deep philosophies, our cosmology, and how that all connects to how we teach and how we go about being in the world. One of the features of colonization in our territories has been that systemic and institutional violence, effected through, for example, the imposition of Christianity, residential schools, resource extraction, Hydro development, the Sixties Scoop, Western education, policing and prisons, and child apprehension, have severed the top of our cultural iceberg from the bottom. So now, many non-Indigenous and Indigenous people's knowledge of our cultures is restricted to its visible and material aspects. The tip of the iceberg has come to define what it means to be Indigenous. Many Indigenous people recognize that decolonization requires repairing that damage and restoring the relationships between our visible and material culture and the deep knowledge, value systems, philosophies, cosmologies and other invisible aspects of our cultures. I do not think you can do that without land-based knowledge. When you look at government policies, whether they're federal, provincial, or even, in some cases, our own governments, it's clear that governments have always known that land is the key to the identity of Indigenous peoples. In Canada, Section 24 of The Constitution Act of 1867 gave the federal government authority over "Indians and lands reserved for the Indians," and, in 1876, the Indian Act detailed the responsibilities the government would assume with respect to the management of these lands. Since that time, the government has repeatedly used the Indian Act to restrict Indigenous peoples' access to our traditional lands and force us to move into reserves, settlements, and cities. In the US, the 1934 Indian Reorganization Act was used for similar ends. In both countries, these Acts have enabled the settler populations to occupy and exploit lands that they see as rich in extractable resources.

I do not know if decolonization is possible and it feels like the term has become a catchphrase. I see decolonization stickers on people's computers and there's an irony in that—a sign that our movement has been branded. I hear people talking now about resurgence (Coburn, 2015) and I understand that term to mean something related to but not necessarily the same as decolonizing. It refers to the ways in which we're bringing to the surface and making room for the deep knowledge that we already have in us. I like that.

Land-Based Education

Laing: Could you talk a little bit about your work developing the land-based education master's program at the University of Saskatchewan?

Wilson: The program came about because elders and others in the community saw the need for real change in what was going on in education. We have had our own education systems and our own ways of teaching and learning that we developed and used over tens of thousands of years. It was only a few hundred years ago that non-Indigenous people arrived in our territories, bringing and ultimately imposing their own ways of teaching and learning on Indigenous people. In the time that has passed since then, the primary purpose of non-Indigenous education systems (as evidenced by the residential school system in particular) has been to forcibly assimilate Indigenous peoples. Over the last half century, however, Indigenous people have demanded and gained more control and autonomy with respect to formal education. This has included, for example, the development of Indian Teacher Education Programs at the University of Saskatchewan (where I work) and other post-secondary institutions. Programs such as these and other initiatives have helped to produce more Indigenous teachers. While post-secondary participation and completion, and other educational outcomes are improving for Indigenous people, they still lag well behind those of non-Indigenous people. We also know that Indigenous-controlled or staffed education systems need to do more than simply replicate the mainstream educational system. It makes no sense to continue doing what has already proven not to work for our people. As Verna Kirkness, who has provided invaluable leadership throughout the fight for Indigenous control of Indigenous education, has observed, unless an Indigenous person "learns about the forces and the history of [their] people, the values, the customs, the language, [they] will never really know [themselves] or [their] potential as a human being" (Pidgeon, Muñoz, Kirkness, & Archibald, 2013, p. 28).

Verna's reminder of our history, values, and customs ties to another reason the land-based master's program was developed. Indigenous communities, lands, and waters are currently facing multiple environmental threats. We are experiencing the impacts of climate change, increased industrialization, hydro development, tar sands extraction activities, development of nuclear energy and contaminant storage, corporatization of land-based practices, hydro development, and the extraction of multiple other resources. The impacts of these activities industries are compounded because they are occurring simultaneously, and because they drive and direct government and corporate policy and investments (and non-investments) in our communities and people. It is critical that we to protect our lands and waters. To do this, all of us, including our teachers, need to understand why they are valuable and how they are threatened. That is how the master's degree program in land-based education came about. Our communities said we need people that understand the land, and the pedagogy of land. How do you teach about land-based education? How do you teach about the land? Many communities have culture camps and people who participate in them can learn traditional skills such as how to filet fish, gather medicines, or tan a hide. What we heard from the community, however, is that there is a need for more than practical skills. We need to foster in our students a deep intellectual understanding of the importance of and our relationships with the land and waters, and the best way to do that is to use land-based pedagogies, where we learn from our experiences on the land. That's what we're trying to offer. They are our future educators.

The land-based program also enables students to remain in their own communities for most of the two or three years it might take them to complete their master's degree. We use a cohort model in which a group of students go through together and can offer each other support. The majority of the classes are structured as intensive field schools that run for a two-week period. The students complete two or three land-based courses in each of the field schools, and in between the land-based components, complete an additional three online courses for a total of 10 courses. The students are typically teachers or have other professional positions in the education system and, as they proceed through the master's program, they can draw on or integrate what they've learned into their own professional practice. Remaining in their home communities also makes it easier for students to access ongoing support from their families and communities.

We are now (again at the request of community members) designing a land-based Ph.D. program for educators. All Indigenous nations have their own strong and distinct intellectual traditions, full of philosophers, engineers, mathematicians, and other big thinkers and doers who searched out the answers and solutions to the challenges their people faced. Living with and on the land requires a kind of intellectual rigor. We didn't just accidentally discover how to make an arrow. We designed it. The Cree people had a mathematical system and calendar based on the number four. Surviving in this harsh landscape and through our long winters took a lot of forethought, planning, and calculation. We constructed a way of life that had minimal negative impact on the environment, and not only sustained us but enabled us to happily thrive as individuals and communities.

Laing: Could you speak about the relationship that you see between land-based pedagogies and the field of Indigenous studies?

Wilson: The field of Indigenous studies has changed for the better in recent years, and that change has been welcomed because in the past the framework of many Indigenous studies or Native studies programs has been a friendly version of the Western gaze ("Hey—let's just see what the natives were doing!"), using historical accounts and occasional interviews. I admit that's an obvious oversimplification—and one that signals my level of disappointment in what some academics have thought worth studying about our peoples. In the past decade, however, the frameworks of most Indigenous studies programs have shifted towards recognizing and validating Indigenous knowledge, knowledge systems, languages, self-determination, and sovereignty. This is a really important shift and, because these areas of interest are all inseparable from our relationships with the land and waters, I would predict that over the next few years an increasing number of Indigenous studies programs will embrace land-based approaches to pedagogy.

Queerness, Indigeneity, and Two-Spirit Research

Laing: Do you see a relationship between the fields of Indigenous studies and queer studies?

Wilson: I've already described some of the inherent problems of the Western model that used to prevail in Indigenous studies. The early departments also had problematic hierarchies in relationship to race and gender. White males were overrepresented in positions such as department chair or full professor, and if a department hired an Indigenous person, it was typically for a lecturer position. That has changed (perhaps out of necessity) but I think there's still work to be done. Indigenous studies needs to queer itself up. By queering, I mean opening up discussion of and challenging the ways in which some within the field of Indigenous studies have reinforced and entrenched binaries and hierarchies related to gender and sexuality. For example, I'm familiar with scholarship that reinforces gender binaries and gender roles, constructing histories that allocate specific tasks to women and reserve other tasks for men. It's as though, intentionally or not, these scholars have just skipped over or avoided validating Indigenous cosmologies that recognize and accept gender fluidity, gender and sexual diversity, and queerness, the kind of understandings that are reflected in the legends or stories of my nation. Now we are starting to see some of our worldviews having more influence and presenting an important challenge to essentialism. We still have a long way to go, though. A significant proportion of my scholarship and activism has focused on two-spirit people. When I started this work, white men, often gay-identified, had authored the vast majority of the literature on the topic. We need to be mindful of the colonial relationship between the people who position themselves as the authors of our stories and ourselves as their (frequently fetishized) subjects. Are they actually writing about us or are they writing about themselves? Do they see themselves as anthropologists? Historians? Or our allies? If they actually are our allies, they need to step back and let us tell our own stories.

Laing: Your work on two-spirit identity is foundational in the field of Indigenous studies, and to the emerging and consistently growing body of Indigenous scholars, including two-spirit and queer-identified Indigenous scholars, who are working in this vein of two-spirit critique. Could you speak a little bit about how this type of research and scholarship has grown?

Wilson: In the early '80s, when in my twenties, I began hanging out in the gay community in Winnipeg. Within about five years, I lost more than 30 friends to AIDS and AIDS-related illnesses, many of whom were First Nations gay-identified men. That experience (as with the elevated suicide rate within the population of Indigenous LGBQT2S young people) really brought home that the outcomes and ongoing impacts of colonization are especially dangerous and too often deadly for Indigenous bodies that challenge Western constructs of gender and sexuality. The impacts of HIV/AIDS on our community was one reason that queer-identified Indigenous people started organizing in the '90s. The term two-spirit came about at that time—out of necessity. We began to question all kinds of institutions, including the white male anthropologists who were talking, theorizing, and writing about our lives. In the literature they produced, we saw that, rather than *our* stories or *our* ideas, they were writing their conclusions about us, based on what they were interested in rather than what mattered to *us*. Their body of work romanticized Indigenous people and Indigenous queerness in our communities, and, from my perspective, did a lot of damage.

The term two-spirit originally referred specifically to people who were LGBTQIA+ and First Nations. The meaning has shifted since then, particularly around gender. My article "How We Find Ourselves: Identity Development and Two-Spirit People" was published in 1996, but it was written a few years earlier when I was an undergrad. Since that time, my thinking has changed around the idea of a masculine and feminine continuum, and now I'm not sure if it even exists or what it means. Two-spirit identity ought to question that continuum but more and more people are now teaching that people have two spirits, a male spirit and a female spirit. I'm not sure where that came from. I've never heard an elder say that or anyone communicate that idea in our Cree language. The idea that we all have a male and a female spirit seems like one more way in which Indigenous people are romanticized. It also feels somewhat homophobic to me, as though, as a two-spirit woman, that I have a "male" part, and it's only that male part that allows me to be with another woman. Binarizing the gender identity of two-spirit people draws us into the ways in which Indigenous women's bodies are regulated. For example, some of the members of our community who lead or organize traditional ceremonies require women to wear skirts if they want to take part in ceremony. People will make an exception to this rule for a two-spirit person who is cisgendered female, with the explanation that, "Oh, well, she is two-spirited and that means she is part male, so she does not have to wear skirt." That is problematic because it essentializes us and, at the same time, sidesteps the real issue, which is that women who do not wear a skirt would be denied access to ceremony.

Currently, Sarah Hunt, Leanne Simpson, and others are really opening up the conversation about what it means to be two-spirit and what it means to be queer.

The term two-spirit was first used in a small circle of people in the prairies. Twenty-some years later, you can now find it in documents like the University of Saskatchewan's anti-discrimination policy and included as an identity in Red River College's demographic section of their admissions application. While there have been lots of (small) positive changes, there's clearly much more work to be done, because the suicide rate in the two-spirit and Indigenous LGBTQIA+ population is not decreasing. In fact, I would say there is hesitancy in some communities to talk about two-spirit or LGBTQIA+ identity. I've already pointed to signs of a shift toward fundamentalism in our communities. This includes our traditional spiritual systems, some of which have become more conservative, taking on very gendered and very binary approaches to spirituality that I never saw when I was a child. Back then, no one was demanding that women wear skirts for ceremonies. In my experience, Indigenous people didn't regulate bodies that way. Now there are issues around women's bodies that never existed before and there are very few safe spaces for two-spirit people in either the mainstream or our own communities or even on social media.

Laing: How can—or perhaps how should—the fields of education and Indigenous studies respond to these realities?

Wilson: The fields of education and Indigenous studies have a responsibility to respond. They *must* respond. If you work in these fields, your job is to challenge and invert hegemony. One way to do that is by providing voice to those who are being marginalized and those who are impacted the most by the whiplash that is happening. Scholars have a responsibility not just to open up the conversations and add things to their syllabi but also to really examine the way that their own practices and the practices of their departments or colleges are structured. Look long and hard at the power dynamics and the power structures and try to undo or unravel some of that.

With respect to the risk of suicide for two-spirit and Indigenous LGBTQIA+ people, those of us working in the field of education have to do something about it. There have been innumerable presentations and lectures on suicide and almost no one mentions the high suicide rates in the queer Indigenous community. Even when they have been told the statistics, they are still afraid to talk about it. There are all these programs that are supposed to prevent or raise awareness around suicide, and almost none of them ever touch on two-spirit people. When we do appear, we are typically presented in this deeply romanticized way—that traditionally two-spirit people were shamans and deeply honored members of their communities. Tell that to the people of Northern Manitoba, where, in 2016, a number of lesbian self-identified youth committed suicide. Their deaths occurred in the context of a suicide epidemic that also claimed the lives of other youth, a crisis that led the First Nation's leadership to declare a state of emergency. The declaration generated promises of support from governments, gained international attention (NoiseCat, 2016), and even resulted in a junior hockey team flying into a northern community to spend a day visiting, talking, and playing hockey with youth. In spite of this flurry of activity and attention, it seemed that no one could speak the word lesbian. Who does that serve? It might serve gendered and heteronormative ideas about what it means to be a kid but it does not serve the kids who need to know that, regardless of their sexual or gender identity, they are valued members of their community.

Scholars and educators have a big role to play. We need to incorporate knowledge mobilization and knowledge translation activities into our work that ensure that our research and our pedagogical practices are accessible and shared with communities. That often happens naturally because most Indigenous scholars have pretty strong connections to their home communities. Unfortunately, much of the work we do to ensure that our work is useful to our communities doesn't fit into the structure or process of the system used to determine who gets tenure and who is promoted within university systems. As academics, we need to work together to push universities to recognize and validate oral knowledge transmission and the importance of relationality and relational accountability in our research activities. I would much rather do an interview, or an oral presentation, than write a paper because they are more accessible, engaging, and interactive formats than words on a page, and they build relational accountability into the knowledge exchange that's taking place between myself and whomever else might be in the room.

I would like to challenge students and scholars to go back to their own languages, histories, and traditions and seek out the stories that aren't usually shared regarding the links between queerness and cosmology, as well as find the ways to tell them that do not reinforce heteropatriarchy. Take, for example, the Weesageychak trickster stories that we grew up with and that remain very popular. When people translate them into the English language, Weesageychak suddenly becomes a male in a little buckskin outfit. Even when these stories are written in Cree, artists' renderings of Weesageychak again portray the character as male. As a result, in most people's minds, Weesageychak is male. But Weesageychak is not male or female. Weesageychak is energy. We need to bring our artists together with those who have this kind knowledge so that our culture can actually be represented. We do not need another statue of Louis Riel or Chief So-And-So. That reinforces heteronormativity and gender supremacy and is another way in which our women have been disappeared. We can find other ways to recognize our cosmology and share the fact that, as a people, we do have deep intellectual traditions that we have developed and sustained for 100,000 years or more, and, as scholars, we come from and continue that tradition. When we step up as public intellectuals, we are demonstrating relational accountability in our lives as academics and should be grateful that we are able to do so.

Laing: I am thinking about all of your observations on the ways that two-spirit has become a meme. That one singular narrative about two-spirit people that gets reproduced, which centers the one mythical, romanticized role that two-spirit people were held as highly revered shamans and healers is so visible. I see that a lot. It gets reproduced so much, and it does not serve us. It is just another romanticization of Indigenous people.

Wilson: Yes, it is like being turned into a mascot. Some people will say, "Well, being a mascot is an honor"—well, no, it's not. We just want to be considered as human. And of course, there are two-spirited or queer people who actually are healers or medicine people but there are also two-spirit people who are not that, who do not want to be that, or for whom that is not part of their life and the meme can easily make those people feel like they must *become* healers or medicine people to be useful. I have also read many places and heard friends (most of them gay men) say that, traditionally, two-spirit people took care of the children. Usually mothers take care of children. There may be instances in which gay men have taken care of children, but I am not aware that this was a widespread practice or a role allocated to gay men. Claiming this as a traditional role for gay men feels like another intrusion of Western heteropatriarchy into our traditional cultures, as men find a sense of self-worth by erasing the contributions of women. Sexism and misogyny are present in and have damaged the two-spirit community. The romanticizing memes about two-spirit people give two-spirit men (and, to a lesser extent, trans women) a kind of power—whether they want it or not. A two-spirit male can be both a man and a superwoman. But two-spirit cisgendered women are sometimes pushed to the side by "traditional" regulations of their bodies, such as the skirt rule described above or menstruation taboos that are used to deny women access to ceremonies or ceremonial items. Two-spirit men, however, seem to have unlimited access. This has left some two-spirit women questioning what that identity means. These issues have been discussed at the annual gatherings of two-spirit people from throughout North America and have also contributed to the decision made by two-spirit women in Saskatchewan and Manitoba to organize their own gatherings. All of this of course would not be an issue if we really did validate and honor a continuum of gender identities.

Laing: The other thing with regard to this singular narrative about two-spirit is that it obscures what you were speaking to just now, the importance of learning our stories and going back to our languages and the teachings of our own nations around gender and sexuality.

Wilson: Yes. People need to remember that our elders, regardless of whether they attended residential schools (and most did), have still been impacted by the education system of that time. Everyone is influenced by mainstream media, education, and other institutions. There is no way around it. At schools, Indigenous children were taught new stories that legitimized the power of the colonial state, the queen, the church, settler economics, racial hierarchies, gender supremacy, and heteronormativity. These stories were overprinted on what they already knew and would continue to learn later from their own families, communities, lands, and waters. On the other hand, our generation has had the luxury of being trained to think critically about what they were taught in the schools and about our cultural teachings about gender and sexual diversity. When we talk to our elders, it can take a while to tease out the concepts of gender and sexual diversity that may exist in their languages and cultures. The presentation on our Cree cosmology and Weesageychak, which was referred to earlier, took over 20 years to piece together (Wilson, 2016). It was not just a single teaching someone gave to me. It was a process of listening to and learning from hundreds of people in my community and beyond, around language to figure out the meaning of the term—a long process of learning from others, developing an understanding, and then going back to them and asking, "Is this what it means?" It wasn't time to share the understanding until the teachers who had shared their knowledge with me gave permission. You do not just go to an elder, ask about sexuality, and they give you the exact answer you were looking for, which you then take out to the world. You have to do hard work to figure this stuff out, to understand what this means in our language. We need to think about how the context of our lands and waters informs the meaning. How does that play out? In my conversations I've learned that traditionally we did not have a concept of "Mother Earth." With that knowledge, I had to learn more about when and why that concept appeared. What is evident is that it is about the relationships and relationality between us and the land and waters. We come from the earth and we rely on the earth to sustain us. When we refer to Mother Earth, we are saying that we have a deep and loving relationship with these lands and waters that we depend upon. Similarly, in our language, the moon is not referred to as "Grandmother Moon." It is just the moon. When we say Grandmother Moon, we are understanding and acknowledging that the moon impacts bodies of water, that we, as humans, are constituted of water, so, of course, the moon impacts us. In Indigenous cultures, the moon might be a brother, a father, or grandmother. We are all right, because the terms we use are a way to acknowledge the relationship we have with the moon. In my family, I was taught that our language does not gender people, but of course we have descriptive terms for "man" and "woman." The existence of those words does not mean that we only acknowledge two genders in general. Rather, they are terms that mark specific gender positions on a continuum.

It takes a lot of work (and much of it is hard work) to learn about our languages and cultures and to do so in a respectful way, especially when the people with the most knowledge in these areas are elders who are first language speakers but have become entrenched in and committed to heteropatriarchy and other wayward teachings from the residential school system and other Western influences. It is challenging for both them and for me because even though they may know their language and have a sophisticated understanding of it, they may not have considered the questions we are asking today around queerness, for example. I have found that most are supportive and encouraging and even excited to contribute to new understandings based on the old knowledge. And when we come to an answer, they then might say, "Oh, yeah, that totally makes sense. I never thought of it that way, but yeah, that's right." You have to keep at it. That is the lesson that I have learned for myself. Just keep at it.

Note

1 St. Denis offers a discussion of how deep knowledge is silenced through multiculturalism discourse.

References

Coburn, E. (Ed.). (2015). *More will sing their way to freedom: Indigenous resistance and resurgence.* Black Point, NS: Fernwood Press.

The Constitution Act, 1867 (UK), 30 & 31 Victoria, c 3.

Faludi, S. (1991). *Backlash: The undeclared war against American women.* New York, NY: Crown Publishing.

The Indian Act, 1867 (Canada).

Indian Reorganization Act, P.L. 73–383, 48 Stat. 984, June 18, 1934 (Washington, DC): Arnold & Porter.

NoiseCat, J. B. (2016, April 12). Canadian first nation suicide epidemic generations in the making. *The Guardian.* Retrieved from www.theguardian.com/commentisfree/2016/apr/12/canadian-first-nation-suicide-epidemic-attawapiskat-indigenous-people

Pidgeon, M., Muñoz, M., Kirkness, V., & Archibald, J-A. (2013). Indian control of Indian education: Reflections and envisioning the next 40 Years. *Canadian Journal of Native Education, 36*(1), 5–35.

St. Denis, V. (2011). Silencing aboriginal curricular content and perspectives through multiculturalism: "There are other children here". *Review of Education, Pedagogy & Cultural Studies, 33*(4), 306–317.

Wilson, A. (1996). How we find ourselves: Identity development and two spirit people. *Harvard Educational Review, 66*(2), 303–318. Doi:https://doi.org/10.17763/haer.66.2.n551658577h927h4

Wilson, A. (2016, December). *Coming in to indigenous sovereignty: Relationality and resurgence.* Presented at the University of Winnipeg Weweni Indigenous Scholars Speaker Series, Winnipeg, MB. Retrieved from http://www.youtube.com/watch?v=XkQo_yr4A_w

9

COLONIAL CONVENTIONS

Institutionalized Research Relationships and Decolonizing Research Ethics

Madeline Whetung (Nishnaabeg) and Sarah Wakefield

Introduction

What makes research ethical? We thought a lot about this question while we navigated the University of Toronto's institutional research ethics process. According to government policy—specifically, the *Tri-Council Policy Statement on Research Ethics: Ethical Conduct for Research Involving Humans (Version 2)*, often known as the *TCPS2*—universities in Canada must evaluate and approve all research that takes place there to ensure it is ethical. The *TCPS2* is required reading for all Canadian researchers planning to talk with people as part of their research, and it is used to guide the decisions of university research ethics boards (REBs). Chapter 9 of the *TCPS2* focuses specifically on "Research Involving the First Nations, Inuit and Métis Peoples of Canada" (*TPCS2*, 2015).

Time and time again, Indigenous scholars have spoken out against the colonizing impact of research (e.g., Deloria, 1969; Pualani-Louis, 2007; Tuhiwai Smith, 1999), and Indigenous communities have fought against their exploitation through research. The institutional research ethics process, and the development of ethics policies specific to Indigenous people (as in Chapter 9 of the *TCPS2*), was intended as a corrective response answering the concerns of Indigenous people.

However, in spite of these specialized policies, people engaged in Indigenous research are continuing to ask how "ethical" the research ethics process truly is. Heather Castledon and Martha Stiegman (2015) state that their attempts to make their research ethical have mostly come about "despite, not because of, the *TCPS2*"; they say that it is too bureaucratic and maintains the university's power over research (2015, p. 2). Likewise, Scott Lauria Morgenson has pointed out that "colonial principles set the legal standard for determining the nature or evidence of "harm" in research with Indigenous people" (2012, p. 807).

We, an Indigenous graduate student (Madeline) and a non-Indigenous professor (Sarah), had many conversations about how our experiences have been shaped by the understandings of research ethics in our university and the *TCPS2*. We attempted to capture these experiences—and discuss how we could build on them to create a *better* process—in a conversation between the two of us, which we recorded and transcribed. We discuss how the existing research ethics process is experienced by researchers, and then consider possibilities for a more genuinely ethical research process that would focus on positionality and relationship to place and people, as well as foster long-term accountability to embedded knowledge.

The original version of our conversation was a dialogue in which we looked for consensus—what Ursula K. LeGuin (1989) calls the "mother tongue," in contrast to the authoritative speech of the "father tongue."[1] However, we decided to take out the "ums," "ahs," and "what do you thinks?" and remove much of the back-and-forth tentativeness and circularity of our original conversation. The chapter still reads as a dialogue, but one in which ideas are presented authoritatively. We made this choice in order to make the text more legible (and substantive) to the academic reader, but this is not a decision without consequences, something we come back to at the end of the chapter.

In this written version, we have also gathered others around us who have considered research ethics by citing their work, to honor their ideas and acknowledge that this conversation is going on in many places. Many of the ideas we discussed in our conversation are not new, and we have worked to acknowledge in this written format those who have influenced our thinking, while still keeping the dialogue as true to its organic process as possible. By maintaining the dialogic format, we seek to model an ethical process of relational engagement, through which we first offer up our own positions and perspectives; consider our relationships to research, place, community, and the university itself; and then approach the issue of long-term accountability to knowledge.

Our Stories as Our Starting Point

Madeline: I write/speak as a Michi Saagiig Anishinaabekwe of mixed descent. I grew up and continue to make my life in Michi Saagiig territory. I am a recent graduate of an MA in geography, through which I conducted elder-guided, land-based research.[2] My frustrations with the ethics process while completing my MA led to many conversations with my supervisor (Sarah) through which we formed this critique. I remember feeling unsure about my place as a person in the ethics review process; for me it was anxiety inducing. As Indigenous student-scholar, when reading the *TCPS2*, it became clear to me that the protocol on research with Aboriginal[3] peoples is presented as though there are not Indigenous people conducting research.[4] One is either a researcher, or a community member, never both. Of course, this is simply not true; Indigenous scholars have been conducting research within the university for some time now. For those of us who are Indigenous and scholar, we are, as Sarah Hunt has indicated, faced with trying to speak up as both, "though it feels impossible to be heard as both at the same time" (2014, p. 21).

My experience reading the ethics protocol made me feel as though it was impossible to embody both at once: I was either colonizing researcher or Indigenous community member: the subject of research. More than this, the university operates from a knowledge-supremacy position where it dis-embeds knowledge that is rooted outside of the academy to bring it into the academy by validating some aspects of it as "research." Ultimately by doing research we are producing something for the academy and so it has to be legible to people who may have no grounding in the kind of information that you are seeking and talking about. And so it winds up being this parallel process—for me it felt like writing a thesis that is just for this place and then doing work that was actually the Indigenous geography itself. That felt like two separate things. These divisions make it feel as though it is difficult to maintain our ethical responsibilities throughout an entire project because it occurs in so many different pieces and it results in a dislocation from self, a reinforcing of colonial dispossession. This made me want to do away with the ethics review process altogether, and it was Sarah's cautions about the importance of ethics review that fueled the discussion here and led us to consider how the ethics review protocol could be reshaped to be less bifurcating for Indigenous students/scholars, as well as less stigmatizing of Indigenous communities.

Sarah: I write/speak as a settler woman (of English/mixed European origin) who was born and continues to live in the territory of the Haudensaunee and Anishnaabeg peoples, in the place I call Hamilton, Ontario, Canada. I work at the University of Toronto in the Department of Geography and Planning. For several years I served as my department's representative on the University's Social Sciences, Humanities, and Education Research Ethics Board (SSHE REB), and then for several more years as the chair of the SSHE REB. During my time on the Board, and particularly my time as chair, I had many occasions to reflect on the strengths and weaknesses of the way research ethics have been institutionalized on campus, and had to work through ethics issues both conceptually and in terms of the "nitty-gritty" of particular projects and procedures.

While on the REB, I saw a lot of poorly conceived and in some cases obviously exploitative "research," and saw the REB encourage researchers to address gaps in their thinking. As just one example, I once had a conversation with a researcher who wanted to investigate an Indigenous economic development project in an urban setting to "see if it was working," but without engaging meaningfully with the community of urban Indigenous people involved. I told the researcher that they should seek approval from the community and have a commitment to making the research meaningful for Indigenous people, and that the REB would expect to see evidence of those things. The researcher was not happy with my answer, saying essentially, "Why is this so complicated? Why is this such a special area? Can't I be trusted to do ethical research?" To me, the answer is that there is a history of colonial relations and extractive, exploitative research with Indigenous people, and this is something that continues to express itself in and through research. This story, in turn, highlights the need for some kind of ethics review that goes beyond the discretion of individual researchers.

However, when Madeline and I started talking about ethics, it forced me to think more carefully about how the research ethics process re-embeds colonial understandings of relationship, respect, and responsibility. To me, the discussions we have had (and which we try to capture here) begin to point the way toward research ethics processes that would be more meaningful.

Beginning the Conversation: The Institutional(ized) Research Ethics Process

Madeline: Sarah's story says a lot about the place-based relations that live in my home territory now. We live in a world where many people don't have the basic information they need to engage ethically with the communities whose land they are living on. Our territories are occupied and in many ways foreign laws have been asserted over Indigenous laws, ethics, and ways of engaging (Simpson, 2011, p. 12; Borrows, 2002, p. 4).[5] The *TCPS2* is a policy that, through its bureaucratic process, also filters relationships between researchers and communities through a Western lens. Through the policy it is difficult to conceptualize ethical engagement outside of the filling out of forms, and the institution's overriding approval.

Difficulties with this process apply not only to Indigenous researchers, but non-Indigenous researchers as well (Castledon & Stiegman, 2015). Due to policy, the boxes are checked as either researcher or researched before the relationship can be engaged in place. The relationship is predetermined based on the ethics review form. Rather than a transgression of the categories of powerful and powerless, privileged and vulnerable, this predetermination results in the maintenance of them. It felt to me as though I was *unable* to engage ethically, because I was unable to embody my multiple positions at once. Indigenous researchers often embody multiple worlds and positions (Fermentez, 2013) and this truth could more effectively be represented in the *TCPS2*.

As it is, I think that the policy itself upholds the idea that settler people *do* research and Indigenous people *are* researched. I think that's a problem. There has to be something else. How do we both acknowledge the colonial history of research with Indigenous people *and* acknowledge the present reality that there are Indigenous people working within the university doing this research that does belong to communities and does have a different set of ethical obligations than complete outsiders would have?

Sarah: I would be the first person to admit that ethical research is not synony- mous with what the Research Ethics Board approves and vice versa, in the same way that what a law says is not the same as justice. In some ways the systems are analogous, in a sense that both are attempts to codify; they are all about having it written down and following the rules, and then if you follow the rules the result is going to be good. But that is not what happens! If you have someone who just jumps through the hoops, the ethics review process as it is now doesn't help.

Reading through the *TCPS2* again after our first conversation did bring home to me how the language of the statement positions the university looking outward to these other places and these other communities, which are very clearly seen as separate. The policy does mention that Indigenous researchers exist, stating that "First Nations, Inuit and Métis scholars attached to academic institutions as fac- ulty members, students or research associates are increasingly engaged in research involving their own communities" and that their "insider relationships and cultural competencies provide unique opportunities to extend the boundaries of knowl- edge" (TCPS2, Ch. 9). However, the whole document is written in a way that doesn't feel connected to Indigenous (or anyone's) lives. It is grounded in—and normalizes—the university as the arbiter of what is ethical in creating knowledge.

This also begs the question of how much of the impetus to create an ethics protocol, to write it out, is just an extension of this need of Western colonial culture to codify and write *everything* out, and to make sure that this record exists outside of the context in which it's being understood? If we look at the history of "research" and the exploitation of people in and through research, it is a story about power, but it is also a story about disembeddedness: it's about people being in a situation where they go and study others, and once they are in that situation, they do things that they would never do if they had responsibilities to an intimate, immediate community. And that impetus to acquire knowledge—I mean, in some ways it is the exact same impetus for colonizing, which is to just look outward and grab a bunch of stuff from other places and try to make it legible to yourself, without necessarily having to be part of it.

Place, Time, Knowledge: Contextualizing Research Ethics

Madeline: Thinking of the university as extractive ties into how we can consider place in ethics processes. Canada and its universities are all built on

Indigenous land. Everyone who lives on Indigenous land has obligations and ethical responsibilities to that land that are related to each
person's particular way of coming to be in that place. The university
is quite literally built overtop of Indigenous places that already carry
knowledge. Considering place recognizes that knowledge comes from
somewhere and it is not necessarily generated within the built walls
of the academy. The university takes knowledge and transcribes it in a
particular way that allows it to be transported "somewhere else." There
is power in taking something and transcribing it, for the consumption
of other people. With that power comes great responsibility, but the
TCPS2 is not framed in terms of responsibility and accountability, it is
framed in terms of "benefits to community" and "minimizing harm."
If we insist on framing research relationships this way indefinitely, we
cannot shift the colonial power dynamic. What if instead of, "How
will you minimize harm?" we asked, "How will you be responsible
to this knowledge and this community with the next seven generations in mind?" Instead of considering the long-term consequences of
research, the *TCPS2* deals only in the present, and in the university as
a place.

Sarah: I don't think I have ever really thought about how colonial modes of
research take knowledge out of time and space. The research is out of
context, in the way that people say, "My quote was taken out of context." You are removing it from where it lives and from the conversation that it was embedded in at the time, so it is not living anymore.
It gives a different meaning to ethical responsibility when you think
about it like that. And then, what is your responsibility to that work
as time passes? The Western colonial way of thinking doesn't require
you to think about it. You are right that the ethics process is front-end
loaded: it gets us to talk about our ethical responsibilities in advance,
but then there's really no follow up. This is something that has been
critiqued in the research ethics literature, saying that there needs to be
more monitoring of what researchers actually do once they get REB
approval (e.g., Norton & Wilson, 2008). But I think what we are talking about goes even further by saying that the researcher's responsibility as to that knowledge doesn't end. I think that is alien to the way
that most Western academics would think about the work that they've
done. When I think about it now, my mind boggles a little bit: I think,
"Oh God, what have I done?" If I knew I had that responsibility, how
would that reshape the work that I do and the way I think about my
research relationships in an ongoing way?

Madeline: I think this idea about the "ongoingness" of knowledge through
relationship to place and people harkens back to really amazing
things about oral history. One important note is that it is of utmost

importance to prevent stories from becoming disembedded from their places and from their social relations (Peacock, 2013, p. 104). The stories we tell and the way we tell and the places in which they're told matter a lot. I think that's what's so difficult to ethically reconcile across apparent different attitudes towards knowledge: the powerful "center of knowledge" intends to universally dis-embed things. For many Indigenous scholars, one ethical obligation might be to prevent this from happening, to not let the academy dis-embed knowledge, to present only what is useful to us and possibly to refuse particular ways of engaging and presenting the knowledge (Simpson, 2014).

Position, Vulnerability, and Shifting the Axes of Power

Madeline: Under settler colonialism, Indigenous peoples are fighting a war on many different battlefields.[6] But you don't have to fight the war at all if you're a non-Indigenous researcher; you don't *have* to do anything. Many Indigenous researchers feel a deep responsibility. This isn't to say that we will all come to the same solution, or that our work is inherently ethical, but hopefully Indigenous researchers come to their research with a sense of this responsibility. And due to our positions, the hope is that we can activate our ethics with our communities in mind in spite of the university protocols that attempt to dislocate us from these relations, and the fact that we are using the academy as a tool.[7]

I wonder if there is a way we can feel like ethical participants, even if we are reluctant participants. At the very least, we need to find a way to prevent protocols from upholding and retrenching the displacement of Indigenous lands and disembodiment of Indigenous peoples. I want to be able to work through the university and remain grounded in Anishinaabe worldviews and culture, especially because all this research takes place in Anishinaabe territory.

When I wrote my ethics application, I attempted to situate my research ethically by foregrounding my own relationship to place and community. I wrote about shifting the center of power. I worked with an elder who has a lot of knowledge about my territory and that's the center of power for me. Obviously you can't just decide that you have power, that's not really how it works in colonized territory, but at the same time in saying, "I'm actually going to do research guided by what my community teachers have shown me is ethical," there is a certain amount of power. It doesn't change what happens with the knowledge and information after, but it shifts the relational process. It centers how one comes to land and community relations and locates the knowledge in its place.

Sarah: I struggle to think of how to get there, though, especially without turning those same tools on power—to fight fire with fire. To jump through these hoops of the academy, but in order to have something that has the power of the academy behind it.

Also, working with non-Indigenous communities, I found it hard to find the forum or venue for discussing those kinds of questions, and even when you do, well, it is hard for a community, in the face of a researcher coming in and saying "We'd like to do this project," to say, "Wait a second. What are you saying?" Usually the response is, "Oh well, you're the expert. I guess you know what you're talking about." So it takes a certain level of empowerment to be able to push back against that. It's hard to say no in the face of power.

Madeline: About this idea of being empowered—there seems to be this attachment of vulnerability to Indigenous people within the research protocol, which says, "Oh, that's such a vulnerable population," in the sense of, "You're so vulnerable to all of my power, you poor Indigenous person." This puts us back in our positions and makes it feel really unchangeable.

Sarah: If you look at our university's research ethics forms and the protocols, there is a question about vulnerable populations, and in my experience of being on the research ethics board, many people interpreted that as if there were categories of people that were inherently vulnerable. Part of my job was to explain, "Well, no, it's not a state of existence, it's a position in relation to the particulars of this research." I think that speaks back to this idea of connection, of relationship. I've been at tables where I've been introduced as a researcher, and if you are just starting a conversation, there is a power dynamic there. You don't know any of these people, they don't know you, but they know that you have this title of university researcher which carries some weight in some segments of society. But if this was a community that I was meaningfully embedded in, where everybody knew me and I knew them and they knew things about my personal life or my personality or whatever, that conversation would be very different. It wouldn't necessarily mean that all those power dynamics would be erased— researchers need to be really careful about how they carry that new identity or that additional responsibility of doing research—but at the same time, people would at least be able to relate to me in a very different way.

Moving Forward: Place, Position, Relationship

Sarah: In order to take the issue of accountability seriously, particularly in relation to Indigenous people, I think institutions need to work harder to de-center the university as the ultimate arbiter of research. The *TCPS2*

(2015) states, "Research ethics review by community REBs or other responsible bodies at the research site will not be a substitute for research ethics review by institutional REBs," but institutions could still develop stronger working relationships with community REBs and could stream-line the institutional process in recognition of the community review. Most universities have a streamlined process for approving research ethics protocols that has been approved at other universities, and sometimes for hospitals as well, so I don't necessarily see that it couldn't be done. Ulti-mately, the *TPCS2* could be changed to give more power and legitimacy to community review.

I can foresee some difficulties. I think those opposed to this move would suggest that community boards are insufficiently rigorous. More importantly, it is a par-ticular kind of community—usually a local government or a more institutional-ized community organization—that has these structures in place. They require at least partial internalizing of dominant models of research ethics review: Is that something we want to promote?

Madeline: I do think we should have more ethics training for people. Not just training in how to fill out forms or on the institutional process, but how to actually *do* ethical engagement.

Sarah: There is training available, but it generally isn't mandatory. There is an online tutorial for the *TPCS2*, but it's easy to do the test without really absorbing the principles. The training right now is often just fre-quently asked questions in relation to the forms: "You have questions about the form, let me tell you how to fill it out." The trainers try to make it more than that, but that's what people are fixated on—not surprisingly, because that's what they actually have to do! So they say, "Tell me how to fill out my stupid form so I don't get in trouble," as opposed to asking, "What are my ethical obligations in this context and how can I meet them?" But if you discuss questions as a group, the positionality of the individuals comes out and can be recognized and taken into consideration in that conversation. There is also more recognition that what can be done by one person maybe isn't what can be done by another person. We all have an obligation to deal with situations ethically, we just can't all deal with them in the same way.

Madeline: I feel there are different pedagogical models that could help people understand how ethics *work*, not just their ethical obligations within the legal bounds of the university. I cannot describe how many of my peers have been completely confused about what ethical engage-ment really means. For me, ethics are ultimately something that we *do*; they actually live in how we conduct ourselves in our relationships and cannot be determined by what is written on a form. If people are struggling with what this looks like, or what it means for their research, they may need specific training. Not training on how to fill out a form, but teachings on how to engage ethically. What about scenario-based training? What if people were required to talk through how they will ethically engage? It's totally different to be put in a position where you have to explain your perspective to a room full of people, versus just writing something down in your ethics protocol. I think there are ways to enact this that could make people consider their ethical responsibilities differently.

That's part of the answer to the question of how to engage in ethical research too—we all have ethical obligations, but we can't all deal with them in the same way, given our different positions. When you have the opportunity to bring that position into the forefront, it really changes how you think about research and the ethics process, because you're allowed to be a person, to say, "I am an agent in this and therefore I have personal connection and a role to play in context." It would have been much easier for me to answer questions like that, questions like, "What is your position in relation to this community, and how is that going to impact the way you engage ethically?" That would've been a much easier question for me to answer than, "Is this a vulnerable population and how are you going to mitigate that vulnerability?" It's not about being Indigenous or non-Indigenous, it's about how you are able to approach things as a community member. And I would have to explain myself: "Who am I and how am I going to conduct myself?"

The notion that good relations emanate out of your own ability to locate your position, the place that you come from, and the people you belong to, is embedded in Anishinaabe ethics. Leanne Simpson (2015) described this perfectly when she spoke on Musqueam, Tsleil-Watuth, and Squamish territory as part of the EMMA talks series. She noted that, by locating herself, she indicates that she's not going to steal their land and that she will do her best to do no harm while in their territories. To me, this is important because, by introducing herself as belonging somewhere else, she automatically brings into the space that she is an outsider there and begins a protocol that has a long history of enabling ethical relations.

Sarah: That's interesting because I never really thought about how *not* self-focused, *not* relational, the ethics forms are. When you fill out the form, you should be thinking all those things through, but then you write them down in a way that completely separates the protocol from your experience. This is all part and parcel of that same colonial knowledge model in a way: "Talk about yourself in the third person."

Madeline: This really explains the sense of displacement that is reinforced through the ethics protocol. It is difficult to see ourselves reflected in the process. And I know it's not just me as an Indigenous person who feels it; ethics protocols cause everyone a ton of anxiety. But they also allow people to pretend that they are not actors in the scenario, right? So going right back to your anecdote at the beginning, having a process where you can talk it through would help people to understand their reasons for engaging or not engaging in certain research: it's their own position in the world and their (lack of) engagement with the other position that they're actually trying to consider.

Conclusion

In this conversation we attempted to work through some of the obstacles to accountability we recognized in the *Tri-Council Policy Statement* that governs research ethics within Canadian post-secondary institutions. Through dialogue, we uncovered the root of our concerns, which lie in the lack of relationality in the current ethics protocol. Though the ethics protocol espouses the value of cultivating relationships, it offers little in the way of *how* to do so and is instead focused on the institutional process of justifying the ethics of the research prior to undertaking it. Dialogically, we have attempted to work through some potential solutions to the colonial conventions of institutional research ethics.

There are both limitations and benefits to the method we have employed to explore decolonizing institutional research ethics. We recognize that this method has limited our engagement in broader academic literature on ethics, which means that the discussion may not offer much of a response to pre-existing critiques. Yet, focusing on the protocol itself and our own experiences with it also allowed us to consider together the practicalities of trying to decolonize research ethics, without abstracting the process. Through conversation, we have had the opportunity to work through and develop consensus, not just about potential solutions, but also how to go about implementing them. In many ways, this dialogic process is reflective of how we view ethical engagement through relationships. By talking out reflections, ideas, critiques, and potential solutions, we were able to go places we may not have considered had we each come to the table committed to particular solutions or ways of doing things and armed with arguments to defend those positions. By engaging with each other across and through our differences, we have been able to represent a form of ethical relating.

The ideas we have worked through together have led us to a (now) shared belief that decolonizing research ethics is ultimately about place, and position, and how those two things lay the groundwork for ethical relationships. Rather than treating research ethics protocols as events that take place within the institutional bounds of the university, we have come to think of research ethics as a process that develops based on the place that we come from, the land that we live on as individuals and as participants in institutions and communities, and the position that each of us holds, both in relationship to the land and to the community we are entering (or a part of). By foregrounding these self-oriented truths, our ethical obligations emerge more readily and seem less "murky" than the way they are currently laid out in the ethics protocol. More than this, if institutional ethics protocols were to be rewritten to foreground positionality, the result would be a less stigmatizing document for those who hold multiple positions, say as both a researcher and a member of an Indigenous community. An ethics protocol that begins with simple self-location (such as the one that Leanne Simpson offered up in her talk as a guest in other Indigenous nations' territories) is a practical and achievable goal. Because decolonization, truly, is not a metaphor (Tuck & Yang, 2012), bringing our individual relationship to people and place (land) into research ethics protocol seems a necessary step to create ethical research relationships to people and their places.

Notes

1 See Ursula LeGuin's Bryn Mawr commencement speech published in *Dancing at the Edge of the World*, wherein she describes the important difference.
2 Chi Miigwetch to Gidigaa Migizi for teaching me, as well as supporting and guiding my research.
3 We [the authors] prefer the term "Indigenous," though the current protocol continues to refer to "Aboriginal" peoples, and when referring to the protocol we will use the term "Aboriginal."
4 This observation was also considered as part of a collective conversation during an Indigenous Geographies workshop facilitated by Sarah Hunt with several graduate students at the University of Toronto on February 6, 2016.
5 Borrows's main argument is that Indigenous laws have been, in many ways, included in Canadian common law, although he does acknowledge that at times "the legal systems of First Nations [have been] ignored, repressed, or concealed" (2002, p. 4).
6 See Glen Coulthard's imagery of struggle over land as a "constellation of power relations" that takes place in many different arenas in *Red Skin White Masks*.
7 This reminds me of something Sarah Hunt said during the workshop on Indigenous Geographies at U of T on February 6, 2016. She indicated that one has to have their own personal sense of how to ethically engage.

References

Borrows, J. (2002). *Recovering Canada: The resurgence of indigenous law*. Toronto, ON: University of Toronto Press.

Castledon, H., & Stiegman, M. (2015). Leashes and lies: Navigating the colonial tensions of institutional ethics of research involving indigenous peoples in Canada. *The International Indigenous Policy Journal, 6*(3), 1–10.

Deloria Jr., V. (1969, reprinted 1988). *Custer died for your sins: An Indian Manifesto*. Norman, OK: University of Oklahoma Press.

Fermentez, K. (2013). Rocking the boat: Indigenous geography at home in Hawai'i. In J. Johnson & S. Larsen (Eds.), *A deeper sense of place: Stories and journeys of collaboration in indigenous research* (pp. 103–126). Corvalis, OR: Oregon State University Press.

Government of Canada. (2015). *TCPS 2—Chapter 9: Research involving the first nations, Inuit and Métis peoples of Canada*. Retrieved from www.pre.ethics.gc.ca/eng/policy-politique/initiatives/tcps2-eptc2/chapter9-chapitre9/

Hunt, S. (2014). Ontologies of indigeneity: The politics of embodying a concept. *Cultural Geographies, 21*(1), 27–32.

Hunt, S. (2016, February 5). *Graduate student workshop with Sarah Hunt hosted by intersections.* Toronto, ON: University of Toronto Press.

Morgenson, S. (2012). Destabilizing the settler academy: The decolonial effects of indigenous methodologies. *American Quarterly, 64*(4), 805–808.

Norton, K., & Wilson, D. M. (2008). Continuing ethics review practices by Canadian research ethics boards. *IRB: Ethics & Human Research, 30*(3), 10.

Peacock, T. (2013). Teaching as story. In J. N. Doerfler, J. Sinclair, & H. Kiiwetinepinesiik Stark (Eds.), *Centering Anishinaabeg studies: Understanding the world through stories* (pp. 103–115). East Lansing, MI: Michigan State University Press.

Pualani Louis, R. (2007). Can you hear us now? Voices from the margin: Using Indigenous methodologies in geographic research. *Geographical Research, 45*(2), 130–139.

Simpson, A. (2014). *Mohawk interruptus.* Durham, NC: Duke University Press.

Simpson, L. (2011). *Dancing on our Turtle's back: Stories of Nishnaabeg re-creation, resurgence and a new emergence.* Winnipeg, MB: Arbeiter Ring Publishing.

Simpson, L. (2015, April 8). Decolonial Love: Building Resurgent Communities of Connection. *EMMA talks.* Retrieved from http://emmatalks.org/talks/

Tuck, E., & Yang, W. (2012). Decolonization is not a Metaphor. *Decolonization, Indigeneity, Education and Society, 1*(1), 1–40.

Tuhiwai Smith, L. (1999, reprinted 2012). *Decolonizing methodologies.* Otago: Otago University Press.

10

DECOLONIZATION FOR THE MASSES?

Grappling With Indigenous Content Requirements in the Changing Canadian Post-Secondary Environment

Adam Gaudry (Métis) and Danielle E. Lorenz

Introduction

The Truth and Reconciliation Commission's (TRC) *Calls to Action* (2015) have had a powerfully disruptive effect on Canadian post-secondary education since their release in December 2015. Unlike numerous previous reports, read only by specialists and journalists, the 94 *Calls to Action* became part of the Canadian public discourse in ways not seen before. Nowhere was this more true than in Canadian universities, where most of the campus leadership—from senior administrators to student government—is conversant in the document. In the years following, campus communities have had sustained discussions on how best to act on these *Calls to Action*, bearing in mind that only a few years ago these policies would have never been seriously considered.

Anticipating the TRC's powerful intervention, two universities—Lakehead University and the University of Winnipeg—started discussing a proactive change to their curriculum: that every undergraduate student be required to take a course focusing on Indigenous issues. The intended result, according to the University of Winnipeg, is to "help . . . students understand the contributions Indigenous people have made to our world, and prepare them to engage in a society where reconciliation is an important reality" (2017, para. 4). In short, these proposals were an attempt to re-boot how universities engaged with Indigenous knowledges, communities, and students in order to produce a tangible change on campus that would in turn engage Canadian society as a whole.

What kind of change this will bring is difficult to foresee. It could be a profound and disruptive change that transforms how universities and colleges engage Indigenous communities. Conversely, it could mark only a change in rhetoric, affecting how Indigenous peoples are addressed, but little beyond that. There is certainly plenty of optimism about the first outcome, but many remain cautious. It's a song we've all heard many times before and experience teaches us that a shift in rhetoric does not necessarily lead to beneficial changes—these new "sunny ways" could also go the way of many other Indigenous-focused policies.

At the forefront of these discussions of Indigenization and the academy is a lively debate over the development and implementation of Indigenous course requirements (ICRs). ICRs are a mandated program or requirements that necessitate students complete a prescribed amount of content focused on Indigenous peoples. There is substantial variety in what this content entails—is it a required Indigenous-focused course or is it selecting a course with some Indigenous content? There is also debate about how to best complete the requirement—is it a standalone course or is it selected from a list of pre-approved courses? Universities are in various stages of developing these policies and some have had program-specific ICRs for years, particularly education and social work programs in western Canada. However, discussions on required Indigenous content for *all* students enrolled at particular universities, regardless of the form that that may take, is a new conversation that has posed new problems and could, some argue, profoundly transform how Canadians understand Indigenous-Canada relations, if properly executed (Gaudry, 2016; Pete, 2016). To gain a broader understanding of what kind of impact these policies would have, we asked the people who are teaching Indigenous content courses. We surveyed Canadian faculty, university administrators, graduate students, and instructors on university Indigenizing strategies via an anonymous online survey, asking respondents to discuss the purposes of ICRs and Indigenization initiatives more broadly. Soliciting participants via social media, we asked respondents if Indigenous content requirements can have a transformative impact in the academy and in Canadian society more broadly. They were also asked whether they thought these policies and their goals were effective in addressing the needs of Indigenous people in a university context. Forty-four individuals completed the survey and we have utilized the emergent themes to structure the rest of this chapter.

The vast majority of those who responded to our request expressed optimism of the potential of transformative education; they felt that their classes have had a positive impact on their students and will have an impact on the world beyond the classroom. In some sense it was surprising to find this level of support for ICR among university instructors, but most were more concerned about institutional policy structures than debating whether or not Indigenous content should be required. This chapter presents a synthesis of the debate around ICRs as discussed by those who teach them. What follows is an analysis of their recommendations on how to move forward successfully with these policies. Examining the pedagogical literature and this Indigenous intellectual commentary, we examine the major concerns around "Indigenous content for everyone," its limitations, and its transformative potential. In terms of public debate, most discussion about ICRs is still in its early stages. Most debates are found on social media, not yet in scholarly volumes or the subject of more detailed studies. As perhaps the first study of its kind, we examine the diverse issues associated with ICR policy and its implementation. To do so, we examine the experiences of our colleagues, who like us are on the frontlines of teaching Indigenous content in post-secondary education.

"100 Ways to Indigenize": Indigenous Scholars Debate Indigenous Content Requirements

Indigenous scholars and intellectuals have debated the efficacy of Indigenous content requirements for some time, although often in less formal forums. It is perhaps not surprising that a great diversity of opinion exists on this, particularly among those who have written on the topic. Regardless of their position, most Indigenous intellectuals see education and Indigenous content courses as the starting point for a larger process of social change.

As the executive lead of indigenization at the University of Regina, Shauneen Pete penned the influential "100 Ways to Indigenize and Decolonize Academic Programs and Courses," which serves as a starting point for discussions of the role of ICRs in the larger transformation of the university and Canadian society. Pete's document aims to

> transform . . . the existing academy by including Indigenous knowledges, voices, critiques, scholars, students and materials as well as the establishment of physical and epistemic spaces that facilitate the ethical stewardship of a plurality of Indigenous knowledges and practices so thoroughly as to constitute an essential element of the university.
>
> *(Pete, 2015, para. 1)*

As go-to reading for any university Indigenization plan, "100 Ways to Indigenize" situates comprehensive curricular reform as a central part of this Indigenization process (Pete, 2015). In particular, Pete notes that "some courses should be required of all learners [to] take up topics associated with settler-Indigenous relations, treaty responsibilities, and actions aimed at reconciliation" (2015, para. 50). While the TRC's *Calls to Action* focused primarily on ICRs in professional schools—medicine, health, teaching—Pete expands on the *Calls* to suggest that *every* student should need to fulfill an ICR to graduate (2015, paras. 25, 27–28). By doing so, Pete centralizes ICRs as part of a broader transformative education project that attempts to reach *all learners*, not just those whose professions require that they interact with Indigenous people.

While many professional programs have mandated particular Indigenous content for years, the idea that curriculum should include Indigenous content for *all* programs is a relatively recent development, spurred on Truth and Reconciliation

Commission's *Calls to Action* (Gaudry, 2016). General cross-university Indigenous content requirements have provoked a new dialogue on the merits and short-comings of requiring all undergraduate students to complete a course (or partial course) that focuses on Indigenous peoples, Indigenous issues, or issues of Canadian settler colonialism. This conversation has been intensified as two Canadian universities, the University of Winnipeg and Lakehead University, have implemented their own policies: as of the 2016–2017 academic year, both institutions require all incoming undergraduate students to take one course that provides sufficient Indigenous content to toward the student's degree.

The public's response to these ICRs has been somewhat mixed; generally, they have been well received on campus. Indigenous academics have debated how these courses could be most effective. While supporting the move to require some Indigenous content across university programs, many Indigenous scholars are equally concerned about superficial changes and intellectual pushback as a result of policy changes. In the midst of rapidly changing policies on university campuses, most of the scholarly debate has occurred on social media. Facebook, scholarly blogs, and online forums have developed a deep analysis of the goals and limitations of ICR proposals. For many Indigenous scholars—those teaching these classes—required content is seen as one part of a larger move to include critical Indigenous knowledges in post-secondary education. Most Indigenous scholars seek to ensure that the larger program of Indigenization and decolonization on university campuses is strengthened, rather than undermined by poorly implemented Indigenous-focused teaching and learning. Many Indigenous scholars express concern that mandatory courses and content is now essentially the main thrust of a broader Indigenization program, displacing a more ambitious goal of decolonizing education that aspires to more fundamentally transform relations of power beyond the academy.

Rauna Kuokkanen, in a widely circulated blog post on *Rabble*, cautions us that the shift to ICRs is not the ideal centerpiece policy as we move to Indigenize the academy. Indigenous intellectuals, she argues, are "selling ourselves short" because "mandatory courses are an easy way out" (2016, para. 2). The academy, Kuokkanen argues, has shown an

> obstinate refusal . . . to go beyond relatively shallow changes in the curriculum to address its academic practices and discourses that enable continued exclusion of other than dominant Western epistemic and intellectual traditions.
>
> *(2016, para. 4)*

The end result is that Indigenization reforms like required Indigenous content "become a quick-fix solution or an item on a list, which once checked needs no further consideration or attention" (Kuokkanen, 2016, para. 5). For Kuokkanen, the fundamental role of Indigenous content requirements has not been adequately addressed in a scholarly or administrative sense, leaving several important unanswered pedagogical questions:

> Will mandatory courses be an end to themselves? Is their objective merely to ensure a disengaged multicultural appreciation of "the other" and colonial containment...? Or will complex and demanding issues such as settler colonialism, land rights, dispossession, state violence, heteropatriarchy, racism and sexism form the core of the curriculum?
>
> *(2016, para. 12)*

In an equally well-read Facebook post, Daniel Heath Justice expressed similar concerns about Indigenous content requirements as "quick-fix solutions that further marginalize the very people they're intended to help" (2016, para. 2). If students are expected to take these classes, he argues, they should do so because the content and conversation promises to be challenging and engaging, while noting that at many western Canadian universities "Indigenous and non-Indigenous students are already demanding these courses and this content . . . the demand is outstripping our capacity to meet it" (Justice, 2016, para. 2). Justice suggests that universities expand on the number of Indigenous course offerings available and avoid "coercive" course selection for students: "Coercion isn't generally necessary—if anything, in my experience, it tends to be counterproductive, disillusioning, and dispiriting for those involved" (2016, para. 10).

Gaudry (2016) writing on *Active History* suggests that a large required Indigenous studies class at the University of Saskatchewan has actually increased interest and enrollment in other Indigenous content courses. As this class has been required by a number of academic programs for over a decade, its existence is normalized so as to make the program-specific ICR uncontroversial. In terms of content, Gaudry observes that, at its most successful, the course transforms student attitudes and encourages future learning. He notes that "there are, of course, students who simply go through the motions, are generally disinterested, or dislike the fact that the course requirement exists, but I've faced little outright resistance and encountered mostly open-minded individuals" (2016, para. 4). His reservations about the implementation of Indigenous content requirements are based on pedagogical concerns. Pedagogically, the course requirement cannot, as many policy proposals seem to presume, prioritize non-Indigenous student experiences at the expense of Indigenous students and Indigenous faculty. Indigenous needs must be central to the development of any Indigenization policies, so as not to further entrench "the kind of colonial relationship we're now supposedly transforming" that has long privileged the needs of settler students over Indigenous people (Gaudry, 2016, para. 16).

In addition to social media dialogue, the post-secondary trade publication *University Affairs* published a feature article in April 2016 that interviewed leading scholars and administrators on the subject of Indigenization, concluding that curricular transformation requires that "the work to be led by Indigenous people, supported by non-Indigenous allies, with everyone sharing and learning from the exchange" and that it is key to "building general awareness among everyone in the university community, and providing plenty of in-service training and pedagogical supports for educators" (Macdonald, 2016, para. 18).

This social media dialogue has a number of parallels with the scholarly work of Indigenous educators who have called for a decolonization of K–12 education for a number of decades (i.e., Battiste, 1998; Battiste, Bell, & Findlay, 2003; Atleo & Fiznor, 2010). The problems within all systems of education is not Indigenous peoples presence (Epp, 2008, 2012); rather, the societal lack of understanding between Indigenous peoples and settlers that exists today is the result of centuries-long processes that favor the narratives of EuroWestern settlers over that of Indigenous peoples. The stories we have now—which are reinforced through curricula in compulsory and post-secondary systems of education—are, simply put, inaccurate tellings of history (Donald, 2009). Indeed, the inaccuracies have been—and in many cases continue to be—present in textbooks (i.e., Cornelius, 1999; Shiu, 2008, 2013) and correspondingly in the lecture content of educators. Moreover, Indigenous students in post-secondary studies report racist microaggressions, specific racist acts, and systemic racism as hostilities they must contend with in the process of gaining their degrees (Hare & Pidgeon, 2011; Sonn, Bishop, & Humphries, 2000).

While there is ample scholarly literature on teaching Indigenous content in university settings and some sustained informal debate about the efficacy of ICRs by Indigenous scholars, we sought to engage a broader range of practitioners. The remainder of this chapter explores a diversity of perspective on this issue and envisions the structural, pedagogical, and ideological issues associated with ICRs. Structurally, we explore the many administrative challenges faced in successfully implementing an ICR policy, surveying those responsible for teaching ICR courses. We look at which faculty and academic units are best situated to teach ICRs and what role Indigenous faculty will play in delivering ICR courses. Pedagogically, we suggest that ICRs should focus on unlearning as much as learning, providing students with opportunities to deconstruct what they "know" about Indigenous people and Indigenous-state relations in order to "clear space" for new, more accurate knowledge regarding both Indigenous peoples and settler colonialism. Ideologically, we examine how the resistance and support of other faculty and students shape required Indigenous courses. We pay particular attention to the debate among respondents on whether raising the consciousness level of non-Indigenous students is effective in the current intellectual climate.

Structural Issues in Implementing ICRs

For most of our respondents, their universities have expressed interest in taking up the Truth and Reconciliation Commission's *Calls to Action* (2015) on ICR development. Despite this notable interest, there remains substantial administrative challenges to successfully implementing an ICR policy. Among faculty and instructors—respondents responsible for delivering Indigenous content courses—there was concern about who would be teaching these high-workload classes, particularly in Indigenous studies units that are already overworked and under-resourced. In order to effectively bring about ICR implementation, respondents envision a broad approach to supporting Indigenous faculty and students beyond just pedagogical innovation, ensuring a reasonable workload geared toward impactful teaching and research.

In pursuit of meaningful transformation of academic norms, respondents generally saw pre-existing Indigenous-focused programs as the ideal entities to take on leadership roles in the Indigenization and ICR implementation process. While there was a general belief that Indigenous faculty should be the ones overseeing these changes, there was also significant concern that additional administrative and teaching burdens would be placed on already overworked and under-resourced individuals. At the core of this leadership is a fundamental tension: a desire by Indigenous faculty to ensure effective change, while also wrestling with a university system that already over-exploits them with numerous other initiatives that require Indigenous representation. ICR implementations risk adding more to already full faculty administrative loads.

One respondent who works in an Indigenous studies unit noted that "the university would be best served by utilizing the knowledge and expertise of Indigenous faculty." Another suggested that to increase enrollment in Indigenous-focused courses, "greater funding for and the development of Indigenous studies programs is central." Leadership by Indigenous studies units and their faculty in implementing ICRs was commonly seen as necessary for both symbolic and practical reasons. One faculty respondent noted that all Indigenization programming "must be Indigenous-led to be an authentic contribution to change," presumably because the shift to Indigenous leadership on this initiative is itself a major change in how the university operates. Many respondents saw the university as "unable to appreciate Indigenous knowledge and self-determination," meaning that "university administrators think they know best, [and so are] refusing to share power." Practically speaking, Indigenous faculty were regularly identified as the most knowledgeable advocates for Indigenous content. The centering of Indigenous expertise permeates the discourse around ICRs, requiring the expansion of Indigenous faculty numbers and increased capacity for Indigenous academic units in order to offer more and larger Indigenous content courses to meet the new demand created by requirements.

Alongside the assumption of leadership by Indigenous faculty was the constant reminder that Indigenous people at the university face greater administrative demands than most non-Indigenous faculty. One respondent noted that "too much of this work is being dropped on already overwhelmed Indigenous staff and scholars. I worry about whether they are receiving appropriate credit and release from other responsibilities." Another wrote that universities "cannot always rely on the [I]ndigenous population to bear the burden and emotional labour of teaching and training non-Indigenous colleagues," while one more was troubled that most academics will only give "lip service . . . without willingness to engage deeply" in the kind of work that Indigenous peoples are expected to carry out. For Indigenous faculty, then, there is a fundamental tension in the implementation of ICRs, in that they are both expected and desirous to be in leadership positions but, without a reallocation of resources, these initiatives will only add to their already over-sized administrative burden. Many respondents were apprehensive that ICRs would only lead to further inequities faced by Indigenous faculty under the guise of an increased involvement of Indigenous people in the university. Without additional resources—both through greater funding for Indigenous programing and an increase in tenure track hires of Indigenous faculty—Indigenization and ICRs run the risk of making the position of Indigenous faculty even more unsustainable.

In order to develop a university structure capable of successfully pursuing an Indigenization strategy, respondents noted that administrative support was key. Funding and resource reallocation seems central to most successful initiatives. As one respondent notes, currently, "funding goes primarily to students and departments who don't need it, often overdetermined by both profit motives and latent white supremacy, settler colonialism, and paternalism." An increase in resources to hire more faculty, then, requires diverting resources from many other programs—often large and well fed—who will likely resist this process. The most common response we received overall was that Indigenization necessitated "the increased presence of Indigenous scholars, teachers, administrators, and students on campuses, and the increased presence of Indigenous knowledges and ways of learning." Given the substantial barriers that Indigenous peoples face, resource reallocation and an increase in the numbers of Indigenous peoples on campus in all capacities is necessary. Without this shift, there seems to be little confidence among respondents that the structural changes necessary for the development of ICR policy will be enough to ensure their success.

Pedagogical Concerns With Implementing ICRs

One respondent indicated that the introduction of ICRs "needs to be primarily about anti-oppression to counter dominance"; something other scholars (Stewart, Cappelo, & Carter, 2014; Stockdill & Yu Danico, 2012) have indicated about academia more generally. Respondents were clear about the need to include more Indigenous course requirements within the overall curricula, though there were differing perspectives on how this should be done. For some, the goal was mandatory content courses that students must complete in order to cross the stage. Other participants advocated for an integrated approach where Indigenous knowledges were made an integral part of existing courses in a variety of fields.

One respondent noted that, "Ideally, Indigenous ways of knowing and content would be completely embedded in each disciplinary curriculum, instead of 'added on' courses or course content." No matter which type is implemented, they must be come from Indigenous understandings of knowing and being: Battiste (1998) criticizes "add-and-stir" models, arguing that Indigenous content changes the scope of courses including their design, implementation, assignments, marking, goals, and delivery. Pedagogically, therefore, ICRs must be anti-oppressive at their core.

A common worry for implementing Indigenous content in mandatory courses is a concern over how racism, oppression, and colonialism are operationalized by instructors in the classroom. When courses are rooted in anti-oppression theory, they examine the ways that oppression manifests while also working to transform curricula, pedagogies, and policies to produce change. Anti-oppressive pedagogical practice works to transform power relations in the classroom, clear space, and recognize place-based histories as well as to amplify the ongoing resistance of local Indigenous peoples, as was suggested by many respondents. Class projects can be used to identify and resist ongoing colonial policies and work to empower Indigenous voices in this struggle (see Kumashiro, 2000). With anti-oppressive pedagogical practice, ICRs can embody transformational education while also assisting in a process of unlearning.

As an educational institution, the university has normalized the experience of students who are white, cismale, heterosexual, middle-to-upper class, lacking dis/abilities, and without children. If a student deviates from these categories, they are more likely to experience oppressive obstructions in the completion of their degree. As one of our participants indicated, there are "generally hostile attitudes towards Indigenous peoples among faculty members, departments, and undergraduate and graduate students" at their institution. What is needed, aligning with anti-oppressive pedagogical practice, is for students—as well as faculty, administrators, and the university as an amalgam of structures—to *unlearn* what they know about the experiences of non-normalized students. This process of unlearning, Cochran-Smith (1995, 2003) describes, is one that challenges the normative assumptions of "how things are," as well as one that must confront the systems of privilege and oppression found within society.

Recognizing that education privileges certain groups over others, processes of unlearning require an engagement with ideas, narratives, and theories that counter the norm. In practice, Indigenous course requirements—as well as Indigenous studies programs—bring forth difficult knowledges into university classrooms since they challenge understandings of Indigenous and settler relationships and common tellings of history. However, in order for settlers to unlearn what they were taught by popular culture and during their K-12 education, they must be willing to accept what is presented to them as a truth.

One very real concern—especially in mandatory Indigenous content courses—is that the students will push back against the instructor because they reject the need for unlearning. One respondent noted in particular that "there is a great deal of resistance to the idea [of Indigenization] in general by many of members of university departments. Many departments remain overwhelmingly male and white, and unless pushed, seldom vary from this pattern." Another participant noted that students resisted what was being presented to them, being "visibly angry that they were required to learn about First Nations and had to hear about Ottawa's deliberate policies of cultural and physical genocide." This same respondent also noted that "a common response among these students after being exposed to the empirical realities of First Nations is either that they claim none of it is true or . . . say that FN peoples 'need to move on.'" Though not all the participants indicated they had negative experiences in the classroom, for those who did, they found that many students are "deeply resistant to anything that challenges the colonial narrative." For many respondents, it was not just a lack of knowledge that could derail ICRs but deeply held settler colonial beliefs in need of disruption.

Ideological Issues in Implementing ICRs

In addition to structural and pedagogical impediments, ideological resistance also constitutes a major obstacle for ICR initiatives and for Indigenization more broadly. Respondents were concerned about conflicts over, on the one hand, being mindful of Indigenous student needs while, on the other, raising the consciousness level of settler students. Respondents had experienced a diverse range of responses to ICRs; unsurprisingly many noted examples of students and faculty who were resistant to the inclusion of Indigenous knowledges and perspectives in university classrooms. Perhaps more surprisingly, many respondents also noted that they encountered no resistance, in addition to general support for Indigenous approaches and content in their courses. Just as commonly, respondents described how initial resistance to Indigenous content in their classes was overcome through effective, persuasive, and transformative learning. In short, most respondents were cautiously optimistic about the transformative impact of required Indigenous content in university learning. Respondents found that it was challenging to teach ICR courses, but usually rewarding when faculty were properly supported by their institutions.

A common response among those teaching required Indigenous content was that many of their students resisted learning about Indigenous issues, citing a number of responses from visible discomfort, to disengagement, to vocal opposition: "this resistance manifests in a variety of ways from refusal to participate, faking it just to pass the course, to actively disrupting the course in any manner they are able." One respondent who had experienced disruptive students found it challenging "to get to the bottom of the issues as most often folks don't have the tools to articulate and analyze why they are feeling a certain way." For many students, resistance extends beyond disputing the course's content, but also in rejecting the need to take the class in the first place. Several respondents noted that students questioned the necessity of learning about Indigenous issues, one writing that "students have come into my office to express their bigotry to [First Nations] peoples and looked to me for assurance that the Indigenous content was there for reasons of 'political correctness.'" This last response shows how administrative and pedagogical messaging are linked, and the necessity of ICRs being adequately communicated to students by the university administration. If not, the pushback will most likely be manifested in the classroom and likely directed at Indigenous faculty and students who had no part in this administrative failing. Administrative messaging and substantial support remains at the heart of effective policy involving an Indigenous initiative, as it needs to overcome engrained student resistance stemming from an often unnamed anti-Indigenous societal racism.

As specialists in teaching Indigenous content, respondents often felt that even though they were well-equipped to deal with student disruptions in the classroom, many found that dealing with opposition to teaching Indigenous content from their colleagues was a far more difficult task. Many faculty respondents expressed a concern that their colleagues were more comfortable with a superficial level of Indigenous content in the classroom, noting a "fear that they won't be able to teach all the content their [sic] used to incorporate," or that an "angry, political, and challenging view" would alienate students and decrease enrollment. Many respondents felt unsupported at times, believed that their concerns were not considered part of their program's core curriculum, and Indigenous knowledge and experience remained something Other—less legitimate, less important, and possessing less explanatory power in their respective disciplines. Attempts to alter the core curriculum—such as teaching Indigenous perspectives on key historical events—was often, as one respondent wrote, "met with derision." Many Indigenous faculty noted what one respondent called "indifference or passive encouragement," akin to the well-noted lip service of administrators mentioned earlier—other faculty were supportive of Indigenous faculty initiatives but were not necessarily keen to invest any of their own energy in them. Many respondents noted similar feelings in their programs but others noted more positive interest among faculty and students.

In terms of hiring, tenure, and promotion of Indigenous faculty, the reception of these classes was a source of concern for their career development. As Daniel Heath Justice notes, ICRs "often tend to be [taught by] sessional instructors or junior faculty—untenured and this more vulnerable to the consequences of negative course evaluations from resentful students" (2016). As with students, opposition from colleagues has very practical career implications for many junior Indigenous faculty (and the majority of Indigenous faculty are junior faculty). One respondent notes in their Indigenous content class that "racism is rampant. There is no support from administration to deal with racism in the classroom. The low student [evaluation] scores [are then treated as] a personal failing of the Indigenous professor." As such, the negative repercussions of structural racism and administrative shortcomings are rarely born by those in the institution with the structural ability to absorb them—like senior administrators and faculty secure in their positions—but rather more vulnerable Indigenous faculty members who are expected to use charisma, charm, and innovative pedagogy to overcome centuries of colonial practice and normalized racism. Administrators and senior colleagues have a particular obligation to support those teaching ICRs and protect them from the negative pushback they may receive, even if they offer excellent courses.

So despite these very real obstacles, many respondents also noted widespread support for required courses, reporting high levels of student engagement. Some respondents noted that they received a lot of encouragement and support from their peers to Indigenize their courses and pointed to support for broader initiatives like ICRs. In class, several were "surprised by the enthusiasm of [their] students," who seem "hungry for understanding." A significant number of respondents reported that, to some degree, "students seem to value the inclusion of Indigenous issues or concerns." Many respondents discussed overcoming initial resistance, turning resisters into proponents of the course material. Once students were exposed to the material they began to engage with it in more meaningful ways. One respondent said that "some of the students that had started by resisting [in a ICR] ended up being the most engaged by the end of the course."

At the core of ICRs or Indigenous issues education for non-Indigenous students is a tension between confronting their own ignorance and a compelling subject matter that can attract many students. Herein lies the challenge with much of this education: if students are able to confront this tension, learn to identify with it, and unlearn their own ignorance, the potential for meaningful education—if not outright transformation—is real. However, most respondents have mixed feelings about the potential for success with ICRs or transformative education more broadly, as it ultimately hinges on this very outcome—will the draw of the material, the efficacy of the content, and the ethical orientation of students overpower the internalized racism and victim-blaming of Canadian societal discourse? If the answer is yes, then ICR policies will likely have an impact on campuses and lead to broader discussions of social justice and decolonization. If the answer is no, and social discourses cannot be overcome, then ICRs will probably only result in additional resistance to the meaningful engagement with Indigenous thought and experience. This is why universities will likely need to work on proactive messaging and other programs that augment any required course, as the attitudes that most non-Indigenous students bring with them have the potential to overpower the more accurate information contained in the course.

There is, of course, a tendency to center non-Indigenous concerns in both policy development and in the classroom. Much of the rhetoric justifying the need for ICRs is aimed at overcoming ignorance or providing a basic working knowledge of Indigenous issues. While this is certainly an important goal, most Indigenous students on campus are not exactly ignorant of these issues, nor do they lack a basic knowledge on the issues that have such dramatic impacts on their lives and the lives of their families. Often lost in this drive to educate settler students is the renewed erasure of Indigenous students in the very classes that aim to make their lives better. Most Indigenous students are able to discuss moments when anti-Indigenous sentiments shared by their peers in class were disruptive, so ICR policy must be implemented in a way that ensures, in the words of one respondent, to "have their histories told and voices heard." If ICRs cannot accomplish this within the classes themselves, or if Indigenous students are expected to take on unofficial teaching roles, placing additional burdens on them, these courses will reinscribe the same power dynamics they aim to dissolve. It is therefore absolutely imperative that all policies have a clear approach to address the needs of Indigenous students. Their experiences in these classes must be privileged if genuinely safe and transformative classrooms are going to be created.

Indeed, the opposition among Indigenous faculty and students to ICRs seems to revolve around this very concern—are these spaces going to effectively transform societal-level power relations which marginalize Indigenous voices? As Daniel Justice notes, ICRs can in effect "further marginalize the very people they're intended to help and often have unintended consequences that do exactly the opposite of the original vision" (2016, para. 2). The success of these courses is, for many, seen as precarious. If the courses are effective, they can be transformative, but if they are not, they risk exposing Indigenous students and instructors to intensified colonialism, which for some respondents is not worth the risk. Much of this likely boils down then to the individual context of the university in question—is there a critical mass of Indigenous faculty? Does campus culture tolerate open racism against Indigenous people? Are university administrators willing to commit to supporting these courses with the full weight of their offices? Is the normalized experience of young white students going to be receptive to these classes, or will ICRs just create majorities of these students who don't want to learn and resent being there? This is the ideological challenge of ICR implementation, much of which relies on structural issues that extend far beyond the individual power of the instructor to transform.

Practical Considerations in Implementing ICRs

In addition to these higher-order concerns, there are also practical issues that departments, faculties, and universities must take into account to make ICRs work. As one respondent noted, "the radical under-representation of Indigenous peoples among faculty is an enduring barrier and needs to be addressed." The Association of Universities and Colleges of Canada (2011) estimates that 1100 Indigenous people have completed a doctoral degree. Assuming these calculations are correct, in a total Aboriginal population of 1,400,685 (Statistics Canada, 2016), only 0.07% have a doctorate. How many of those with Ph.Ds. are in the academy is unclear; yet, data from the National Aboriginal Achievement Fund Scholars Study as reported in the Urban Aboriginal Peoples Study (2010) indicates that although 46% of respondents reported having no Indigenous instructors in their post-secondary studies, others reported that "some (10%) or all/most (3%) of their instructors in college or university were Aboriginal" (p. 134).

As previously noted, there is an expectation for Indigenous faculty—of which there are substantially and statistically less—to do the majority of the work around ICRs, on top of their already-existing duties and roles, some of which go beyond normalized professor-student relationships. As one respondent explained, "white faculty turn to Indigenous faculty to develop Indigenous content courses instead of working on these as well. We do it off the side of our desks as we care for Indigenous students." The reason settler faculty are likely to engage in this behavior is due to the perception that Indigenous peoples' cultural backgrounds make them "experts" on Indigenous histories and knowledges rather than their cultural knowledges and academic training. Since the onus of Indigenizing work is thrust on to Indigenous faculty, there is a much greater likelihood of overwork and, in turn, burnout within this smaller labor pool. With the work needed to make ICRs function—intellectual, emotional, and mental given the sometimes personal nature of the content—at times being very difficult, the biggest practical concern that comes with implementing ICRs is that there are simply not enough Indigenous peoples who can do the work in an equitable way. Whether settlers are adequately trained in the academic areas of study and are able to teach the content in an equitable way—that is, thoroughly understanding anti-oppression pedagogy—is another matter.

Conclusion

If requiring a minimum amount of Indigenous content in university degrees is in our future, those on the frontline have shown us there's a minefield ahead. One respondent offered a terse piece of advice, which was echoed in almost every response we read: "proceed carefully." The point is that, if we're going to do this, we need to do it collaboratively and with the support of the highest levels of administration. If half-baked programming is implemented or if programs are rushed before there's adequate capacity to deliver them, ICRs are not going to work. Or worse, their failure will set us back, perpetuate mistruths, or destroy interest in actually engaging with Indigenous peoples and Indigenous histories. Successful ICR policies will be successful because they listened to the guidance of those who have the most to lose or gain from their implementation: Indigenous faculty, students, and communities.

As we've already noted, we're at a time where post-secondary institutions have grabbed onto the TRC's *Calls to Action* (2015) and we're in a moment in time where change is possible. We now need to decide what kind of change that will be. Will it be superficial, mostly rhetorical change? Or will we finally begin the long process of transformative actions that right the perpetual wrongs done to Indigenous peoples by Canadians? ICRs certainly aren't going to change the world, but they may lay the foundation for a different kind of discussion and a different kind of relationship between Indigenous peoples and Canadians outside of the classroom. Perhaps those on the frontline of transformative Indigenous content education can offer us the most. Because despite all their concerns, there is a general optimism that with the right combination of administrative support, transformative pedagogy, ideological shifts, and targeted Indigenous hiring, we could start to tackle some of these major social, political, economic, and cultural injustices. It's probably as good a first step as any.

References

Association of Universities and Colleges of Canada. (2011). *Trends in higher education: Volume 1—Enrollment*. Retrieved from www.cais.ca/uploaded/trends-2011-vol1-enrolment-e.pdf

Atleo, M. R., & Fitznor, L. (2010). Aboriginal educators discuss recognizing, reclaiming, and revitalizing their multi-competences in heritage/English-language use. *Canadian Journal of Education, 32*, 13–26.

Battiste, M. (1998). Enabling the autumn seed: Toward a decolonized approach to Aboriginal knowledge, language, and education. *Canadian Journal of Native Education, 22*(1), 16–27.

Battiste, M., Bell, L., & Findlay, M. (2003). Decolonizing education in Canadian universities: An interdisciplinary, international indigenous research project. *Canadian Journal of Native Education, 26*(2), 82–95.

Cochran-Smith, M. (1995). Uncertain allies: Understanding the boundaries of race and teaching. *Harvard Educational Review, 63*(4), 541–570.

Cochran-Smith, M. (2000). Blind vision: Unlearning racism in teacher education. *Harvard Educational Review, 70*(2), 13–24.

Cochran-Smith, M. (2003). Learning and unlearning: The education of teacher educators. *Teaching and Teacher Education, 19*(1), 5–28.

Cornelius, C. (1999). *Iroquois corn in a culture-based curriculum: A framework for respectfully teaching about cultures*. Albany, NY: State University of New York Press.

Donald, D. T. (2009). The curricular problem of Indigenousness: Colonial frontier logics, teacher resistances, and the acknowledgement of ethical space. In J. Nahachewsky & I. Johnson (Eds.), *Beyond 'presentism': Re-imagining the historical, personal and social pages of curriculum* (pp. 23–41). Rotterdam, NE: Sense Publishers.

Epp, R. (2008). *We are all treaty people: Prairie essays*. Edmonton, AB: University of Alberta Press.

Epp, R. (2012). "There was no one here when we came": Overcoming the settler problem. *The 2011 Bechtel Lectures*, University of Waterloo, Waterloo, ON. Retrieved from https://uwaterloo.ca/grebel/sites/ca.grebel/files/uploads/files/cgr-30-2-s2012-2.pdf

Gaudry, A. (2016). Paved with good intentions: Simply requiring Indigenous content is not enough. *Active History*. Retrieved from http://activehistory.ca/2016/01/paved-with-good-intentions-simply-requiring-indigenous-content-is-not-enough/

Hare, J., & Pidgeon, M. (2011). The way of the warrior: Indigenous youth navigating the challenges of schooling. *Canadian Journal of Education, 34*(2), 93–111.

Justice, D. H. (2016). Untitled blog post. *Facebook*. Retrieved from www.facebook.com/daniel.justice.7393/posts/535094576666580

Kumashiro, K. K. (2000). Toward a theory of anti-oppressive education. *Review of Educational Research, 70*(1), 25–53.

Kuokkanen, R. (2016). Mandatory indigenous studies courses aren't reconciliation, they're an easy way out. *Rabble.ca*. Retrieved from http://rabble.ca/blogs/bloggers/campus-notes/2016/03/mandatory-indigenous-studies-courses-arent-reconciliation-theyre?utm_content=buffer8da8a&utm_medium=social&utm_source=twitter.com&utm_campaign=buffer

Macdonald, M. (2016). Indigenizing the academy: What some universities are doing to weave indigenous peoples, cultures and knowledge into the fabric of their campuses. *University Affairs*. Retrieved from www.universityaffairs.ca/features/feature-article/indigenizing-the-academy/

Pete, S. (2015). 100 ways to Indigenize and decolonize academic programs and courses. *University of Regina*. Retrieved from www.uregina.ca/president/assets/docs/president-docs/indigenization/indigenize-decolonize-university-courses.pdf

Pete, S. (2016). 100 ways: Indigenizing & decolonizing academic programs. *Aboriginal Policy Studies*, *6*(1), 81–89.

Shiu, D. P-Y. (2008). *"How are we doing? Exploring Aboriginal presentation in texts and Aboriginal programs in Surrey secondary schools.* (Unpublished doctoral dissertation). Vancouver, BC: University of British Columbia.

Shiu, D. P-Y. (2013). Misrepresentating aboriginal peoples in textbooks. *Social Justice Newsletter: BC Federation of Teachers*. Retrieved from https://bctf.ca/uploadedFiles/Public/SocialJustice/Publications/SJ-Newsletter/Winter2013.pdf

Sonn, C., Bishop, B., & Humphries, R. (2000). Encounters with the dominant culture: Voices of Indigenous students in mainstream higher education. *Australian Psychologist*, *35*(2), 128–135.

Statistics Canada. (2016). *Aboriginal peoples in Canada: First nations people, Métis and Inuit* [Catalogue No. 99–011–X]. Retrieved from www12.statcan.gc.ca/nhs-enm/2011/as-sa/99-011-x/99-011-x2011001-eng.cfm

Stewart, M., Cappelo, M., & Carter, C. (2014). Anti-oppressive education and the trap of 'good' intentions: Lessons from an interdisciplinary workshop. *Critical Education*, *5*(14), 1–19.

Stockdill, B. C., & Danico, M. Y. (2012). The ivory tower paradox: Higher education as a site of oppression and resistance. In B. C. Stockdill & M. Y. Danico (Eds.), *Transforming the ivory tower: Challenging racism, sexism, and homophobia in the Academy* (pp. 1–30). Honolulu, HI: University of Hawai'i Press.

Truth and Reconciliation Commission. (2015). *Calls to action*. Retrieved from www.trc.ca/websites/trcinstitution/File/2015/Findings/Calls_to_Action_English2.pdf

University of Winnipeg. (2017, July). *Indigenous course requirement*. Retrieved from www.uwinnipeg.ca/indigenous-course-requirement/

Urban Aboriginal Peoples Study. (2010). *Urban aboriginal peoples study: Main report*. Retrieved from www.uaps.ca/wp-content/uploads/2010/04/UAPS-FULL-REPORT.pdf

11

E KORE AU E NGARO, HE KĀKANO I RUIA MAI I RANGIĀTEA (I WILL NEVER BE LOST, I AM A SEED SOWN FROM RANGIĀTEA)

Te Wānanga o Raukawa as an Example of Educating for Indigenous Futures

Kim McBreen (Waitaha, Kāti Mamoe, Ngāi Tahu)

Acknowledgments

This chapter writes about the work of the ART confederation in imagining and building Te Wānanga o Raukawa. The writing relies heavily on unpublished documents and conversations, and would not have been possible without support, in particular, from Kahukura Kemp, Aneta Wineera, Ani Mikaere, Āneta Rāwiri and Whatarangi Winiata and whānau. Thanks also to Ani Mikaere, Linda Smith and Philip Wills for comments on previous versions of this manuscript.

E Kore Au e Ngaro, He Kākano i Ruia mai i Rangiātea:*
Te Wānanga o Raukawa as an Example of Educating for Indigenous Futures

This chapter explores the experiences and vision of Te Wānanga o Raukawa in Aotearoa/New Zealand as a case study for decolonizing Indigenous education. The Wānanga is a Māori tertiary education institute that opened in 1981 with the goal of ensuring the survival of Māori, managing matters in ways that the ancestors would recognize as Māori. It is an example of creativity, experimentation and faith.

There are three types of tertiary education institutions that the New Zealand state now considers public (New Zealand, 2016). Eight universities focus on bachelor's degree and postgraduate teaching and research, and account for 132,000 equivalent full-time students (EFTS). Eighteen polytechnics focus on vocational training, certificate- and diploma-level teaching, and account for 77,000 EFTS. Three wānanga provide learning and research based on Māori practices and philosophies; they have each developed their own priorities, with one concentrating on vocational training, certificate and diploma level, and two on bachelor's degree and postgraduate level; together they account for 23,100 EFTS. Te Wānanga o Raukawa is one of these wānanga.

The Wānanga was established by a confederation of three iwi (nations)—Te Āti Awa, Ngāti Raukawa and Ngāti Toa Rangatira—as part of a larger plan of tribal development.[1] In 1975, from the verge of cultural extinction, those iwi (known as the ART confederation) looked to build their own solution to their own problem—how to get their young people to engage with their language and culture. The Wānanga's role was building skills and knowledge, as well as supporting critical analysis necessary for whānau (family groups) and hapū (clans) to live as Māori.

Although the term "decolonization" is not commonly used at Te Wānanga o Raukawa, the challenges it was designed to confront are the result of 200 years of colonization. By returning to the wisdom of the ancestors, the Wānanga has experimented with unique, innovative solutions. While it accepts Crown funding, it is primarily accountable to its three founding nations. This has costs and many benefits. Prioritizing the aspirations of the ART confederation, the Wānanga is imagining and creating, critically re-inventing Māori processes and measures of success. For every people, the solutions will be different. The Wānanga is an example of exploring the past and trusting in our ancestors to create possibilities of decolonized futures.

Background

Māori are the Indigenous people of Aotearoa/New Zealand. By 1769, when the first Europeans set foot on these shores, Māori laws, knowledge systems, language, economies, health and governance had developed into unique, thriving systems. In 1840, when the British Crown brought their treaties, those systems were still thriving, having integrated useful European ideas and technologies. Te Tiriti o Waitangi, written by the Crown and signed in 1840 by over 500 Māori leaders (representing a fraction of Māori communities), affirmed the authority of those leaders (rangatiratanga) and allocated a lesser, separate authority to the Crown to govern its own people (kāwanatanga). Even before the Crown had finished collecting signatures, it began dismantling Māori authority and expanding its own, tearing down Māori systems and building up the New Zealand state's colonizing systems in their place, endangering Māori survival.

By the early 1970s, the ART confederation, with an estimated 40,000 descendants of the three iwi, realized that all their Māori language speakers were over 30 years of age. Two generations were growing up without their language. This was a crisis—the confederation was on the brink of losing its ability to speak its language. In the words of James Henare, "Ko te reo te mauri o te mana Māori" (language is the essence of Māori dignity) (New Zealand, 1989, p 34). Language is an indicator of cultural well-being and carries much of a people's culture (Rāwiri, 2012). Without the language, holding on to all that it carries—the knowledge, values, even practices—becomes harder.

In response to this crisis, in 1975 the confederation launched a 25-year development plan to prepare for the 21st century (Winiata, 1979). It also aimed to close the gap in educational achievements between its young people and the wider community, and to rejuvenate meeting houses throughout the region. Whakatupuranga Rua Mano—Generation 2000 was a visionary, ambitious and wide-ranging plan; it may also have been described by some as wildly unrealistic.

Whakatupuranga Rua Mano had three missions: Pākehā, ART and education.

Pākehā mission focused on gaining support from non-Māori for Māori survival and self-determination. While it consumed a great deal of time and energy during the early years of Whakatupuranga Rua Mano, it was eventually abandoned in favor of the other two missions, which were felt to represent a more productive use of limited resources (Walker, 2011).

At that time, few people in the confederation had the knowledge and language needed for cultural survival. ART mission aimed to share and grow that knowledge among younger generations. It developed four principles for rejuvenating the confederation (Winiata, 1979):

a. The marae[2] is our principle home; it must be maintained and respected.
b. The language is a treasure; it must be protected and revived.
c. The people are our wealth; they must be developed and retained above all else.
d. Strive for self-determination.

ART mission has been credited with rejuvenating the confederation. Regular "young people's hui"[3] hosted thousands of teenagers—more than 60 week-long gatherings between 1976 and 2000, most of them implementing total immersion in Māori language (Winiata, 2000). This mission grew the number of Māori language speakers under 30 in the confederation, from none in 1976 to approximately 600 by 1995, and to an estimated 4000 in 2010 (Walker, 2011). By 1999, every marae in the confederation had refurbished or rebuilt their meeting house; many added playgrounds for young people and lounges for elders (Mikaere, 2016).

Whakatupuranga Rua Mano also identified educational achievement as important. It would improve future decision-making within the confederation and enhance the confederation's ability to influence decisions at a national level. Education mission aimed to undo conditioning that directed Māori students into non-academic subjects, to raise expectations of young Māori so that they would consider professional careers and positions of influence (Winiata, 1979).[4] The confederation regularly organized meetings with students in the final years of high school, and with senior staff of schools, to discuss career aspirations and pathways. Students were supported and mentored at school and in further education.

In 1981, Te Wānanga o Raukawa opened as a center of learning to further this mission and to retain young people who otherwise might leave for education but never return to serve the confederation.

Te Wānanga o Raukawa—Putting the Principles Into Action

Te Wānanga o Raukawa adopted a well-known proverb as a "forever" statement: E kore au e ngaro, he kākano i ruia mai i Rangiātea—I will never be lost, I am a seed sown from Rangiātea.[5] This proverb has special significance to the ART confederation and Te Wānanga o Raukawa,[6] and connects Māori survival to ancestors, demanding a future that honors them. The "au" ("I") of the statement refers to the survival of Māori as a people, which requires that Māori culture, knowledge and language also survive. It compels us to use the past to imagine and prepare the future. This section explores how the Wānanga used this statement and the principles of Whakatupuranga Rua Mano to design an educational program for cultural resurgence and to ensure the survival of Māori as Māori.

How Can the Wānanga Contribute to Reinvigorating Marae as Our Principal Home?

By the 1970s, many marae were neglected, not just in the ART confederation, but all around Aotearoa. Many people had little relationship with their marae. They may have known little about their marae, may have never visited their marae, may have taken their marae for granted—expecting that it would be there when needed. For many, the marae was not beloved, familiar or nurturing, deserving of the term home; it was strange, intimidating, filled with people who we feared would judge us for our ignorance and lack of commitment. This created a spiral, where people found it harder and harder to return to and support their marae, meaning there was less to go back for, and within few generations the marae were being abandoned. The effects of this process are still being felt by many Māori today.

The Wānanga response was the development of Iwi and Hapū studies. Students are supported to learn the history and practices of their own people, to interview their elders, to visit their marae and write about its history and current use. Iwi[7] and Hapū[8] studies is compulsory and accounts for at least a quarter of total coursework. It encourages students to familiarize themselves with their marae and to honor the people sustaining them. The implications of this work for relationships, especially with elders, make assignments demanding. While students typically find Iwi and Hapū studies challenging and time-consuming, many acknowledge that it is uniquely rewarding, resulting in new and stronger relationships among families.

In the early years, the Wānanga followed the precedent set by Whakatupuranga Rua Mano with much of the teaching held at local marae. By bringing people and income to those marae, the Wānanga contributed to their reawakening. So much so that many are no longer available for hosting courses and teaching has moved to the Wānanga Ōtaki campus or one of its external teaching hubs (known as marae-based studies sites).

Two courses that are still typically taught at marae are the certificate courses in karanga and whaikōrero (the ceremonial speaking roles of women and men, respectively), where local experts come together with the students to discuss their roles and contribute to the ability of those marae to perform their ceremonial functions. In many cases, these courses create an ongoing commitment to learning local history and oral traditions (Mikaere, 2016, p. 276).

How Can the Wānanga Contribute to Reinvigorating the Māori Language as a Treasure?

Most Māori do not speak the Māori language. Again, this is not a problem specific to the ART confederation. When Whakatupuranga Rua Mano began, an estimated 18% of Māori were fluent in their language and almost none were young children (New Zealand, 2010, p. 7). That remains largely unchanged (Statistics New Zealand, 2013). With so few competent speakers, and ever fewer native speakers, the language is threatened, especially local variants (New Zealand, 2010, p. 48). The state of the language was the crisis that triggered Whakatupuranga Rua Mano and it remains a priority for the Wānanga. In order to halt the decline and reinvigorate the language, there need to be classes and opportunities to speak.

Te Wānanga o Raukawa aims to produce bilingual graduates and is committed to exploring strategies for teaching the language. Whakatupuranga Rua Mano's six- to 10-day Māori language immersion hui was a successful and popular innovation and continues to be central to Māori language learning at the Wānanga. Each undergraduate year of study at the Wānanga includes two of these hui. In 1995, the Wānanga introduced weekly language classes at locations in the ART confederation area; distance learning for those outside it was introduced in 1999. Marae-based studies has meant that regional variants can be taught off campus and an online certificate-level course was introduced in 2012.

Compulsory language study makes up at least a quarter of total undergraduate coursework. In addition, Māori language is part of all courses—in songs, opening and closing formalities, introductions, blessings and assessments. Students are encouraged to use Māori language as much as they can and graduate students are expected to be competent speakers. Some graduate courses are delivered entirely in the Māori language, the remainder include Māori language components, such as papers designed to enrich and deepen students' language skills. The Wānanga also now offers full-time diploma, bachelor's and graduate-level courses on the language.

How Can the Wānanga Contribute to Developing and Retaining People, Honoring People as Our Most Valued Asset?

The New Zealand state education system has been a tool of colonization. Nearly all of the state's educational resources have promoted the English language and European episteme (Winiata, 1995; see Kuokkonen, 2007 on colonization and Indigenous epistemes), and prepared young Māori for low-paid, physical employment (Barrington, 1988). Generations of Māori have been taught that they are simple and practical, and that anything more than a basic education would be wasted on them. Generations of Māori have been excluded from the skills and knowledge that are necessary for planning and succeeding in the European world, while being told that their lack of success is innate. Universities are especially foreign and intimidating, and that disorientation contributed to very low success rates for the few Māori who made it into the institutions, reinforcing the narrative that Māori are not intellectually capable.

The Wānanga needed to overcome the sense of failure and worthlessness that many Māori people carry as a result of their education experience. It needed to first consider what success would look like, then how it could be measured and supported.

Success would be growing people's skills to contribute to their communities.

The Wānanga decided on two strategies. First, there would be open entry: previous lack of educational success would not preclude enrollment and all students would receive academic counseling to ensure they enrolled in the appropriate course at the appropriate level. Second, no student would fail: too many Māori had experienced failure in the colonizing system, so the Wānanga should not allow them to fail as Māori in a Māori system. The Wānanga committed to designing courses to meet student and community needs, develop Māori minds and encourage excellence, while welcoming students whose education has not prepared them for tertiary education and finding ways for them to succeed.

The Wānanga does not assume that students enter with the skills they will need and courses are designed to consider the best methods for the required learning. Students are supported to learn the skills they need, such as critical reading, writing, interviewing and using kaupapa[9] to think critically. Staff are in regular contact with students, checking on their progress and needs and helping with assignments. Several times each year, students are invited for a week of intensive support to complete coursework. For most subjects, long reading lists do not produce the most prepared graduates. Most courses are taught in small groups, with discussion a major tool, allowing adult students to share their knowledge and experience, as well as test their ideas. Discussion allows tutors to learn from students, to adjust the coursework to suit the group of students and to discover the specific assumptions students need to unlearn from their experience of colonizing education.

The Wānanga uses achievement-based performance standards to assess students' learning (Leach, Neutze, & Zepke, 2003). Learning outcomes are provided for each course and students can demonstrate that they have met those standards in a variety of ways, including class discussions, set assignments or tasks that are suited to the course aim (such as composing or performing songs, as well as producing art, essays or presentations, or role plays). They receive detailed feedback on the quality of their work over a range of criteria, from excellent to unsatisfactory. Students know what is required and how they can improve. If the work does not demonstrate that the standard has been met, students can repeat assessments as many times as needed, for as long as they need until successful. It may seem like a semantic distinction, but there is a real difference between an institution failing a student and a student choosing whether or not to continue. Students can opt out and not submit work; the Wānanga will continue to encourage and allow them to complete the assessment when they are ready. A number of students attend the same classes year after year, participating in all exercises and discussions, but not completing assessments. They are often encouraged to delay enrolling until they have work to submit.

Higher education pulls young people from the provinces, enriching university cities and draining the hometowns and communities of their future. The purpose of the Wānanga is to grow people's knowledge and skills for use in their communities—the confederation wanted to retain people, not send them away. The Wānanga predicted that the people most wanting the education it offered were adults who were already employed, already raising families. It needed to provide education that could fit around those commitments and allow students to stay in their own communities. The solution has been to teach courses in blocks of three to seven days, often over weekends, with accommodation and food provided, including for support people or dependents. Despite the focus on building the confederation, the Wānanga is open to students from all nations.

Each course has been developed by considering the needs of Māori communities. The first course, "Māori and Administration," recognized that marae and Māori-resurgence projects needed skilled administrators who were culturally Māori. It aimed to provide an intensive course in Māori culture so that, after three years, a student who had started with little experience of Māori culture would graduate with skills and knowledge as if they had grown up in the culture.

How Can the Wānanga Contribute to Self-Determination?

Since setting itself up as the state, the Crown has attempted to define what is best for Māori. Consistently, the answer has been assimilation and the education system has been used to encourage this, rewarding Māori who achieve in the way the Crown wants. Skills, knowledge and projects that are in line with Crown values lead to success; skills, knowledge and projects that aren't are not recognized.

The Wānanga continues from Whakatupuranga Rua Mano as a model of self-determination. As unrealistic as it must have seemed to set up a tertiary education center of learning with no support from the state, the confederation attempted it. The Wānanga could have affiliated to a university, but it remained independent, accountable only to the confederation. It was the first of its kind, and the confederation found ways to make it work, with largely voluntary teaching. Because it came out of the education mission of Whakatupuranga Rua Mano, the focus was on raising educational expectations as well as providing practical skills, on the confederation's terms. This was not an institution for producing low-waged Māori labor, nor for preparing Māori for university. "Developing the Māori mind" was the goal, preparing leaders and strategic thinkers, confident in the Māori knowledge system. Courses prioritize oral literature, as well as local, Māori and other Indigenous material, and encourage students to do the same. At the time, the Wānanga was the only "private" tertiary education institution conferring degrees, the content and quality of which was determined by the confederation, not the state.[10]

Te Wānanga o Raukawa initially offered one degree, the bachelor's of Māori and Administration, designed to produce bilingual and bicultural administrators needed for the confederation. Two students enrolled in 1981, with around 60 volunteers from several Māori nations to teach them. With no external support, the Wānanga continued to attract low numbers of students from the confederation— by 1991, around 40 students were enrolled. This changed when the state recognized the Wānanga as a tertiary education institution in 1993, making students eligible for allowances and loans. By 1996, the Wānanga had 600 equivalent full-time students (EFTS), 1200 by 2006 (Walker, 2011). The Wānanga has remained small, with 1500 equivalent full-time students representing more than 3300 actual students, around 90% of whom are Māori, with a median age of 39 (Te Wānanga o Raukawa, 2015, p. 23). While it now has paid teaching staff, it continues to use volunteers with recognized knowledge and expertise to contribute to learning; around 300 kaiāwhina serve in this way. Courses offered include the equivalent of six certificate-level courses; 15 diploma-level courses, 13 of which can be continued to the bachelor's level and five to the master's level (Te Wānanga o Raukawa, 2015, pp. 92–95); and the highest course offered, the kāurutanga, which has no mainstream equivalent.

Even though the Wānanga now receives some funding from the state, and almost all courses are now recognized by the state, the state has no role in deciding whether courses will be offered, nor in deciding course content. The confederation continues to determine the need, relevance and value of each course. Several have been developed without state approval, including the already mentioned certificate-level courses on karanga and whaikōrero, as well as the kāurutanga. Ngā Purutanga Mauri were concerned that the confederation maintain control over these, rather than allowing them under the Crown regime (the karanga course is now Crown recognized, but the others remain outside the Crown system).

Resistance, Safety, and Growing the Knowledge Continuum

Te Wānanga o Raukawa's path into the future has been to critically re-search the legacy of the ancestors—the principles and practices that make up a Māori theory of existence (Mikaere, 2011). It is not framed as decolonization but is nevertheless a decolonizing pathway, setting goals, finding solutions and measuring success based in Māori knowledge and understandings. It is an experiment (Winiata, 2016), with several innovations enabling its success. Many strategies have developed in order to keep the project safe in a hostile, colonizing environment.

Te Wānanga o Raukawa is at a disadvantage in the tertiary education sector. With 1500 EFTS, it is tiny; income from those students has to support all the administrative and support functions of the organization—staff and other resources are stretched thin. Many students did not complete high school and most have been out of education for years—out of practice at sitting, concentrating to read, listen and discuss for long periods. The Wānanga must incorporate foundation skills into its courses, as well as rebuilding stamina for study. These are realities that require more from wānanga than universities; however, the Wānanga is funded at a much lower rate than universities, receiving 53% to 63% of university funding per EFTS.[11]

Teaching and learning is only one aspect of the Wānanga and its responsibility to Māori survival. In order to succeed, the Wānanga must also actively resist colonization and expand the Māori knowledge system.

The Natural Tension

Te Tiriti o Waitangi is a treaty signed between the Indigenous peoples of Aotearoa and the British Crown at time when the population was 98 to 99% Indigenous. That treaty confers kāwanatanga (self-governance) to the Crown and confirms Indigenous tino rangatiratanga (absolute authority). "The natural tension" is a phrase Whatarangi Winiata uses to describe the stand-off between the Crown's determination to govern everyone and Māori nations' resolve to remain self-determining. In particular, Winiata (2013) is concerned with how that tension affects the Wānanga. He offers a way forward—for the parties to negotiate as equals in order to find a fair and enduring solution. Whenever the Crown seeks to impose a decision or policy on the Wānanga, the concept of the natural tension operates as a touchstone to remind the Wānanga of its authority and responsibility to self-determination. The Wānanga has not wavered, refusing to compromise time and again, and, in so doing, it has maintained its integrity of purpose.

The Wānanga has contributed to two claims against the Crown. In 1999, the three wānanga successfully claimed that the Crown had failed to provide them with capital establishment grants, unlike every previously established tertiary education institution (New Zealand, 1999). In 2008, after 10 years of "negotiations," Te Wānanga o Raukawa received over NZ$50 million in redress.

The Crown's Performance Based Research Fund (PBRF) has led to a more comprehensive claim (Winiata, 2013). Since 2004, tertiary education providers in Aotearoa/New Zealand have been partially funded through the PBRF, which rates institutions on their research output as assessed by the Crown's criteria (largely based on number of publications in high-impact academic journals) and rewards them accordingly.[12] The purpose of the Wānanga is to support the resurgence of knowledge and excellence of Māori nations, so publication in international journals is an invalid measure. If the Wānanga were to accept the PBRF's assessment tool, its accountability and purpose would inevitably become blurred. When the PBRF was proposed, the Wānanga informed the Crown that its performance could only be assessed against the proverb "e kore au e ngaro, he kākano i ruia mai i Rangiātea." The Crown has not accepted this approach, so, despite its focus on growing Māori knowledge, the Wānanga has refused to participate in PBRF. Attempts to negotiate with the Crown have been unsuccessful. The PBRF has increased government research funding to universities and decreased funding to all other tertiary institutions—particularly the three wānanga, whose research funding decreased by 70% (New Zealand, 2008). The Wānanga is currently preparing a claim for:

- Acknowledgment that the Māori episteme has been disadvantaged by Crown actions for 170 years;
- Resources to remedy that disadvantage, bringing the knowledge system to where it might be had it not been disadvantaged;
- Resources so that it will not be disadvantaged into the future.

Ngā Purutanga Mauri

By 1990, young people involved in Whakatupuranga Rua Mano were looking for a way to honor the group of elders whose hard work, passion for their people, and knowledge and experience had ensured the success of Whakatupuranga Rua Mano and Te Wānanga o Raukawa. These elders became Ngā Purutanga Mauri, keepers of the mauri.[13] It is far from an honorary group: Ngā Purutanga Mauri are recognized as the link between the generations who have gone and those of the future—carrying their elders' examples and teachings, as well as providing example for younger generations. They are responsible for the integrity, reputation and spiritual safety of the Wānanga, and for ensuring that the practices of the Wānanga uphold the integrity, reputation and spiritual safety of the three nations of the confederation (Nicholson, 1998). The group therefore has input into all matters at the Wānanga, with representatives on every committee, decision-making body and academic program review.

An example is te kāurutanga, the Wānanga's highest qualification. Ngā Purutanga Mauri oversee every stage, from evaluating prospective candidates and their projects, determining who may enroll, to monitoring their progress and determining how they will be assessed. Ani Mikaere (2017), one of the first recipients of the kāurutanga, reflects on her relationship with Ngā Purutanga Mauri:

> The whakapapa[14] relationships between myself and each of the Purutanga Mauri bring with them multiple layers of understanding about the way in which the project should be conducted and about the mutual obligations that bind us together as the work progresses. These understandings may be largely unarticulated, but that fact renders them no less potent: being a niece or a mokopuna[15] of Purutanga Mauri, past and present, has a way of sharpening one's focus on the issue of responsibility in a particularly forceful and enduring manner.
>
> *(p. 11)*

Ngā Purutanga Mauri take their responsibility seriously, balancing the need to ensure that the Wānanga is at all times acting and making decisions consistent with the needs and values of the confederation, while allowing the Wānanga to do its job efficiently. Despite this responsibility, those who work with Ngā Purutanga Mauri describe them as relaxed, open to questioning, and to giving their views and advice. Representatives of Ngā Purutanga Mauri are present at all major events at the Wānanga, from symposia and conferences to graduation, where all available members are on stage for the full day, personally acknowledging every graduating student. Their participation is crucial to the success of those occasions.

Te Kawa o te Ako

As Te Wānanga o Raukawa grew, it needed a formal process for dealing with issues that threatened the learning environment and experience of staff and students. Rather than adopt a familiar Western style code of conduct, the Wānanga looked for their own solution. Kawa guides behavior at traditional meeting grounds to ensure a safe and productive environment. It can include both rules about what is acceptable as well as more general expectations. The Wānanga implemented Te Kawa o te Ako,[16] promoting a culture for teaching and learning. Te Kawa o te Ako requires Wānanga staff and students to consider the effects of their actions—do they contribute to or detract from a culture of teaching and learning? Whenever anyone's ability to work, teach or learn is affected by another person's behavior, they may choose to publicly or privately challenge the person, or to complain formally to Te Kawa o te Ako committee (Raureti, 2009). If a complaint is made, the committee will speak to all parties and require those who created the problem to provide an appropriate resolution and assurance that they will not create more problems. Until the process is resolved, people may be excluded from the Wānanga. This process has been used in diverse situations including theft, sexual assault, alcohol and drug taking, and malicious gossip. It has resulted in a significant shift in behavior and attitude of people on campus, requiring that people prioritize the collective's well-being (Raureti, 2009).

Kaupapa Here

After 20 years of experimenting with Māori education under the direction of the confederation and the principles of Whakatupuranga Rua Mano, the Wānanga reflected on its experience of self-determination. Pakake Winiata (n.d.) identified 10 kaupapa[17] that were constantly involved in decisions. These have become the "kaupapa here," usually translated as guiding kaupapa, but more literally the binding kaupapa of Te Wānanga o Raukawa. They are an explicit part of decision-making, planning and reporting at the Wānanga. From course design and employment contracts to the Wānanga's statutorily required audit, the Wānanga is measured against its kaupapa. These have proven so useful that the model has been exported to many Māori organizations (Winiata, 2016).

Conclusions

Te Wānanga o Raukawa has a unique role in decolonization and Indigenous education in Aotearoa/New Zealand. The ART Confederation was approaching extinction when it established Te Wānanga o Raukawa. With determination and vision rooted in our language, values and knowledge system, the Wānanga has led a cultural resurgence.

The Wānanga continues to experiment. Even as it has adopted many structures of Western education institutions, it explicitly rejects their assumption of superiority and is developing uniquely Māori ways of operating within the tertiary education environment, guided by the principles of Whatatupuranga Rua Mano and its kaupapa here.

The Wānanga continues to resist. Even as it has accepted funding from the state, it has maintained explicit opposition to the state's assumption of power. It has led one successful claim against the Crown, arguing that Māori can define their own educational institutions and that the state must resource them as they do their own institutions. It is leading another claim, a claim that challenges foundations of colonizing philosophy, arguing that the Crown's actions have consistently devalued and dismantled the Māori knowledge continuum, while at the same time resourcing and venerating Western knowledge systems.

Te Wānanga o Raukawa is many things. Most obviously, it is an educational institution, rebuilding a Māori skill base, and encouraging students to critically explore what it means to be Māori in the 21st century and beyond. It is an experiment, identifying problems, suggesting solutions based on Māori philosophies and values, testing those solutions, adjusting and learning from the experience. It is a haven for many, where recognizing the injustice and violence of colonization is considered both healthy and normal, where talking about values and emotional and spiritual needs is encouraged. It is a critical intervention, questioning colonizing assumptions, demonstrating Māori solutions, shifting norms, rebuilding confidence in Māori philosophies and practices. It is a model of decolonization and Indigenous futurities (e.g., Arvin, Tuck, & Morrill, 2013), shaped by the future that the ART confederation imagines, where cultural survival and success is assured. It is also grounded in the past, demonstrating the responsibility of current generations to acknowledge the ancestors, their gifts, knowledge, language, their dreams for the future. It is just one example of how Indigenous nations, even from the brink of cultural extinction, can rebuild themselves, decolonizing as they go.

Notes

1 This was the terminology in the 1970s. Now "iwi and hapū" would be preferred over "tribal."
2 Marae = ancestral gathering place(s), usually including a meeting house, dining hall, large grassed area for encountering visiting groups; may also include houses and community facilities.
3 Hui = gathering(s).
4 Eleven professions were identified as essential for a self-determining confederation and goals were set for graduates in each of them over the 25 years of the plan.
5 In some migration traditions the name Rangiātea is associated with the launching point of waka carrying the ancestors to Aotearoa. In some creation traditions it is the name of the house of learning (whare wānanga) where all knowledge originated.
6 For example, the first church built by the ART confederation is called Rangiātea. It was completed in 1851 (destroyed by arson in 1995 and rebuilt) and now neighbors Te Wānanga o Raukawa.
7 Iwi = nation(s).
8 Hapū = clan(s).
9 Kaupapa = Māori values, principles.
10 The success of this model has been demonstrated. Only a few years later, an organization that would become Te Wānanga o Aotearoa, which concentrated on practical skills for the community such as Māori arts and trades training, would lobby the Crown to recognize wānanga as a category of tertiary education institution (Te Wānanga o Aotearoa, n.d.). It is now one of the nation's largest tertiary education providers. Soon after, a third was established, Te Whare Wānanga o Awanuiārangi.
11 In 2014, universities received NZ$12,698 per effective full-time student (EFTS), plus NZ$267 million from PBRF; Te Wānanga o Raukawa received NZ$7948 per EFTS (63% of a university EFTS), with no money from PBRF (53% compared to university EFTS and PBRF funding combined) (New Zealand, 2014).
12 PBRF accounts for nine percent of total tertiary education funding.
13 Mauri = spiritual integrity, vital essence.
14 Whakapapa = the web of relationships that connects us to all of creation; in this case, close kin.
15 Mokopuna = a person two or more generations younger, usually a close relation.
16 The kawa of teaching and learning.
17 Kaupapa = values, principles.

References

Arvin, M., Tuck, E., & Morrill, A. (2013). Decolonizing feminism: Challenging connections between settler colonialism and heteropatriarchy. *Feminist Formations, 25*, 8–34.
Barrington, J. M. (1988). Learning the dignity of labour: Secondary education policy for Maoris. *New Zealand Journal of Education Studies, 20*, 151–164.
Kuokkanen, R. (2007). *Reshaping the university: Responsibility, indigenous epistemes and the logic of the gift.* Vancouver, BC: UBC Press.

Leach, L., Neutze, G., & Zepke, N. (2003). Course design and assessment for transformation. In N. Zepke, D. Nugent, & L. Leach (Eds.). *Reflection to transformation: A self-help book for teachers*. Palmerston North, Aotearoa: Dunmore Press.

Mikaere, A. (2011). From Kaupapa Māori research to re-searching kaupapa Māori: Making our contribution to Māori survival. In *Kei Tua o te Pae Hui proceedings: The challenges of Kaupapa Māori Research in the 21st Century* (pp. 29–37). Wellington, Aotearoa: New Zealand Council for Educational Research.

Mikaere, A. (2017). *Like moths to the flame? A history of Ngāti Raukawa resistance and recovery*. Ōtaki, Aotearoa: Te Tākupu. New Zealand, Ministry of Education. (2008). *How the PBRF has shifted research funding*. Retrieved from http://thehub.superu.govt.nz/sites/default/files/42160_Funding_factsheet_0.pdf

New Zealand, Tertiary Education Commission. (2014). *Tertiary education performance report*. Tertiary Education Commission. Retrieved from www.tec.govt.nz/assets/Reports/The-Tertiary-Education-Performance-Report-2014.pdf

New Zealand, Waitangi Tribunal. (1989). *Report of the Waitangi Tribunal on the te reo Maori claim (WAI 11)* (2nd ed.). Wellington, Aotearoa: Author.

New Zealand, Waitangi Tribunal. (1999). *The wānanga capital establishment report (WAI718)*. Wellington, Aotearoa: Author.

New Zealand, Waitangi Tribunal. (2010). *Waitangi Tribunal Report 262: Te reo Māori*. Wellington, Aotearoa: Author.

Nicholson, I. (1998, May 11). *Teenei mea "Te Purutanga Mauri."* Unpublished internal document, Te Wānanga o Raukawa.

Raureti, H. (2009). Te Kawa o te Ako: Kaupapa and tikanga Māori as regulators of behaviour and interaction in a modern context. In *Mā te rango te waka ka rere: Exploring a kaupapa Māori organisational framework*. Ōtaki, Aotearoa: Te Wānanga o Raukawa.

Rāwiri, Ā. (2012). *Te Wānanga o Raukawa: Restoring mātauranga to restore ecosystems*. Ōtaki, Aotearoa: Te Tākupu.

Statistics New Zealand. (2013). *Census QuickStats about Māori*. Retrieved from www.statistics.govt.nz/Census/2013-census/profile-and-summary-reports/quickstats-about-maori-english/maori-language.aspx

Te Wānanga o Raukawa. (2015). *Te pūrongo 2015*. Ōtaki, Aotearoa: Author.

Walker, P. (2011). *Whakatupuranga Rua Mano 1975–2000: He tirohanga whakamuri*. Ōtaki, Aotearoa: Te Tākupu.

Winiata, P. B. (2000). *Whakatupuranga Rua Mano*. (Unpublished Master of Mātauranga Māori thesis). Te Wānanga o Raukawa, Ōtaki, Aotearoa.

Winiata, P. C. (n.d.). *Guiding kaupapa of Te Wānanga-o-Raukawa*. Retrieved from www.wananga.com/images/pdf/Guiding_Kaupapa.pdf

Winiata, W. (1979). Whakatupuranga Rua Mano Generation 2000: An experiment in tribal development. *Planning Paper No. 4*. Wellington, Aotearoa: New Zealand Planning Council.

Winiata, W. (1995, June 28). *Treaty of Waitangi: Towards 2000: Economic progression and the interconnection between Maori and Tauiwi development*. Unpublished internal document, Te Wānanga o Raukawa.

Winiata, W. (2013, October 2). *The natural tension*. Unpublished internal document, Te Wānanga o Raukawa.

Winiata, W. (2016). Building Māori futures on kaupapa tuku iho. *Whakatupu mātauranga, 1*, 21–42.

12

DESIGNING FUTURES OF IDENTITY

Navigating Agenda Collisions in Pacific Disability

Catherine Picton and Rasela Tufue-Dolgoy

Educate yourself enough
So you may understand
The ways of other people
But not too much
That you may lose
Your understanding
Of your own

—*Lemalu Tate Simi, "Identity" (1995)*

The conceptualization and experience of disability is unique and diverse—among individuals and importantly, among cultures. This is especially true in Samoa where the unique cultural context, the Fa'asamoa (the Samoan way), intersects with multiple and frequently incongruous conceptualizations of disability. Some disability perceptions are relics of a colonial history. Others are more contemporary perspectives influenced by global constructions of disability. These intersections do not always occur as an effortless integration. They are sometimes felt as collisions of agendas; where multiple perspectives encounter and impact one another. These collisions have implications for the social, political, economic, cultural, and individual identities of people with disabilities.

Beyond a historical "ableist"[1] view of disability in Samoa reported by Anesi (2015), the past decade of disability policy development has been driven by a global human rights approach. In particular, the UN's Convention on the Rights of People with Disabilities (UNCRPD) (United Nations, 2006), ratified by Samoa in 2016, has been a significant driving force. A measure of success has been achieved in shifting societal perceptions of disability through the integration of a global human rights ethos into Samoan disability policy. However, Samoa's unique cultural nuances are not necessarily reflected (Picton, 2015). This highlights the need for a new approach to the development of disability policy and raises a logistical question: Is it possible to develop disability policy that reflects the value and relevance of the cultural context while simultaneously incorporating diverse and alternative views?

Over the past several decades, the value, role, and function of Indigenous knowledge and perspectives has been increasingly recognized as critical to Pacific development. Tuhiwai Smith's (2012) view of decolonization in research frames Indigenous voices as critical to Indigenous futurities. While her frame is neither exclusive to Samoa or disability, it offers a powerful theoretical position from which to think about the issues that Samoan people face in reclaiming cultural epistemological and ontological spaces from ongoing colonizing practices. This decolonizing perspective, when interwoven with disability, is an opportunity for critical knowledge and experiences of Indigenous disability to be voiced by Indigenous people with disabilities.

It is important to clarify the focus of this chapter specifically pertains to the Samoan culture and, in this case, the use of the term "Indigenous" refers only to only Samoans. As Tuhiwai Smith (2012) importantly cautions, the broad use of the term "Indigenous" contributes to the production of homogenized views of Indigenous cultures. The nuances that exist between Indigenous cultures do not, however, exclude them from potential agenda collisions of the nature that Samoa is currently facing.

This chapter will journey through the collisions of Samoan disability conceptualizations. First, it describes the unique interplay between cultural ontological perspectives of identity and their collision with disability conceptualizations arising in part from colonizing influences. Second, the chapter will locate disability in Samoa in a broader global context, as well as examine the agenda collisions of culture, disability, and the global homogenization of disability constructs. Third, methods of policy development will be explored, highlighting the importance of promoting Indigenous intellectual autonomy in securing valued Indigenous identity spaces. Finally, the Tutusa framework will be proposed as a tool to navigate these agenda collisions and to foreground issues that are relevant and valuable to Samoans with disabilities. The Tutusa framework is a discussion tool to co-construct disability conceptualizations and to discuss issues relevant to the lived experience of disability in Samoa. Playing on the Samoan meaning of Tutusa, meaning "to be the same, equal" (Milner, 1992), the framework aims to ensure that all stakeholder voices are considered equal. It provides tools to evaluate all stakeholder perspectives, with a focus on what is valuable to Samoans with disabilities. This view can then be used in the broad development of policies relevant to Samoans with disabilities and positively influence Samoan futurities.

Disability and Samoa: A Journey of Conceptualizations

> *The demands of modernization and globalization have exposed Samoan culture to*
> *influences from a plethora of other sources and have resulted in pressures for social and*
> *cultural change, both good and bad.*
>
> —Unasa Leulu Felise Va'a (2006, p. 125)

The Independent State of Samoa, located in the South Pacific Ocean, forms part of the Polynesian triangle in the wider Oceania region. With an on-island population of nearly 190,000 it is surprising that the prevalence of disability is reported at just two percent (Faafeu-Taalogo, Lene, Nuanua o le Alofa, & Inclusion International Asia Pacific Region, 2002) given the UN estimate that 18.2% of the global population have a disability (World Health Organisation, 2011). This discrepancy may emanate from a genuine under-representation of the incidence of disability in the recently developed island nation. It may also emanate from potential limitations of statistical reporting and data collection techniques that fail to identify people with disabilities according to globally recognized measures (Bornman, 2004). This feature of statistical reporting in itself deeply discriminatory (Mittler, 2015).

Statistical reporting on disability in Samoa is additionally complicated by disparate societal beliefs, arising from the intersection of culture, colonizing influences, and globalizing influences, as well as resulting in implications for identity development (Picton, 2016). This is both problematic for the way that people experience disability and for the development and acceptance of policy. Understanding the interplay between cultural and alternative views of disability is an important link to recognizing the impact of agenda collisions. Samoa's settler colonial history features as a significant influence on contemporary disability conceptualizations.

In the times prior to colonization, it can be assumed that disability was conceptualized within a frame of the Fa'asamoa. This deeply rooted all family members, disabled or otherwise in a complex and unique cultural script, imbuing a sense of culture, connectedness, and identity.[2] Samoan identity is collective, binding individuals in kinship arrangements that nurture a deep sense of belonging, well-being, shared community status, financial stability, and reciprocal networks (Kolone-Collins, 2010; Kruse-Vaai, 1998; Seiuli, 2012; Tufue-Dolgoy, 2010). These collective practices are inclusive and provide security, prosperity, love, and unity for all family members.

Samoans are still predominantly embedded in the practices of the Fa'asamoa. It has adapted to colonizing and globalizing influences, but not without repercussions. Conceptualizing disability in a way that is different to the collective, potentially risks cultural identity, and in turn, access to the prosperity of the collective (Picton, 2015). For example, Thornton, Binns, and Kerslake (2013) identified an agenda collision between church membership and customary land ownership.

They report that where people choose to adopt beliefs outside of the collective, they are denied access to customary land, a birthright of being part of a collective identity and enjoying the security and prosperity of kinship inclusion.

Significant to current Samoan conceptualizations and experiences of disability is the beliefs brought to Samoa during the colonial era. The arrival of English missionaries and traders in the 1830s caused widespread cultural disruption (Meleisea, 2012; Va'a, 2006) and collisions of agendas. For example, the introduction of Christianity challenged established Indigenous spiritual belief systems (Thornton et al., 2013; Va'a, 2006), and a new education system dismantled traditional, nonformal practices, as well as restricted the usage of the Samoan language in educational settings (Coxon, 2007; Kolone-Collins, 2010). This period of colonization coincided with the medical model era in Europe, characterized by an ableist view of disability as an illness (Clapton & Fitzgerald, 1997). A moral view, characterized by the belief that disability is an act of God (Creamer, 2012) was also a way to conceptualize disability in Europe during this era as a charity model, depicting people with disability as in need of help or objects of pity (Clapton & Fitzgerald, 1997). All views remain in contemporary Samoan society (Lameta, 2013; Picton, 2015; Tufue-Dolgoy, 2010). These conceptualizations represent collisions of agendas and perspectives not only with the Fa'asamoa but also with each other. For example, a Samoan moral perspective may conceptualize disability as either a curse or a blessing (Picton, 2015); a conflict within a single view. These incongruities challenge contemporary societal cohesion by thwarting the acceptance of new policy and impacting the experience of disability.

The medical model of disability was particularly pervasive in Samoan society and became the foundation for policy development until recently. Anesi (2015) reports disability policy in the 1970s as being framed in ableist rhetoric, causing a collision of agendas. Cultural approaches such as village schools promoted inclusion; formal schooling excluded people with disabilities. This ableist rhetoric prompted the establishment of a Samoan community group who advocated for and created a formal education system for children with disabilities (Anesi, 2015), marking a return to some semblance of cultural ideology. Government policy provisions for inclusive education were not nationally implemented until 1992. The policy was still largely a borrowed one (Tufue-Dolgoy, 2010) and did not foreground the voices of Samoans with disabilities. A policy from either an Indigenous or human-rights perspective was still nearly a decade away.

For the 2005 to 2015 period the Samoan Ministry of Education, Sports, and Culture (MESC) implemented the Strategic Policy and Plans (2005–2015) and for the first time addressed equity in education through the inclusion of an Inclusive Education policy (Ministry of Education Sports and Culture, 2006; Tufue-Dolgoy, 2010). With intellectual input from Samoan educational practitioners, its aim was to improve curriculum delivery, pedagogical quality, and school infrastructure (Tufue-Dolgoy, 2010). However, parts of the policy were still largely borrowed and funding was allocated by Australian and New Zealand donor partners (Afamasaga-Fuata'i et al., 2012) with inherent obligations, complications, and collisions. The ambition of this policy was to combine progressive national development goals with Indigenous knowledge and brings to mind Tuck's and Yang's (2012) caution that viewing decolonization and national improvements as mutually exclusive is a rigid assumption. This monumental step in education policy reflected a political shift toward a social model of disability, characterized by a view of society as limiting and inadequate in its accommodation of all citizens (Clapton & Fitzgerald, 1997), and suggests that the removal of barriers mitigates the experience of disability. However, there was still no overarching disability policy in Samoan society. In 2011, Samoa implemented its first national policy on disability.

Culture, Policy, and the Generic Globalization of Disability

> *Take up the fight against the global production of disability.*
> —*Helen Meekosha, Contextualizing Disability (2008, p. 16)*

The Samoan National Policy for Persons with Disabilities (SNPD) was implemented for the 2011 to 2016[3] period, signaling an unequivocal political shift of ideology (Ministry of Women Community and Social Development, 2009). As a broad societal vision for equity, the policy was based upon the UNCRPD and promotes robust global ideologies. It ostensibly reflects Samoan cultural concepts of alofa (love), fa'aaloalo (respect), and tautua (service) (Lameta, 2013), although it remains largely a borrowed policy. A growing body of research indicates resistance to borrowed disability policy, resulting from the subjugation of Indigenous knowledge and perspectives (Lameta, 2013; McDonald & Tufue-Dolgoy, 2013; McKinstry, Price, & Setareki, 2012; Picton, 2015; Tufue-Dolgoy, 2010). For example, from a human rights perspective, the SNPD *addresses* issues of discrimination and prejudice, but from a cultural perspective, the SNPD *challenges* epistemological and ontological constructs.

Developing and recently developed countries like Samoa are increasingly vulnerable to the worldwide homogenization of disability, considered the global "gold standard" (Merriam, 2007) of knowledge. The prioritization of global notions of social justice, as a concept ostensibly differing from Indigenous social justice concepts, reinforces Indigenous intellectual contributions as illegitimate to knowledge production (Tuhiwai Smith, Maxwell, Puke, & Temara, 2016). This issue is compounded by the significant financial contributions made by regional aid partnerships and the ensuing obligations and accountability to the region expected from recipient countries.[4] This is yet another example of an agenda collision where regional and global development agendas are prioritized over Indigenous ones. Rather than empowering people with disabilities, homogenizing approaches to disability create a landscape where disability is not a Samoan concept, subjugating cultural ideas and practices, and effectively removing disability from the cultural bedrock. The absence of actively incorporating Samoan perspectives of disability was compromising policy implementation. Tufue-Dolgoy (2010) recommended further examination of Samoan disability conceptualizations as necessary to the effective development of policy.

Anesi (2015) published such research in 2015; however she reports perspectives of disability from the 1970s and 1980s, identifying an ableist history in Samoa as a contributing factor in the experience of discrimination for people with disabilities. Also in 2015, Picton published research on more contemporary perspectives of disability in Samoa.[5] She found diverse and frequently incongruous views of disability that challenged the broader cultural and socio-political context views of disability. The range of perspectives of disability, drawn from cultural, colonizing, and contemporary global views include moral, charity, social, and cultural[6] frames. They all represent collisions of agendas. They also foster a lack of shared understanding of disability (Anastasiou & Kauffman, 2011; Clapton & Fitzgerald, 1997; Garrick Duhaney & Salend, 2010; Kudlacova, 2008) and impact upon the way that disability is experienced.

Reaching a more nuanced view of the experience of disability in Samoa involves valuing the important voices of Samoans with disabilities. Knowing what is valuable and relevant to Samoans with disability is critical to effective development and implementation of policy. However, the incorporation of this knowledge is yet to be fully realized.

Creating Identity Spaces: Combining Culture and Policy

So'o le fau i le fau
(Join the hibiscus fiber to hibiscus fiber; strength in unity.)

—*Samoan Proverb*

Creating space for valued experiences, views, and identities, even where this presents global or cultural challenges, is important to formulating futurities for Samoans with disabilities. Gaining momentum within the academy of critical disability studies is the examination of the intersectionality of disability with cultural conceptualizations and notions of citizenship (Ghai, 2002; Lang, 2001, Meekosha, 2011; Meekosha & Soldatic, 2011). Meekosha and Soldatic refer to a "global counter-hegemonic movement" (2011, p. 1392) that ruptures the global dominant discourse of disability.

In advocating and prioritizing culture as a challenge to global hegemonic paradigms, Hollinsworth (2013) identified a concerning assumption that cultural beliefs and practices are deterministic, rather than flexible and progressive. This is unfounded in the Samoan context; the Fa'asamoa is flexible, inclusive, and responsive to change (McDonald & Tufue-Dolgoy, 2013; Siauane, 2004) where change is relevant and valued. However, the current available models of culturally responsive policy development are limited; they do not provide a roadmap to challenge assumptions and perspectives.

Two models of policy development, specifically for the Samoan disability context, have been recently proposed. First, the "Blended Policy Development Model" (Duke et al., 2016) resulted from a recent donor-funded project conducted in Samoa. Theoretically constructed outside of Samoan cultural frameworks, the model is intended as a tool to analyze the initial stages of policy adoption and design (Duke et al., 2016). It demonstrates the complexities and agenda collisions that Samoa is tasked with navigating where donor funding has attached regional expectations and responsibilities. Aside from acknowledging the existence of cultural traditions as a perspective, it does not foreground the perspectives and experiences of people with disabilities, nor does it prioritize Samoan intellectual autonomy as a driving force in reclaiming ownership of Samoan disability futurities.

A second model of policy integration, the "Education Policy Borrowing System Development" model (McDonald & Tufue-Dolgoy, 2013) shown in Figure 12.1 demonstrates the process of identifying areas for reform, engaging stakeholder perspectives, implementation, and the continued monitoring and management of the policy. It offers a broad overview of the cycle of policy adoption: attraction to policy, the incorporation of stakeholder perspectives, implementation, and monitoring, with overarching consideration of the local and global contexts.

Both models assume that policy will be borrowed, rather than newly developed, a concerning assumption given that "borrowed," "introduced" or "imposed" policy comes pre-packaged with non-Indigenous values. Neither model specifies how stakeholder perspectives will be considered, returning us to the question of whether it is possible for policy to simultaneously navigate cultural, global, and individual agendas, while foregrounding Indigenous intellectual autonomy and the voices of people with disabilities. The Tutusa framework is a tool to achieve this goal through promoting the value of decolonizing revolutions, and incorporating valued alternative knowledge systems.

Navigating Agenda Collisions Through the Tutusa Framework

The success of a society is to be evaluated . . . primarily by the freedoms that members of the society enjoy.

—Amartya Sen, Development as Freedom (1999)

The Tutusa framework (Figure 12.2) promotes Samoan identity spaces and knowledge production as fundamental to the development of disability

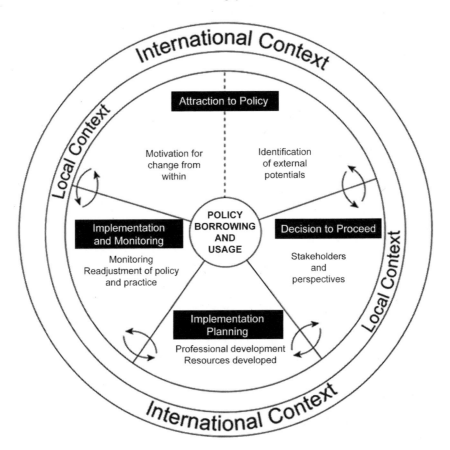

FIGURE 12.1 Education Policy Borrowing System Development Model

Source: McDonald and Tufue-Dolgoy (2013)

conceptualizations and policy. It offers a robust tool for the development of a unique Samoan perspective of disability through navigating the space between cultural, colonizing, and globalizing ideological agendas. A culturally responsive Talanoa method guides stakeholder discussion, simultaneously valuing and responding to individual, societal, global, and cultural aspirations. A structured approach to Talanoa is offered through a series of evaluation filters, influenced by the Capabilities Approach (CA) (Nussbaum, 2007; Sen, 1979; Terzi, 2005). This process represents the "stakeholder perspectives" phase of policy development.

The engine of the Tutusa framework is the Talanoa approach (Otsuka, 2006; Vaioleti, 2006, 2011). Rooted in Indigenous practice, Talanoa literally means "to talk"; a culturally important and collaborative decision-making process to co-construct meaning (Vaioleti, 2006). Aside from its obvious cultural relevance, Talanoa has much to offer progressive policy development. Through the sharing of individual, practical, and cultural experiences and ideas, Talanoa is a platform to co-construct meaning, alongside social, national, and political perspectives. The CA filters (middle section of the framework at Figure 12.2) guide the Talanoa process, prioritizing the voices of an extensive stakeholder community. For example, stakeholders may debate the value of cultural obligations, or the real opportunities of society to implement initiatives, or even the issues around economy and policy. These potentially disparate voices are collectively valued, yet equally subject to robust debate. The Talanoa can occur at a village, organizational, and government level, ensuring that all stakeholders have an opportunity to voice their perspectives. For example, nominated representatives of village Talanoa sessions will report the village perspective at district Talanoa sessions. Samoans with disabilities and their families are critical to this phase of Talanoa in sharing their lived experience of disability. Those perspectives will then be reported by representatives to Talanoa sessions held by advocacy groups and organizations. Through these sessions, all stakeholder perspectives are being equally valued and evaluated. Finally, government Talanoa, with input from all representatives, would be conducted. This government Talanoa would consider perspectives generated from village, community, and organizational stakeholders. It would also evaluate other stakeholder views such as educational, economic, and donor relationships perspectives. The collision of agendas is inherent in this process; thus the Tutusa framework uses a series of filters to navigate such collisions.

The Talanoa process is guided by concepts drawn from the CA. The CA focuses upon what concepts are valued by individuals and recognizes that human diversity is a natural state (Nussbaum, 2007; Sen, 1979; Terzi, 2005). The CA was originally designed as a model of moral evaluation, human development, and welfare economics, and later developed as a tool with which to assess and evaluate human development and well-being within the context of disability (Harnacke, 2013; Nussbaum, 2007; Terzi, 2005, 2014). Its focus is to determine what functions are intrinsically valued by the stakeholder groups and, most importantly, are valued by Samoans with disabilities. The seemingly exhaustive pursuit of mitigating societal barriers and hurdles, many of which are identified through the lens of global disability conceptualizations, seems futile if the goals beyond the barriers and hurdles are not actually valued within the unique cultural context. The right to choose what is contextually valued presents a more liberating pathway to lived experience with disabilities.

The Tutusa framework also focuses on value and offers a series of filters, influenced by the CA, to guide the evaluation of stakeholder perspectives. The filters include the evaluation of value, capabilities, opportunity, social factors, and available commodities. Where a concept or perspective is considered valuable, it must then be evaluated according to individual and societal capability. This is an important point of reflection; if an individual or society does not have the immediate capability to carry out a valued function, an evaluation of barriers must ensue. Immediate action may be restricted by both individual and societal

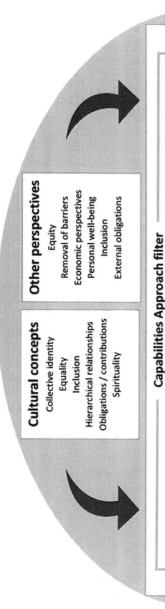
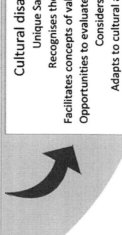

FIGURE 12.2 The Tutusa Framework

Source: Picton (2015)

opportunities and freedoms, the influence of societal values, and the availability of resources and commodities. These three filters are of particular significance to developing and recently developed countries as they navigate culture, economic circumstances, broader national and regional development goals, and the agenda collisions and obligations of donor relationships. The identified barriers to valued functions become the goals toward the ongoing development and implementation of policy that respond to all stakeholder perspectives.

Ongoing development, resulting from the Tutusa framework, is part of a cycle of critical evaluation; a systematic process that must be revisited as individual, social, cultural, and political circumstances shift, particularly where new policy successfully redresses marginalization. While some suggestions of cultural and other perspectives are offered within the framework as examples of the capabilities of the Tutusa framework, these may or may not represent stakeholder views. In practice, what is evaluated is the product of extensive stakeholder Talanoa to determine what bears relevance to the debate around policy development specific to disability in terms of rights, capabilities, functioning, and culture.

Designed specifically as a tool for Samoan disability policy development, the Tutusa framework has a broad transdisciplinary and transcultural application. By changing the concepts to be evaluated, the Tutusa framework could, for example, evaluate culture and tourism, or the economy and the environment. It could also be used in other cultural contexts that face similar collisions of agenda in national development.

The Tutusa framework brings about a transformative space where culture ceases to merely underpin policy that wallows beneath the weight of global "gold standards" (Merriam, 2007). It realizes a level of ideological cohesion and solidarity previously unattainable through traditional policy blending. It firmly locates the production of knowledge within Indigenous parameters and foregrounds the intellectual contributions of Samoans with disabilities as critical stakeholders. This is a roadmap for Samoans with disabilities to secure identities of value and empowerment.

There is a salient urgency to acknowledge the narratives of disability as valuable contributions to the rich and diverse tapestry of Samoan society. As key stakeholders, Samoans with disabilities are central voices in the construction of disability and subsequent policies. It is their rightful choice as to which identity spaces to value and occupy. Policy can support this empowerment where it co-constructs disability with all stakeholder perspectives and prioritizes the voices and choices of people with disabilities.

Disability policy is charged with the responsibility of constructing and disseminating disability conceptualizations to create societal cohesion and unity. The Tutusa framework is a viable tool to entrench the voices of Samoans with disabilities into Pacific futures. It provides ongoing opportunities to rethink the way that disability as an individual, social, cultural, and global experience is approached. Locating the choice of what is valued firmly within contemporary

Samoan epistemological and ontological frames offers the greatest choice of cultural futurity.

Notes

1 Anesi (2015) uses several sources to frame ableism in her work. Most notably she draws on Kluth (2006), defining ableism as an inherently negative view of impairment and disability as a condition to be "cured" or fixed.
2 A brief overview of the Fa'asamoa offers insight into the agenda collisions of culture and other perspectives of disability. For a comprehensive description of the Fa'asamoa, see Va'a (2006).
3 An updated policy based upon the 2011 to 2016 version is in development.
4 Australia and New Zealand have strong donor relationships with Samoa. Aid is distributed for a variety of national development priorities. Forecasted Australian aid for Samoa for the 2017–2018 period is $37.2 million (www.dfat.com.au), and New Zealand forecasts $38 million in bi-lateral funding during the same period (www.mfat.govt.nz).
5 Picton's research drew heavily on participant voice through a culturally embedded Talanoa process.
6 Samoan cultural conceptualizations of disability prior to the arrival of missionaries is undocumented, but a contemporary cultural frames is based on Samoan concepts of equality, rather than equity, contributions, and collectivism (Picton, 2015).

References

Afamasaga-Fuata'I, K., Afamasaga, G., Esera, E., Fa'afeu-Hope, T. E., Schuster, L. T., Shon, L. E. F., & Polu, A. L. (2012). Aspects of social development. In L. M. Meleisea & P. S. Meleisea (Eds.), *Samoa's journey 1962–2012 aspects of history* (pp. 141–172). Wellington, New Zealand: Victoria University Press.

Anastasiou, D., & Kauffman, J. (2011). A social constructionist approach to disability: Implications and special education. *Exceptional Children, 77*(3), 367–384. doi:10.1177/001440291107700307

Anesi, J. (2015). *Trying times: Disability, activism, and education in Samoa, 1970–1980.* (Doctoral dissertation), Syracuse University. Retrieved from http://surface.syr.edu/cgi/viewcontent.cgi?article=1418&context=etd

Bornman, J. (2004). The World Health Organisation's terminology and classification: Application to severe disability. *Disability and Rehabilitation, 26*(3), 182–188. doi:http://dx.doi.org/10.1080/09638280410001665218

Clapton, J., & Fitzgerald, J. (1997). The history of disability: A history of "otherness." *New Renaissance Magazine, 7*(1), 1–3. Retrieved from www.ru.org/human-rights/the-history-of-disability-a-history-of-otherness.html

Coxon, E. (2007). Schooling in Samoa. In C. Campbell & G. Sherington (Eds.), *Going to school in Oceania* (pp. 263–314). Connecticut: Greenwood Publishing Group.

Creamer, D. (2012). Disability theology. *Religious Compass, 6*(7), 339–346. doi:10.1111/j.1749–8171.2012.00366.x

Duke, J., Pillay, H., Tones, M., Nickerson, P., Carrington, S., & Ioelu, A. (2016). A case for rethinking inclusive education policy in developing countries. *Compare: A Journal of Comparative and International Education, 46*(6), 906–928. doi:10.1080/03057925.2016.1204226

Faafeu-Taalogo, M. T., Lene, D., Nuanua o le Alofa, & Inclusion International Asia Pacific Region. (2002). *Samoan adult 15+ disability identification census report & key recommendations: Statistical report*. Retrieved from Apia, Samoa. Nuanua o le Alofa and Inclusion International Asia and Pacific Region.

Garrick Duhaney, L. M., & Salend, S. J. (2010). History of special education. In P. Peterson (Ed.), *International encyclopedia of education* (3rd ed., (pp. 714–720). Retrieved from http://vs7pm8vz2k.search.serialssolutions.com/?V=1.0&L=VS7PM8VZ2K&S=JCs& C=TC_005077253&T=marc&tab=BOOKS

Ghai, A. (2002). Disability in the Indian context: Post-colonial perspectives. In M. Corker & T. Shakespeare (Eds.), *Disability/postmodernity: Embodying disability theory* (pp. 88–100). London, UK: Continuum.

Harnacke, C. (2013). Disability and capability: Exploring the usefulness of Martha Nussbaum's capabilities approach for the UN disability rights convention. *Journal of Law, Medicine & Ethics, 41*, 768–780. doi:10.1111/jlme.12088

Hollinsworth, D. (2013). Decolonizing indigenous disability in Australia. *Disability and Society, 28*(5), 601–615. doi:10.1080/09687599.2012.717879

Kluth, P. (2006). *Toward a social model of disability: Disability studies for teachers*. New York, NY. Center on Human Policy.

Kolone-Collins, S. (2010). *Fagogo: Ua molimea manusina: A qualitative study of the pedagogical significance of the fagogo—Samoan stories at night—for the education of Samoan children*. (Master's thesis). Retrieved from http://aut.researchgateway.ac.nz/handle/10292/1034

Kruse-Vaai, E. (1998). *Producing the text of culture: The appropriation of English in contemporary Samoa*. (Doctoral dissertation). University of New South Wales, Australia.

Kudlacova, B. (2008). From repression to inclusion: Historical models and approaches to disabled people in the European context. *Problems of Education in the 21st Century, 8*, 68–78. Retrieved from www.scientiasocialis.lt/pec/files/pdf/Kudlacova.Vol.8.pdf

Lameta, E. (2013). *Samoan inclusive education situational analysis: Students with disabilities*. Retrieved from Apia, Samoa. Ministry of Education, Sports and Culture.

Lang, R. (2001, June). *Understanding disability from a South Indian perspective*. Paper presented at the 14th Annual meeting of the Disability Studies Association, Winnipeg, Canada.

McDonald, L., & Tufue-Dolgoy, R. (2013). Moving forwards, sideways or backwards? Inclusive Education in Samoa. *International Journal of Disability, Development & Education, 60*(3), 270–284. doi:10.1080/1034912X.2013.812187

McKinstry, G., Price, P., & Setareki, M. (2012). *Review of disability legislation in the Pacific*. Fiji: Pacific Islands Forum Secretariat:

Meekosha, H. (2008, September, 2–4). *Contextualising disability: Developing Southern/global theory*. Paper presented at the 4th Biennial Disability Studies Conference, Lancaster, England.

Meekosha, H. (2011). Decolonising disability: Thinking and acting globally. *Disability and Society, 26*(6), 667–682. doi:10.1080/09687599.2011.602860

Meekosha, H., & Soldatic, K. (2011). Human rights and the global south: The case for disability. *Third World Quarterly, 32*(8), 1383–1398. doi:10.1080/01436597.2011.614800

Meleisea, M. (2012). Introduction. In L. M. Meleisea, P. S. Meleisea, & E. Meleisea (Eds.), *Samoa's journey 1962–2012: Aspects of history* (pp. 13–17). Wellington, New Zealand: Victoria University Press and the National University of Samoa.

Merriam, S. (2007). An introduction to non-Western perspectives on learning and knowing. In S. Merriam (Ed.), *Non-Western perspectives on learning and knowing*. Florida: Kriegar Publishing Company.

Milner, G. B. (1992). *Samoan dictionary*. Auckland, New Zealand: Pasifika Press.

Ministry of Education Sports and Culture. (2006). *Strategic policies and plans, July 2006-June 2015*. Apia, Samoa: Author.

Ministry of Women Community and Social Development. (2009). *Samoa national policy for persons with disabilities*. Apia, Samoa: Author.

Mittler, P. (2015). The UN convention on the rights of persons with disabilities: Implementing a paradigm shift. *Journal of Policy and Practice in Intellectual Disabilities, 12*(2), 79–98. doi:10.1111/jppi.12118

Nussbaum, M. (2007). Human rights and human capabilitites. *Harvard Human Rights Journal, 20*, 21–24. doi:10.1080/14754835.2013.824268

Otsuka, S. (2006). *Talanoa research: Culturally appropriate research design in Fiji*. Paper presented at the Australian Association for Research in Education [AARE] International Education Research Conference: Creative Dissent-Constructive Solutions Melbourne, Australia.

Picton, C. (2015). *Conceptualising disability from a Samoan epistemological and cultural reference frame*. (Doctoral dissertation, Central Queensland University). Retrieved from http://hdl.cqu.edu.au/10018/1059606

Picton, C., Horsley, M., & Knight, B. A. (2016). Exploring conceptualisations of disability: A Talanoa approach to understanding cultural frameworks of disability in Samoa. *Disability, CRB and Inclusive Development (DCID)*, 17–32. doi:10.5463/DCID.v27i1.502

Seiuli, B. (2012). Uputaua: A therapeutic approach to researching Samoan communities. *The Australian Community Psychologist, 24*(1), 24–37. Retrieved from http://researchcommons.waikato.ac.nz/handle/10289/9826

Sen, A. (1979). Equality of what? In S. McMurrin (Ed.), *The Tanner lectures on human values* (Vol. 1). Paper presented at the Tanner Lecture on Human Values, Cambridge University, 22 May (pp. 197–220). Cambridge University Press, Cambridge.

Sen, A. (1999). *Development as freedom*. London, UK: Oxford University Press.

Siauane, L. (2004). *Fa'aSamoa: A look at the evolution of the Fa'aSamoa in Christchurch*. (Master's thesis). University of Canterbury, Christchurch, New Zealand. Retrieved from https://ir.canterbury.ac.nz/bitstream/handle/10092/899/thesis_fulltext.pdf?sequence

Simi, T. L. (1995, May 30). Identity. *Samoan Observer*.

Terzi, L. (2005). Beyond the dilemma of difference: The capability approach to disability and special educational needs. *Journal of Philosophy of Education, 39*(3), 443–459. doi:10.1111/j.1467–9752.2005.00447.x

Terzi, L. (2014). Reframing inclusive education: Educational equality as capability equality. *Cambridge Journal of Education, 44*(4), 479–493. doi:10.1080/0305764X.2014.960911

Thornton, A., Binns, T., & Kerslake, M. T. (2013). Hard times in Apia? Urban landlessness and the church in Samoa. *Singapore Journal of Tropical Geography, 34*(3), 357–372. doi:10.1111/j.1467–8373.2010.01410.x

Tuck, E., & Yang, W. K. (2012). Decolonization is not a metaphor. *Decolonization: Indigeneity, Education & Society, 1*(1), 1–40.

Tufue-Dolgoy, R. (2010). *Stakeholders' perspectives of the implementation of the inclusive education policy in Samoa: A cultural fit*. (Doctoral dissertation, Victoria University). Retrieved from researcharchive.vuw.ac.nz/xmlui/handle/10063/1539

Tuhiwai Smith, L. (2012). *Decolonizing methodologies: Research and indigenous peoples* (2 ed.). London, UK: Zed Books.

Tuhiwai Smith, L., Maxwell, T. K., Puke, H., & Temara, P. (2016). Indigenous knowledge, methodology and mayhem: What is the role of methodology in producing indigenous insights? A discussion from Matauranga Maori. *Knowledge Cultures*, *4*(3), 131–156. Retrieved from www.addletonacademicpublishers.com

United Nations. (2006). *The convention on the rights of persons with disabilities.* Author. Retrieved from www.un.org/disabilities/convention/conventionfull.shtml

Va'a, L. F. (2006). The fa'asamoa. In A. So'o, U. F.Va'a, & T. Lafotanoa (Eds.), *Samoa National human development report 2006: Sustainable livelihoods in a changing Samoa* (pp. 113–135). Apia, Samoa: National University of Samoa.

Vaioleti, T. (2006). Talanoa research methodology: A developing position on Pacific research. *Waikato Journal of Education*, *12*, 21–34. Retrieved from http://researchcommons. waikato.ac.nz/handle/10289/6199

Vaioleti, T. (2011). *Talanoa, manulua and founga ako: Framework for using and enduring Tongan educational ideas for education in Aotearoa/New Zealand.* (Doctoral dissertation, University of Waikato). Retrieved from http://researchcommons.waikato.ac.nz/handle/10289/5179

World Health Organisation. (2011). *World report on disability.* Geneva: Switzerland. Author.

13

DECOLONIZING EDUCATION THROUGH TRANSDISCIPLINARY APPROACHES TO CLIMATE CHANGE EDUCATION

Teresa Newberry and Octaviana V. Trujillo (Yaqui)

Introduction

According to Vine Deloria (1999), "life is not scientific, social scientific, mathematical, or even religious; life is a unity, and the foundation for learning must be the unified experience of being a human being." In this chapter, we propose that transdisciplinary education is a decolonizing methodology since it serves an antidote to the reductionism that is an artifact of Western scientific approaches to knowledge whereas traditional knowledge is holistic, synthetic and multi-contextual. This chapter seeks to uncover educational approaches that transcend standard reductionist and analytical approaches in favor of Indigenous methodologies (Smith, 1999). We introduce a transdisciplinary climate change education module that can serve as a model of "true learning" which according to Cajete (2005) incorporates technical knowledge as well as an emphasis on reciprocal relationships with both human and natural communities. The movement toward a culturally responsive understanding of global climate change interpreted through an Indigenous lens has been limited and this work aims to shed light on methodologies and approaches that incorporate Indigenous worldviews in the context of education of American Indian/Alaska Native students at tribal colleges. We believe that these approaches are critical to providing holistic, culturally sustaining science education and it is our hope that this work will serve as a guide for others engaged in this work.

Global climate change is inherently a transdisciplinary problem that requires input from multiple scientific disciplines and consideration of socio-ecological systems in order to achieve sustainable, long-term solutions. While the differentiation and fragmentation of science into separate disciplines over the past several 100 years has yielded essential knowledge, methods and tools, an integration of knowledge is now required to address complex scientific problems (Buizer, Arts, & Kok, 2011; Holm et al., 2013; Lang et al., 2012; Mauser et al., 2013). This can explain the current trend toward transdisciplinary research in climate change science (Hellstein & Leydesdorff, 2016). Transdisciplinary research is defined by Brandt et al. (2013) as research that incorporates multiple scientific disciplines as well as input from practitioners outside of academia. Similarly, transdisciplinary education goes beyond interdisciplinary content and includes the interactions between knowledge from academics and knowledge from practitioners in order to promote a mutual learning process (Mitchell & Moore, 2015; Steiner & Posch, 2006). The need for diverse perspectives underscores the paramount importance of incorporating traditional ecological knowledge (TEK) or Indigenous knowledges (IK) in understanding and finding solutions to global climate change. In addition, leading scholars in science and environment education for Native Americans agree that pedagogy that incorporates traditional Indigenous knowledge is a crucial component of Native American student success in math and science courses.

TEK is "a cumulative body of knowledge, practice, and belief, evolving by adaptive processes and handed down through generations by cultural transmission, about the relationship of living beings (including humans) with one another and with their environment" (Berkes, 2008). TEK is a form of knowledge based on relationships and connection (ways of being in the world), in contrast to the "parts and wholes" reductionist approach typically employed under Cartesian-influenced aspects of Western science (Pierotti & Wildcat, 2000). This means that TEK can provide insights into the functioning of local ecosystem processes and to organismal responses to changing environmental conditions, both of which are important in understanding some of the major environmental problems facing all societies in today's changing world. One of the strengths of TEK is that it assumes that local environments and climate are continuously changing in a non-equilibrium fashion and that living organisms, including humans, must be flexible in their ability to respond.

IK is a bit broader than TEK and refers to a complete body of knowledge and practices maintained and developed by peoples who are locally bound and Indigenous to a specific area (Battiste & Henderson, 2009; Berkes & Berkes, 2009; Brayboy & McCarty, 2010; Nakashima, 2000; Sillitoe & Marzano, 2009). IK is situational, tacit, culture- and context-specific knowledge that is orally transmitted from generation to generation, and is dynamic, adaptive and holistic in nature. IK is rooted in the community and incorporates Indigenous goals of living "a good life" which is sometimes referred to as striving "to always think the highest thought." This metaphor refers to the framework of a sophisticated epistemology of community-based, spiritual education in which the community and its traditions form the primary support for its way of life and quality thinking. Thus, the community becomes a kind of center and context for learning how to live spiritually (Cajete, 2000) and Indigenous education is always situated within a community context.

Indigenous cultures possess vital place-based knowledge, which includes a history of adapting to highly variable and changing social and ecological conditions, concepts of adaptation and change at much longer time scales than sometimes available via methods in the natural sciences (Intergovernmental Panel on Climate Change, 2014; McNeeley & Schultzski, 2011; Maldonado et al., 2016). Transdisciplinary approaches that incorporate TEK and IK ensure its inclusion in the generation of new knowledge (Gould, González, Walker, & Ping, 2010).

Ways That Transdisciplinary Approaches Promote Student Educational Success

Legitimizing Traditional Knowledge

Transdisciplinary research and education reflects a move from the investigation of science on society but with society and a shift toward equivalencies of competencies from academic expertise and expertise of non-scientists including values (Steiner & Posch, 2006). Hence, transdisciplinary curriculum serves to legitimize the knowledge of students through the incorporation of local, cultural knowledge and by allowing students to become co-constructors of knowledge. Transdisciplinary approaches are an antidote to the deficit model, which only recognizes knowledge from European/Western societies and instead promotes transformational learning (Habermas, 1979; Mezirow, 1994; Mezirow, 1996) that values multiple perspectives and removes hierarchical frameworks for knowledge, thereby empowering Indigenous students as legitimate knowledge holders.

Mediation of Border Crossings

For Native students, everyday life is situated in Indigenous worldviews and there is an apparent great cultural divide between their culture and the culture of science. For these reasons, success in science is dependent on how well students can transcend the cultural borders between the disparate worldviews of their everyday life and science (Ezeife, 2003; Jegede & Aikenhead, 1999). The predominant mainstream perspective in science education typically results in an assimilationist approach and can result in Native students feeling alienated by science (Aikenhead, 1996) and perceiving success in science as an either/or proposition (Gates, 2006). In order to be successful in science many students are faced with a potential loss or erosion of identity in order to perform in a knowledge system that does not value or incorporate their cultural heritage. According to Jegede and Aikenhead (1999), culturally sensitive curriculum supports the students' life view and mediates a smooth border crossing whereas science curriculum that is incongruent to the students' life-world culture can be disruptive to a student's worldview and lead to abandonment and marginalization of their culture. This might result in short-term success in science, but ultimately leads to loss of culture and assimilation.

Collateral learning refers to how students resolve two or more schemata simultaneously held in long-term memory (Jegede & Aikenhead, 1999). Transdisciplinary approaches to science education can mediate border crossings and promote desirable collateral learning. Since transdisciplinary curriculum presents content in a high-context, integrated manner, it prevents compartmentalization of knowledge where the student masters the concept in the classroom but is unable to apply it within their everyday life that is part of their life-world experience. Instead it facilitates the students' ability to achieve simultaneous collateral learning wherein learning a concept in one domain of knowledge or culture can improve the learning of a similar concept in another domain (Aikenhead & Jegende, 1999). In this latter situation, the two worldviews can act to augment and enrich knowledge in the other domain. Transdisciplinary approaches also promote simultaneous collateral learning because transdisciplinary education incorporates real-world, authentic learning, giving the students the opportunity to connect their learning to their own unique life-world culture. It also includes opportunities to explore answers using all their knowledge, including relational knowledge, value systems and spiritual interconnectedness; thus reinforcing connections between the two knowledge systems and empowering students to make their own unique connections and bridges between Western science and Indigenous knowledges.

Incorporation of Core Values

Gregory Cajete (1999), arguably the foremost scholar in this area, contends that for science and math courses to be effectively taught for American Indian students, they must use instructional strategies that incorporate values common to most Native American tribal nations and connect mathematical and scientific concepts to real-world issues and problems. Cajete (1999) argues:

> Because core values invariably affect education outcomes, it is important that the teacher, teaching methods, and curricular content reflect this dimension of the learner. It follows then, that an effective and natural way for learning to begin is to help students become aware of their core values. This can be accomplished when the teacher shows the students how the content presented in a particular subject area (such as science) is relevant to or otherwise enhances an understanding of the student's core values.
>
> *(p. 139)*

TEK is by its very nature holistic knowledge, which not only includes multiple discipline areas but also integrates spiritual and ethical dimensions in its knowledge system. Therefore, transdisciplinary approaches that include TEK provide mechanisms for the inclusion of value systems.

Incorporation of High-Context, Problem-Based Learning

In identifying traditional Native American values and behaviors, Cajete includes several that are congruent with both problem-based learning and characteristics of high-context learners and three are particularly relevant: "orientation to the present, practicality, and holistic orientation." Those same three factors are also components of an approach to learning that has gained attention of educators from K-12 to colleges and universities, known as "engaged civic learning." Engaged civic learning is an approach to learning that is problem centered, using authentic problems, inter- or multidisciplinary, and connected to communities (holistic, to use Cajete's term). Problem-based learning is an approach to educating students where they are presented with real-world problems that require solutions. Students evaluate the problem, gather data, identify possible solutions and present their conclusions. Because of the problem/solution focus, education in this context usually crosses academic disciplinary borders, a characteristic of transdisciplinary education.

Cajete's call for an Indigenous pedagogy also resonates with Ibarra's (2001) argument for pedagogy that is effective for multi-contextual student populations. As Ibarra (2001) notes, both low-context learners and high-context learners exist in society, but pedagogy in institutions of higher education is often effective only for low-context learners. According to Ibarra (2001) and others, low-context learners are those who learn best by following directions, where learning is oriented toward the individual, information is compartmentalized and can be separated from social and other context, and where culture is not critical in reasoning and new ideas. In contrast, according to Ibarra (2001) and others, high-context learners are those who learn best by demonstration, application and experience; where comprehensive thinking is important; where learning is collaborative and practical; where interconnected thinking is important; where culture is critical to understanding difference and new ideas; and where information is unreliable if it is separated from context. Ibarra (2001) further notes that Native American and Hispanic students, in particular, tend to be high-context learners. In summary, curriculum must be culturally relevant and include practical applications of the complex theoretical concepts being taught to authentic problems that resonate with students' lives.

Monhardt (2000) offers an illustrative example of the importance of context for new ideas and information by comparing an attempt to teach outsiders (non-Navajos in this case) how to play the Navajo shoe game. Without a proper context and points of reference for information, it is impossible for one to understand the game, even if someone was provided a written set of rules for the game. Absent the necessary context for the information or a partner or mentor who is an insider (Navajo, in this case), one cannot even effectively participate, much less win:

> As an Anglo woman, I was a bit confused when I first read about this game, and I reread the directions several times trying to understand it. I had many

questions about exactly how to play. Finally I realized that the basic rules of the game are clearly described, but no matter how many times I read the directions, I still just didn't quite "get it." . . . you hide rocks in shoes, you say the right words, and you try to guess where the rocks are. It seemed like an incredible amount of effort just to find some rocks. But of course, my world view is not rooted in Navajo culture. . . . To a Navajo, on the other hand, this description of the game may be very understandable . . . it is a sacred game that stems from the Navajo creation stories of how day and night came to be. It has a point—a very important one.

(p. 18)

Monhardt (2000) contends that effective educational practices for minority students (including Native American students) and women in science must create and include "equitable contexts for learning," including discussions of incorporating traditional Indigenous knowledge into curricula and instruction. Other scholars have noted the importance of context for effective learning in mathematics for particular groups, including Barton and Frank (2001), who explore how Indigenous languages may explain differences in how Indigenous students understand spatial relationships, quantity concepts and more. Barton and Frank (2001) reviewed the literature in ethnomathematics and noted that some have explored the idea that "mathematics manifests itself differently in different social or cultural contexts" as part of understanding the puzzle of differences among groups in mathematics achievement (Barton & Frank, 2001, p. 136). Cajete, as well as other leading scholars in the field of American Indian Education, particularly STEM education for Native American students, continue to point to the need for effective pedagogies for American Indian student success in higher education.

Overview of the Curriculum and Tribal Colleges and Universities

Thirty-eight Tribal Colleges and Universities (TCUs) serve over 20,000 Native American undergraduate students across the US. The tribal college movement began in response to the need for self-determination and tribal sovereignty; therefore, tribally controlled education is an act of cultural restoration (Crazy Bull, 2010) and reconciliation through deconstructing and challenging the dominance of Western knowledge (Kanu, 2006; Wilson, 2004). Each tribal college has a dual mission to preserve tribal culture and to provide students a high-quality post-secondary education while serving the needs of its community and tribal members (Tierny, 1992; American Indian Higher Education Consortium, 2001). Tribal community colleges play a pivotal role in training Native American ecologists by providing them with the expertise to address the environmental challenges faced by their communities, such as climate change. Undergraduate science curriculum at tribal colleges is designed to be relevant to the culture of Native students because this is essential for developing the local experts and scientifically literate populace needed to address specific challenges faced by Native communities.

Tohono O'odham Community College (TOCC) is one of the 38 tribally controlled colleges and universities in the US and is the institution of higher education of the Tohono O'odham Nation. Located in the heart of the Sonoran Desert of southern Arizona and northern Mexico, the Tohono O'odham Nation is home to the Tohono O'odham, or "Desert People." At TOCC, the science curriculum has been developed under the premise that science is part of the cultural heritage of each student, as every culture has relied upon processes for gathering and making meaning of information about the natural world (TEK). A cornerstone of TOCC's science program is a global change biology course. which teaches climate change from an Indigenous perspective. This is accomplished through the incorporation of the Tohono O'odham language and stories, an analysis of Western science and Indigenous ways of knowing, inclusion of traditional ecological knowledge and place-based learning. This course includes a transdisciplinary module that was developed as part of a cross-institutional collaboration with Northern Arizona University for the National Council for Science and the Environment's Climate Change Adaptation, Mitigation and eLearning (CAMEL) site and piloted in TOCC classes in spring 2012 (Newberry & Trujillo, 2012). The module was enhanced through the incorporation of a mathematical component under the Southwest Native Lands Project funded by the National Science Foundation and, most recently, has continued to be refined and adapted based on the unique "Man in the Maze" education model for problem-based learning (Newberry, Quijada, Guarin, & Lopez, 2016).

Climate Change, Water and Traditional Ecological Knowledge in the Southwest: A Transdisciplinary Approach to Climate Education

Since the impacts of climate change are falling disproportionately on tribal communities in the US—particularly in Alaska and the southwestern states (Wildcat, 2013)—our motivations for the curriculum include addressing issues of climate justice, legitimizing traditional knowledge, and encouraging interdisciplinary dialogue across science, policy, student and elder circles. The fundamental problem addresses adaptation to changes in water availability due to climate change impacts and exploring strategies for including Indigenous knowledge and cultural traditions that respect the rights of nature in water policy. We created a model that incorporated elder input, science input and policy input to meeting future water needs in the Southwest under current and project climate change scenarios (Figure 13.1).

Specifically, this transdisciplinary module integrates social science, water policy, traditional ecological knowledge and climate change science in the

Model Incorporating Input from Elders, Scientists, and Policy Makers about Solutions for Meeting Future Water Needs.

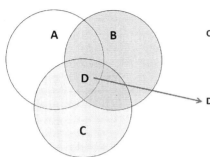

A. **Elder Knowledge of Water**
  - Embedded in sacred history, ceremonial cycles, and specific language
  - Traditional Ecological Knowledge of Water

B. **Water Policy**
  - Tribal Law and Policies
  - State Law and Policies
  - Federal Law and Policies

C. **Scientific Knowledge of Climate Change Impacts on Water**
  - Predicted and measured changes in temperature and precipitation
  - Impacts on watersheds

D. **Strategies for Tomorrow**
  - Water Policy Incorporating both scientific and traditional knowledge
  - Adaptation plans incorporating scientific knowledge plus traditional knowledge and values

FIGURE 13.1   Model Incorporating Elder Input, Science Input, and Policy Input to Meeting Future Water Needs

context of the Tohono O'odham Nation. The goal of this module is to examine strategies for including Indigenous knowledge and cultural traditions into water policy and environmental decision-making. This is accomplished by providing the students a background on the Tohono O'odham cultural perspectives on water from the perspectives of Tohono O'odham elders, geographical orientation and creation stories. It incorporates the spiritual values related to water as sacred and central to the Tohono O'odham culture. It includes traditional uses of water in the context of traditional lifeways and farming as well as the modern uses of water by the Tohono O'odham. The students then learn about current and predicted climate change patterns such as drought, increased temperature, changes in overall and seasonal precipitation patterns, and extreme weather events. The students then apply this knowledge to predicting potential impacts of these environmental changes to each water source on the Tohono O'odham Nation. Finally, using the model that incorporates elder knowledge, water policy, and climate change science, they develop water policy scenarios, adaptation plans and tribal resolutions addressing climate change impacts on the food and water resources on the Tohono O'odham Nation. The students are required to incorporate Indigenous viewpoints on water and Tohono O'odham cultural core values (T-So:son) in their final projects. Since this curriculum is available to mainstream institutions via the CAMEL site, mainstream students are also afforded the opportunity to learn science from a multicultural perspective.

Conclusion

We feel that transdisciplinary approaches to climate change education are vitally important to promoting resiliency in Indigenous communities (Aldunce, Bórquez, Adler, Blanco, & Garreaud, 2016). Transdisciplinary approaches provide students opportunities to make connections between different types and forms for knowledge and allow them to examine concepts of culture, knowledge and power through an Indigenous lens, which in turn promotes self-education and sovereignty (Brayboy, 2006). Transdisciplinary education trains students to be active and competent participants in transdisciplinary research since they will be competent in both IK and community knowledge as well as scientific knowledge. Furthermore, they will know how to navigate between to the two knowledge systems and be well versed in methodologies to incorporate IK and community knowledge alongside scientific knowledge toward the production of new knowledge. This is vitally important because the resilience of Indigenous communities facing threats of climate change is strengthened when Indigenous peoples shape climate policies, are included in natural resource management, strengthen tribal economies, and engage in sustainable development (Maldonado et al., 2016).

On a broader scale, well-trained Indigenous ecologists who also have a strong grounding in their own cultural knowledge can provide the scientific community with unique multi-contextual, Indigenous perspectives on the science of ecology through TEK. Since TEK includes human interactions and is holistic in nature, transdisciplinary curriculum including the social science dimension is a natural outcome of teaching science from an Indigenous perspective. Furthermore, the inclusion of traditional ecological knowledge across disciplines encourages integrative, multi-contextual thinking and promotes the interdisciplinary dialogue necessary to finding solutions to the global environmental problems facing humanity.

References

Aikenhead, G. S. (1996). Science education: Border crossing in the subculture of science. *Studies in Science Education, 27*, 1–52.

Aldunce, P., Bórquez, R., Adler, C., Blanco, G., & Garreaud, R. (2016). Unpacking resilience for adaptation: Incorporating practitioners' experiences through a transdisciplinary approach to the case of drought in Chile. *Sustainability, 8*(9), 905.

American Indian Higher Education Consortium (AIHEC). (2001). *Building strong communities: Tribal Colleges as engaged institutions.* Retrieved from www.aihec.org/our-stories/docs/reports/TCUsAsEngagedInstitutions.pdf

Barton, B., & Frank, L. (2001). Mathematical ideas and Indigenous languages. In B. Atweh, H. Forgasz, & B. Nebres (Eds.), *Sociocultural research on mathematics education: An international perspective* (pp. 135–150). Mahwah, NJ: Lawrence Eribaum Associates, Inc.

Battiste, M., & Henderson, J.Y. (2009). Naturalizing Indigenous knowledge in eurocentric education. *Canadian Journal of Native Education, 32*(1), 5–18, 129–130.

Berkes, F. (2008). *Sacred ecology* (3rd ed.). New York, NY: Routledge.

Berkes, F., & Berkes, M. (2009). Ecological complexity, fuzzy logic, and holism in Indigenous knowledge. *Futures, 41*(1), 6–12.

Brandt, P., Ernst, A., Gralla, F., Leuderitz, C., Lang, D., Newig, J., & von Wehrden, H. (2013). A review of transdisciplinary research in sustainability science. *Ecological Economics*, *92*, 1–15.

Brayboy, B. K. J. (2006). Toward a tribal critical race theory. *Education The Urban Review*, *37*(5). doi:10.1007/s11256–11005–10018-y

Brayboy, B. K. J., & McCarty, T. L. (2010). Indigenous knowledges and social justice pedagogy. In T. K. Chapman & N. Hobbel (Eds.), *Pedagogy across the Curriculum: The practices of freedom* (pp. 184–200). New York, NY: Routledge.

Buizer, M., Arts, B., & Kok, K. (2011). Governance, scale, and the environment: The importance of recognizing knowledge claims in transdisciplinary arenas. *Ecology and Society*, *16*(1), 21.

Cajete, G. (1999). The Native American learner and biocultural science education. In K. Swisher & J. Tippeconic III (Eds.), *Next steps: Research and practice to advance Indian education* (pp. 139–140). Charleston, WV: Clearinghouse on Rural Education and Small Schools.

Cajete, G. (2000) *Native science: Natural Laws of Interdependence*. Santa Fe, New Mexico: Clear Light Publishers.

Cajete, G. (2005). American Indian epistemologies. In M. J. T. Fox, S. C. Lowe, & G. S. McClellan (Eds.), *Serving native American students, new dimensions for student services* (pp. 69–78). Hoboken, NJ: Wiley & Sons.

Crazy Bull, C. (2010). Cultural integration at Northwest Indian college: An experience of cultural Restoration. In E. Boyer (Ed.), *Ancient wisdom: Modern science: Integration of native knowledge in math and science at tribally controlled colleges and universities* (pp. 27–41). Pablo, MT: Salish Kootenai College Press.

Deloria, V. (1999). Knowing and understanding. In *Spirit and reason* (pp. 137–143). Golden, CO: Fulcrum Publishing.

Ezeife, A. (2003). The pervading influence of cultural border crossing and collateral learning on the learner of science and mathematics. *Canadian Journal of Native Education*, *27*(2), 179–194.

Gates, M. (2006, Summer/Fall). Native Americans find their niche in technology. *Diversity/ Careers in Engineering & Information Technology*. Retrieved October 19, 2008, from www.diversitycareers.com

Gould, W., González, G., Walker, D., & Ping, C. (2010). Commentary, integrating research, education, and traditional knowledge in ecology: A case study of biocomplexity. *Arctic Ecosystems. Arctic, Antarctic, and Alpine Research*, *42*(4), 379–384.

Habermas, J. (1979). *Communication and the evolution of society*. Boston, MA: Beacon Press.

Hellsten, L., & Leydesdorff, L. (2016). The construction of interdisciplinarity: The development of the knowledge base and programmatic focus of the journal climatic change, 1977–2013. *Journal of the Association for Information Science and Technology*, *67*(9), 2181–2193.

Holm, P., Goodsite, M. E., Cloetingh, S. A.P. L., Agnoletti, M., Moldan, B., Lang, D. J., . . . Zondervan, R. (2013). Collaboration between natural, social and human sciences in global change research. *Environmental Science & Policy*, *28*, 25–35.

Ibarra, R. (2001). *Beyond affirmative action: Reframing the context of higher education*. Madison, WI: University of Wisconsin Press.

Intergovernmental Panel on Climate Change (IPCC). (2014). *Fifth assessment report: Impacts, adaptation, and vulnerability*. Retrieved from http://hcl.harvard.edu/collections/ipcc/ar5/

Jegede, O., & Aikenhead, G. S. (1999). Transcending cultural borders: Implications for science teaching. *Research in Science & Technological Education*, *17*(1), 45–66.

Kanu, Y. (2006). *Curriculum as cultural practice: Postcolonial imaginations.* Toronto, ON: University of Toronto Press, Scholarly Publishing Division.

Lang, D. J., Wick, A., Bergmann, M., Stauffacher, M., Martens, P., Moll, P., & Thomas, C. (2012). Transdisciplinary research in sustainability science: Practice, principles and challenges. *Sustainability Science, 7*(1), 25–43. doi:10.1007/s11625–11011–10149-x

Maldonado, J., Bennett, T. M. B., Chief, K., Cochran, P., Cozzetto, K., Gough, B., & Voggesser, G. (2016). Engagement with indigenous peoples and honoring traditional knowledge systems. *Climatic Change, 135,* 111. doi:10.1007/s10584-015-1535-7

Mauser, W., Klepper, G., Rice, M., Schmalzbauer, B. S., Hackmann, H., Leemans, R., & Moore, H. (2013). Transdisciplinary global change research: Co-creation of knowledge for sustainability. *Current Opinion in Environmental Sustainability,* 420–432.

McNeeley, S. M., & Shulski, M. D. (2011). Anatomy of a closing window: Vulnerability to changing seasonality in Interior Alaska. *Global Environmental Change, 21,* 464–473.

Mezirow, J. (1994). Understanding transformation theory. *Adult Education Quarterly, 44*(4), 222–232.

Mezirow, J. (1996). Contemporary paradigms of learning. *Adult Education Quarterly, 46*(3), 158–173.

Mitchell, R. C., & Moore, S. (2015) Muse, ruse, subterfuge: Transdisciplinary Praxis in Ontario's post-secondary Bricolage? *Review of Education, Pedagogy, and Cultural Studies, 37*(5), 393–413. doi:10.1080/10714413.2015.1091257

Monhardt, R. (2000). Fair play in science education: Equal opportunities for minority students. *The Clearing House, 74*(1), 18–23.

Nakashima, D. J. (2000). What relationship between scientific and traditional systems of knowledge? In A. M. Cetto (Ed.), *Science for the twenty-first century: A new document* (pp. 432–444). Paris: UNESCO.

Newberry, T., Quijada, A., Guarin, J., & Lopez, C. (2016). The man in the maze: An indigenous education model. *Tribal College and University Research Journal, 1*(1), 1–19.

Newberry, T., & Trujillo, O. (2012). *Climate change, water and traditional ecological knowledge in the Southwest.* A Web-based Learning Module. [Blog post]. Retrieved from www.camelclimatechange.org/resources/view/174754/?topic=71692

Pierotti, R., & Wildcat, D. (2000). Traditional ecological knowledge: The third alternative. *Ecological Applications, 10,* 1333–1340.

Sillitoe, P., & Marzano, M. (2009). Future of indigenous knowledge research in development. *Futures, 41*(1), 13–23.

Smith, L. T. (1999). *Decolonizing methodologies: Research and indigenous peoples.* Otago: University of Otago Press.

Steiner, G. & Posch, A. (2006). Higher education for sustainability by means of transdisciplinary case studies: An innovative approach for solving complex real-world problems. *Journal of Cleaner Production, 14,* 877–890.

Tierney, W. G. (1992) An anthropological analysis of student participation in college. *The Journal of Higher Education, 63*(6), 603–618.

Wildcat, D. R. (2013). Introduction: Climate change and indigenous peoples of the USA. In J. K. Maldonado, B. Colombi, & R. Pandya (Eds.), *Climate change and indigenous peoples in the United States.* Cham: Springer.

Wilson, A. (2004). Reclaiming our humanity: Decolonization and the recovery of Indigenous knowledge. In D. Mihesuah & A. Wilson (Eds.), *Indigenizing the academy: Transforming scholarship and empowering communities* (pp. 69–87). Lincoln, NB: University of Nebraska Press.

14

WITH ROOTS IN THE WATER

Revitalizing Straits Salish Reef Net Fishing as Education for Well-Being and Sustainability

Nicholas XEMŦOLTW̱ Claxton (Tsawout) and
Carmen Rodríguez de France (Kickapoo)

> *We have been here a long time. During that time we lived with the sea songs, the elements, the lands. Our ancestors continue to teach us through our ancient language through our presence here.*
>
> —STOLȻEȽ (Dr. John Elliot, Sr.)

The W̱SÁNEĆ People have been living on their territory for thousands of years tracing their existence back to the time of creation, living sustainably, and in prosperity according to their teachings, philosophies, beliefs, and principles. The SX̱OLE, or Reef Net Fishery, was at the core of this existence; an integral piece for maintaining balance and a sense of well-being. As a knowledge system, the Reef Net defined their existence and relationship to the land. This knowledge system was effectively dismantled through the colonizing efforts of Western education and schooling, and was nearly lost after being outlawed by the Colonial Government of Vancouver Island roughly 100 years ago.

This chapter will describe the process of revitalizing the W̱SÁNEĆ Reef Net Fishery at The LÁU,WEL,NEW Tribal school where community members, school administrators, and teachers have been involved in exposing the students to the principles and philosophy of the W̱SÁNEĆ people, their worldview, and ways of being as a way to reignite ways of life prior to contact. The school is located in the Territory of the W̱SÁNEĆ People, on Southern Vancouver Island in British Columbia, and serves five surrounding First Nations communities: Tsarlip, Tsawout, Tseycum, Malahat, and Pauquachin.

Through practical examples, main author Nicholas Claxton will describe how he has been working at the Tribal school along with elders and knowledge keepers in order to maintain and sustain relationships with the land, the people, and the culture as a W̱SÁNEĆ man who began revitalizing Reef Net fishing three years ago in his community at Tsawout, and as the focus of his doctoral work at the University of Victoria. Carmen Rodríguez, Indigenous scholar with heritage from the Kickapoo Nation working at the University of Victoria, will discuss how this cultural practice has shown great potential in informing the future directions of education using Indigenous knowledge to support decolonization. Through these experiences and examples, the authors will emphasize the shared responsibilities to the environment as Indigenous Nations and non-Indigenous citizens of what is now known as Canada.

The SX̱OLE and the W̱SÁNEĆ People: Situating W̱SÁNEĆ Reef Net Fishing Practice

According to W̱SÁNEĆ oral history, the W̱SÁNEĆ people lived sustainably, peacefully, and in prosperity according to the teachings, philosophies, beliefs, and principles of XÁLS the Creator. The SX̱OLE, or Reef Net Fishery, was at the core of this existence; it was the "backbone" of the W̱SÁNEĆ traditional society.

Fishing for Pacific Salmon with a Reef Net is an ancient fishing technology and practice. This fishing method was unique to the Straits Salish People, and practiced in what is now known as the Salish Sea (the waters in and around the Southern Gulf Islands and the San Juan Islands). The Reef Net was W̱SÁNEĆ Peoples main fishing technology. In SENĆOŦEN (the Saanich language), the Reef Net was called the SX̱OLE. This name both refers to the material with which the net was constructed (the inner bark of the Pacific Willow) and the net itself. The W̱SÁNEĆ utilized the Reef Net as the main method for salmon fishing (particularly Sockeye and Pink), which was conducted in the tidal waters of the Salish Sea rather than in rivers and streams. The Reef Net technology was very sophisticated technology, requiring people to have an in-depth knowledge of the salmon (their habits and travel routes), tides and currents, weather, plants, and a solid foundation of the laws and beliefs inextricably linked to this practice. The Reef Net Fishery could not be successful without the W̱SÁNEĆ people's deep respect for the salmon, the earth, and each other. Fishing with the SX̱OLE instilled and reinforced W̱SÁNEĆ philosophies and worldview.

The SX̱OLE was hand constructed from natural materials specifically harvested from the local landscape. The Reef Net itself consisted of a lead and a net. The lead of the Reef Net consisted of cedar log buoys, cedar ropes to form the sides and the floor of the lead, and specially made rock weights. Dune grass would be threaded through the twinning of the ropes that formed the floor and the sides, which would appear to the salmon as if they were actually swimming near the bottom. This made the salmon feel safe. Ropes to permanent anchors secured the front of the lead, and the rear of the lead was connected to the fishermen's canoes and to the net itself. The lead also served to funnel salmon into a net that was suspended between two canoes, and it would bag out with the flow of the tide. The net was anchored in specific (hereditarily owned family) locations, usually at the mouth of a south-facing bay. The sterns of the canoes were also secured to the bottom with ropes and anchors. When the net was hauled and fishing was stopped, the rear of the lead was tied to those rear anchors and the lead of the Reef Net remained in the water, usually for the duration of a season, unless repairs had to be made. The gear would also remain there for the entire fishing season by the use of giant rock anchors. During the entire salmon fishing season, the Saanich people would also remain at those fishing locations thus connecting the people to their territorial homelands. This is a simple description of a very complex fishing technique, and a very sophisticated and sustainable way of life. Simply put, the SX̱OLE, or Reef Net Fishery formed the core of the W̱SÁNEĆ traditional society, including the core of the W̱SÁNEĆ traditional educational system or way, which fostered a deep knowledge, connection, beliefs of the people to the salmon and to the lands and waters.

According to Dr. Verna Kirkness (1999), prior to contact, education was rooted in the community and the natural environment, and was strongly linked to the survival of the family and the community. Learning was aimed at gathering knowledge necessary for daily living. Through observation and practice, people learned how to hunt, trap, fish, farm, and gather food. The elders and members of the community transmitted such knowledge in informal ways, through storytelling, ceremony, ritual, and celebration, which provided youth the skills and attitudes necessary for daily life. While it is important to acknowledge that Aboriginal communities are diverse and are immersed in beliefs, traditions, languages, and practices that differ, it is also important to remember that there are shared cosmologies, values, and ways of doing and being that are similar among nations. Hawaiian scholar Aluli Meyer (2008) describes these differences as universality and specificity of culture, suggesting that universality is based on spirituality and knowledge while specificity relates to one's ancestors and one's "local" understandings of the world, which includes one's landscape. Meyer argues that land is not just a physical place but also a space where knowledge emerges and where knowledge is contextualized. She continues to say that, to her people, the way in which one interacts with the land or the ocean reveal aspects of one's identity, shaping, in turn, one's values, ways of thinking, and ways of being. In learning from and with the land, one is more disposed to learning about oneself and to reorganize knowledge in meaningful ways. This can be challenging when, as Gregory Cajete (2000) affirms, place is taken for granted or if it is conceived as the same for everyone. Within Western perspectives, place is represented through criteria established and agreed upon a priori (i.e., maps and scientific notions). Cajete says that in order to know any kind of physical landscape, one has to experience it.

In his book Saltwater People (1990), Dave Elliot Sr. recounts how life used to be for the W̱SÁNEĆ people who depended on the sea, the marshes, and the lands for sustenance, and how the movement from one place to the next during the summer and winter months exemplified the values and beliefs of his people of taking from the land and sea only what one needs and respecting the territories of other communities with whom the land was shared. "We were saltwater people. We lived on islands and water so that made us fishermen, sailors, navigators, boat builders, travellers, and workers of the sea" (Dave Elliot Sr., 1990, p. 55). Elliott says there were no boundaries among people until 1856 when an international boundary was established by the Treaty of Washington, and later when the territories were separated due to the treaty with the Hudson Bay Company.

In 1852, the W̱SÁNEĆ signed a treaty with then-Governor of Vancouver Island Sir James Douglas. From the W̱SÁNEĆ people's perspective, this treaty was an agreement between the two nations. Also, the Douglas Treaty states that the Saanich People were entitled to "carry on their fisheries as formerly," a sustainable practice that formed the foundation for the W̱SÁNEĆ identity and way of life as a nation. With the arrival of the colonizers, the opportunities that children, youth, and communities had to experience land and seascapes changed drastically, preventing knowledge from being contextualized, experienced, and reorganized. Colonization brought along new ways of thinking and being, new ways of reading the land (a pragmatic view based on economic development and gain), and new ways of organizing knowledge. Colonization also robbed people of their physical space, their livelihood, their sustenance, and their organized cultural ways that formed the bases of their existence. Along with the imposition of new ways of learning from the land, colonization established a new world order and structure where people and communities were uprooted from their original homes and transplanted into foreign landscapes, hence being forced to adapt to a different context, rely on alternative modes of subsistence, and conform to imposed ways of being and understanding the world.

Learning was no longer aimed at gaining knowledge for life. With the establishment of residential schools, education and learning became a set of organized and structured activities that carried little or no relevance either for life or for people's immediate context. This was in complete contrast to the ways in which learning took place prior to contact and in which expertise developed. Reminiscing about his childhood, Elliott (1990) describes how Reef Net fishing was a form of livelihood, and how much one needed to learn in order to become an accomplished fisherman: "those people were the equivalent to today's engineers, because they understood the tide, the wind, stress strength of the ropes. How much material would stand that strong tide, that strong wind?" (p. 56)

The winds of change brought about different ways of understanding the world. However, in revitalizing cultural practices, languages, and other ways of life, we have begun to reclaim traditional ways of being, knowing, and learning that need to be connected to the land and the sea, to worldview, language, culture, beliefs, and homelands of the W̱SÁNEĆ people to help the community regain a sense of wellness and well-being.

According to Cajete (2000), Aboriginal education should seek "to heal and transcend the effects of colonization" (p. 181). Further, Hampton (1995) suggests that Aboriginal education must address the issue of colonization in order to decolonize. To stave off the continued onslaught of assimilation, nationhood "requires a nation to be confidently rooted in their culture, and be bodily and spiritually strong to be able to survive on their lands independently, in order to support our traditional models of government" (Alfred, 2005, p. 31).

Education for Revival and Transcendence: Bringing Back the Saanich Reef Net Fishery

We are living in times of reconciliation where we aspire to create a shared future for Aboriginal and non-Aboriginal people. Learning how to live in harmony with the land and with each other will require unlearning and re-learning new ways of looking at the world and raising awareness of the importance of protecting Indigenous knowledge. We ought to heed the advice of elder Albert Marshall whose approach, called "Two Eyed Seeing," invites us to include Indigenous knowledge within the curriculum so that Indigenous and non-Indigenous perspectives and knowledges be available to everyone, and thus benefit and enrich all peoples.[1]

The revitalization of the W̱SÁNEĆ Reef Net Fishery as a practice, belief system, and knowledge system is essential to the restoration of the well-being of the W̱SÁNEĆ people. This journey of the resurgence of the SX̱OLE began in 2014. Restoring the Saanich practice of fishing as formerly is essential to the restoration of Saanich educational way, and it is essential to Saanich identity and way of life. Restoration of traditional practices such as the Saanich Reef Net Fishery is important coming at a time when Senator Sinclair, the Chair of the Truth and Reconciliation Commission, has "invited" us all as Canadian citizens to explore ways in which, together, Aboriginal and non-Aboriginal people can create paths for a shared future. Consequently, reconnecting Indigenous peoples to their territorial lands and waters will restore the well-being and sustainable existences as nations. This reconnection will bring back a sense of identity through re-establishing traditional practices, ceremony, language, and beliefs that come with the connection to the territory. More specifically, to revive the Saanich Reef Net Fishery will also restore the transmission of Saanich culture, spiritual knowledge, and teachings from the elders to the Saanich children and youth.

Restoring the Saanich Reef Net Fishery will also contribute to an increased reliance on a diet based on more traditional foods like salmon. In pre-contact times, the Saanich peoples sustained themselves on everything from the local territory and salmon was one of the most important sources of food. To catch more salmon, especially in a way that honors the rich history of the local territory, will lead to eating more salmon and restoring traditional sources of diet. It will also create the sense of well-being that comes from relating deeply and spiritually as a community since the Saanich Reef Net formed the core of Saanich traditional society.

Over the short and long term, restoring this traditional fishing practice has many positive implications. While it restores the traditional governance system, it can also restore the foundation in which the Saanich people can interact with the settler state. By honoring the traditional practice that is protected by the treaty, it can also reformulate the relationship back to a nation-to-nation relationship with the state. This could also contribute greatly to the well-being and sustainability of the Saanich community. In the long term, it could also provide the economic opportunity to re-establish a sustainable economy on the fishery.

The restoration of the Saanich Reef Net is a way for the Saanich people to strengthen and renew identity and nationhood, which was nearly destroyed, sadly neglected, and almost forgotten as a result of the success of the colonizers' strategies. Hopefully this can inform and inspire other First Nations in British Columbia and Canada to initiate the restoration of their own practices in their communities and on their lands.

The construction of the ceremonial Reef Net within the school as a part of the Reef Net revitalization project is consistent with and falls within the W̱SÁNEĆ School Board's philosophical statement, which states that the SENĆOŦEN culture must be maintained, perpetuated, and protected. This Reef Net revitalization project was meant to realize those philosophical statements by bringing the Reef Net technology back to the center of the W̱SÁNEĆ society, starting with the education of W̱SÁNEĆ children in the School. This was the premise of this project.

Starting in the spring of 2014, I (Claxton) started to spend time with STOLȻEȽ (language teacher and knowledgeable elder) in his SENĆOŦEN language and culture class at the ȽÁU,WEL,ṈEW̱ Tribal School. His class was held over three hours on Fridays. I attended most Fridays during the Spring of 2014, though STOLȻEȽ continued to work with his students on the project during the times that I could not attend. Together with the students, we harvested some SX̱OLE, or willow. We brought it back to the classroom, where we taught the children the technique and process of harvesting the fibrous inner bark used for twine construction.

First, we went out to a local wetland to gather some willow. This was a way for us and for the students to reconnect with the local territory. STOLȻEȽ reinforced the knowledge that the willow tree was a living entity; he taught some sacred prayer words that were spoken to the tree before harvesting its branches. Through harvesting the willow, we learned that the best willow to harvest was the long and straight branches of the new growth in the spring time. The bark came off easily and the rough outer bark could be scraped off quite effortlessly. Through working with their hands, the students ended up with a nice supply of long strands of the inner bark of the willow tree. With this, the students were then able to make cordage, using a twisting technique, which creates a strong, yet, fine two-ply cord. We spent a few classes harvesting willow branches and stripping the outer bark off, until we had an adequate supply for the length of cordage we required to begin making the net.

The students worked with their hands, and while that was going on there was the chance for some informal teaching of stories and history, as well as just a chance to visit. A comfortable learning environment was organically created. Perhaps opening each class with a prayer, which was a spiritual grounding, created this environment. Opening in this way also acknowledged the spiritual nature of the Reef Net and the Reef Net model. STOLȻEȽ noted that many of the students that were normally disruptive in his classroom on many of the other days would settle down and work on the net. I believe that the students felt the meaning and the significance of the work, and it was something that they could connect to through their ancestral connections. We concur with Basso (1996) when he says that dwelling consists of the "multiple 'lived relationships' that people maintain with places, for it is solely by virtue of these relationships that space acquires meaning" (p. 54).

For much of the classes, the students worked with their hands and even worked together twisting the bark to make twine. They expressed a sense of pride and accomplishment in their production. While making twine was the focus of the initial stages of the project, there was ample opportunity for language and culture learning in the classroom in formal and informal ways.

The project, which ran from January 2014 through to the end of the year, became a focal point for the school. For example, some of the students who showed interest in carving began to carve the canoes that would be a part of this model under the guidance of STOLȻEȽ. Others created model halibut hooks and other fishing tools, and even carved miniature salmon. The learning and teaching was fueled by creativity and by cultural connection and relevance.

Momentum within the school continued around the project. During this spring of 2014, one of the other three teachers in the school began to shift the teaching of their subject around the project. Berkeley Lott, the science/social studies teacher in the school, taught his social studies unit based on the Saltwater People text and paid particular attention to the Reef Net chapter in that text. This connection allowed the students to engage with the Reef Net technology in a deeper and more meaningful way; students weren't just learning about it in one subject area, but across the subject areas. This project was not as much about creating a curriculum of the Reef Net, but enacting it in experiential and practical ways, making it a living curriculum versus one that is in print. This project is an excellent example of how the First Peoples Principle of Learning can be explored and lived by Aboriginal and non-Aboriginal teachers, students, and community members. Among the nine principles, we found the following to best represent the learning that had taken place as a result of participating in the project:

Learning supports the well-being of the self, the family, the community, the land, the spirits, and the ancestors;

Learning is holistic, reflexive, reflective, experiential, and relational (focused on connectedness, on reciprocal relationships, and a sense of place);

Learning involves generational roles and responsibilities;
Learning recognizes the role of Indigenous knowledge;
Learning is embedded in memory, history, and story.
Learning involves patience and time.

The result of the project within the school was the creation of an adequate amount of twine for the ceremonial Reef Net model. STOLȻEȽ talks about his students' hands-on efforts and participation in making the twine as their "prayers" for Reef Net revitalization. In this sense, their contributions and their learning (and teaching) were their prayers. Without this, the revitalization of the Reef Net could not have happened.

The Reef Net revitalization project continues into the current academic year. The project continues to teach the students about the Reef Net technology. This academic year, the LÁU,WEL,ṈEW̱ Tribal School has implemented an overall curricular model that is similar to British Columbia's New Curriculum, which was also implemented this year, with a new focus on "Big Ideas" and Curricular "Competencies." In the Tribal School, the SXOLE has been situated as one of those "Big Ideas" in the curriculum. In this way, the W̱SÁNEĆ people continue to decolonize their education system and ultimately the minds of the W̱SÁNEĆ students in a very real and tangible way. The Reef Net Project is allowing young people to learn from each other, from the elders, and from the land, along with the changes in landscapes, perspectives, and the emergence of newer technologies.

Environmental educator David Orr (1994) writes about "the problem of education, rather than problems in education" (p. 4). He states that our education systems have prepared us to think about the natural world in industrial and unsustainable ways. The driving force behind mainstream educational reform has been about preparing our young to be successful in and contribute to the global economy, rather than living sustainably in our homelands. For Indigenous people, educational reform is about retaining, restoring, and revitalizing our traditional lifeways. As Basso (1996) suggests, one needs to "deeply root these practices in tradition, wrapped up in relations of reciprocity, respect, and spirit" (p. 54). With roots in the water, the W̱SÁNEĆ people are revitalizing the Reef Net Fishery both as education and a way of life.

Note

1 As explained in a blog post from 2004, at www.integrativescience.ca/Principles/TwoEyedSeeing/

References

Alfred, G. R. (2005). *Wasáse: Indigenous pathways of action and freedom*. Peterborough, ON: Broadview Press.

Basso, K. (1996). Wisdom sits in places: Notes on a Western Apache landscape. In S. Feld & K. Basso (Eds.), *Senses of place* (pp. 13–52). Santa Fe, NM: School of American Research Press.

Cajete, G. (2000). Indigenous knowledge: The Pueblo metaphor of indigenous education. In M. Battiste (Ed.), *Reclaiming indigenous voice and vision* (pp. 181–191). Vancouver, BC: UBC Press.

Elliott, D. Sr. (1990). *Saltwater People*, as told by Dave Elliott Sr.: A resource book for the Saanich native studies program. In J. Poth (Ed.), Saanichton, BC: School District 63 (Saanich).

Hampton, E. (1995). Towards a redefinition of Indian Education. In M. Battiste & J. Barman (Eds.), *First nations education in Canada: The circle unfolds* (pp. 5–46). Vancouver, BC: UBC Press.

Kirkness, V. (1999). Aboriginal education in Canada: A retrospective and a prospective. *Journal of American Indian Education, 39*(1), 14–30.

Meyer, M. A. (2008). Indigenous and authentic: Hawaiian epistemology and the triangulation of meaning. In N. K. Denzin, Y. S. Lincoln, & L. T. Smith (Eds.), *Handbook of critical-land indigenous methodologies* (pp. 217–232). Thousand Oaks, CA: Sage Publications, Inc.

Orr, D. W. (1994). *Earth in mind*. Washington, DC: Island Press.

15

WAŁYAʕASUKʔI NAANANIQSAKQIN

At the Home of Our Ancestors: Ancestral Continuity in Indigenous Land-Based Language Immersion

chuutsqa Layla Rorick (Hesquiaht)

Seven years ago, I experienced a metaphysical interaction with a crab on the beach which informed my learning path.

My own language revitalization journey began with an encounter on the beach with a crab who yelled at me "Learn your language! Do whatever it takes!" That was an admonition that shook me to my very core with its absolute urgency and truth. I would say I accepted my life's work at that moment when I replied "Ok, I'll do it," even though I had not considered the possibility or even the viability that I could learn my own language since I was a child, listening to elders tell us that we needed to save our language. When I told my elders about Crab who yelled at me, they said it was probably my ancestor čuucqa speaking to me through the crab. That encounter with Crab on the beach allowed me to *feel* for the first time the reality of my living Indigenous language, which caused me to seek out methods by which a language could be acquired (Rosborough & Rorick, 2017, p. 13).

My desire to return our ancestral language back to our people, and back to the places from which our language has originated, has impetus in a series of spiritual occurrences or metaphysical encounters on the beach (Rorick, 2016; Rosborough & Rorick, 2017). Though surprising to me at the time of occurrence, those experiences have been verified in discussion with elders to be consistent with ancestral Nuu-chah-nulth (nuučaańuł) interaction with the metaphysical or spiritual realm. Spirituality, inclusive of supernatural communication, is one of four major nuučaańuł learning strategies (Atleo, 2004; Atleo, 2009; Nuu-chah-nulth Tribal Council, 1995; Rorick, 2016; Rosborough & Rorick, 2017). nuučaańuł language and worldview have grown out of a coastal location and contain environmental markers that tie our language and our daily actions to the land and seascape. nuučaaňuɫ worldview allows for human interaction with the natural and metaphysical world; when I speak in my language about what I learned from spiritual experiences, not only is the sentence order and content different from the English language, but my word endings place those occurrences on the beach, which helps the listener to envision and connect to the place in my story.

None of my generation grew up as speakers of our nuučaaňuɫ language; though at home on Hesquiaht Indian Reserve #6 on the west coast of Vancouver Island, we often heard elders speak on the declining state of our language and culture. I began learning Hesquiaht language (ḥiḥiškwiiʔatḥa) as an adult seven years ago, by creating my own nuučaaňuɫ language-learning programs with elders Lawrence and Angela, because none were available. At that time, nobody had yet become a speaker as an adult. As my proficiency advanced, like many other Indigenous activists in the province of British Columbia (BC), I put efforts into advancing the speech of other language learners under the guidance of fluent elders who are concerned with passing on our distinctly Indigenous ways of knowing. At the same time, through graduate studies, I have been researching language immersion teaching approaches and practices that can aid in transmitting our teachings to the next generations.

As a language activist, I would like my efforts to align with nuučaaňuɫ ancestral ways. Success in nuučaaňuɫ ways is something that comes with diligence; it is essential that leadership qualities are developed and applied over time in order to be regarded as successful. Toward this direction, "we have to undertake a journey of learning, unlearning and relearning, and this journey is difficult because we are inundated with the continuing effects of colonialism every moment of every day" (Absolon, 2011, p. 141). It seems that in order for our Indigenous knowledge systems to survive, we must become successful concurrently in both worlds, thereby convincing ourselves and others of our worth.

Key to the resurgence of ancestral Indigenous knowledge systems, through decolonizing educational approaches, is recovering and re-strengthening connections to our languages, our relationships with our ancestral homelands, and our spirituality. This chapter will discuss motivations for Indigenous educational programs to be designed from a base of Indigenous knowledge and will outline some reasons why we have not yet seen the proliferation of educational experiences that align with Indigenous ancestral ways. The advantages of designing Indigenous place-based and decolonizing educational opportunities to create positive impacts in Indigenous populations is then discussed. Following this, I describe the planning, delivery and subsequent effects on my teaching practice that resulted from delivering a place-based, grassroots ḥiḥiškʷiiʔatḥa course on ancestral ḥiškʷiiʔatḥ land. Additionally, I will explore the intersections between Indigenous language, place-based knowledge, and spirituality in the context of educational program development and delivery before explaining the theory and methodologies employed in developing my practice as an emerging language immersion teacher.

Ancestral Continuity in Place-Based Language Revitalization

"Creation is a continuity. If creation is to continue, then it must be renewed" (Little Bear, 2000, p. 78). The work of Indigenous scholars shows me that Indigenous philosophies still exist in a strong state, even if in diminished capacities that need re-strengthening and sometimes sharing between tribes and nations due to the continuing impact of colonial governments under which we live in North America. Little Bear's (2000) assertion that creation is continuity and continuity is renewal recalls for me my ḥiškʷiiʔatḥ elders' assertion that we, ḥiškʷiiʔatḥ, are ʔiqḥmuut: we are ancient and continuing.

An ancestral nuučaańuł pathway to success can involve continuing to search out and share who I am now, who we once were as nuučaańuł people, and who we can become, based in seeking understanding of the way our ancestors have envisioned our continuation. For contemporary learning programs to be consistent with ancestral nuučaańuł ways, they must be developed on a foundation of our own Indigenous knowledge, which according to Battiste (2008) comprises "a distinct knowledge system, with its own concepts of epistemology [, a term that refers to ways of knowing and the experience of truth] and scientific and logical validity" (p. 85). nuučaańuł people, like other First Nations, experienced cultural and linguistic losses throughout the Indian Residential School (IRS) era and its ensuing period. In order to live in continuity with our ancestors, we must continue to pass our ancestral nuučaańuł language on for our next generations. Our language is spoken by 14 First Nations tribes on Vancouver Island, and at the time of this writing we have just 1.7% fluent nuučaańuł speakers remaining (First Peoples' Cultural Council [FPCC], 2014), down from 100% fluent speakers before the advent of IRS (TRC, 2015). Because of the legacy of IRS and other compounding factors, all 34 BC Indigenous languages are now listed as critically endangered, nearly extinct, or sleeping (FPCC, 2014). All parents and grandparents on my reserve had been raised in residential school and, when I was a child, our parents were the first generation to have their children growing up in the home since the 1880s. Languages have mostly not been taught in the home as a residual effect of IRS experiences, so Indigenous children have not been able to access effective Indigenous language-learning environments for several decades (Bougie, 2010; Canadian Heritage, 2005; FPCC, 2014). McIvor, Napoleon, and Dickie (2009) studied the effects of language and culture loss on the health of Indigenous peoples, identifying six protective factors against Indigenous health issues: land and health, traditional medicine, spirituality, traditional foods, traditional activities, and language. A shift away from Indigenous language affects shifts in health by directly affecting cultural and spiritual practices, as well as disrupting Indigenous knowledge continuity and relationship with the land. When the decline of Indigenous languages negatively affects our social and natural world relationships, it affects our quality of mutual human understanding as well.

Community efforts in the schools, for the most part, have been ineffective at revitalizing our language in the past 40 years, in my opinion. I feel that we always had the right people and the right talent to revive our own language, but we did not have access to effective approaches or a sufficient amount of language study time that would have resulted in greater language proficiency for students. I attended ḥiškʷiiʔatḥ's elementary school, and since none of us children became nuučaaňuɫ speakers, I believe my language-learning experience there to be common to that of other ḥiškʷiiʔatḥ students: In language class, we were taught for a half hour daily through the English language, and most instruction took place inside the school. I want to be clear that I experienced our language teachers as talented and engaging, but I completed my years in those classes with the feeling that I still didn't know what they know. Studies show that connecting comprehensive educational applications of Indigenous knowledge that are grounded in Indigenous ways of thinking and experiencing the world will contribute toward the revitalization of Indigenous languages and cultures (Canadian Heritage, 2005; Michel, 2012), yet we did not have access to resources resulting from those understandings. I propose that new and freely available nuučaaňuɫ language teaching resources and approaches that help students develop an understanding of the nuučaaňuɫ world through reconnection to the environment, reconnection to ancestral activities on the land, and reconnection with nuučaaňuɫ language are required components of comprehensive nuučaaňuɫ educational opportunities that can be continuous with ancestral nuučaaňuɫ ways.

A Place-Based ḥiḥiškʷiiʔatḥa Course

The opportunity to learn the language of the land on which one lives means that a different set of ideas, knowledge, and wisdom can be shared and proliferated to influence a change in the future; a different way to organize our ideas and approaches to living on this land. For this initial place-based ḥiḥiškʷiiʔatḥa course, I wanted to combine the language knowledge I gained from fluent elders with my parents' outdoor education and group management experience at Hooksum Outdoor School on our ancestral ḥiškʷiiʔatḥ homeland to inform the creation and delivery of this distinctly ḥiḥiškʷiiʔatḥa resource.

Ultimately, I want people to take the language back onto the land: to reconnect and *remember* a nuučaaňuɫ ʔiqḥmuut, or ancient and continuing. The course reminded participants of a need to bring our children onto the land to understand and to connect with our identities and our respective responsibilities as ḥiškʷiiʔatḥ people. It verified the directions we have been given so many times from our elders in the last several decades that we are responsible to pass on ancient teachings. When designing language lessons, foremost in my mind is fostering a safe environment for learners to move from silence to speech. Learners want to partake in the passing of teachings and they desire to become speakers of the language, which requires engaging their voices. To create speakers, it is important to provide immediate repetitive language examples to the whole group, and then literally stand each person up to speak at the beginning of each day. This can then be followed by individual speech-mirroring support and exaggerated, often silly gestures by the activity leader with concurrent positive feedback. This provides learners with a voice to carry throughout the lesson. Perley (2013) uses the italicized term *remember* (p. 244) and its derivatives to counteract the *dismemberment* or disembodiment of language from the community of practice. Language revitalization must actively *remember* Indigenous language into all the relations we have within Indigenous families and communities, including our living Indigenous world, our stories, landscapes, and spirituality. This course with my kinkʷaaštaquml family was an opportunity to interact and learn through our language and culture, our lands and waters in the same relational way that we have since the beginning of time.

Much of the language taught in this course and case study stemmed from my language immersion work with ʔuʔuʔaałuk nuučaańuł Language Nest, which I volunteered to create and coordinate alongside ḥiškʷiiʔatḥ elders Julia Lucas and Maggie Ignace in Port Alberni, BC. Some of the language came from memories of home, from a pre-language course visit to inventory places and items to be included, and from the input of the ḥiškʷiiʔatḥ elders who helped to correct my list of target language. I am able to do this work and continue my language growth because of the initial foundation of language I was taught over a period of three years by ḥiškʷiiʔatḥ elders Lawrence Paul and Angela Galligos. Throughout my learning over the past several years I have wanted to reach a level of language proficiency where I could bring the lessons outside.

With this course in the winter solstice of 2015, I explored the four domains of language use, derived from the physical areas that exist for language teaching in ʔayisaqḥ: hitinqis: the beach, hitiił: in the house, hitaaqƛas: in the forest and hiłačišt: on the sea. For example, we used two kitchens during this course; the siquwił "kitchen in the house" was spoken of with the "in the house" suffix ending, and the siquwis "kitchen on the beach" was spoken with the "on the beach" suffix ending. Each planned activity, then, needed to take into account the location(s) of delivery. While facilitating a lesson in the forest, I needed to use the "in the forest" suffix ending to say, for example, "under the fir tree-in-the-forest" or hiẏapuẇas maawi, because even within basic communication, our language integrates location information that directly connects speech to place.

In my own language learning as an adult, I have pieced together mutually compatible methods of learning at different times with accessible fluent speakers and used various language media. For this course, it was important to me that the language being delivered employed various teaching approaches and that the planned language was verified with more than one fluent speaker. I knew that my experience as an emerging teacher was not unique, because through reading and conversations, I found that Indigenous language activists across the continent find it necessary to overlap their language learning with the creation of learning tools (Hermes, Bang, & Marin, 2012; Hinton & Hale, 2008; Johnson, 2012). When I was attending Master-Apprentice program training with my elders, Leanne Hinton demonstrated using full sentences through shorter skits while making meaning through gestures and actions. The Master-Apprentice approach developed by Hinton (2002) has been effectively modified for application in groups or families (Hinton, 2013).

Combining the language knowledge I gained in my three-year experience in the role of Apprentice and my two years as an assistant in the Language Nest, which is a language immersion space for families with young children to interact with fluent speakers, I was able to develop a pilot model. The pilot language course engaged students in very minimal reading, and only in conjunction with games, but spelling was deliberately done in standardized nuučaaṅuł orthography and not an English-based writing system that approximates the sounds of our language, so that the lesson outlines that resulted from the course could still be useful in a decade or more, and so that nuučaaṅuł people could feel confident in looking at the created resource without the burden of requiring further corrections or verifications with regard to pronunciation and accuracy. Toward this end, it was helpful for my work to undergo the scrutiny of fluent speakers and a linguist. My experience with learning through the Master-Apprentice immersion approach (Hinton, 2002), and then delivering immersion teaching based loosely on a synthesis of that approach with dramatic skits and the Paul Creek method (Peterson et al., 2014), had not formally connected ḥiḥiškʷiiʔatḥa content with the ḥiškʷiiʔatḥ environment until I engaged in the planning and delivery of this course with my kinkʷaaštaqumł family.

It was my first experience as an independent teacher and it gave me insights into the ways in which teaching differs from using ancestral language in the home during daily activities. I felt that I was engaged in an acting performance while teaching, and I gave myself permission to act more dramatically. I noticed that the delivery of language lessons differed markedly in increased effort level. Through the lessons preparation and interaction with learners during the lessons delivery, I gained insight into scaffolding lessons to build on learners' knowledge. The lesson structure and the planning process helped me to stay in immersion during planned sets during this course. As ḥiškʷiiʔatḥ, we all have a role in the retention and recovery of our language and culture, so it makes sense that a ḥiḥiškʷiiʔatḥa course would respect and integrate the individual strengths of those involved. My father's well-placed contributions in delivering the cultural teachings during the course, combined with my mother's collaboration with him and the rest of the family to ensure logistical viability and forethought for the best learning scenarios, allowed for everyone to contribute our time and respective knowledge in a safe way that added to everybody's learning. During the course, I gauged the receptiveness of our family of learners to the lessons, the suitability of the setting with regard to weather, and made plans with the group accordingly. The language lesson summaries were adjusted from my elder-checked language plans and were then formalized to include as immersion sets in the appendices of my Masters project (Rorick, 2016). I would say that the preparation process, including the data gathering, verification with elders, practice and delivery of the lessons, provided me with a foundation from which to continue building a teaching vocabulary and a language knowledge base that interacts with the surrounding environments, thereby daily re-strengthening the ties between my language and the environment.

This place-based language course delivered and created a teaching resource that has begun to contribute to and expand into teaching nuučaańuł language in primary, elementary, and community classes. I still carry the feeling and determination I had when I came away from the course that the language our ancestors spoke in those very same places can be *remembered* and renewed for our offspring, and thus we remain ʔiqḥmuut-ancient and continuing.

Indigenous Language, Place-Based Knowledge, and Spirituality

> Language shapes [our epistemology:] the way we think, perceive, and organize the world in culturally meaningful ways, and our First Nations languages provide irreplaceable ways of organizing the social, natural, [and metaphysical] world, based on [our ontology, which is] the ancient, cumulative human experience and associated assumptions of First Peoples.
>
> (Ignace, 2015, p. 12 in Rosborough & Rorick, 2017)

When younger generations have access to tools and resources to carry our ancient Indigenous knowledge systems forward, then it can be said that Indigenous knowledge systems have continuity. Indigenous knowledge lives on through ancestral teachings as they are lived, spoken, demonstrated, and deliberately shared. Indigenous knowledge is relational, which means not only must we repair our damaged relationship to our languages, but it means we must at the same time maintain and constantly renew our human, metaphysical, and natural world relationships. In my opinion, ancestral nuučaańuł continuity of human relationships reaches back beyond the most recent period of colonial violence against Indigenous peoples to continue on in the pre-contact way of nuučaańuł ancestors who welcomed the first European explorers. ʔiqḥmuut or nuučaańuł ancestral continuity in action can contribute toward the resurgence of Indigenous languages and cultures.

nuučaańuł scholar Umeek Atleo (2004) found that Indigenous language and Indigenous scholarship are transformational for improving understandings and relationships between Indigenous peoples and settlers. With regard to research, Atleo (2004) found that "[settlers] have made their gifts of science and technology evident and recognizable to all, while our gifts of relationality and *isaak* (respect for all life forms) have only now begun to emerge" (p. 134).

Our language itself holds a knowledge and understanding of the nuučaan̓uł world, including how we approach relationships with others and with our environment. My father, Stephen Charleson, told me in preparing for our 2015 family language immersion course that over the last century we have been subjected to constant shifts and changes in the ways we learn in schools and within our families (Rorick, 2016). Our relationship to nuučaan̓uł knowledge has been stifled and limited by social and political factors, most principally by Indian residential schools and by geographical challenges caused by industries and natural disasters. I have come to believe that in order to preserve ancestral knowledge continuity in Indigenous languages, in spirituality and in our relationship to ancestral land and seascapes, we must actively seek to re-strengthen those tenets of Indigenous knowledge in our everyday practice.

It can be difficult to differentiate the truth about Indigenous knowledge from Western imaginings upon what can be understood from looking at the surface of our cultural beliefs and behaviors. Western understandings view the metaphysical realm as the end of what can be understood and are therefore not useful; I believe that those who lean away from Western understandings can develop deeper understandings when efforts are made to continually renew and connect to Indigenous worldview(s), especially through connecting language to place in order to reveal Indigenous understandings and truths. I have heard it said that Western religions had their evolutionary beginnings in a type of spirituality similar to that practiced by Indigenous peoples; Indigenous spirituality is perceived as a state of disorganization and uncertainty, and by contrast Western religions are characterized as supreme linear pillars of organization and certainty. This idea contributes to the Western myth that Native peoples are primordial and that our knowledge systems are thusly equivalent or comparable to outdated Western, "more developed" systems. Instead, I see the ancient commonalities between our knowledge systems and theirs, acknowledge that they each developed under the constant influence of socio-cultural forces across the ages, resulting in the development of separate understandings and worldview, including the higher degree of importance Indigenous peoples assign to drawing understandings from specific place(s). An immersive, extended educational effort is required in order to process understandings in the context of their place(s) of origin. Indigenous knowledge is not something that can be understood while maintaining an outside perspective that can only imagine from a look at the surface of Indigenous cultural beliefs.

Petitions, sometimes called "prayers," to the metaphysical, as well as spontaneous encounters with metaphysical elements are part of a nuučaan̓uł ancestral system of knowledge management and transmission. According to nuučaan̓uł scholar Umeek Atleo (2004), "supernatural [metaphysical] experiences were necessary for an effective management of reality" (p. 72). Encounters in the realm of the metaphysical are most often viewed by the dominant culture as unreal, as pathological, and therefore not useful or even sane. Those kinds of experiences have been sometimes defined as unfounded, labeled "supernatural" or outside of the natural, and not part of reality. I have come to believe that Indigenous relationships with the metaphysical over the ages strengthened our systems of metaphysical petition on the west coast of Vancouver Island and likely elsewhere in Indigenous communities around the world. Locally, this is manifested in the various types of ceremonial petition used by nuučaańuł people, which involve specific places, actions, intense focus of the mind toward certain aims to achieve success in various mediums. The successful result of a metaphysical petition can result in certainty for the petitioner about a correct course of action in relation to their circumstance. In my opinion, an educational practice based in Indigenous understandings would enrich the practice and daily realities of those who live on these lands.

Indigenous Place-Based Education as a Decolonizing Practice

Indigenous place-based education can be a decolonizing practice in multiple ways. In employing a decolonizing practice, I seek to privilege Indigenous, rather than dominant colonizing knowledge bases to guide my work. Tuck and Yang (2012) define colonialism as

> the biopolitical [which I interpret as the intervention of authority on life] and geopolitical [which I see as the intersections of living land and authority] management of people, land, flora and fauna within the "domestic" borders of the imperial nation.
>
> *(pp. 4–5)*

Settler colonialism has sought to remove Indigenous peoples from desirable land through a process of belittling, dehumanization, and misinformation and/or silence about Indigenous peoples (Tuck, McKenzie, & McCoy, 2014). Decolonizing practice combats the cultivated settler colonial-cultivated view of Indigenous people as being low aptitude, lacking intelligence and possessing weak character by challenging the underlying assumption of the superiority of dominant systems. "Eurocentric knowledge systems have displaced Indigenous knowledge, languages, and cultures, making invisible, our distinct Indigenous knowledge systems which should, but does not enjoy a place of parity with dominant systems" (Battiste, 2008). Operating in an Indigenous context creates a comfortable learning environment for Indigenous learners and it is efficient for direct conveyance of Indigenous knowledge; it eliminates dominant educational dialogue around Indigenous people that can cause discord for Indigenous learners. In order to bring awareness to nuučaańuł models of learning and success, educational discourse and research should directly reflect models of nuučaańuł success from a nuučaańuł context. Thompson (2012) reminds me that Indigenous knowledge systems have developed independent of Western systems across the ages, and we are in need of emergent leadership that is revitalizing and confirming Indigenous worldview and knowledge systems. As Indigenous peoples, closing the educational "achievement gap" between minorities and whites should not, as Ladson-Billings (2006) argues, result in Indigenous peoples becoming more white. A decolonizing approach privileges an Indigenous knowledge base from which to build educational approaches that are specifically nuučaaňuɫ in order to strengthen the learning of nuučaaňuɫ learners.

For a variety of reasons, the mostly widely discussed of those being a cultivated cultural inferiority complex, we have some violated and distrusting nuučaaňuɫ people who would rather die with Indigenous knowledge and resources than share with others. Familial animosities, histories, and socio-political forces are at risk of overtaking the place of traditional knowledge systems as the foundation from which we draw strength if we allow those forces to silence ancestral knowledge. I do not deny that there are symptoms of continued oppressions within my community, but I would instead like to acknowledge their current place in our relationships and focus on where we can become able to live peacefully in our language once again. I believe the role of the language activist is to make peaceful actions in community, even if the way our communities are currently surviving does not sit well with the spirit. I believe that nuučaaňuɫ educators and knowledge keepers can apply a decolonizing approach by focusing on strengthening and revitalizing precolonial Indigenous knowledge-based teachings, connecting the past with the present and the future, and connecting people with the land and spirituality: passing on our teachings in ancestral continuity.

Indigenous Theories and Methodologies That Guide My Language Efforts

In taking a decolonizing approach that is based in Indigenous knowledge, I looked to the work of Indigenous scholars whose research is guided by Indigenous paradigms, worldviews, processes, and contexts to re-create and re-theorize methodologies (Absolon, 2011; Rosborough, 2012; Smith, 1999; Wilson, 2008). Indigenous researchers undertake qualitative research that is grounded in building and keeping relationships (Absolon, 2011; Kovach, 2009; Brayboy & Deyhle, 2000), and our embeddedness in the community means that in the pursuit of knowledge we ask deeply informed questions (Brayboy & Deyhle, 2000). My qualitative, community-based Indigenous research in delivering the place-based ḥiḥiškwiiʔatḥa language course was informed by nuučaaňuɫ knowledge, locally applied decolonizing theory, and the field of Indigenous language revitalization. Three qualitative research methods were employed in the study of that language course: interview, reflective-writing, and participant observation. I used journaling to reflect on and to analyze the lesson format in order to include considerations and instructions for future teaching of the lessons in an outdoor setting. "Ultimately, an exploration of traditional Indigenous education is an exploration of a nature-centered and community-responsive philosophy of research.

Education, in this context, becomes education for "life's sake" (Cajete, 1994) and is founded on environmental learning because it all relates to the "deep ecology" and "relationships of place" (Cajete, 2008). The finalized lessons from the language course were informed by my experience in developing and teaching the language lesson sets in partnership with my extended family members at our ancestral home at ʔayisaqḥ. They reflect the combination of place-based outdoor education at Hooksum Outdoor School, as communicated to me by my parents, and the observation of place-based learning during the language course on ancestral land.

Moving forward in Indigenous language revitalization scholarship, I search for ways that Indigenous knowledge can contribute to improved management of our lands and seascapes with the addition of more wide-reaching inclusiveness and acceptance of strengthened relationships to the natural and metaphysical realms. I am particularly interested in ways that nuučaańuł knowledge systems can contribute to the formation of Indigenous social, political, and economic foundations for developing Indigenous worldview-based curriculum through educational research; research that contributes toward redressing colonial dispossession of Indigenous lands, languages, and worldviews. Future research that contributes to the resurgence of a more widely applied Indigenous knowledge cultivation that is consciously integrated by non-Indigenous people, and which strengthens the conditions for transmission of ancestral knowledge in Indigenous communities, would strengthen educational approaches in this country.

I aspire to give back to my children, to my family, to my community, to neighbors, and to the elders who have given their time over the past several years. I understand this pattern of receiving and redistribution of knowledge to be an Indigenous way, and a crucial element of Indigenous research.

Conclusion

I want my ancestors to recognize me as their own, speaking our language on the land from which we have sprung. I think that if it makes you feel alive as an Indigenous person to live in that way, then those Indigenous values live on to create continuity through you. For me, as a nuučaańułʔaqsup "nuučaańuł woman," success is seeking strength in spirituality, in connection to all that our ancestors held up as valuable. I see lasting success and leadership happening for our people only when we stand on a firm foundation brought forward by our ancestors. Indigenous land-based education and language revitalization efforts that are reflective of deep investment in outcomes will contribute toward the *remembering* of our languages, relationships, and Indigenous knowledge systems.

Service toward the revitalization and sharing of Indigenous knowledge systems that have survived colonial violence has a healing and restorative role in education. Though the language lessons resulting from the place-based language course I discussed here could be delivered out of territory, it would likely exclude lessons about place names until suitable resources are created that make a fitting connection between the names and places that integrate the way one actually experiences a place from our situation on the land or on the water, and not strictly from an aerial view provided by looking at maps. Making a presence on ancestral lands, however, remains for me a core tenet of wholistic learning about the ḥiškʷiiʔatḥ world, especially when learning through ḥiḥiškʷiiʔatḥa.

It is my desire to continue as one of the people who is helping to drive our Indigenous language forward in the long term, applying collaborative efforts to create new speakers and supporting other emerging language immersion teachers. Like many other Indigenous language activists, I will continue efforts alongside fluent elders to create and deliver free learning resources and training with an eye toward contributing to the restoration of our language. I would like to be a contributor toward the restoration of our language to a place where sophisticated ʔiqḥmuut oratory and higher-thinking in our language undergoes renewal, and I hope my research and efforts toward the advancement of Indigenous language revitalization in my own nuučaaňuɫ community will contribute to increased knowledge of respectful researcher engagement with a community of Indigenous knowledge keepers and improved nuučaaňuɫ language acquisition resources. I want to help develop and provide models of practice that contribute toward the continuation of ancestral nuučaaňuɫ language and understandings of the world. As a permanent member of the community, taking on a small role in a specifically nuučaaňuɫ way, I reach into the past to look for better working models for the future of our relationships with each other and our relationships to this place, seeking to illuminate and to draw from ignored Indigenous knowledge systems and from ʔiqḥmuut, the ancient but continuing worldview of Indigenous peoples, right here, on this land.

Language immersion can be one of the tools that gives people that feeling of *remembering*, that experience or further understanding of what it means to be ʔiqḥmuut. The goal of the Indigenous language immersion environment is to provide the space, the freedom and the safety to reconnect to living our lives in our language, on our land. Taking our rightful place(s) as ʔiqḥmuut ḥiškʷiiʔatḥ calls us to engage the language of the land in ancestral continuity, informing our continual reconnection to the spiritual and natural world.

References

Absolon, K. (2011). *Kaandossiwin: How we come to know*. Winnipeg, MB: Fernwood Publishing.

Atleo, E. R. (2004). *Tsawalk: A Nuuchahnulth perspective*. Vancouver, BC: University of British Columbia Press.

Atleo, M. R. (2009). Understanding aboriginal learning ideology through storywork with elders. *Alberta Journal of Educational Research, 55*(4), 453–467.

Battiste, M. (2008). The struggle and renaissance of Indigenous Knowledge in Eurocentric Education. In M. Villegas, S. R. Neugebauer, & K. R. Venegas (Eds.), *Indigenous knowledge and education: Sites of struggle, strength, and survivance* (pp. 85–91). Cambridge, MA: Harvard Education Press.

Bougie, E. (2010, September 9). *Family, community and Aboriginal language among young first nations children living off reserve in Canada.* Canadian Social Trends, Component of Statistics Canada Catalogue no. 11–008-X. Statistics Canada. Government of Canada.

Brayboy, B. M., & Deyhle, D. (2000). Insider-outsider: Researchers in American Indian communities. *Theory Into Practice, 39*(3), 163.

Cajete, G. (1994). Final Thoughts. *Look to the mountain: an ecology of indigenous education.* Durango, CO: Kivakí Press.

Cajete, G. (2008). Sites of strength in indigenous research. In M. Villegas, S. R. Neugebauer, & K. R. Venegas (Eds.), *Indigenous knowledge and education: Sites of struggle, strength, and survivance* (pp. 204–208). Cambridge, MA: Harvard Education Press.

Canadian Heritage. (2005). *Towards a new beginning: A foundation report for a strategy to revitalize first nations, Inuit and Métis languages and cultures.* Report to the Minister of Canadian Heritage by the Task Force on Aboriginal Languages and Cultures. Ottawa. Catalogue no. CH4–96/2005.

First Peoples' Cultural Council. (2014). *Report on the status of B.C. First Nations languages.* 2nd ed. Retrieved from www.fpcc.ca/files/PDF/Language/FPCC-LanguageReport-141016-WEB.pdf

Hermes, M., Bang, M., & Marin, A. (2012). Designing indigenous language revitalization. *Harvard Educational Review, 82*(3).

Hinton, L. & Hale, K., Eds. (2001). *Green book of language revitalization in practice.* San Diego, CA: Academic Press.

Hinton, L., Vera, M., & Steele, N. (2002). *How to keep your language alive: A commonsense approach to one-on-one language learning.* Berkeley, CA: Heyday Books.

Hinton, L. (Ed.). (2013). *Bringing our languages home: Language revitalization for families.* Berkeley: Heyday Books.

Johnson, Michele S7imla7xw (2013). n'łəqwcin (clear speech): 1,000 hours to mid-intermediate N'syilxcn proficiency (Indigenous language, Syilx, Okanagan-Colville, n'qilxwcn, Interior Salish). Retrieved from http://circle.ubc.ca/handle/2429/45453

Kovach, M. (2009). *Indigenous methodologies: Characteristics, conversations, and contexts.* Toronto, ON: University of Toronto Press.

Ladson-Billings, G. (2006). From the achievement gap to the education debt: Understanding achievement in US schools. *Educational Researcher, 35*(7), 3–12.

Little Bear, L. (2000). Jagged worldviews colliding. In M. Battiste (Ed.), *Reclaiming indigenous voice and vision* (pp. 77–85). Vancouver, BC: UBC Press.

McIvor, O., Napoleon, A. & Dickie, K. M. (2009). Language and culture as protective factors for at-risk communities. *International Journal of Indigenous Health, 5*(1): 6–25.

Michel, K. A. (2012). *Trickster's path to language transformation: Stories of Secwepemc immersion from Chief Atahm School.* (Doctoral dissertation). Retrieved from https://open.library.ubc.ca/cIRcle/collections/ubctheses/24/items/1.0105178

Nuu-chah-nulth Tribal Council. (1995). *Wawaačakuk yaqwiiʔitq quuʔas: Sayings of our first people.* Penticton, BC: Theytus Books.

Perley, B. (2013). Remembering ancestral voices: Emergent vitalities and the future of Indigenous languages. In E. Mihas, B. Perley, G. Rei-Doval, & K. Wheatley (Eds.), *Responses to language endangerment: In honor of Mickey Noonan: New directions in language documentation and language revitalization* (pp. 243–270). Amsterdam: John Benjamins.

Peterson, Sʕamtícaʔ S., Wiley, L. & Parkin, C. (2014). *N'sel'xcin Curriculum Project.* Series of 6 N'sel'xcin textbooks, audio CDs, and teaching manuals: *N'sel'xcin 1: A beginning course in Okanagan; Captikʷł 1: Okanagan stories for beginners; N'sel'xcin 2: An intermediate* course in Okanagan Salish; Captikʷł 2: Okanagan stories for intermediate students; N'sel'xcin 3: An advanced course in Okanagan Salish; Captikʷł 3: Okanagan stories for advanced students (in press); Teacher's Manual: Direct acquisition lesson activities; Lesson plans. Keremeos, B.C. and Spokane, WA: The Salish School of Spokane, Paul Creek Language Association and Lower Similkameen Indian Band. Retrieved from www.interiorsalish.com

Rorick, c. L. (2016). wałyaʕasukʔi naatnaniqsakqin: At the home of our Ancestors: Hesquiaht second language immersion on Hesquiaht Land. (Master's project). Retrieved from www.uvic.ca/education/assets/docs/Rorick_Layla_MEd_2016.pdf

Rosborough, P. C. (2012). K'angextola sewn-on-top: Kwak'wala revitalization and being Indigenous. (Doctoral dissertation). University of British Columbia, Vancouver, BC.

Rosborough, T., & Rorick, c. L. (2017). Following in the footsteps of the Wolf: Connecting scholarly minds to ancestors in indigenous language revitalization. *Alternative: An International Journal of Indigenous Peoples.* doi:1177180116689031

Smith, L. T. (1999). *Decolonizing methodologies: Research and indigenous peoples.* New York, NY: Zed Books.

Thompson, J. C. (2012). *Hedekeyeh Hots'ih Kahidi—"Our Ancestors are in us": Strengthening our voices through language revitalization from a Tahltan Worldview.* (Doctoral dissertation). University of British Columbia, Vancouver, BC.

Truth and Reconciliation Commission of Canada (TRC). (2015). *Truth and reconciliation commission of Canada: Calls to action.* Retrieved from Truth and Reconciliation Commission of Canada website www.trc.ca/websites/trcinstitution/File/2015/Findings/Calls_to_Action_English2.pdf

Tuck, E., McKenzie, M., & McCoy, K. (2014). Land education: Indigenous, post-colonial, and decolonizing perspectives on place and environmental education research. *Environmental Education Research, 20*(1), 1–23. Retrieved from https://doi.org/10.1080/1350 4622.2013.877708

Tuck, E., & Yang, K. (2012). Decolonization is not a metaphor. *Decolonization: Indigeneity, Education & Society, 1*(1), 1–40.

Wilson, S. (2008). *Research is ceremony: Indigenous research methods.* Halifax, NS: Fernwood Publishing.

AFTERWORD: MEETING THE LAND(S) WHERE THEY ARE AT

A Conversation Between Erin Marie Konsmo (Métis) and Karyn Recollet (Urban Cree)

Sometimes we want to go home, but "returning to the land" is more difficult than we often acknowledge.

—Chelsea Vowel

The bodies of our communities are under siege by forces that leverage violence and ableism at every turn. Ableism is connected to all of our struggles because it undergirds notions of whose bodies are considered valuable, desirable and disposable. How do we build across our communities and movements so that we are able to fight for each other without leveraging ableism?

—Mia Mingus

In the pages that follow, Erin Marie Konsmo and Karyn Recollet weave together moments and spaces for breathing, imagining, creating, and blossoming on lands, water and sky. These moments aim to disrupt the multiple ways in which settler colonialism continues to try and define our relationships with all of creation.

Erin: My partner and I joked recently about how if "you have a copper IUD you are busy water walking every day." It's important to keep a sense of humor when we sometimes take "returning to the land" so seriously. We joke about how "my family's been water walking for generations!" which speaks to how many generations of women have had IUDs in my family. This isn't to diminish the work of grandmothers like Josephine Mandamin walking for the water, but to acknowledge the many ways that women, trans and two-spirit people maintain their own personal connections and care for the water, which includes their reproductive autonomy.

Yarrow is a medicine that can be used during menstruation and in support of the uterus, among many other uses. As I waited at a bus stop in amiskwacîwâskahikan (Edmonton) on a hot sunny day, head down, feeling shy out in public, I found myself staring at a section of yarrow that had sprouted. As one of the first plant medicines I learned about and with its connections to reproductive health I was delighted! In that moment, I took a photo, yarrow in hand, bus bench and sign behind. I posted it to social media and immediately had a response that warned me of picking medicines in the city, at risk of them being sick, impacted by negative energy and to ensure I only picked in areas where they were "pure/untouched." Purity narratives appear in many forms and are often further reinforced by whiteness, misogyny, homo/transphobia, NIMBY and ableism. For any deviations from the normative—white, male, heterosexual, cisgender and able-bodied—are seen as less pure. I want us to consider how these notions are projected further in relation to Indigenous lands and especially as it relates to Indigenous resurgence on the land.

What does it mean to shame those who pick medicines in cities or at bus stops? In a conversation with a friend about my experiences being shamed for picking medicines at a bus stop, she responded, "What does that mean for our people who live in the cities? are they not medicine?" (See Figure 16.1.)

This conversation taught me a lot about the ways in which both ableism and purity are being reflected in our relationships to medicines, ceremony and culture. Medicines that are sick or contaminated are often left behind and the ability to access pure forms of resurgence on the land are becoming minimal. We know that resource development and pollution exist in almost all the spaces of our territories, whether that's the city, the reserve or in rural areas. Cities already function in ways to erase Indigenous people and disjoint us from being "connected to the land." And yet cities are also built on Indigenous land, and Indigenous peoples continue to live in our own territories whether they be urban or rural. In the face of massive land theft, dispossession and destruction, Indigenous people should be encouraged to nurture whatever medicines we can find, wherever we can find them.

Karyn: I like to archive migration glyphs in the city of Tkaronto where I work, and where Gracie saw her first murals and drank her first sips of soy chai latte (yes I gave my 5-year-old a taste of that sweet urban elixir!). I started to think about the city as an Indigenous space through the ways that murals started speaking to us—particularly the work of Fiya Bruxa, Chief Lady Bird, Aura Last, and others whose ancestor pieces reminded me of what it was to be home, as home can be a space of movement, fluidity and the insights of these choreographies. When I approach city glyphs spray painted on walls in our beautiful, imaginative urban spaces, I think about the coded texts that teach us how to be good future kin in the world, and how these are ways to intervene on harmful practices such as ableism that destroy relationships with lands and with each other.

FIGURE 16.1 Yarrow at the Bus Stop

Erin: We are in a time where water defense is an ever-increasing movement in the face of pipelines, nuclear waste disposal and boil water advisories. "Water is Life" posters and art fill Instagram feeds and are carried at direct action camps. Intervening in harmful practices like ableism means we all have a responsibility to ensure meaningful participation for differently abled people to be recognized as contributing to land and water defense. I see that fluidity you speak of at the safer injection sites in both Moss Park in Tkaronto (Toronto) and near Byward Market in Odawa (Ottawa) as a response to the public health emergency of opioid overdoses. These pop-up safe injection sites are volunteer-\ run and a place where people can safely use drugs with support in the event that they overdose. They are an emergency response to the overdose crisis led by community due to a lack of action by the state. Naloxone, a medication used at these sites, is used to block the effects of opioids, especially in the case of opioid overdose. It is an overdose prevention medication that anyone can be trained to administer and is life saving/giving. For me, harm reduction has and will continue to provide life for our people, before we even make it to the water, so that we can make it to the water. It's about meeting community where they are at, free of stigma, and holding space for the value of every life. It is also about helping keep each other safe under colonialism. If we are really committed to protecting life, then we need to take care of our people in all the fluid forms of resurgence. We need harm reduction for our people to make it through to access the water/land, to protect it and ultimately our nations. I appreciate Tara Williamson's words on the value of every life:

I have learned that people under the influence of drugs or alcohol should not be using the "sacred" medicines (sage, cedar, tobacco, sweetgrass). Yet, in my work as a social worker, and truly in my own life, it is sometimes those times that I need the help of medicine most. Who am I to say that the drunk man on the street cannot breathe the sweet smell of wiingashk?

(2013)

Before I ever heard the phrase "water is life," I knew the phrase "harm reduction is life." It taught me about bringing water to where our people are at. People who use drugs and alcohol, access safer injection sites, and should be loved and not stigmatized. There are calls for the need for water bottles at sites, whether they are land defense camps or safer injection sites. Both of these places can teach us about the water. Ultimately many of our kin who use drugs are also there and naloxone is also life giving. Naloxone can be both injected or inhaled in a nasal spray. In both forms, this life-giving substance is in a liquid state, just like water. The "water is life" and "harm reduction is life" movements are both doing critical work to care for our nations and have much to teach us about our relationships to each other and the water.

Karyn: Erin, your words are urgent in this moment—we need to make sure that we are all alive so that we can make it to the water. I wonder—what are the choreographies, the practices that we can employ "at the water's edge" so that we can make sure that no one gets left behind? What are the shapes of our gatherings[1] when we center the practices of harm reduction at the water's edge? There is a need to practice consensual relationship building with the waters, the stars and each other—especially in the work that we do as movement makers, creators of social movements and those who help to hold space for them. Establishing intimacies with lands' destruction can mean that we are re/embodying and re/imagining our bodies beyond—as other worlding through jumping scale from the boundedness, as our bodies/lands seep outward. Some of us have been used to the tiny details, the gestures, the languages that we employ to fall in love with the ruptures within. We oftentimes find ourselves in joy, love and hope in the wasteland.

Erin: Harvesting medicines even where they may be harmed can be a practice of harm reduction. So many times I've found medicines beside gravel pits, under power lines, close to a man camp where resource development workers are living, in the wake of logging devastation or in the meridian of a busy highway. Picking medicines in each of these areas involves some level of risk. Some people will tell you not to pick medicines in these areas because they aren't as strong or impacted by pollution. By stating our loving intentions and offering tobacco to these medicines, no matter how impacted by industry, we can begin to heal the medicines while they begin to heal us. How does our relationship to land, plants and animals who have been hurt teach us about how we also treat and view those who are not normative (i.e., not cisgender, not straight, not male, not white, not able-bodied)? For many of my queer, two-spirit and trans kin, disability, illness and sickness are a part of our experiences of colonialism, including when we are on the land or water. I believe our gender/sexualities were made exactly for these futures. Sara Ahmed speaks about queer objects and how "to live out a politics of disorientation might be to sustain wonder about the very forms of social gathering" (p. 24). At a time in which harm is almost inescapable, the work of folks advocating harm reduction is critical to the ways we theorize going "back to the land and water." Harm reduction shows us on the land that we can return to the land and our ceremonies and not be shamed for how we do that. Harm reduction meets people where they're at with compassion and looks beyond labeling people as "addicts" or labeling medicines as "bad." Our medicines are seen as tools to help heal us. We are now in a time where we have to contend with the reality that they'll also be impacted by the forces of colonialism and resource development. Each person in our families and nations is a medicine. Differently abled people, trans, queer, and two-spirit people, and those that use substances and live with addictions, all have gifts to offer.

Karyn: I look to dark matter to show me choreographies of the gravitational pull—how to make kin . . . even if I am shy about it all. I too have been changed, and in some ways—charged from the rubble . . . perhaps my city migrations are akin to being born from a milky way created of dirt, and bone fragments, swirling and gently nudging me towards those spaces I most revere/fear. Perhaps going *back* to the land is not really the answer, as it presupposes a linearity that is associated with structures and systems that have not served us well. What I am thinking here is "meeting the land(s) where they are at" and thinking through our processes of consensual kin making with them. We have all been impacted so that our bodies (as in bodies of water) need radical love to have affect in our future pasts—and present futures.

Yes, Erin, what if we saw the magic of the land/water/plants in every space we were? What if we felt the presence of underground waterways teeming with fresh water salmon and eels . . . fishing weirs to gather magic we all hold space for—kinstillatory—we need all of us in our gorgeous complexities.

Erin and Karyn: Our ideas of the land and what is "natural" or "sacred" is often wrapped up in ableism. We need to consider lands' overflow—as land that evades singularity, creating migration glyphs as it flows deep and celestially. In order to love and build good relations through ongoing colonialisms and environmental destruction, we need to rid ourselves of the technologies and practices associated with purity, which also ultimately harm our city kin, and gender- and sexuality-complex folks and people with disabilities.

Rarely do we hear people talk about environmental justice and disability as relational to ways in which "purity" is mobilized in land protection movements. Coming to terms with and identifying purist essentialisms as destructive within Indigenous spaces is necessary as we risk embedding others in narratives of purity in our relationships with water or land, or purity around cultural and ceremonial knowledge. Since we are in a space/time where our bodies are entangled in infrastructure, we need to not force dogmatic practices of land/water on our people, because it is ultimately ableist, creating shame if you don't meet that standard, and leaves very specific people behind; the very people whose bodies negotiate multitudinous relationships to lands' overflows.

We need to reimagine not only our cities, but also bodies of all abilities as being good on the land/water. We can reimagine these plant medicines that persevere in the ruins of environmental devastation as part of our kin, and ultimately still valuable in assisting our bodies and spirits. (See Figures 16.2 and 16.3.)

Erin: On a rainy afternoon, I spent time harvesting birch bark with my two-spirit Anishinaabe partner on their territory just south of Lac Seul First Nation/Obishikokaang. The birch that we were harvesting was from trees that had been logged and left in the rubble. Discarded by the logging companies that left as quickly as they clear cut, the fallen birch trees caught our attention as if they needed some love, care and reciprocity.

For me, this felt like ethical harvesting inside a world that continues to be destroyed by extreme extractivism. It spoke to me because I felt like those trees are similar to the people who are left behind in the rubble of colonialism. Trees that had been through logging devastation but still had ways to contribute. I can't help but hope that whenever I'm left in the rubble that someone will still be able to see me for what I can share and the medicines I provide.

FIGURE 16.2 Harvesting Birch Bark

If our homelands are left in the rubble/forever changed by cityscapes, how will we see them? How will we still care for what is left behind? Do we abandon ourselves? How many kin, either human, animal or plants, do we leave behind when we enforce ideas about "damaged goods"? Our communities will be stronger and our people will be healthier when we begin to enforce an ethic of caring for all. While I'm not advocating for futures of destruction, I am advocating for futures that will make space for all of us if destruction continues.

My partner reminds me that fields of blueberries often grow in the wake of logged land and shared that some Anishinaabe grandmothers even grow excited

FIGURE 16.3   Harvesting Birch Bark

at the prospect of a new road being cut through the bush, knowing that abundant blueberries will follow in a few short years. This is not so different from customary Anishinaabe practices of controlled forest fires to stimulate growth and renewal of the plants and trees. There is an understanding that, sometimes, environmental change can lead to new and beautiful beginnings. Cree language speaker Mary Cardinal Collins from Saddle Lake First Nation once told me that blueberry in the language was referred to as the "healing berry." Berries are already teaching us about the ways in which we can exist under these realities of destruction. That we can harvest that which heals our bodies in the ruins of extreme wreckage.

I continue to see the ways that some essentialist resurgence narratives are difficult and make Indigenous resurgence inaccessible. In this case, the "return to the land/waters" narrative has also become difficult, for myself included. Whenever I feel those narratives come up, I'm reminded of the words of Sarah Hunt, and her response to Glen Coulthard's *Red Skin White Masks*:

> although we might agree with Coulthard's rejection politics, the lives of many Indigenous people remain bound up in state systems, both ideologically and materially, such that they cannot simply turn away from them. Today, right now, we know that 40% of women in federal prisons are Indigenous and more than 50% of kids in care in BC are Indigenous.
>
> *(2014)*

Erin and Karyn: How do "return to the land" narratives impact those who are incarcerated? Is there any space in these discourses for those who are held in prisons on Indigenous lands? As a community we need to consider those who are entangled in state systems, often without their consent. Being critical of purity recognizes that few in our community are sufficiently privileged to completely escape the colonial mechanisms that bind. Folks who live in the cities are often excluded from Indigenous lands discourses. What does it mean, for instance, to orient ourselves to the CN tower in Tkaronto as that which gestures celestially, tentacularly, and is rhysomatically rooted to the underground flows? A "return to the land" narrative disembodies the relationships between urban Indigenous peoples their relationships with the stewards of Indigenous lands that cities are occupying, and with the lands themselves. Likewise, for people living with chronic illnesses, a "pure" return to the land can remove them from life-sustaining medicines and demand levels of physical labor of which they are not necessarily able. Indigenous people in Canada experienced HIV at rates about 3.6 times higher than other Canadians in 2008, and at this time their quality of life is significantly improved with access to anti-retroviral medicines.[2]

Erin: As someone coming to terms with a chronic illness while also grappling with how we return to the land, no moment stood out more for me on the land than wading through the dump on Obishikokaang traditional territory with my partner, looking for eagle feathers. In a place seen as dirty and smelly, where people discard what is seen as worthless and no longer of value, we climbed through trash with the most beautiful bald eagles flying overhead. The trees along the edge of the dump were filled and abundant, holding streams of garbage like nests for eagles to rest. As I walked through, I met a groundhog hiding in the rubble of concrete and medical waste. It came out to visit and watch me. This moment stood out for me, grounded me and haunted me. It was a place where it was ok to hold all the contentions of our ill bodies, colonialism, consumerism and realities while still being on the land with animal kin. It may not have been the pristine moments captured in notions of "back to the land," but it felt perfect. In the very least, we (including animal kin) were together on the land, in the destruction together. No one more or less sacred. It allowed my ill body to exist on the land without shame or stigma. The feathers we gathered there were later gifted to both two-spirit, trans and gender-complex youth, as well as a young survivor of sexual violence (see Figure 16.4).

Most of the work I've been taught to do has been intimate care work including supporting survivors of violence in my life, making space for two-spirit people, building up tools of harm reduction and meeting community where they're at.

FIGURE 16.4   Harvesting Feathers

While these practices at the water's edge may not regularly be seen as part of the "land" narrative, I can't help but ask myself: How does this care work provide us with tools for when we return to the land? A mentor of mine once asked me, *"What are we saving the land for if there are no women and two-spirit people left?"* This refers to the ways in which Indigenous land rights are always prioritized over addressing the impacts of gender-based violence upon our communities. Some of these very environmental spaces and land defense movements were also spaces where men who were known abusers were constantly upheld. My mentor's words have stuck with me, forever engrained and present in any space that flattens discussions about the land and doesn't connect it to ongoing realities of violence on our bodies.

As we return to the land we need to address rape culture and misogyny. We can be back on the land and still have rapists, misogyny and homo/transphobia plague our nations. They don't magically disappear as we step into the bush. Many of us are hurt people returning to the land. The land and water don't magically wash away that hurt as we return to it, it is not some magical Christian land baptism.

Karyn: What happens when we continuously rebuild land/water resurgent narratives that don't intimately work in our bodies? Can we care for the land/water if our bodies are not cared for? What happens when intimate care falls apart on the land? Between each other?

I am thinking about what clan teachings scrolled out on the fractals of urban concrete had to teach me of what it means to be a good relative (see Figure 16.5). I want to be a good relative . . . this, from my initial rupture between my birth mother and I when I was born. One day as I was walking on Anishinaabe and Haudenosaunee territory in Tkaronto, my kinship with more than human beings made their introduction through cardboard origami on this urban wasteland. Perhaps, this fractal was a way of communicating how human and more than human beings make makeshift homes on this urban wasteland using whatever materials are at hand.

Nehiyaw philosopher Erica Violet Lee teaches us, "when we make a home in lands and bodies considered wastelands, we attest that these places are worthy of healing and that we are worthy of life beyond survival" (2016). I feel that we gravitationally pull love and kinships from the rubble.

Can we care for the land/water if our bodies are not cared for? How might these practices of care-giving manifest in the urban space? My Nehiyaw/Anishinaabe daughter Gracie activates urban cedar cleansing every time we walk past cedar saying, "look momma, medicine" as she gently tugs and fills her little pockets. In this way she is looking after us so that we no longer yearn, desire and cry for fire keepers outside of our own flame.

FIGURE 16.5   Deer Clan on Concrete

So what does happen when intimate care falls apart on the land—between each other? I have asked myself repeatedly what would it mean if I were to fall into radical love with a star, and think about this space as part of lands' overflow. This dreaming up of the possibilities is not to wish for a utopic promise, but rather to think about our bodies and relationships with land as non-binary, multitudinous in its formations and shapes of love.

City kin may fall in love with land differently—perhaps it is a falling, rather than a grounding—we have oftentimes fallen from some other place as perpetual visitors. We have practices and protocols of visiting that are migrations glyphed onto our skin, braided in our hair, and imprinted on our sneakers. Like that fallen star we need to relate to each other and this land through kin-making strategies—like your gorgeous offering of birch bark earrings so that I can walk lands through my kinship with you. These gestures and symbologies matter to us as we carve our futures using patterns of relationality, formed as sister kinships. These ethics are our future past traditions as they manifest and imprint on the skin.

Our migration practices, the way that land overflows themselves into all the realms—celestial, sub aqueous—remind us of our capacities to jump scale. I like to throw rocks to the sky—so that they too can jump scale from misogyny and other forms of settler colonial violences that our bodies—theirs and mine—have been subjected to. Sometimes I think that as star people we should exercise our rights to flight in our bodies as vessels of time travel.

Erin: As we go back to the land and water we need to consider how ableism, gender and sexuality are constructed in these spaces. As we live under forces of destruction, we must also contend with how ableism and purity are created on the land and our bodies.

The binaries that we put on gender and people's bodies are also seen in other spheres of our communities. When we put binaries on "back to the land," we also perpetuate ableism on those whose bodies have been forever changed from the rubble, specifically two-spirit, queer and trans kin. Binaries that also force heteronormativity onto land, water, plants and animals. After all, gender normativity wasn't only forced onto our bodies but also onto our lands simultaneously. Queerness on the land is also about our relationships to destruction, to imagining our bodies beyond a city/bush divide, to making space for all of creation. Queerness is about living in responses to the world that's been created around us, to finding ourselves in spaces like the city dump and meeting our animal kin there.

It is also about us taking the lead of those most ill when it comes to land/water resurgence. I don't want to return to lands and waters where we make invisible those whose bodies, genders and abilities aren't part of the future.

I'm grateful for my partner and the ways we are able to make space for each other on the land and water, and for every moment where I can be on the land/ water without shame or ableism and have my gender, sexuality. To not have my body shamed and make offerings to the beavers, muskrats and fish in the water. These are some of the things being queer teaches you about going back to the land.

Karyn: Narratives of lands' overflow can potentially be a site to critique ongoing realities of violence on our bodies, so that environmental spaces and land defense movements can become accountable spaces. Land defend-her. How we activate lands in our practices of land defense is intimately tied to how we are in relationship with each other.

Misogyny is a bad land practice—period. We need to stop upholding toxic masculinity in all spaces, but especially those that house our futurity bundles (kinships with human and more-than-human that have yet to be).

Movement makers, repeat after me. Consensual-ity . . . say it aloud slowly . . . say it sexily . . . it's a gorgeous, generative world-making word . . . say it often—build from it—always.

Notes

1 I witnessed Dine body somatic practitioner Nazbah Tom ask this question during a session at the University of Toronto and it has stuck with me ever since.
2 Aboriginal HIV and AIDS Statistics. http://caan.ca/regional-fact-sheets/

References

Ahmed, S. (2006). *Queer phenomenology: Orientations, objects, others*. Durham, NC: Duke University Press.

CAAN. (2017, November 30). *Aboriginal HIV and AIDS statistics*. Retrieved from http://caan.ca/regional-fact-sheets/

Hunt, S. (2014, October). *Red skin, White masks: Rejecting the colonial politics of recognition*. Panel discussion at Simon Fraser University, BC.

Lee, Erica Violet. (2016, November 30). In defense of the wastelands: A survival guide. *GUTS Issue 7, LOVE*. Retrieved from http://gutsmagazine.ca/wastelands/

Mingus, M. (2011). *Changing the framework: Disability justice how our communities can move beyond access to wholeness*. [Blog post]. Retrieved from https://leavingevidence.wordpress.com/2011/02/12/changing-the-framework-disability-justice/

Vowel, C. (n.d.). *niwî-kîwânân: We will go home*. [Blog post]. Retrieved from http://workingitouttogether.com/content/niwi-kiwanan-we-will-go-home/

Williamson, T. (2013). Of Dogma and ceremony. *Decolonization: Indigeneity, Education & Society*. Retrieved from https://decolonization.wordpress.com/2013/08/16/of-dogma-and-ceremony/

CONTRIBUTORS

Giovanni Batz (K'iche' Maya)

Giovanni was born and raised in Los Angeles, California, and is the son of Guatemalan working-class immigrants and paternal grandson of K'iche' Maya. His research interests include: extractivist industries and megaprojects in Latin America, Guatemalan-Maya migration, displacement and diaspora, Indigenous social movements, and human rights. Giovanni received his Ph.D. in Social Anthropology at the University of Texas at Austin. His dissertation, "The Fourth Invasion: Development, Ixil-Maya Resistance, and the Struggle against Megaprojects in Guatemala," is based on a resistance movement among the Ixil-Maya in Cotzal, Guatemala against the construction of a hydroelectric dam. He has also worked with Guatemalan-Maya youth in Los Angeles, as well as conducted research on deportations and migration of K'iche' Maya from Almolonga, Quetzaltenango. Giovanni served as a tutor and facilitator at the Ixil University between 2013 and 2015. In 2016, he received a grant by the Guatemalan Human Rights Commission in order to raise awareness on the human rights situation in Guatemala. Giovanni is currently a Visiting Assistant Professor in the Department of Anthropology, and Global and Intercultural Studies (Latin American, Latino/a, and Caribbean Studies) at Miami University. Giovanni was awarded the 2018-2019 Anne Ray Resident Scholar Fellowship at the School for Advanced Research, where he will work on a book manuscript on his research on megaprojects in Cotzal and Guatemala.

Nicholas XEMŦOLTW̱ Claxton (Tsawout)

Nicholas's Indigenous name is XEMŦOLTW̱ and he was born and raised in Saanich (W̱SÁNEĆ) Territory. He is a member of Tsawout, one of the Saanich First Nation bands on Southern Vancouver Island. Nicholas received his master's in Indigenous Governance and his doctorate through the Faculty of Education at the University of Victoria. He is currently Assistant Teaching Professor in Indigenous Education in the Faculty of Education. His research interests are in revitalizing the traditional fishing and environmental knowledge and traditions of Reef Net fishing in his community. He draws knowledge from his late uncle Dr. Earl Claxton (YELḰÁTŦE), his uncle John Elliott (STOLȻEȽ), and his father Lou Claxton (SELEMTEN), who participated first-hand in the Saanich Reef Net technology. He teaches through experiential learning and likes to be out on the lands and waters of his territory.

Kelsey Dayle John (Diné)
Yá'át'ééh! Biliganna nishłį. Tł áashchi'i báshíshchíín. Biliganna dashicheii. Bit'ahnii dashináli. Kelsey Dayle John yinishyé. Teec Nos Pos déé' naashá. (Hello, I am white, born for the Red Bottom clan, my maternal grandfather is white, and my paternal grandfather's clan is Within His Cover Clan. I'm originally from Teec Nos Pos). Kelsey is a doctoral candidate at Syracuse University and a National Science Foundation Graduate Research Fellow. Her dissertation is on the Navajo horse. Currently, she lives in Farmington, NM and works with a Navajo Tribal University. When she's not working she runs with her dog June bug and spends as much time on horses and with her family as she can. Alongside her research, she is learning Diné Bizaad (the Navajo language).

Adam Gaudry (Métis)
Adam Gaudry's family is from Sioux Narrows on the Lake-of-the-Woods, he was born and raised in southern Ontario. He is Assistant Professor in the Faculty of Native Studies and Department of Political Science at the University of Alberta. At the University of Saskatchewan he taught Canada's largest required Indigenous studies course, 300 students and required for teacher candidates, nursing students, and future social workers in Saskatchewan. He is a practitioner of decolonial and community-based learning, currently working with Gwich'in people to build a youth-focused bush camp school in Teetl'it Zheh. He also studies Métis political thought, history, identity, and governance.

Noelani Goodyear-Ka'ōpua (Kanaka Maoli)
Noelani is an educator, author, activist, and parent who works as Associate Professor of Indigenous Politics at the University of Hawai'i at Mānoa. Her research, teaching, and activism focus on Hawaiian social movements and Indigenous resurgence. Her first book, *The Seeds We Planted: Portraits of a Native Hawaiian Charter School* (University of Minnesota Press, 2013), discusses the creation of Hawaiian culture-based public schools within and against settler state structures, and provides a case study of the school Noelani co-founded. She has also co-edited *A Nation Rising: Hawaiian Movements for Life, Land and Sovereignty* (Duke University Press, 2014) and *The Value of Hawai'i, 2: Ancestral Roots, Oceanic Visions* (University of Hawai'i Press, 2014). She writes with the blog collective Ke Kaupu

Hehi Ale and enjoys volunteering with community organizations doing land- and ocean-based cultural resurgence work, including the Kānehūnāmoku Voyaging Academy, which focuses on Hawaiian sailing and navigation traditions, and the Hui o Kuapā, which cares for Keawanui fishpond on Molokaʻi.

Erin Marie Konsmo (Métis)

Erin Marie is a non-binary prairie queer from Alberta, an Indigenous Full Spectrum Doula, community-based artist, and helper at the Native Youth Sexual Health Network. They spend their time learning more about cervical mucus and menstrual supports, creating tools for culturally safe sex education, and harvesting birch, medicines, and roots from the land.

Marie Laing (Kanyen'kehá:ka)

Marie is a queer Kanyen'kehá:ka (Six Nations of the Grand River Territory) writer of mixed Haudenosaunee and Irish, Scottish, and South African settler ancestry. Raised in Kingston, Ontario, she holds a bachelor's degree in Sexual Diversity Studies from the University of Toronto and is currently working toward a master's degree in Social Justice Education at the Ontario Institute for Studies in Education. She lives in Toronto.

Danielle E. Lorenz

Danielle Lorenz, a first-generation Canadian of mixed European descent, grew up in Caledon, Ontario. Currently in the process of completing her Ph.D. in Educational Policy Studies at the University of Alberta, she is also the 2018 Managing Editor (English) of the *Canadian Journal for New Scholars in Education*. Her examination of Indigenous-settler relationships in educational systems through an intersectional and anti-oppressive praxis is complemented by her lived experiences as someone with a dis/ability and chronic illness. As an intermediate-level cat herder, she is often looking for a lint roller.

Kyle T. Mays (Saginaw Chippewa)

Kyle T. Mays is a Black American and Saginaw Chippewa scholar and activist, currently residing in Los Angeles, California. Since he was an undergraduate, he has worked with young men of color, including teaching a "Learning History through Hip Hop" Course at a Juvenile Detention Center. In addition to his intellectual and activist work, he regularly listens to the latest Hip Hop, including listening to Beyonce's *Lemonade* and Jay-Z's *4:44* side-by-side for hours.

Kim McBreen (Waitaha, Kāti Mamoe, Ngāi Tahu)

Kim is part of Te Whare Whakatupu Mātauranga at Te Wānanga o Raukawa. The goal of Te Wānanga o Raukawa is Māori surviving as a people. The Whakatupu Mātauranga team contributes to that goal by supporting work that grows our understanding and expression of kaupapa, the principles that underpin Māori knowledge, and returning that knowledge to communities. Critically working with kaupapa includes unpicking the effects of all the oppressions introduced with colonization. Kim cannot quite believe that she is paid to contribute to that project.

Marissa Aki'Nene Muñoz (Xicana Tejana)

Marissa is a mother/daughter/granddaughter activist educator scholar, tracing her roots to Tlaxcalteca, Coahuilteca, and Wixarika communities of the present-day Texas/Mexico frontera. Her current research focuses on critical storying, testimonio, and collective memory as community strategies that have protected rich mesoamerican intellectual traditions from colonization. Building upon Indigenous scholarship and frontera-specific methodologies, Marissa's research moves toward mobilizing ancestral knowledges of water as a means of community revitailzation toward healing, in response to the environmental racism, cultural ethnocide, and ever-increasing military occupation of the the US-Mexico frontera communities.

Teresa Newberry

Teresa is Academic Chair of Science, Mathematics, and Health at Tohono O'odham Community College (TOCC) where she has developed a culturally relevant Associate of Science program using innovative approaches that bridge traditional ecological knowledge (TEK) and Western science. Her work at TOCC focuses on the preservation and transmission of TEK in the tribal college setting. Her research interests include preservation of biocultural diversity, Indigenous education, and ecosystem responses to climate change. As an internationally recognized scholar in the area of Indigenous science education and TEK, Teresa has been an invited faculty member with University of Arizona's American Indian Language Development Institute. She has partnered with National Council for Science and the Environment, Northern Arizona University, and the American Indian Higher Education Consortium on numerous projects to create culturally relevant, transdisciplinary curriculum in science, math, and traditional knowledge, particularly in the areas of climate change and water. She has also authored an atlas of plants of the Tohono O'odham Nation that incorporates scientific, linguistic, and cultural information as a tool for engaged pedagogy and preservation of biocultural diversity. Recently, as an NSF Fellow in the Opportunities for Underrepresented Scholars program, she developed an Indigenous education model for teaching science from a holistic, culturally based perspective.

Naadli Todd Lee Ormiston (Northern Tutchone, Tlingit)

Wáa sá iyatee. Yoo xat duwasaakw Naadli. (Hello. How are you? My Indigenous name is Naadli, which means "new beginnings" in Tutchone.) Naadli is Northern Tutchone from Yukon and Tlingit from Alaska. I acknowledge that I am a visitor in the territory of the Songhees, Esquimalt and W̱SÁNEĆ peoples of the

Coast Salish Nation. It is an honor and privilege to work as a visitor in Coast Salish Territory. I graduated with my Doctorate in Education at the University of BC. I am currently the Chair of Indigenous Education at Camosun College in Victoria, BC. Much of my work focuses on Indigenous leadership pedagogies in higher education. I am committed to learning as a lifelong process and constantly engaging in new learning. While it is clear from my own experiences, I see a real imperative of the need to learn about identities and cultures, of "coming to know" who we are, where we come from, what our traditions are. This occurs through many teachings, including Indigenous education within post-secondary institutes. How might this be facilitated in a holistic way? I am committed to connecting holistic land-based and experiential education with and inside post-secondary settings that ultimately centers Indigenous ways of knowing and being.

Catherine Picton

Catherine is a Research Fellow at the University of the Sunshine Coast in Queensland, Australia. After completing bachelor's degrees in Arts and Education, Catherine spent six years teaching in Samoa, providing support and advocacy for students with disability. She has a Ph.D. in Social Anthropology, exploring cultural conceptualizations of disability in Samoa. Catherine's research interests include culture, disability, Pacific policy development, and student well-being and engagement. Catherine has worked with local community groups in Australia to support school students with disability in Samoa and Vanuatu. When she is not researching and writing, Catherine likes to spend time with her young son exploring beaches, bush trails, and restaurants across the Sunshine Coast region in South East Queensland. She also enjoys visiting Pacific Island countries to enjoy the sounds, tastes, and cultures of the Pacific. She can be contacted at cpicton@usc.edu.au.

Karyn Recollet (urban Cree)

Karyn is Assistant Faculty Member in Women and Gender Studies at the University of Toronto. She is mother to Gracie Maya, who is 6-years-old. Karyn researches in the areas of Indigenous arts and aesthetics, urban Indigenous land relationships, and Indigenous feminist activations—including dance practices.

Carmen Rodríguez de France (Kickapoo)

Carmen has been a grateful visitor on the land of the Coast Salish and Straits Salish people for 20 years. At the University of Victoria, she facilitates courses on Indigenous education, knowledge, and ways of being, and collaborates with other programs across campus such as Social Justice and the Latin American Studies Program. Her career spans 33 years with participation in a broad range of educational, community service, and research activities. Carmen works with Aboriginal children, youth, and adults in diverse educational contexts, and more recently has partnered with various community organizations to support the enactment of the Calls to Action from the Truth and Reconciliation Commission Report (TRC). As an immigrant of Indigenous heritage from the Kickapoo Nation, Carmen is interested in strengthening collaborations between Indigenous and non-Indigenous people in Canada aiming to create a shared future.

chuutsqa Layla Rorick (Hesquiaht)
chuutsqa is a Hesquiaht (pronounced Hish-kwee-ut) First Nations woman from the Nuu-chah-nulth (pronounced New-chaa-nool-th) people. chuutsqa has dedicated the last seven years to creating and maintaining free, community-based language and culture initiatives that preserve and enhance a living Nuu-chah-nulth culture. She began by co-creating her own language-learning programs with elders Lawrence Paul and Angela Galligos because none were available. chuutsqa completed a three-year Mentor-Apprentice language immersion program, co-authored free Hesquiaht language dictionaries, and went on to start a grassroots Language Nest immersion program with elders Julia Lucas and Maggie Ignace. After graduating with a master's degree of Education in Indigenous Language Revitalization, chuutsqa began to facilitate community language immersion classes and teach immersion sets in elementary school. Through these efforts, with the help of fluent speakers, she has progressed from being a non-speaker who grew up on her Hesquiaht First Nations reserve at Hot Springs Cove to being a high-intermediate speaker who supports others to become speakers and immersion teachers. chuutsqa began doctoral studies at the University of Victoria in 2016. Her doctoral work aims to improve language proficiency within her family and community by engaging fluent speakers in language immersion planning and implementation.

Sandra Styres (Kanien'kehá:ka)
Sandra is of Kanien'kehá:ka (Mohawk), English, and French descent and resides on Six Nations of the Grand River Territory. Dr. Styres is Assistant Professor of Indigenous Education with the Department of Curriculum, Teaching, and Learning at OISE, University of Toronto and Adjunct Professor with the Department of Child and Youth Studies at Brock University. Dr. Styres's research interests specifically focus on various aspects of Indigenous education that include: decolonizing Land-centered approaches to Indigenous pedagogies and teaching practices; literacies of Land; teacher-student interactions, learning through various modalities and the pedagogical implications of those modalities; issues concerning social justice, racism, and construction of race in teaching and learning contexts; integration of Indigenous teaching and learning in higher education with both Indigenous and non-Indigenous students; pre-service and in-service teacher development; Indigenous philosophies and knowledges; culturally aligned methodologies and theoretical approaches to Indigenous research; Indigenous and non-Indigenous research collaborations; as well as addressing issues of ethics and protocols that guide the work between Indigenous peoples, communities, and universities.

Eve Tuck (Unangax)

Eve is Associate Professor of Critical Race and Indigenous Studies in the Department of Social Justice Education, Ontario Institute for Studies in Education, University of Toronto. She is Canada Research Chair of Indigenous Methodologies with Youth and Communities, and is a William T. Grant Foundation Scholar (2015–2020). Tuck is the author of *Urban Youth and School Pushout* (2012), and co-author with Marcia McKenzie of *Place in Research* (2015). She is co-editor with K. Wayne Yang of *Youth Resistance Research and Theories of Change* (2014) and *Toward What Justice?* (2018).

Rasela Tufue-Dolgoy

Rasela is Senior Education Lecturer at the National University of Samoa (NUS). She received her master's degree in Education from Newcastle University, Australia and her Ph.D. from Victoria University of Wellington, New Zealand. She also holds a Diploma for Teaching English as a Second Language (TESL) from Victoria University of Wellington. Rasela currently teaches undergraduate and postgraduate educational courses at the National University of Samoa. In addition to teaching, she is also keen to research, present, and publish widely on contemporary issues in education. Some of her publications concern policy issues in relation to "inclusive education" as well as "parental support in children's education." She recently co-authored and published papers on Open Distance Learning (ODL) as an alternative service delivery model as well as transfer of training as it relates to teacher professional development. Rasela is also keen to write for young children, having authored and published a book for the development of young children's literacy in the Samoan language. She has presented at several conferences held nationally, regionally, and internationally. She currently resides in Samoa and can be contacted at *r.tufue-dolgoy@nus.edu.ws*.

Linda Tuhiwai Smith (Ngāti Awa, Ngāti Porou)

Linda is Professor of Education and Māori Development and served as Pro-Vice Chancellor Māori at the University of Waikato. She has worked in the field of Māori education for many years as an educator and researcher and is well known for her work in Kaupapa Māori research. Linda has published widely in journals and books. Her book *Decolonising Methodologies Research and Indigenous Peoples* has been an international best seller in the Indigenous world since its publication in 1998. More recently, Linda was a Joint Director of Ngā Pae o Te aramatanga, New Zealand's Māori Centre of Research Excellence and a Professor of Education at the University of Auckland. She is well known internationally as a public speaker. Linda is from two iwi in New Zealand: Ngāti Awa and Ngāti Porou.

Octaviana V. Trujillo (Yaqui)

Octaviana is Founding Chair and Professor of the Department of Applied Indigenous Studies at Northern Arizona University. Octaviana is a former Chairwoman of the Pascua Yaqui Tribe and in 2011 was Visiting Fellow at the Rachel Carson Center for Environment and Society at the Ludwig-Maximilian University in Germany. She is Principal Investigator (community outreach) on the National Cancer Institute, Partnership for Native American Cancer Prevention and research, and education and training director of the Center for American Indian Resilience, which explores resiliency to reduce American Indian health disparities. Octaviana, the National Council for Science and Environment, and American Indian Higher Education Consortium have partnered to develop science and math learning materials at Tribal Colleges and Universities. Octaviana has served on national and international boards, including Farmworker Justice (empowering migrant and seasonal farmworkers to improve their living and working conditions, immigration status, health, and access to justice) and the Global Diversity Foundation (promoting agricultural, biological, and cultural diversity around the world through research, training, and social action). She was appointed by President Obama to serve as a member of the Joint Public Advisory Committee for the North American Commission on Environmental Cooperation.

Sarah Wakefield

Sarah is an associate professor at the University of Toronto. In her research, she seeks to understand how individuals and organizations work together to create just, healthy, and sustainable communities. She is specifically interested in activism: what motivates activist work, what sustains it, and how it can be most effective. She is trying to learn how to be a good ally to Indigenous people, within the university and in her community.

Kevin Whalen

Kevin Whalen is an assistant professor of American Indian Studies and History at the University of Minnesota, Morris. He is the author of *Native Students at Work: American Indian Labor and Sherman Institute's Outing Program, 1900-1945.*

Madeline Whetung (Nishnaabeg)

Madeline is engaged in anti-violence community work in her home-place, Nogojiwanong. She is a PhD student in Geography at the University of British Columbia interested in community responses to violence. Most recently her work has taken her to Denendeh to support Dechinta Bush University developing Indigenous consent curriculum. Madeline is a citizen of the Nishnaabeg Nation and a member of Curve Lake First Nation of Michi Saagiig, Scottish and English descent.

Alex Wilson (Opaskwayak Cree Nation)

Alex is a professor with the Department of Educational Foundations and the Academic Director of the Aboriginal Education Research Centre at the University of Saskatchewan. Her scholarship has greatly contributed to building and sharing knowledge about two spirit identity,'coming-in' theory, history and teachings, Indigenous research methodologies, and the prevention of violence in the lives of Indigenous peoples. She is one of many organizers with the Idle No More movement, integrating radical education movement work with grassroots interventions that prevent the destruction of land and water. She is particularly focused on educating about and protecting the Saskatchewan River Delta and supporting community based food sovereignty efforts. Having co-developed a Masters program in Land-Based Education at the University of Saskatchewan, Dr. Wilson is now in the process of creating an international Indigenous Land–based PhD program. I acknowledge that I live and work on the traditional territories of the Neyinowak Inniwak (Cree) and Metis peoples.

K. Wayne Yang

Wayne writes about decolonization and everyday epic organizing, particularly from underneath ghetto colonialism, often with his frequent collaborator, Eve Tuck, and sometimes for an avatar called La Paperson. Currently, he has an appointment as Associate Professor in Ethnic Studies at UC San Diego. He is excited to collaborate with the Land Relationships Super Collective, the Black Teacher Project, and Roses in Concrete.

INDEX

Note: Page numbers in *italic* indicate a figure on the corresponding page